METROPOLITAN COLLEGE OF N-
LIBRARY, 12TH FLOOR
431 CANAL STREET
NEW YORK, NY 10013

Worldly Provincialism

Social History, Popular Culture, and Politics in Germany
Geoff Eley, Series Editor

A History of Foreign Labor in Germany, 1880–1980: Seasonal Workers/Forced Laborers/Guest Workers, Ulrich Herbert, translated by William Templer
Reshaping the German Right: Radical Nationalism and Political Change after Bismarck, Geoff Eley
The Stigma of Names: Antisemitism in German Daily Life, 1812–1933, Dietz Bering
Forbidden Laughter: Popular Humor and the Limits of Repression in Nineteenth-Century Prussia, Mary Lee Townsend
From Bundesrepublik *to* Deutschland: *German Politics after Unification,* Michael G. Huelshoff, Andrei S. Markovits, and Simon Reich, editors
The People Speak! Anti-Semitism and Emancipation in Nineteenth-Century Bavaria, James F. Harris
The Origins of the Authoritarian Welfare State in Prussia: Conservatives, Bureaucracy, and the Social Question, 1815–70, Hermann Beck
Technological Democracy: Bureaucracy and Citizenry in the German Energy Debate, Carol J. Hager
Society, Culture, and the State in Germany, 1870–1930, Geoff Eley, editor
Paradoxes of Peace: German Peace Movements since 1945, Alice Holmes Cooper
Jews, Germans, Memory: Reconstruction of Jewish Life in Germany, Y. Michal Bodemann, editor
Exclusive Revolutionaries: Liberal Politics, Social Experience, and National Identity in the Austrian Empire, 1848–1914, Pieter M. Judson
Feminine Frequencies: Gender, German Radio, and the Public Sphere, 1923–1945, Kate Lacey
How German Is She? Postwar West German Reconstruction and the Consuming Woman, Erica Carter
West Germany under Construction: Politics, Society, and Culture in Germany in the Adenauer Era, Robert G. Moeller, editor
A Greener Vision of Home: Cultural Politics and Environmental Reform in the German Heimatschutz Movement, 1904–1918, William H. Rollins
A User's Guide to German Cultural Studies, Scott Denham, Irene Kacandes, and Jonathan Petropoulos, editors
Catholicism, Political Culture, and the Countryside: A Social History of the Nazi Party in South Germany, Oded Heilbronner
Contested City: Municipal Politics and the Rise of Nazism in Altona, 1917–1937, Anthony McElligott
The Imperialist Imagination: German Colonialism and Its Legacy, Sara Friedrichsmeyer, Sara Lennox, and Susanne Zantop, editors
Framed Visions: Popular Culture, Americanization, and the Contemporary German and Austrian Imagination, Gerd Gemünden
Triumph of the Fatherland: German Unification and the Marginalization of Women, Brigitte Young
Mobility and Modernity: Migration in Germany 1820–1989, Steve Hochstadt
Building the East German Myth: Historical Mythology and Youth Propaganda in the German Democratic Republic, 1945–1989, Alan L. Nothnagle
The German Problem Transformed: Institutions, Politics, and Foreign Policy, 1945–1995, Thomas Banchoff
Worldly Provincialism: German Anthropology in the Age of Empire, H. Glenn Penny and Matti Bunzl, editors

Worldly Provincialism

German Anthropology in the Age of Empire

H. GLENN PENNY AND MATTI BUNZL, EDITORS

THE UNIVERSITY OF MICHIGAN PRESS
Ann Arbor

Copyright © by the University of Michigan 2003
All rights reserved
Published in the United States of America by
The University of Michigan Press
Manufactured in the United States of America
♾ Printed on acid-free paper

2006 2005 2004 2003   4 3 2 1

No part of this publication may be reproduced,
stored in a retrieval system, or transmitted in any form
or by any means, electronic, mechanical, or otherwise,
without the written permission of the publisher.

A CIP catalog record for this book is available from the British Library.

Library of Congress Cataloging-in-Publication Data

Worldly provincialism : German anthropology in the age of empire / H.
  Glenn Penny and Matti Bunzl, Editors.
    p. cm. — (Social history, popular culture, and politics in
  Germany)
    Includes bibliographical references and index.
    ISBN 0-472-11318-6 (cloth : alk. paper) — ISBN 0-472-08926-9
  (paper : alk. paper)
    1. Anthropology—Germany—History. I. Penny, H. Glenn. II.
  Bunzl, Matti, 1971–   III. Series.
  GN17.3.G47 W67   2003
  301'.0943—dc21   2002015818
    ISBN13 978-0-472-11318-7 (cloth)
    ISBN13 978-0-472-08926-0 (paper)
    ISBN13 978-0-472-02524-4 (electronic)

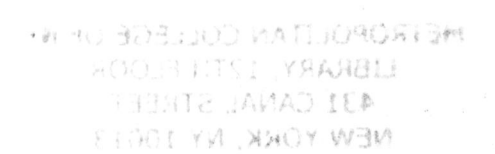

Contents

Introduction: Rethinking German Anthropology, Colonialism, and Race MATTI BUNZL AND H. GLENN PENNY 1

Coming of Age in the Pacific: German Ethnography from Chamisso to Krämer HARRY LIEBERSOHN 31

Völkerpsychologie and German-Jewish Emancipation MATTI BUNZL 47

Bastian's Museum: On the Limits of Empiricism and the Transformation of German Ethnology H. GLENN PENNY 86

Spectacles of (Human) Nature: Commercial Ethnography between Leisure, Learning, and *Schaulust* SIERRA A. BRUCKNER 127

Adventures in the Skin Trade: German Anthropology and Colonial Corporeality ANDREW ZIMMERMAN 156

Turning Native? Anthropology, German Colonialism, and the Paradoxes of the "Acclimatization Question," 1885–1914 PASCAL GROSSE 179

Anthropology at War: Racial Studies of POWs during World War I ANDREW D. EVANS 198

Colonizing Anthropology: Albert Hahl and the Ethnographic Frontier in German New Guinea RAINER BUSCHMANN 230

Gathering the Hunters: Bushmen in German (Colonial) Anthropology ROBERT J. GORDON 256

Priests among the Pygmies: Wilhelm Schmidt and the Counter-Reformation in Austrian Ethnology SUZANNE MARCHAND 283

Bibliography 317

Contributors 343

Index 347

Introduction: Rethinking German Anthropology, Colonialism, and Race

MATTI BUNZL AND H. GLENN PENNY

This book complicates what we know about the history of anthropology and its role in the colonial arena. In the conventional chronology, the discipline's nineteenth-century foundations appear as manifestations of a quintessentially colonial science, while its twentieth-century articulations move toward an ever more progressive, anticolonial stance. It is a powerful narrative, to be sure. But in characterizing the history of anthropology on a global scale, it obscures its overwhelming focus on the Anglo-American and French tradition. Germany, this book argues, does not fit the paradigmatic trajectory of anthropology's history. On the contrary, it seems to reverse the dominant periodization. As the contributions in this volume begin to document, nineteenth-century German anthropology was neither characterized by colonial concerns, nor interested in organizing the world's peoples according to evolutionary sequences.[1] Instead, it was a self-consciously liberal endeavor, guided by a broadly humanistic agenda and centered on efforts to document the plurality and historical specificity of cultures. This liberal humanism stood in marked contrast to Anglo-American and French variants; but while those traditions moved

---

1. In this essay, we use *anthropology* as an overarching term that encompasses both physical anthropology and ethnology, or what we now more commonly refer to as cultural anthropology. In nineteenth-century Germany, however, *Anthropologie* (physical anthropology) and *Ethnologie* (cultural anthropology) were considered two distinct fields. Most of the actors discussed in this volume would have defined themselves as ethnologists. Consequently, we refer to them as ethnologists throughout this essay.

toward pluralistic frameworks in the first decades of the twentieth century, German anthropology took the opposite route. Around the turn of the century, its practitioners began to abandon the discipline's cosmopolitan heritage; and after World War I, a narrowly nationalistic and overtly colonialist orientation became virtually hegemonic, culminating in the discipline's willing involvement in the Nazi machinery. The German tradition thus differs in surprising and illuminating ways.

But if the history of German anthropology is thus characterized by a kind of *Sonderweg,* it also allows us to rethink the general relationships between anthropology, colonialism, and theories of race. That this should be so is largely a function of nineteenth-century German anthropology's importance. Germans, this book contends, played a formative role in the shaping of international anthropology. As theorists and institution builders, they were centrally involved in anthropology's codification, both as discipline and practice. And in consequence, the actions of German ethnologists and anthropologists have much to tell us about the history of anthropology in general.

Moreover, the history of German anthropology also affords us a unique perspective on the history of Germany itself. That the overwhelming majority of German ethnologists and anthropologists were liberal champions of cultural pluralism during the imperial period (1871–1918) separates them from their counterparts in the rest of liberal Europe. That the majority were not racist, but strongly opposed to biologically based theories of human difference, however, goes to the heart of German historiography. Given the turn toward race science in the early twentieth century and the complicity of many German anthropologists in Nazi race crimes, the liberalism of nineteenth-century anthropology seems counterintuitive. Yet this is another critical intervention performed by this collection. It argues against readymade teleologies that locate the origins of Nazi ideology in late-nineteenth-century constellations. In contrast to prevailing views that regard Germans' involvement in the colonial contest as a direct precursor to Nazi atrocities, this volume calls for a rethinking of Germany's figuration in postcolonial studies as a precondition for a more nuanced understanding of modern German history.

Germans in the History of Anthropology

The essays in this book are a product of particular interests that arose among anthropologists and historians in the 1980s and 1990s. During those decades, American anthropologists developed a growing concern for the history of their discipline, which ultimately led to the establishment of the history of anthropology as a recognized subfield.[2] At the same time, historians increasingly turned to questions of identity, colonialism, and the role of the Other in Western self-perceptions in an effort to address global issues of power and inequality.[3] These trends, combined with the rapid growth of cultural history and cultural studies during these decades, made anthropology, anthropological theory, and the history of the discipline particularly appealing to historians. The fact that the contributors to this volume all turned to the history of anthropology more or less independently during the early 1990s is one indication of the pervasiveness of this appeal—that and the realization that although the dominant paradigm of American cultural anthropology could be traced to intellectual and institutional antecedents in nineteenth-century Germany,[4] most of the work on the history of anthropology has focused on Britain, the United States, and France.[5]

---

2. In addition to the increasing number of essays devoted to the history of the profession in leading anthropological journals, the greatest indication of the salience of this new field is the success of the History of Anthropology series edited by George Stocking (and more recently Richard Handler) and published by the University of Wisconsin Press since 1983, and the creation of the journal *History and Anthropology* in 1984.

3. For a good introduction to these interests see Nicholas B. Dirks, Geoff Eley, and Sherry B. Ortner, eds., *Culture/Power/History: A Reader in Contemporary Social Theory* (Princeton: Princeton University Press, 1994).

4. Here we are referring of course to the Boasian tradition. A number of scholars have focused on Boas's intellectual debt to the German sciences, but the most thorough account is unquestionably Douglas Cole, *Franz Boas: The Early Years, 1858–1906* (Seattle: University of Washington Press, 1999); see also inter alia George W. Stocking Jr., ed., *Volksgeist as Method and Ethic: Essays on Boasian Ethnography and the German Anthropological Tradition* (Madison: University of Wisconsin Press, 1996).

5. It would be impossible to render a complete bibliography of the ever-growing historiography of British, American, and French anthropology. Recent works that have helped define the canon, however, can be listed (albeit incompletely). Aside from the volumes in the History of Anthropology series published by the University of Wisconsin Press, they include George W. Stocking, *Race, Culture, and Evolution: Essays in the History of Anthropology* (Chicago: University of Chicago Press, 1968); Stocking, *Victorian Anthropology* (New York: Free Press, 1987); Stocking, *The Ethnographer's Magic and Other Essays in the History of Anthropology* (Madison: University of Wisconsin Press, 1992); Stocking, *After Tylor: British Social Anthropology, 1888–1951* (Madison: University of Wisconsin Press, 1995); Henrika Kuklick, *The Savage Within: The Social History of British Anthropology, 1885–1945* (Cambridge: Cambridge University Press, 1991); Jack Goody, *The Expansive Moment: Anthropology in Britain and Africa* (Cambridge: Cambridge University Press, 1995); Adam Kuper, *Anthropology and Anthropologists: The Modern British School* (London: Routledge and

Germans, in other words, have been largely left out of the story, and this volume begins to address and obviate that absence.[6] To be sure, Germans have been attributed a long history of scientific engagement with the wider world. Scientific travelers such as Georg Forster and Alexander von Humboldt, for example, are well known and repeatedly

---

Kegan Paul, 1983); Curtis M. Hinsley Jr., *Savages and Scientists: The Smithsonian Institution and the Development of American Anthropology, 1846–1910* (Washington, D.C.: Smithsonian Institution Press, 1981); Lee Baker, *From Savage to Negro: Anthropology and the Construction of Race, 1896–1954* (Berkeley and Los Angeles: University of California Press, 1998); Regna Darnell, *And Along Came Boas: Continuity and Revolution in Americanist Anthropology* (Amsterdam: John Benjamins, 1998); Darnell, *Invisible Genealogies: A History of Americanist Anthropology* (Lincoln: University of Nebraska Press, 2001); Peter Pels and Oscar Salemink, eds., *Colonial Subjects: Essays on the Practical History of Anthropology* (Ann Arbor: University of Michigan Press, 1999); Joan Vincent, *Anthropology and Politics: Visions, Traditions, and Trends* (Tucson: University of Arizona Press, 1990); James Clifford, *Person and Myth: Maurice Leenhardt in the Melanesian World* (Berkeley and Los Angeles: University of California Press, 1982).

6. Over the last few years, a trickle of work on the history of German anthropology has begun to be published in English (much of it by contributors to this volume). See Woodruff D. Smith, "The Social and Political Origins of German Diffusionist Ethnology," *Journal of the History of the Behavioral Sciences* 14 (1978): 103–12; Smith, "Friedrich Ratzel and the Origins of *Lebensraum*," *German Studies Review* 3, no. 1 (1980): 51–68; Smith, *Politics and the Sciences of Culture in Germany, 1840–1920* (Oxford: Oxford University Press, 1991), esp. chaps. 5, 6, 8, and 9; James Whitman, "From Philology to Anthropology in Mid-Nineteenth-Century Germany," in *Functionalism Historicized: Essays on British Social Anthropology*, ed. George W. Stocking, History of Anthropology, no. 2 (Madison: University of Wisconsin Press, 1984), 214–30; Robert Proctor, "From *Anthropologie* to *Rassenkunde* in the German Anthropological Tradition," in *Bones, Bodies, Behavior: Essays on Biological Anthropology*, ed. George W. Stocking, History of Anthropology, no. 5 (Madison: University of Wisconsin Press, 1988), 138–79; Matti Bunzl, "Franz Boas and the Humboldtian Tradition: From *Volksgeist* and *Nationalcharakter* to an Anthropological Concept of Culture," in Stocking, *Volksgeist*, 17–78; Bennoit Massin, "From Virchow to Fischer: Physical Anthropology and 'Modern Race Theories' in Wilhelmine Germany," in Stocking, *Volksgeist*, 79–154; Suzanne Marchand, "Orientalism as *Kulturpolitik*: German Archeology and Cultural Imperialism in Asia Minor," in Stocking, *Volksgeist*, 198–336; Marchand, "Leo Frobenius and the Revolt against the West," *Journal of Contemporary History* 32, no. 2 (1997): 153–70; H. Glenn Penny, "Municipal Displays: Civic Self-Promotion and the Development of German Ethnographic Museums, 1870–1914," *Social Anthropology* 6, no. 2 (1998): 157–68; Penny, "Fashioning Local Identities in an Age of Nation-Building: Museums, Cosmopolitan Traditions, and Intra-German Competition," *German History* 17, no. 4 (1999): 488–504; Andrew Zimmerman, "Anti-Semitism as Skill: Rudolf Virchow's *Schulstatistik* and the Racial Composition of Germany," *Central European History* 32, no. 4 (1999): 409–29; Zimmerman, "German Anthropology and the 'Natural Peoples': The Global Context of Colonial Discourse," *European Studies Journal* 16, no. 2 (1999): 85–112; Zimmerman, *Anthropology and Antihumanism in Imperial Germany* (Chicago: University of Chicago Press, 2001). See also the special volume of *Pacific Arts* 21–22 (July 2000) devoted to German anthropology in the Pacific.

evoked by scholars in an array of disciplines. But the ubiquitous interests in the non-European world among Germans living in even the most provincial places in Germany are less frequently remembered. During the middle of the nineteenth century, a range of naturalists followed in Humboldt's footsteps, and travel reports became common in German newspapers and bookstores. Ethnographic accounts from the Amazon, the islands of Yap, and equally far-off places began to frequent the pages of the *Illustrirte Zeitung* and other middle-class journals, which devoted entire sections to *Länder- und Völkerkunde* by the 1850s. This period also witnessed the emergence of popular natural science associations. In their wake, zoos and natural history museums became commonplace, and by the 1870s, museums devoted to ethnology were being founded all across Germany.[7] Indeed, in 1873, the first free-standing museum in the world devoted wholly to ethnology was conceived in Berlin, and it soon contained some of the world's largest and most comprehensive collections of ethnographic artifacts. At the same time, *Völkerschauen,* or what Sierra Bruckner has called "commercial ethnography," brought non-Europeans themselves to Germany in events that became part of everyday life by the end of the nineteenth century.[8] Moreover, German ethnologists and anthropologists played formidable roles in creating the international networks of collection and exchange that linked scientists throughout Europe and the United States; they launched some of the world's largest anthropological expeditions; they sent a string of ethnologists into South America, Africa, Asia, and the Pacific; they were a powerful presence at international conferences; they founded a number of internationally recognized periodicals devoted to anthropology and ethnology; and they actively engaged in international debates about human history, environmental assimilation, and race.

These contributions to anthropology and its history, however, have been largely obscured by events in the twentieth century. In the British

---

7. On the rise of natural science associations see Andreas W. Daum, *Wissenschaftspopularisierung im 19. Jahrhundert: Bürgerliche Kultur, naturwissenschaftliche Bildung und die deutsche Öffentlichkeit, 1848–1914* (Munich: R. Oldenbourg, 1998). On the zoological gardens see Annelore Rieke-Müller and Lothar Dittrich, *Der Löwe Brüllt Nebenan: Die Gründung Zoologischer Gärten im deutschsprachigen Raum, 1833–1869* (Cologne: Böhlau Verlag, 1998). On the development of ethnographic museums see H. Glenn Penny, "Cosmopolitan Visions and Municipal Displays: Museums, Markets, and the Ethnographic Project in Germany, 1868–1914," Ph.D. diss., University of Illinois, 1999.

8. Sierra A. Bruckner, "The Tingle-Tangle of Modernity: Popular Anthropology and the Cultural Politics of Identity in Imperial Germany," Ph.D. diss., University of Iowa, 1999.

context, the hegemonic position of structural-functionalism has repressed the disciplinary memory of more historicist variants. For the heirs of Bronislaw Malinowski and A. R. Radcliffe-Brown, the normative trajectory of social anthropology usually began with the repudiation of history and collecting as unscientific—a situation that systematically concealed the contributions of nineteenth-century German anthropologists.[9] The situation was more complex in the American context. There, Franz Boas implemented a historicist project rooted in nineteenth-century German social thought. German scholarship was a central component of Boas's own teaching at Columbia University, and his students often saw their work as continuous with nineteenth-century German traditions.[10] As anti-Boasian trends grounded in structural-functionalism and neo-evolutionary thought came to the fore in the 1940s and 1950s, however, German anthropology began to fade quickly from the American scene.[11]

A central factor in the disappearance of German contributions from the Anglo-American canon was the state of German anthropology itself. Simply put, German anthropology never recovered from World War I. The war led to the loss of German colonies, destroyed the funding sources of German ethnology, and eradicated the international networks German scholars had built up over the previous four decades. Moreover, while the United States, Britain, and France produced the guiding lights of twentieth-century anthropology, Germany's great

---

9. For a paradigmatic example, see Edward Evans-Pritchard's posthumously published *A History of Anthropological Thought* (New York: Basic Books, 1981), which ignores the German tradition entirely.

10. Both Alfred Kroeber and Margaret Mead touch on Boas's emphasis on Germanic scholarship in teaching. See Kroeber, "Franz Boas: The Man," *American Anthropologist*, Memoir Series no. 61 (1943): 5–26; Mead, "Apprenticeship under Boas," in *The Anthropology of Franz Boas: Essays on the Centennial of His Birth*, ed. Walter Goldschmidt (Menasha, Wis.: American Anthropological Association, 1959), 29–45. Robert Lowie's *The History of Ethnological Theory* (New York: Holt, Rinehart and Winston, 1937) gives a good indication of the place of nineteenth-century German anthropology in the Boasian canon. The book contains extended discussions of Gustav Klemm and Theodor Waitz and features an entire chapter on Bastian.

11. This process can be observed, for example, in the discipline's shifting internal historiography. In Marvin Harris's massive treatise *The Rise of Anthropological Theory* (New York: Thomas Crowell, 1968), nineteenth-century German anthropology appears as cursory context for the work of Boas, but receives no treatment in its own right. In contrast to the dominant tendency, George Stocking has consistently emphasized the formative role nineteenth-century German anthropology played in the work of Boas, and hence the history of twentieth-century American anthropology at large. See, esp., *Race, Culture, and Evolution*.

men—Adolf Bastian and Rudolf Virchow—appeared in the late nineteenth century, and after their passing, no single individual emerged as a genuine leader of the discipline. Even more importantly, interwar German anthropology came to be more and more dominated by racialist thinking, which ran counter to the progressively liberal designs emerging in other national traditions. As a result, Germans became increasingly isolated in the international world of anthropology, and by the 1930s their time seemed to have passed. And if that was not exactly true, then the complicity of German anthropologists in Nazi race crimes seemed to make them well worth forgetting for subsequent generations of scholars. The consequence of these trends is a relative paucity in the historiography of German anthropology, limited, as it has been with two exceptions to be discussed below, to institutional histories of individual museums and biographies of a few leading men.[12]

---

12. See inter alia K. Krieger and G. Koch, *Hundert Jahre Museum für Völkerkunde Berlin* (Berlin: Reimer, 1973); Wolfgang J. Smolka, *Völkerkunde in München: Voraussetzungen, Möglichkeiten und Entwicklungslinien ihrer Institutionalisierung (c. 1850–1933)* (Berlin: Dunker und Humboldt, 1994); and Jürgen Zwernemann, *Hundert Jahre Hamburgisches Museum für Völkerkunde* (Hamburg: Museum für Völkerkunde, 1980). Comprehensive works also appeared, such as Michael Hog, *Ziele und Konzeptionen der Völkerkundemuseen in ihrer historischen Entwicklung* (Frankfurt am Main: Rit G. Fischer Verlag, 1981). A number of biographies of Bastian have appeared over the years. See, for example, Annemarie Fiedermutz-Laun, *Der Kulturhistorische Gedanke bei Adolf Bastian: Systematisierung und Darstellung der Theorie und Methode mit dem Versuch einer Bewertung des Kulturhistorischen Gehaltes auf dieser Grundlage* (Wiesbaden: Franz Steiner Verlag, 1970); and Klaus-Peter Koepping, *Adolf Bastian and the Psychic Unity of Mankind: The Foundations of Anthropology in Nineteenth Century Germany* (London: Queensland Press, 1983). Virchow has also seen repeated attention, although less for his efforts as an anthropologist than for his importance as a pathologist and politician. The standard work is Erwin H. Ackerknecht, *Rudolf Virchow: Doctor, Statesman, Anthropologist* (Madison: University of Wisconsin Press, 1953); a more comprehensive biography is forthcoming: Constantin Goschler, "Rudolf Virchow. Eine biographische Studie über Naturwissenschaft, Liberalismus und die Kultur des Fortschritts," Habilitationsschrift, Humboldt-Universität, Berlin, 2001. Other work focusing on individual figures includes Johannes Steinmetzler, *Die Anthropogeographie Friedrich Ratzels und ihre ideengeschichtlichen Wurzeln* (Bonn: Geographisches Institut, 1956); Gunther Buttmann, *Friedrich Ratzel: Leben und Werk eines deutschen Geographen, 1844–1904* (Stuttgart: Wissenschaftliche Verlagsgesellschaft, 1977); Hans-Jürgen Heinrichs, *Die fremde Welt, das bin ich: Leo Frobenius, Ethnologe, Forschungsreisender, Abenteurer* (Wuppertal: P. Hammer, 1998). Some of the more notorious characters in German anthropology have also received this kind of attention. See, for example, Niels C. Lösch, *Rasse als Konstrukt: Leben und Werk Eugen Fischers* (Frankfurt am Main: Peter Lang, 1997).

Germans in Postcolonial Studies

As with the history of anthropology, Germans have been relatively neglected by the field of postcolonial studies. Traditionally, its practitioners have focused overwhelmingly on Britain and France—the obvious sites for any critical engagement with modern Europe's colonial entanglements. In this analytic context, Germany was often ignored as a late and secondary imperialist power. Edward Said has rendered this stance paradigmatically, listing "the Germans" among those people who did not have a "long tradition of . . . *Orientalism.*"[13]

This view of German exceptionalism and relative noninvolvement was challenged in the 1990s by the pioneering research of several influential German literary scholars. Turning the critical apparatus developed in the field of postcolonial studies to the investigation of Germany itself, they sought to challenge the implicit assumption of a German colonial *Sonderweg.* Susanne Zantop thus forcefully argued for the constitutive presence of "colonial fantasies" in the German national imagination long before the country's formal entry into the colonial contest.[14] Nina Berman similarly held that the pervasiveness of literary orientalism, instantiated most famously in the omnipresent novels of Karl May, evidenced Germany's colonial mind-set quite independently of actually existing colonies.[15] Along with the fellow literary scholars who contributed to the important and similarly themed collection *The Imperialist Imagination: German Colonialism and Its Legacy,* Zantop and Berman have thus effected a kind of normalization.[16] In their interpretive schema, Germany might have been a latecomer to the colonial contest; but the cultural trajectory of its engage-

---

13. Edward Said, *Orientalism* (New York: Vintage, 1978), 1. Most other canonical work in postcolonial studies ignores the German dimension of European colonialism as well. See, e.g., Homi Bhabha, *The Location of Culture* (London: Routledge, 1994); Ann Laura Stoler, *Race and the Education of Desire: Foucault's "History of Sexuality" and the Colonial Order of Things* (Durham: Duke University Press, 1995); Ania Loomba, *Colonialism/Postcolonialism* (London: Routledge, 1998); Gayatri Spivak, *A Critique of Postcolonial Reason: Toward a History of the Vanishing Present* (Cambridge: Harvard University Press, 1999); Robert Young, *Postcolonialism: An Historical Introduction* (Oxford: Blackwell, 2001).

14. Susanne Zantop, *Colonial Fantasies: Conquest, Family, and Nation in Precolonial Germany, 1770–1870* (Durham: Duke University Press, 1997).

15. Nina Berman, *Orientalismus, Kolonialismus und Moderne: Zum Bild des Orients in der deutschen Kultur um 1900* (Stuttgart: Metzler, 1997).

16. Sara Friedrichsmeyer, Sara Lennox, and Susanne Zantop, eds., *The Imperialist Imagination: German Colonialism and Its Legacy* (Ann Arbor: University of Michigan Press, 1998).

ment with non-Europeans essentially followed that of other European colonial powers.

Taken as a collectivity, the literary scholarship on German colonialism has produced compelling arguments; and in many ways, the present volume is profoundly indebted to its insights. At the same time, it diverges from the recent work in important ways. On the one hand, the shift from literature to anthropology and from textual to historical modes of interpretation brings new concerns for the cultural specificity of intellectual and institutional practices. Rather than reading Germans' interests in the rest of the world in terms of a generalized European expansionism, the contributors to this volume allow for the relevance of nationally particular historical trajectories. On the other hand, the following essays display a keen concern for the analytic complexities attained by the careful contextualization of real actors in their various circumstances. In this manner, the present collection draws on the disciplinary commitments of the cultural historians and anthropologists who contributed to it and who sought to pose anew the pressing questions surrounding Germany's colonial history.

Why, then, were Germans interested in their multiple "Others"? The essays in this volume suggest that it was not simply for precolonialist or colonialist reasons. Their concerns were driven by much more than colonial fantasies, imperialist imaginations, or yearnings for power. The German interest in non-Europeans—in their cultures, their religions, their physiognomy, their physiology, and their history—were tightly bound up in a range of intellectual traditions that were much richer and more multifarious than a simple colonialist drive. These included humanism, liberalism, pluralism, monogenism, and a persistent desire to know more about the world that went hand in hand with the German commitment to *Bildung*. All these elements played significant roles in Germans' desire to connect with the wider world, and one of the goals of this volume is to propose this insight as a starting point for further discussion. For one, we need to understand what happened to these progressive forces—how they were altered, co-opted, or displaced—if we hope to understand the history of anthropology, as well as the catastrophic history of Germans' relationship with its racialized Others.

The assertion that there was more to German anthropology than the colonial experience, however, will not suffice. Indeed, we need to find the specific constellations that propelled the discipline in the imperial era; and the essays in this volume emphasize the negotiations that took place on the continent and within parameters that ranged from anthropologists' intellectual agendas and professional opportunities to the striking shifts that characterized their institutional landscape. In this sense, the present volume functions as a critical corrective to a recent literature in postcolonial studies that emphasizes the colonial dimensions in the constitution of modern Europe.[17] Certainly, colonial articulations shaped the metropole in important ways. But the essays in this volume complicate this picture by showing that the German metropole also had its own intellectual momentum—a momentum that was critical to the changing dynamics within the discipline of anthropology.

Even the turn toward race by many German anthropologists in the early twentieth century gained its most powerful impetus from within the German context rather than from Germans' experiences abroad. Swift and surprising when set against the discipline's nineteenth-century history, it was propelled by particular changes in Germany's intellectual and institutional contexts. Indeed, further analysis of the history of German anthropology may well change our understanding of the history of race in Germany. The essays in this volume already provide us with such a striking range of historical trajectories within this single discipline that we gain a new appreciation for the contingent nature of its dramatic reorientations.

The most decisive of those, of course, was the early-twentieth-century shift from a broadly liberal to a more narrowly nationalistic and *völkisch* orientation. In many ways, this development poses the central questions for many of the essays contained in this volume: why did nineteenth-century German anthropology favor a pluralistic, progressive stance, and why did that tendency fade from prominence so quickly after the turn of the century? Why, to put it differently, did Germans initially emphasize culture, plurality, and plasticity, and why did that give way to a new emphasis on biology, hierarchy, and invariance? These are the crucial questions in regard to the disciplinary dynamics of German anthropology. But the answers also have much to tell us about the history of anthropology more generally, the rise of race science in Germany, and the connections between science, culture, and society in Central Europe.

---

17. See, e.g., Antoinette Burton, *Burdens of History: British Feminists, Indian Women, and Imperial Culture* (Chapel Hill: University of North Carolina Press, 1994); Anne McClintock, *Imperial Leather: Race, Gender, and Sexuality in the Colonial Contest* (New York: Routledge, 1995).

A Cosmopolitan Discipline

The unique ways in which Germans approached non-Europeans in the late nineteenth and early twentieth century provide us with important insights into a complex intellectual and cultural trajectory from Herder to Hitler—a trajectory that reveals a particular sensitivity to difference, even if it does not provide us with an obvious path from the first to the second. From our twenty-first-century perspective, it is thus striking to observe the historical continuity of a basic intellectual position that valorized the particularity of each national and ethnic entity. What is even more remarkable is that this German attitude figured in persistent opposition to Western European ideas. Herder had formulated his Counter-Enlightenment credo of cultural pluralism in critical response to the homogenizing tendencies of such French philosophes as Voltaire and Condorcet.[18] Against their inclination to view all of humanity as progressing along a set path toward civilization, Herder posed a vision of historical specificity and cultural incommensurability. This position was embedded in a cosmopolitan framework that accepted the basic unity of mankind, but saw it expressed in difference rather than sameness. Universal reason, in this manner, was not posited as an abstract standard; and as a result, human groups could not be ordered according to developmental schemes.

This Counter-Enlightenment stance persisted through the emergence of German anthropology and ethnology as scientific disciplines in the second half of the nineteenth century.[19] While British anthropologists like Edward B. Tylor and John McLennan championed cultural evolutionism along the lines of Enlightenment progressivism, Bastian and Virchow vigorously opposed any and all developmental theories.[20] Instead of the creation of evolutionary hierarchies, they advocated large-scale research that would chart the specificities of all the world's peoples, followed, in turn, by a determination of those aspects of human life that were truly universal. Bastian and Virchow, much like Herder, the brothers Humboldt, and a range of nineteenth-century German scholars before them, ultimately viewed human diversity

---

18. On Herder and the German Counter-Enlightenment tradition, see Isiah Berlin, *Vico and Herder* (London: Hogarth Press, 1976); Berlin, *Against the Current* (Oxford: Oxford University Press, 1981).

19. Bunzl, "Boas and the Humboldtian Tradition."

20. On the history of nineteenth-century British cultural evolutionism, see Stocking, *Victorian Anthropology.*

through a specifically German lens; and what they saw was the result of particular histories rather than stages on the progressive march of reason.

For German ethnologists, heirs to the Herderian *Volksgeist* tradition, culture was something people everywhere possessed. Neither did Europeans have a monopoly over it, nor did other groups strive unsuccessfully to attain it. This concept of culture informed Germans' interactions with non-Europeans on a variety of different levels and framed the most essential parameters of German ethnology as a science. It was this concept that, as Harry Liebersohn and Rainer Buschmann show in their respective essays, led to Germans' interest in salvaging particular cultures in Micronesia and Samoa, and to a form of empire building in the Pacific that was based on fundamentally different principles than those employed by Britain and France. This culture concept also accounted for the widespread agreement among Germans that the corruption of indigenous cultures should be blamed on the West, as well as a strong belief that "pure" cultures might still be discovered even in the final moments of the nineteenth century.

Germans' fascination with the plurality of cultures, however, was not limited to their engagement with "exotic" areas of the world. It also played an important role in their more introspective, midcentury endeavors to make sense of European cultures. *Völkerpsychologie,* for example, was a discipline focused on European cultures and their complicated natures. It deployed the intensive study of language and literature to elucidate the connections between individuals and groups and to delineate the relationships between culture, nation, and *Volk.* As Matti Bunzl stresses in his essay in this volume, Heymann Steinthal and Moritz Lazarus founded *Völkerpsychologie* in an effort to locate themselves within German culture, to understand and justify their own identities as German Jews. But in so doing they also captured the more general attempts in Germany to create cultural sciences that unified humanist impulses with the more positivist character of the modern age.

Ethnologists who focused on non-Europeans showed the same prominent interest in the mixing of cultures, and emphasized each culture's historicity. Indeed, for Bastian, who dubbed himself a "psychological traveler" [psychologischer Reisender] in 1860,[21] the preemi-

---

21. Adolf Bastian, "Meine Reise um und durch die Welt," *Illustrirte Zeitung* 35 (1860): 219–22.

nence of culture, the processes of collective thought, and the relationship between individuals and groups framed his ideas and efforts. As H. Glenn Penny shows us, much of Bastian's ethnology was focused on a quest to better understand the workings of the human mind. In contrast to Lazarus and Steinthal, however, Bastian moved beyond the confines of the written text and traveled abroad for his sources. Embracing the natural sciences, he took his questions into the field where material artifacts could be collected as the new definitive "texts" of human history. A number of Bastian's counterparts in Britain and the United States were engaged in similar efforts of artifact collection (even though they themselves began traveling abroad at a much later date). What set Bastian and his colleagues apart from the Anglo-American tradition, however, was a desire to use the collected material to provide new answers about humanity at large rather than validate old truths about European superiority.[22] Indeed, the pervasive tendency to seek out new information about human cultures and to use it to refashion oneself, not only helps to account for the worldliness that could be found even in the most provincial of German places,[23] it also allows us to understand the generous support Bastian and his counterparts received in an array of German cities.[24]

German intellectual traditions were thus markedly different from those found in Western Europe, and as a result, so were Germans' encounters with non-Europeans. Indeed, as Harry Liebersohn reminds us in his contribution to this volume, there is no justification for presupposing that Europeans shared a common cultural code while abroad or to assume that they would behave similarly during their

---

22. For a discussion of anthropologists' goals in the Smithsonian, for example, and the motivations behind their displays, see Hinsley, *Savages and Scientists.* Cf. Penny, "Cosmopolitan Visions," 51–54.

23. This forward-looking tendency is well established in much of the historiography on German history. See, for example, Modris Eksteins, *Rites of Spring: The Great War and the Birth of the Modern Age* (Boston: Houghton Mifflin, 1989); Rudy Koshar, "The *Kaiserreich's* Ruins: Hope, Memory, and Political Culture in Imperial Germany," in *Society, Culture, and the State in Germany, 1870–1930,* ed. Geoff Eley (Ann Arbor: University of Michigan Press, 1996), 487–512; Koshar, *Germany's Transient Pasts: Preservation and National Memory in the Twentieth Century* (Chapel Hill: University of North Carolina Press, 1998); Peter Fritzsche, "Nazi Modern," *Modernism/Modernity* 3, no. 1 (1996): 1–21.

24. In addition to the big museums in Germany's largest cities, Hamburg, Berlin, Leipzig, and Munich, a number of smaller museums were also founded during the imperial period in smaller cities: Bremen, Cassel, Darmstadt, Karlsruhe, Lübeck, Stuttgart, Freiburg, as well as medium-sized cities such as Dresden, Cologne, and Frankfurt. For a fairly complete listing see Hog, *Völkerkundemuseen,* 92–106.

interactions with non-Europeans. Germans' encounters were generally different from those of the French or the British because, for most of the nineteenth century, they were informed first and foremost by their notions of culture rather than their political preconceptions and colonial concerns.

External, geopolitical factors thus contributed to the persistence of Germans' emphasis on culture. Their initial encounters and theoretical meditations predated the formation of the German Empire by a considerable period. Indeed, it mattered a great deal that Germans had to wait until the middle of the 1880s to transition from being individuals who benefited from the umbrella of imperialism while traveling, trading, and working outside of Europe, to citizens of a nation-state actively engaged in acquiring lands and peoples for the purpose of political and economic domination. Largely as a result of these historical contexts, the Herderian *Volksgeist* tradition continued to shape many educated Germans' encounters abroad as well as their theorizing at home, even after Imperial Germany was founded and began to emerge as a colonial power of its own.

The enduringly cosmopolitan orientation of late-nineteenth-century German anthropologists was particularly evident in their selection of ethnographic sites. Where people did their anthropology not only made a significant difference in terms of knowledge production of course, but functioned as a direct reflection of larger political constellations. By the late nineteenth century, ethnographers from other countries worked overwhelmingly in their own spheres of colonial influence: the French in Africa; the British in Africa, India, and Australia; and the Americans among American Indians. German anthropologists, by contrast, were far more likely to pursue their interests beyond the colonial reach of the *Kaiserreich*. Working on every continent, Germans thus produced the vast majority of ethnography on the indigenous peoples of Brazil and other South American states during the nineteenth century,[25] while Leo Frobenius received funding from at

---

25. In the decades around the turn of the century the German ethnologists who participated in large-scale expeditions to Brazil included, among others, Karl and Wilhelm von den Steinen (1884, 1887–88), Paul Ehrenreich (1887–88), Hermann Meyer (1895–99), Max Schmidt (1901–27), Fritz Krause (1908), and Theodor Koch-Grünberg (1899–1924), all of whom made successful careers out of their ventures. For an annotated list of well-known ethnologists who explored Brazil before 1914 see John Hemming, *Amazon Frontier: The Defeat of the Brazilian Indians* (Cambridge: Harvard University Press, 1987), 483–512. His list, however, is not comprehensive.

least three major German museums to work in French and British territories in North and West Africa as late as the first decade of the twentieth.[26]

On the one hand, such efforts were an articulation of the general intellectual vision behind German anthropology: the commitment to inductive science, an empirical methodology that stressed the need to gather as much information as possible before attempting to generate theories about human difference, and the Herderian attempt to cover the various manifestation of *Volksgeist* as completely as possible. But on the other hand, they were also a by-product of the fact that while Germany had a cosmopolitan tradition it could build on, it was itself a young nation-state. Together, these factors meant that German ethnologists and anthropologists were, at least initially, less committed and tied to the advancement of a national community. Instead, their dedication was to international scientific ideals, with the result that Germans were eager to practice anthropology all over the world and felt comfortable doing so.

If German anthropology was marked by the persistent worldliness of its ethnographic engagement, it was also characterized by a remarkable provincialism. Much more than in Western Europe and the United States, anthropology actually took place outside the major metropolitan centers. This situation reflected German anthropology's beginnings in a self-consciously polycentric nation where municipal and regional support was critical for the success of local universities and the rise of the German sciences.[27] Germany's polycentric nature ultimately accounted for the growth of the numerous regional centers of anthropology, located in such cities as Leipzig, Hamburg, Stuttgart, Munich, and Cologne, as well as in Berlin and, in the realm of the Habsburg Monarchy, Vienna. Museums, rather than universities, were the predominate institutional setting for the development of ethnology, and each of these cities' respective museums—funded by municipal and regional governments as well as local and international supporters—had their own regional flavors. The museum in the harbor city of Hamburg, for example, became famous for its collections from the South Seas, while its counterpart in the "cultural center" of Munich was renowned for artifacts from East Asia. Only the museum

---

26. Jürgen Zwernemann, "Leo Frobenius und das Hamburgische Museum für Völkerkunde," *Mitteilungen aus dem Museum für Völkerkunde Hamburg* 17 (1987): 111–27.

27. Joseph Ben David, *The Scientist's Role in Society: A Comparative Study* (Englewood Cliffs, N.J.: Prentice Hall, 1971).

in the imperial city of Berlin had truly significant collections from all around the globe (in part because the institute enjoyed privileged access to collections from the colonies). But all of the museums actively sought to take in the entire world.

Indeed, the provincialism of Germany's ethnological museums was remarkably worldly. A similar worldliness was also apparent outside the museums, in the many German cities that celebrated the arrival of *Völkerschauen* in their parks and squares. Even small and medium-sized towns were eager to host these events, not simply for the titillating experience of observing exotic others, but as part of a genuine craving for a knowledge of, and experience with, the larger world. This experience was also critical for the cities' reputations and self-images. The arrival of *Völkerschauen* in Basel, for example, was hailed in local newspapers as a marker that their city was no longer a provincial town, but a *Grossstadt* in the most modern sense.[28] To be sure, the enthusiasm for *Völkerschauen* had much to do with a stereotypically Western fascination for the "primitive"; but it also reflected a particularly German craving for *Bildung* as the defining feature of respectable middle-class existence in and beyond the major urban centers.[29] Together, these impulses produced a veritable industry of *Völkerschauen:* events that—as Sierra Bruckner shows in her essay—were both exotic spectacles of the kind found in other European and American cities and uniquely German occasions whose success was gauged by their scientific and educational quality.[30]

---

28. Balthasar Staehelin, *Völkerschauen im Zoologischen Garten Basel 1879–1935* (Basel: Basler Afrika Bibliographien, 1993), 136.

29. On this aspect of *Bildung* see Georg Bollenbeck, *Bildung und Kultur: Glanz und Elend eines deutschen Deutungsmusters* (Frankfurt am Main: Suhrkamp, 1996).

30. See Bruckner in this volume. See also Sibylle Benninghoff-Lühl, "Die Ausstellung der Kolonialisierten: Völkerschauen von 1874–1932," *Andenken an den Kolonialismus,* Ausstellungskataloge der Universität Tübingen, no. 17 (1984), 52–64; Benninghoff-Lühl, "Völkerschauen—Attraktionen und Gefahr des Exotischen," *SOWI—Sozialwissenschaftliche Informationen* 15, no. 4 (1986): 41–48; Stefan Goldmann, "Wilde in Europa," in *Wir und die Wilden: Einblicke in eine kannibalische Beziehung,* ed. Thomas Theye (Reinbeck bei Hamburg: Rowohlt, 1985), 243–69; Wolfgang Haberland, "'Diese Indianer sind Falsch,' Neun Bella Coola im Deutschen Reich 1885/6," *Archiv für Völkerkunde* 42 (1988): 3–67; Barbara Hey, "Vom 'dunklen Kontinent' zur 'anschmiegsamen Exotin,'" *Österreichische Zeitschrift für Geschichtswissenschaft* 8, no. 1 (1997): 186–211; Bernth Lindfors, ed., *Africans on Stage: Studies in Ethnological Show Business* (Bloomington: Indiana University Press, 1999); Hilke Thode-Arora, *Für fünfzig Pfennig um die Welt: Die Hagenbeckschen Völkerschauen* (New York: Campus, 1989); Michael Wiener, *Ikonographie des Wilden: Menschen-Bilder in Ethnographie und Photographie zwischen 1850 und 1918* (Munich: Trickster Verlag, 1990).

Were German ethnology and anthropology significantly different because of the diversity of cosmopolitan and provincial places at which they were practiced? This collection cannot offer a definitive answer to that question, but the contributions to the volume do indicate that the diversity of places had much to do with the liberal orientation of these German sciences in the late nineteenth century as well as their turn to a national and eventually racial orientation in the early twentieth.

The Turn toward Nation and Race

The rather abrupt shift after the turn of the twentieth century from a liberal preoccupation with the plenitude of the world's peoples to a more narrow concern with the nation's specific Others stands at the heart of German anthropology's historiography; and several of the essays in this volume address it directly. In general terms, our contributors concur that it was shifting national and international contexts that engendered the transformation. Having undergone a "scientization" as humanism went disciplinary in the last decades of the nineteenth century, ethnology and anthropology moved closer to the nation's colonial project; and in the process, its practitioners began to engage in debates that paved the way for a fundamental rearticulation, not just of anthropological theory, but also of Germany's relationships to its various Others. All contributors thus readily agree on the basic facts: that most German anthropologists and ethnologists abandoned the liberal humanism of Virchow and Bastian after the turn of the century, and that they embraced an increasingly *völkisch* vision, dominated by the various "struggles" for Lebensraum, both outside and within Europe instead. Where the authors of the following essays enter into productive disagreements and dialogues, however, is in their respective accountings for this development.

Penny, for one, emphasizes that the critical shift was not simply a move from liberal to illiberal science. Rather, he argues that the development that matters was a fundamental transition in conceptions about what constituted good science. Charting the transformation in the context of Germany's ethnological museums, he traces a generational shift that turned an earlier emphasis on empirical induction and global human psychology into a more limited and mechanical concern for the location and comparison of distinct cultural groups and their respective histories. This move took place after the turn of the twentieth century for a number of reasons; and Penny identifies professional pressures, institutional limitations, and concerns about the pace and viability of Bastian's empirical project as crucial factors in the shift that was to affect the meaning of human difference at the most basic level.

Popular demands were a critical factor in this transition as well, and indeed, when we combine Penny's essay on museums with Bruckner's discussion of commercial ethnography, we not only see a striking parallel in the trajectory of these two forms of ethnographic display; we also gain an increased appreciation for the transformative power that public opinion could bring to German science. Both the museums and the *Völkerschauen* were driven initially by a similar quest for knowledge. But around the turn of the century, both institutions went through analogous transitions that reflected their location in a rapidly changing public sphere. When Germany was refashioned by the forces of modernity—the onset of mass culture and commercial consumption, the democratization of visual culture, and the rise of the socialist parties—German ethnology was refashioned as well. Its visual displays moved toward a more imperialistic kind of entertainment in both their popular and professional variants, and that affected the character of ethnology as a science.

The liberal focus on culture, plurality, and plasticity, however, was not lost only in the museums and at the *Völkerschauen*. As a number of other contributors show, the development extended to other disciplinary domains, particularly the subfield of physical anthropology. Dating the transformation at a particularly early moment, Andrew Zimmerman argues that anthropology lost its humanist commitments as soon as the scientization of the disciplines began to take shape. While he thus agrees with Penny that the political trajectory of German anthropology, and its eventual usefulness for fascism, cannot be reduced to a shift from a more liberal to a less liberal science, he ultimately offers a more radical reinterpretation. Rather than relating the emergence of a *völkisch* science to institutional developments and transformations of the public sphere, he indicts an earlier movement toward an ostensibly objective anthropology, one based on the precepts of natural science and associated most prominently with Virchow. For Zimmerman, the increasingly colonial dimensions in the work of German anthropologists thus stands as a cipher for a basic inhumanity that linked the project of objective measurement to the systematic destruction of Germany's Others. In this interpretive framework, German South West Africa not only emerges as a laboratory for genocide, but as a reminder of anthropology's complicity in Germany's trajectory. For it was the power relations within colonial territories (especially their hospitals, prisons, and graveyards) that at once yielded the docile subjects for anthropologists' measurements as well as the ultimate sites for the collection of body parts—the central objects of their desires. The acquisition of these body parts thus not only produced anthropology and colonialism as mutually constitutive practices, but it rendered the new objectivity itself a veritable building block in an antihumanist trajectory that would lead to the catastrophic treatment of non-German people as objects rather than subjects.

Pascal Grosse tells a somewhat different story. He, too, is concerned with transformations in the attitudes toward non-Europeans; but in his focus on debates about acclimatization, he figures the increasing link between anthropology and colonial politics in different terms. According to Grosse, as physical anthropologists turned to the question of Europeans' ability to survive in tropical climates, they did prepare the way for many of the biological theories favored by the National Socialists. But in contrast to Zimmerman, Grosse dates the crucial shift to the turn of the century when anthropologists began to link their work to colonial politics, biology, and eugenics. Grosse thus sees the transformation in German anthropology apart from the commitment to objective science. In fact, he emphasizes that the willingness to draw affirmative connections between race, climate, and colonial ambitions was a radical departure from Virchow's stance. Along with his liberal supporters, Virchow had actually harnessed anthropology to argue against Bismarck's colonial designs, suggesting that European settlements were futile in light of a biologically proven inability to adapt to tropical climates and reproduce in sufficient numbers. Proponents of German colonialism, in contrast, sought to breed this problem away, arguing in favor of a biological solution—a process of eugenic selection that would identify Germans who were tropically fit.

In the course of the acclimatization debate, the procolonial faction gained the upper hand. With growing political interest in settler colonies, acclimatization in tropical colonies was cast as a step toward a solution for the pressing population problems at home. As a result, the discourse on acclimatization not only linked biology and eugenics, but produced a focus on the selection and creation of human beings who would at once adapt to new environments and maintain their "German" character. The critical difference between Grosse's and Zimmerman's explanations, however, is that Grosse sees the triumph of the procolonial faction as a function of politics rather than science. German anthropology, his interpretation suggests, was less an agent of historical change than a mirror of larger social developments.

Grosse and Zimmerman's disagreements on the origins of a nationally driven anthropology notwithstanding, they do concur on the centrality of colonial concerns in the process. And yet, on the road to race science and a new focus on biology, colonial actions and debates were not the only context for changes in intellectual orientation and scientific praxis. Indeed, much of what we can find in the behavior and attitudes of physical anthropologists in the colonies Andrew Evans has also found in Austrian and German prisoner-of-war camps during World War I. The disparate power relations, the distancing between the observer and the observed, the reduction or elimination of the prisoner's subjectivity, all occurred between German anthropologists and their European subjects in the camps.

But war not only put some Europeans into positions usually occupied by colonized peoples. According to Evans, it created the very conditions that led to the erosion of the categories that had been at the heart of the liberal anthropological project. Prior to the war, and despite the movement toward natural science, German anthropology was still dominated by the liberal conviction that there was no direct connection between race and human faculty—a stance that inhibited, indeed made all but impossible, the positing of racial hierarchies. Racial types were not linked to cultural categories, and the sciences of ethnology and anthropology maintained their separate domains. The camp experience, Evans argues, broke down the division. In particular, it was the anthropologists' practice of measuring and objectifying Europeans, whom they organized and differentiated according to national (political) categories, that initiated the conflation of race, nation, and *Volk*. Occurring in the fervent context of the Great War, these practices also suggest how German anthropologists, who had purposefully isolated themselves from the race debate and drawn on the authority of their science to debunk racial theories, could turn, so quickly and dramatically, to an acceptance of race science. Evans thus offers yet another explanation of how anthropologists became complicit in creating the racial space Germans occupied in the Weimar and Nazi periods.

The essays on German anthropology's turn to nation and race thus present a multiplicity of contributing factors. In so doing, they underscore that race science did not necessarily emerge because of orientalist discourses, but despite the many alternatives. Local causes and immediate contingencies were clearly of immense importance, more so, arguably, than long dureé intellectual or cultural trajectories.

But even if the analytic focus is on the shift toward nation and race itself, causation remains an issue of debate. Was the shift from culture, plurality, and plasticity to biology, hierarchy, and invariance a function of context, actions, or ideology? Again, there is no consensus on the question, not even among the essays focused on physical anthropology. Grosse emphasizes the role of political contingencies that redirected the discourse on acclimatization, taking anthropologists with it. Zimmerman stresses the importance of scientific practice, particularly the fateful decision by liberals to embrace a new objectivity that undermined humanism within the colonial context and beyond. Evans agrees that contingencies and contexts, in this case the scientific practices in prisoner-of-war camps, mattered greatly in the transformation of German anthropology. But he also argues that in the end, the move away from liberal categories and precepts was neither inadvertent nor accidental. It was the result of conscious choice, a willingness to abandon liberal ideals during and after the experience of the camps.

Ideology, in short, mattered a great deal, as two of the other contributors to this volume suggest as well. Like Evans, Penny argues that the transformation of German ethnology depended first and foremost on the willingness of a younger generation to abandon their predecessors' ideological convictions about the sanctity of a particular scientific method. He, too, argues that this move was a conscious choice that reflected a shift in principles, not unlike the new willingness among anthropologists in the camps to entertain a link between biology and human faculty.

Similarly, as Suzanne Marchand shows us, a conscious, ideological commitment to pluralism prevented Austria's anthropological establishment from following suit. Because of his Catholic convictions, Wilhelm Schmidt's turn toward diffusionism did not bring him closer to colonialist ideals or hierarchies of race, as was the case with some of his German counterparts. Quite the contrary, institutional and religious contexts in Austria provided him with an alternative space for his decision making; and his strong personal beliefs encouraged him to eschew colonialist efforts and race theories right up through World War II. In all these cases, conscious, ideological choices either facilitated or prevented the turn toward race.

The ideological refusal of race became a minority position in Germany. Ironically, however, it also emerged as the most enduring legacy of that country's nineteenth-century tradition. As the liberal tenets of Virchow and Bastian were abandoned in Germany itself, they became the cornerstone of the anthropology developed in the United States by Franz Boas. A quintessential nineteenth-century scholar who had trained with the luminaries of Germany's liberal anthropology, Boas not only adhered to the strict separation between race, language, and culture, but made it the programmatic center of an antievolutionary, anticolonial, and antiracist project that always retained the progressive character of a *Kulturkampf*.[31] In Germany, ideological breakdowns led to anthropology's abandonment of liberal principles and the discipline's eventual complicity with Nazi race crimes. In the United States, ideology mattered too; but there, it led in the very opposite direction, away from racialist prejudice and toward a more pluralistic, democratic society.

Religion and Anthropology

To gloss the antiracist commitments of such figures as Schmidt and Boas under the rubric of "ideology" is necessarily vague. Greater specificity might be achieved by taking a closer look at an understudied variable in the history of German anthropology, namely religion. Indeed, the essays by Marchand and Bunzl in this volume remind us that the opposition to race science in Central Europe often had religious valences. Marchand demonstrates that it was largely the belief systems at the base of Schmidt's religiosity that account for the critical differences between Austria's leading ethnologist's brand of diffusionism and that of his counterparts in the North. Schmidt's Catholicism, in other words, shaped the essential parameters of his science, making it all but impossible for him to support race science.

Paradigms based in different religious traditions also matter in Bunzl's discussion of the German-Jewish orientation informing the discipline of *Völkerpsychologie*. In that case, however, religious effects are more complicatedly mediated, surfacing less as a set of beliefs than as an overarching cultural orientation, itself the effect of the encounter between a religious/cultural system (Judaism) and a social/cultural system (the German middle-class culture of *Bildung*). That encounter

---

31. Stocking, "Anthropology as *Kulturkampf*: Science and Politics in the Career of Franz Boas," in *Ethnographer's Magic*, 92–113.

deserves further elucidation, not least because, as Bunzl suggests in conclusion of his essay, it identifies the configuration of Boasian anthropology as a specifically German-Jewish phenomenon.

Both Marchand and Bunzl thus underscore the relevance of religious difference in German anthropology. Their focus on the impact of belief systems in shaping the science of Catholics and Jews, however, is not meant to imply that religion was only operative among members of more or less marginal groups. On the contrary, their contributions encourage us to think about the impact of religion more systematically; and it is in this vein, that they pave the way toward future work on the religious dynamics underlying the dominant sciences forged at such Protestant strongholds as Berlin and Hamburg.

Even more, however, the essays by Marchand and Bunzl point beyond Germany to the relevance of religious difference in the history of anthropology at large. Some work exists—Stocking's remarks on Quakerism, Clifford's analysis of Maurice Leenhart—but the function of religion in the constitution of modern anthropology's history remains insufficiently understood.[32] The essays by Marchand and Bunzl thus provide us with a new incentive to investigate how religion channeled and shaped the legitimating power of science with regard to cultural hierarchies, colonial ambition, and concepts of race. The fact that anthropology in the United States and Great Britain, as well as in most of Germany, took shape overwhelmingly within a Protestant context, for example, has received remarkably little attention; and much work thus needs to be done to elucidate the various connections between religious configurations and anthropological knowledge production.

Colonialism and Anthropology

While the relationship between religion and anthropology remains underexplored, the question of anthropology's role vis-à-vis colonialism has been center stage for several decades. This ongoing interest, however, has not always led to clarification of the vexed issue. Even a cursory analysis of the available literature reveals a striking disjuncture between the arguments advanced by scholars engaged in postcolonial

---

32. Stocking, *Victorian Anthropology;* Clifford, *Person and Myth.* For an analysis of early modern encounters that does pay attention to the importance of religion, see Anthony Pagden, *The Fall of Natural Man: The American Indian and the Origins of Comparative Ethnology* (Cambridge: Cambridge University Press, 1982).

studies and those who have focused more specifically on the history of anthropology. Practitioners of both disciplines emphasize the preeminent importance of the relationship between anthropology and colonialism; but the commonality often ends there. As Frederick Cooper and Ann Laura Stoler have argued, scholars engaged in postcolonial studies tend to privilege binary oppositions, especially self/other polarities, that draw on a model posited decades ago in Said's *Orientalism*.[33] In consequence, a majority have failed to give enough attention to "the plurality of competing visions by which Europeans in the colonies fashioned their distinctions, conjured up their 'whiteness,' and reinvented themselves."[34] An intellectual myopia thus often reigns.

Moreover, as Cooper and Stoler go on to note, many practitioners of postcolonial studies continue to essentialize the function of anthropologists in colonialism, painting them overwhelmingly as the handmaidens of colonial domination and paying little attention to the more nuanced approaches developed by historians of anthropology over the last twenty years.[35] Indeed, recent work on the history of anthropology has given our understanding of the relationship between colonialism and anthropology much greater complexity.[36] A new emphasis on differentiations in regard to time, region, and individuals is only the most important result of these efforts, which have also begun to challenge the simple binaries and predictable characterizations often found in postcolonial studies.

The present volume is conceived in the spirit of Cooper and Stoler; and as such, it intervenes in the available literature on the relationship between colonialism and German anthropology. That literature has largely followed the intellectual trends set by British and American postcolonial scholars—resulting in work organized around totalizing

---

33. Said himself has complained that this is a model that has been reified by many of his followers. Frederick Cooper and Ann Laura Stoler, "Between Metropole and Colony: Rethinking a Research Agenda," in *Tensions of Empire: Colonial Cultures in a Bourgeois World*, ed. Cooper and Stoler (Berkeley and Los Angeles: University of California Press, 1997), 9–10, 16–18.
34. Ibid., 16.
35. Ibid., 14.
36. The most important contributions are Talal Asad, ed. *Anthropology and the Colonial Encounter* (Atlantic Highlands, N.J.: Humanities Press, 1973); George W. Stocking, ed., *Colonial Situations: Essays on the Contextualization of Ethnographic Knowledge,* History of Anthropology, no. 7 (Madison: University of Wisconsin Press, 1991); Nicholas Thomas, *Colonialism's Culture: Anthropology, Travel, and Government* (Cambridge: Polity Press, 1994); Pels and Salemink, *Colonial Subjects.*

arguments designed to either condemn or exonerate German anthropology from the charge of colonial complicity.[37] Few scholars, to date, have thus paid attention to the variability of colonial contexts; and in consequence, we know little about the specific roles German anthropologists played at different times and in particular colonial settings.

The present volume cannot address these issues comprehensively. But a number of essays do revisit the links between German anthropology and German colonialism to show that their relationship was far from monolithic. These essays are not designed to rehabilitate a science gone astray. Rather, the goal of this work is to approach German ethnology and anthropology as disciplines that took shape within a particular national context as well as the more overarching imperialist one, and to use the differences that we can identify between the Germans and their more frequently scrutinized British, French, and American counterparts to shed light on broader questions in the history of anthropology as well as Germans' interests in, and relationships with, non-Europeans.

The contributions by Rainer Buschmann and Robert Gordon are excellent examples of this approach. Buschmann presents us with a vision of German New Guinea in which colonialism and anthropology were tightly connected—but not in the most obvious ways. He shows that the sciences of ethnology and anthropology were harnessed by the colonial governor Albert Hahl as a means for helping to repopulate German territories and improving relations between colonizer and colonized. Hahl not only supported anthropologists, took an active interest in their work and tried to turn it to his advantage; he also partici-

---

37. Within the German literature the first substantive inquiry into the colonial question came from East Germany, where the analysis of the relationship between colonialism and anthropology (or other related sciences) was less of a taboo topic. Ingeburg Winkelmann, "Die Bürgeliche Ethnographie im Dienste der Kolonialpolitik des Deutschen Reiches (1870–1918)," Ph.D. diss., Humboldt-Universität, Berlin, 1966. Two decades later a similar argument was posited in the West by Manfred Gothsch in *Die deutsche Völkerkunde und ihr Verhältnis zum Kolonialismus: Ein Beitrag zur kolonialideologischen und kolonialpraktischen Bedeutung der deutschen Völkerkunde in der Zeit von 1870 bis 1945* (Hamburg: Institut für Internationale Angelegenheiten der Universität Hamburg, 1983). Indeed, Hamburg seems to have led this later movement in introspection, producing both Hans Fischer's *Die Hamburger Südsee Expedition. Über Ethnographie und Kolonialismus* (Frankfurt am Main: Syndikat Verlag, 1981), and the rather trenchant retorts by Volker Harms, such as "Das Historische Verhältnis der deutschen Ethnologie zum Kolonialismus," *Zeitschrift für Kulturaustausch* 4 (1984): 401–16; see also Woodruff D. Smith, "Anthropology and German Colonialism," in *Germans in the Tropics: Essays in German Colonial History*, ed. Arthur J. Knoll and Lewis H. Gann (Westport, Conn.: Greenwood Press, 1987), 39–58.

pated in refashioning anthropological theory and practice by urging a number of young German anthropologists in the direction of a functionalist anthropology that de-emphasized the quest for collections in favor of extended, in situ analysis.

Buschmann's example is instructive in a number of ways. In suggesting that the dialog between anthropologists and colonial officials may have been more fruitful than generally imagined, it provides us with one instance where colonial authorities had a significant impact on methodology and theory. In this manner, Buschmann documents a powerful exception to Talal Asad's well-known claim that "the role of anthropologists in maintaining structures of imperial domination" has "usually been trivial," the "knowledge they produced" being "too esoteric for government use."[38] Hahl, Buschmann explains, found plenty of uses for anthropological knowledge and made significant strides in exploiting it. But he pushed German ethnologists toward functionalism, not toward a science based on biological concepts of race or one meant to legitimate colonial hierarchies of power.

Gordon's essay on the interrelation of science and colonial respectability in South West Africa offers another set of surprises, centered on the fact that metropolitan ideas sometimes took on unexpected resonance in the shifting colonial contexts of the early twentieth century. In South West Africa, the German settlers who had initially colonized the territory found themselves occupied by a new colonial power following World War I. In an interesting twist on the relationship between settlers, indigenous peoples, and the science of German anthropology, Gordon illustrates how, over the course of a few decades, the peoples who had been the target of the eliminationist policies detailed by Zimmerman, the Nama or Bushmen, became the objects of new interest for German settlers. These settlers sought to use the Nama and what they deemed to be a quintessentially German science to assert their own character against the British and South Africans. Once considered a collective menace, these "authentic primitives" were quickly transformed into a national scientific treasure, something to be used in political efforts to set post-German Namibians apart from the interloping South Africans. Over time, the Bushmen were thus harnessed for a variety of new uses, and so too were the Germans. The names of German and Austrian scientists from an earlier

---

38. Talal Asad, "From the History of Colonial Anthropology to the Anthropology of Western Hegemony," in Stocking, *Colonial Situations*, 315.

era found their way onto street signs in Windhoek; and Eugen Fischer, the notorious race theorist who was shunned by the world in light of his role during the Third Reich, was hailed for his achievements in *Rassenkunde* and invited to lecture in this tiny part of the postcolonial world at a time when his reputation in Europe had seriously waned.

Such strange twists in German anthropology's colonial dynamics complicate the formulation of generalized insights on the relationship between anthropology and colonialism. Instead, the disjunctures between anthropological trends in the metropole and practices in many colonial spaces alert us to the contingencies and contradictions that characterized the different paths pursued by German ethnologists and anthropologists during the age of empire. Rather than search for an overarching pattern of German colonial anthropology, we thus need to recognize the many changes that led to the variously localized constellations, both in regard to the disciplines and the different sites of the colonial contest. All this indicates that we can locate the answers to our questions on the relationship between German anthropology and German colonialism (and, for that matter, anthropology and colonialism in general) in the shifting intersection of particular agendas—not in grand oppositions.

Nazism and Anthropology

Given the unquestioned centrality of National Socialism and the Holocaust in German history, it is not surprising that much of the literature on German ethnology and anthropology, especially that produced in the German-speaking world itself, addresses that darkest of historical periods.[39] The importance of this work is self-evident, even though it has significant historiographical limitations. Often written in the form of individual or institutional reckoning, the scholarship on Nazi

---

39. The most comprehensive treatise on the relationship between anthropology and National Socialism is Hans Fischer, *Völkerkunde im Nationalsozialismus. Aspekte der Anpassung, Affinität und Behauptung einer wissenschaftlichen Disziplin* (Berlin: Reimer Verlag, 1990). See also Markus Mosen, *Der koloniale Traum: Angewandte Ethnologie im Nationalsozialismus* (Bonn: Holos, 1991); Peter Linimayr, *Wiener Völkerkunde im Nationalsozialismus: Ansätze zu einer NS-Wissenschaft* (Frankfurt am Main: Peter Lang, 1994); Thomas Hauschild, ed., *Lebenslust und Fremdenfurcht: Ethnologie im Dritten Reich* (Frankfurt am Main: Suhrkamp, 1995). Much has also been written about the relationship between folklore and National Socialism. See esp. Wolfgang Jacobeit, Hannjost Lixfeld, and Olaf Bockhorn, eds., *Völkische Wissenschaft: Gestalten und Tendenzen der deutschen und österreichischen Volkskunde in der ersten Hälfte des 20. Jahrhunderts* (Vienna: Böhlau, 1994).

anthropology tends to treat the Third Reich in relative isolation; and in consequence, comparatively little attention has been paid to the long-standing intellectual and institutional processes that led to the discipline's complicity in Nazi crimes.

The pioneering work on the genealogies of Nazi anthropology was actually undertaken by scholars outside the German-speaking world; and we owe much to the efforts by Benoit Massin and Robert Proctor, who have elucidated the transition from a self-consciously liberal physical anthropology to an overtly nationalist *Rassenkunde*.[40] Prior to this volume, their essays constituted the most extensive investigations of the decisive shift in early-twentieth-century German anthropology. But in linking the transition to the eventual emergence of Nazi anthropology, their work also transported a teleological conceptualization, especially in the absence of research into the intellectual and political diversity of the discipline in turn-of-the-century Germany. Reading the discipline's trajectory through latter-day National Socialists is bound to produce a deep genealogy of Nazi thought qua anthropological race science. And while such an interpretation is valid for figures like Eugen Fischer, it would be misleading to see all the developments of early-twentieth-century German anthropology as part of a seamless march toward the Kaiser Wilhelm Institute for Anthropology, Human Descent Theory, and Eugenics.

Much of the literature produced on Germany by postcolonial studies scholars gives rise to similar concerns regarding teleological reasoning. For the editors of *The Imperialist Imagination*, to take the paradigmatic example, the Holocaust is the "central and unavoidable fact of German history"; and that situation necessitates a search for antecedents and precedents.[41] Ever since Hannah Arendt's famous pronouncements, German colonialism—with its agenda of national expansionism and the protosearch for *Lebensraum*—has been seen as a late-nineteenth-century laboratory of Nazi policy; and it is that connection which animates much of the scholarship on Germans' relations with their non-European Others during the imperial era.[42] In that con-

---

40. Massin, "From Virchow to Fischer"; Proctor, "From *Anthropologie* to *Rassenkunde*."

41. Friedrichsmeyer, Lennox, and Zantop, *The Imperialist Imagination*, 4.

42. Hannah Arendt, *The Origins of Totalitarianism* (New York: Harcourt, Brace, Jovanovich, 1973). In many ways, Susanne Zantop's groundbreaking work on Germans' "colonial fantasies" set this analytic trend. She, and those who followed her, have attempted to extend Arendt's pronouncements about the connection between colonialism and National Socialism. Drawing on the texts produced by (some) German writers, a number of these

text, too, seminal work has been done; but the concern to locate the nineteenth-century origins of Nazism in Germany's colonial encounters invariably flattens the complexities inherent in these situations.

None of this is to say that we should abandon the search for Nazism's history or be oblivious to the turn-of-the-century shifts that laid much of its groundwork. Indeed, the present volume contains a number of essays that identify late-nineteenth-century constellations as precursors of Nazi ideology and practice, the pieces by Zimmerman and Grosse foremost among them. But these essays are complemented by other research that traces several of the alternative paths taken by German anthropologists in the early twentieth century. Some of these paths, such as that of Marchand's Pater Schmidt, avoided the turn to nation and race even as it was part of larger theoretical developments, in this case the often racialized concern with diffusion.[43]

As German history remains concerned with the turn toward biological racism and the links between German colonialism, imperialism, National Socialism, and genocide, the essays in this volume show that we need the kind of differentiations historians of anthropology have brought to bear on their subject matter. Only such an attention to complexity will allow us to understand these relationships beyond simple binaries and stereotyped representations. In this manner, the history of German anthropology dramatizes a problem that is not unique to the discipline, but characteristic of most research on nineteenth-century

---

scholars have attempted to show that there was a long, colonialist engagement between Germans and non-Europeans that might, in Zantop's words, explain "that racist, xenophobic, and sexist models for action did not emerge in a vacuum but were firmly implanted in the imagination of 'precolonial' Germans" (*Colonial Fantasies,* 16). See also Berman, *Orientalismus, Kolonialismus und Moderne.*

43. In making her argument, Marchand joins other scholars who have emphasized that not all ethnologists and anthropologists in Central Europe made the turn toward race in the early twentieth century and that a number of them remained staunchly committed to alternative visions. Bastian's and Virchow's opposition to race science, of course, is well known, and Felix von Luschan's opposition to race, despite his interest in eugenics and his vocal support of colonialist and nationalist projects, has also received recent attention. (See, inter alia, Malgorzata Irek, "From Spree to Harlem: German Nineteenth Century Anti-racist Ethnology and the Cultural Revival of American Blacks," *Sozialanthropologische Arbeitspapiere,* Freie Universität, Berlin Institut für Ethnologie, Schwerpunkt Sozialanthropologie, 27, 1990; Massin, "From Virchow to Fischer"; Smith, *Politics.*) But there were other German ethnologists, such as Paul Ehrenreich, Karl von den Steinen, Eduard Seler, Georg Thilenius, and Karl Weule, who also resisted central aspects of the new racial anthropology. These individuals, however, have been largely overlooked by historians of German anthropology; and in consequence, we continue to know little about what clearly was the contested road from liberal to Nazi anthropology.

Germany. Readers demand to know the connections to what follows, and often weigh the importance of scholarship based on what it can tell us about the path toward National Socialism. As the essays in this volume illustrate, however, no clear trajectory can be drawn from the complex and multiple constellations that characterized imperial anthropology to the race science embraced by the Nazis. That might be disappointing to some; but it is a realization that needs to be made. Instead of a nineteenth-century explanation for the crimes of the twentieth, this volume ultimately illuminates German ethnology and anthropology as local phenomena, best approached on the terms of their own worldly provincialism.

Coming of Age in the Pacific: German Ethnography from Chamisso to Krämer

HARRY LIEBERSOHN

Pacific travel narratives of the late eighteenth and early nineteenth centuries belonged to the "rituals of conquest" by which Europeans established legitimate claims to extra-European territories—rituals that, as Patricia Seed has shown for an earlier era, had highly particular and national stylizations.[1] The sighting, mapping, and naming of new places, as set down in travelers' diaries, logs, and printed reports, bolstered claims of priority over other European powers in the occupation of places around the world. Beyond this well-known function of asserting first dibs, travel accounts could also have a more subtle but perhaps in the long run more powerful effect. They could affirm the "special relationship" between European power and newly encountered people. An especially clear case is the British relationship to Tahiti. Captain Cook visited the island on all three of his circumnavigations. He recognized that he was encountering foreign and complicated political institutions, but nonetheless decided that the local ruler of his landing point, Matavai Bay, was the "king" of the island. Especially in his account of his second circumnavigation, Cook propagated the legend that this ruler, who came to be known as Pomare I, was the island's

---

I wish to thank Vanessa Agnew, Matti Bunzl, Janet Keller, and Glenn Penny for criticizing earlier drafts of this essay. I have not been able to include all their suggestions, but the essay has benefited greatly from exposure to their different perspectives.

1. Patricia Seed, *Ceremonies of Possession in Europe's Conquest of the New World, 1492–1640* (Cambridge: Cambridge University Press, 1995).

rightful and benevolent monarch. Later British captains and missionaries built on this ideology, while Pomare and his family for their part made shrewd use of their British allies to further their political ambitions. Part of an untidy mixture of wishful thinking, colonial strategy, and opportunism, travel accounts contributed to the invention of a dynasty that hung on until the end of the nineteenth century.[2] Tahiti was not the only place where this kind of collaborative creation of monarchy took place; George Vancouver was even more successful at co-inventing monarchy in the Hawaiian islands by narrating Britain's special relationship to the future Kamehameha I in his voyage account.[3] A *political* idea, monarchy, in the paternalistic-enlightened packaging of the late eighteenth century, linked Polynesians and Europeans in these stately official voyage accounts.

Britain's strategy of forming political partnerships with Polynesian powerholders can serve as a starting point for a comparative examination of German colonialism. To what extent can we observe the fashioning of a "special relationship" to define its colonialism in the Pacific when it began almost a century later? Our answer relies on ethnographers from two different historical moments: Adelbert von Chamisso (1781–1838) and Augustin Krämer (1865–1941). Chamisso was the naturalist on an early-nineteenth-century Russian voyage of scientific discovery; Krämer made his first Pacific visit as a doctor on a German warship. Within the narrow compass of these two figures, one from the age of revolution and restoration, the other from the imperial era, we can discern pieces of a pattern that diverges from Anglo-French examples and suggests a distinctive German cultural mission.

We turn first to Chamisso and his relationship to "Germany." It was of course not a nation-state, but a culture that he entered into as a for-

---

2. This process of collaboration was extremely complex, and I can offer no more than a sketch of it here. See Douglas L. Oliver, *Ancient Tahitian Society,* vol. 3, *Rise of the Pomares* (Honolulu: University of Hawaii Press, 1974) for a detailed portrayal of the establishment of the Pomare dynasty. The critical moment of legitimation by Cook comes in his *A Voyage Towards the South Pole, and Round the World, Performed in his Majesty's Ships the Resolution and Adventure in the years 1772, 1773, 1774, and 1755,* 2 vols. (London: Strahan and Cadell, 1777), 351.

3. See George Vancouver, *A Voyage of Discovery to the North Pacific Ocean and Round the World, 1791–1795,* ed. W. Kaye Lamb, 4 vols. (London: Hakluyt Society, 1984), 3:1180–82. Vancouver was on Cook's second and third circumnavigations, and it is not unreasonable to see him as absorbing the great man's political example.

I have used *Hawaiian Islands* or *Hawaii* to refer to the entire archipelago, *Hawai'i* to refer to the island of that name.

eigner and made his own. Born into an old French noble family, Chamisso had fled as a child with his family from their home in Champagne before the armies of the French Revolution.[4] Dragging their way across Europe, they finally found a place of refuge in Berlin. As a boy he ended his formal schooling early to become a page to Queen Luise, the gracious, cultivated wife of Frederick William III. The impoverished aristocrat took up a commission as lieutenant in the Prussian army, a position that introduced him to the rigors and virtues of his adopted country while also leaving him time for poetry and companionship with fellow intellectuals in Berlin. He and his friends were part of the literary movement of Romantic intellectuals in Berlin and North Germany around 1800.[5] They represented romanticism at its most cosmopolitan, with the brothers Schlegel especially notable for their interest in world literature. Formative for Chamisso's education was a lecture series by August Wilhelm Schlegel in 1803 on the history of what we would today call comparative literature. Born a Catholic aristocrat, Chamisso enjoyed close friendships with Jewish Berliners, identifying closely enough with Jewish marginality that the misadventures of his greatest literary success, Peter Schlemiel—named after the shtetl-ghetto folk type of the bumpkin—bore an unmistakable resemblance to Chamisso's own inglorious career.[6] Chamisso's early years, then, were an ongoing experience of crossing places and confessions and classes, with a good dose of Romantic wit about the strangeness of it all.

Four years after resigning from his officer's commission in 1808,

---

4. For biographical background on Chamisso see Harry Liebersohn, "Discovering Indigenous Nobility: Tocqueville, Chamisso, and Romantic Travel Writing," in *American Historical Review* 99, no. 3 (1994): 746–66, with references to further literature; and Klaus Neumann, "Schlemihl's Travels: 'Hasty Contact' at Rapanui and the Context of a European Biography," *History and Anthropology* 10, nos. 2–3 (1997): 139–84. In addition, readers will find helpful orientation in the editorial apparatus of Adelbert von Chamisso, *Sämtliche Werke*, vol. 2, *Prosa*, ed. Werner Feudel and Christel Laufer (Munich: Hanser, 1982); and Chamisso, *Sämtliche Werke*, vol. 2, ed. Jost Perfahl and Volker Hoffmann (Munich: Winkler, 1975). Both contain the texts of Chamisso's voyage accounts as well as other relevant writings, commentaries, and notes. Hereinafter, references are to the Feudel and Laufer edition. See also the excellent notes and translation in Adelbert von Chamisso, *A Voyage around the World with the Romanzov Exploring Expedition in the Years 1815–1818, in the Brig Rurik, Captain Otto von Kotzebue*, trans. and ed. Henry Kratz (Honolulu: University of Hawaii Press, 1986). I have relied on all three editions for the following remarks about Chamisso and the *Rurik* voyage.

5. An excellent starting point is still Rudolf Haym, *Die Romantische Schule. Ein Beitrag zur Geschichte des deutschen Geistes*, 5th ed. (Berlin: Weidmann, 1928).

6. "Peter Schlemihls Wundersame Geschichte," in *Sämtliche Werke*, 2:17–79.

Chamisso began studying the natural sciences at the University of Berlin. By chance—when the scientist originally appointed fell sick—Chamisso was signed on to be the official voyage naturalist on a Russian expedition, the *Rurik,* which sailed around the world from 1815 to 1818. This expedition, like many official voyages of the period, had double aims, imperial and scientific. The Russian autocracy was in a phase of continental and overseas expansion. After two decades of conflict, it could consider itself the victor, and indeed the savior of Europe, in the struggle to push back Revolutionary and Napoleonic France. With the prestige of victory to back up its demands, at the Congress of Vienna it extended its influence in Eastern Europe. In the same period Russia began a remarkable series of circumnavigations in search of commercial and strategic advantage in the Pacific. Beginning with the 1803–6 voyage of the *Nadeshda* and the *Neva,* commanded by Adam von Krusenstern, Russian voyages furthered the Pacific fur trade, looked in on outposts in Kamchatka, pushed into the Bering Straits, stopped in San Francisco, and went island hopping through Oceania. The *Rurik* was one of the culminating voyages at a moment when Russian ships announced their country's ambition of rivaling France and England in the pursuit of world empire.[7] It had a distinctly scientific character, supporting Chamisso as naturalist and Louis Choris as artist, and a physician, Johann Eschscholtz, who shared Chamisso's passion for collecting plants and later became a professor at the University of Dorpat (today Tartu) in Estonia.[8]

What did Chamisso make of the mélange of peoples and places the ship encountered? Let us first turn to his "scientific" contribution. He wrote it shortly after his return to Berlin in 1818, and it appeared as part of the official, multiauthor account of the expedition published under Kotzebue's name.[9] He hoped to have the work published as a

---

7. For convenient summaries see the biographical entries on Krusenstern and other Russian navigators in John Dunmore, *Who's Who in Pacific Navigation* (Honolulu: University of Hawaii Press, 1991). See the many books on Russian expansion in the Pacific by Glynn Barratt, especially *Russia in Pacific Waters, 1715–1825: A Survey of the Origins of Russia's Naval Presence in the North and South Pacific* (Vancouver: University of British Columbia Press, 1981), *The Russian View of Honolulu, 1809–26* (Ottawa: Carleton University Press, 1988), and *Russia and the South Pacific, 1696–1840: The Tuamotu Islands and Tahiti* (Vancouver: University of British Columbia Press, 1992).

8. A lieutenant Morton Wormskiold also joined the ship as an independent naturalist, but quarreled with the other scientific members of the expedition and left board in Kamchatka. *Sämtliche Werke* 2:95, 97, 116–17.

9. Otto von Kotzebue, *Entdeckungs-Reise in die Sued-See und nach der Berings-Strasse zur Erforschung einer nordoestlichen Durchfahrt. Unternommen in den Jahren 1815, 1816,*

separate volume, but found himself ordered—by Count Rumiantsev, Russian statesman and official sponsor of the voyage—to publish it in the Kotzebue account and submit to Kotzebue's editorial direction.[10] It was a frustrating experience for Chamisso, although not an unusual one for official voyage naturalists, whose notes and collections were often considered to be the property of the voyage sponsor.[11]

Whatever the constraints, Chamisso packed in cosmopolitan insights. His comments on taboo regulations, for example, challenged his readers to think beyond simplification of foreign ritual practices:

> The attempts to trace the sacred, largely prohibiting customs and laws of the taboo—which segregate the sexes, raise unbreakable walls between the classes of the people, and differ in the different peoples, although they are always in the same spirit the foundations of social order—back to one principle and one source and to understand these human statutes in their context or to derive them from the religious and civil system of other known nations will probably always be in vain. Here writing is unknown, and if we did not have the written document at hand, who would have been able to detect the gentle spirit of the Mosaic Law in the similar prohibitions and customs of the Jews, a law that even gives animals well-measured rights and in which, moreover, the idea of pure and impure seems unfounded to us? Also, we are far from assuming that civil or religious order proceeded as a complete whole from one mind: such a structure is often built up by history, which receives the stones for it by accident. And do we not ourselves see silly man turn from a purely spiritual religion back to polytheism, and put his vain, earthly trust in a material object, stone and wood? Is it not easier for us ourselves, like other peo-

---

1817 and 1818, auf Kosten Sr. Erlaucht des Herrn Reichs-Kanzlers Grafen Rumanzoff auf dem Schiffe Rurick unter dem Befehle des Lieutenants der Russisch-Kaiserlichen Marine Otto von Kotzebue... (Weimar: Hoffman, 1821).

10. See Chamisso's letter to Rumiantsev, 3 September 1819, 5 June 1820, and an undated draft; and Rumiantsev to Chamisso, 21 September 1819, 12 November 1819, 10 December 1819, and 29 January 1820, in Nachlass Chamisso, Deutsche Staatsbibliothek—Berlin, K.30/Nr. 22.

11. In his 1830s voyage account Russia figures as a symbol of political oppression in a world struggling to realize the Revolutionary ideal of liberty. See especially Chamisso's remarks on his stay in St. Petersburg at the conclusion of the voyage, where the police were first reluctant to let him in and then were reluctant to let him go. See *Sämtliche Werke*, 2:366–69.

ples of the world, to believe magic, lies, and the word than to adhere to the spirit?[12]

Chamisso's close companionship (and indeed identification) with Jews at home contributed to his sensitivity abroad. Whether in distant islands or nearby isolation, insiders worked out customs less neat and more humane than outsiders' *esprit de système* allowed. Later we shall see that Krämer too turned to Jews as exemplars of difference, but with a different lesson in mind.

One of the recurring themes of Chamisso's later memoir, the *Tagebuch*, is life's curious twists and disruptions of status. On board the Russian military expedition he himself bobbed up and down, one moment a privileged gentleman, the next a superfluous civilian. He and Choris and Eschscholtz befriended Kadu, a Caroline Islander they took on board, with the patronizing kindness of a superior civilization; yet Chamisso also noted the moment of reversal when Kadu saw the *Rurik* captain and scientist humbled in the presence of a more powerful man than they, Kamehameha I, the majestic unifier of the Hawaiian Islands, and "a man of his race and color."[13] Later on the same stay on Hawai'i, Chamisso could assume the role of master when Kamehameha's adviser Kareimoku provided him with a native guide and a boy for his botanical wanderings around the island. A quick comeuppance was the answer when he tried to assume a colonial tone:

> I once had reason to be dissatisfied with my guide, who, as we went into the mountains and I needed him most, had me go ahead with the boy and didn't follow along after us at all, so that I had to turn around and find him. I shot up the whole quiver of my O-Waihian vocabulary in an angry address in which I reminded him of his duty and threatened with Kareimoku, who had put him under my orders. The man, as is the right of an O-Waihian, laughed immoderately at my clumsy speech, which, however, he very well understood, and he gave me no further opportunity to pour out my eloquence in the course of the trip.[14]

An anecdote this aristocratic liberal recorded with pleasure, for it illustrated a native spirit of liberty.

---

12. Chamisso, *Voyage,* 258.
13. Ibid., 303.
14. Ibid., 187.

Another theme is the failures of communication of a cross-cultural voyage. Looking backward, we expect difficulties between "Europeans" and "Others"—yet what is to guarantee that Europeans will have a common cultural code? Nowhere in the *Tagebuch* is the breakdown of understanding more pronounced than in the dealings of the blueblood French aristocrat turned Prussian scientist, Chamisso, with the *arrivé* Baltic German service noble, Kotzebue. They started out with a spontaneous liking toward one another and parted with a warm handshake. In between, on board the *Rurik,* their troubles began with an argument about space: "The captain protests against collecting on the voyage because the ship's space does not permit it, and an artist is at the disposition of the naturalist to draw whatever the latter might desire. The artist, however, protests that he has to take orders only directly from the captain."[15] Chamisso was often better at understanding Pacific Islanders than at feeling his way into Kotzebue's situation. The captain had to maintain the rigorous discipline of a fighting ship; Chamisso felt slighted by the mildest reproach. The captain had diplomacy to conduct; Chamisso could not acknowledge its delicacy or success. On the Hawaiian islands a Russo-German adventurer, Dr. Scheffer, had raised the Russian flag over the semiautonomous island of Kauai. Kotzebue had to persuade Kamehameha I, the monarch of the islands, that the Russian government had not sponsored Scheffer's challenge to his authority. Only Kotzebue's skill at reassuring Kamehameha and his advisers made it possible for Chamisso to wander freely during the time they spent on the islands.

What was German about all of this? Tensions between captain and scientist were more the norm than the exception, built into the conflicting aims of command and knowledge-gathering. They were accentuated, though, by Chamisso's situation as a non-Russian subject on a Russian expedition. He belonged to that overproduction of German intellectuals who since the mid–eighteenth century had offered their knowledge to foreign rulers and on occasion found their scientific mission at odds with their masters' political aims.[16] In many ways he looks

---

15. Ibid., 21.
16. There is a good overview of early German ethnography in Wilhelm E. Mühlmann, *Geschichte der Anthropologie,* 2d ed. (Frankfurt am Main: Enke, 1968). One of the most important ventures was Johann Reinhold Forster's investigation for Katherine II's government of the condition of the German settlers in the Lower Volga in 1765–66. Forster's frank revelation of the poor conditions of the immigrant colony displeased his Russian patrons, who refused to pay him for his report. See Ulrich Enzensberger, *Georg Forster. Ein Leben in Scherben* (Frankfurt am Main: Eichborn, 1996), 16–22.

back to eighteenth-century German travelers like J. R. Forster and Georg Forster rather than to a strictly delimited national tradition. Precisely Chamisso's nonnational or fuzzily national character adds to the interest of including him in our story. With this character in mind, we can ask how a later generation could nonetheless elaborate on his writings and treat him as a German "founder."

Exit Chamisso; exit the age of a provincial Germany, on the margins of power, shipping its surplus of intellectuals like Chamisso on foreign enterprises like the *Rurik*. We now cross over into the second half of the nineteenth century and enter an age of economic expansion, national unification, creation of a German navy, and a quickening interest in the wealth and prestige of colonies. Whereas Chamisso came from an aristocratic family that had plummeted down to economic misery, a discrepancy between status and class that breeds ironists, Krämer had the self-importance of a man on his way up in the world. His father, from a town near Stuttgart, came from a family of millers, but had made money during a few years in Chile and returned to his native Württemberg a prosperous man. In a big social leap, Augustin went through Gymnasium and on to the university. Chamisso had become a lieutenant for want of a choice; Krämer enjoyed the status that went along with being a navy doctor. Overseas he turned into an artifact collector, one of the many in his generation, who in Germany and elsewhere were ransacking the globe for idols and instruments to load onto ships and take back home.[17] In his native Württemberg he was an early booster of plans for an ethnological museum, which opened in 1911. Krämer gave his artifacts to the Linden Museum (named after its founding figure, who died the preceding year) and later served as its director.[18] Chairman of the German Anthropological Society from 1911 to 1915, after World War I he taught in the newly founded ethnological institute at the University of Tübingen, which he himself had played a role in founding.[19]

---

17. See H. Glenn Penny III, "Cosmopolitan Visions and Municipal Displays: Museums, Markets, and the Ethnographic Project in Germany, 1868–1914," Ph.D. diss., University of Illinois, 1999.

18. On Karl Heinrich Graf von Linden see the biographical entry in *Biographisches Jahrbuch und Deutscher Nekrolog* 15 (1913): 510; microfiche copy in *Deutsches Biographisches Archiv,* Neue Folge, card 815, 446–49.

19. For biographical background, see Edwin Hennig, *Württembergische Forschungsreisende der letzen anderthalb Jahrhunderte* (Stuttgart: Linden Museum, 1953); the autobio-

Krämer made five trips to the Pacific before World War I, the first as physician aboard the warship *Bussard* during the years 1893–95. The ship moved in a triangle between Samoa, New Zealand, and Australia. Krämer started out as a scientist interested in studying plankton; during his twelve months in Samoa he fell in love with the people and the place.[20] His diaries for these years alternate between upper-class amusements and ethnological education. During the *Bussard*'s stay in Samoa they record practice writing Samoan, tennis and dinner with the German consul, and dove hunting with a Samoan named Ui and his wife.[21]

The first voyage whetted Krämer's appetite for more. He envisioned a second Pacific voyage devoted to natural science, ethnography, and collecting. An inheritance from his recently deceased parents paid for much of the journey, supplemented by funds from a Stuttgart philanthropist for museum acquisitions and by generous help from the navy, including transportation from place to place. In Hawaii and Samoa Krämer could turn to German consuls for help. How different this backing from private wealth, navy, and state officials was from Chamisso's sullen collaboration with his Russian employers!

Krämer's memoir of this journey of apprenticeship, *Hawaii, East Micronesia, and Samoa* (1906), is a detailed account, over five hundred pages long, of a trip that lasted from April 1897 to 1899.[22] Krämer's account of this voyage took significant, if ambivalent, notice of his predecessor. He painstakingly criticized the errors in Chamisso's account, as when he analyzed in detail the sexual tyranny of chiefs over the women on their islands, a dimension of Micronesian life that Chamisso (and the other *Rurik* travelers) failed to see. At the same time Krämer held up Chamisso as the epitome of the humane traveler. In

---

graphical remarks in Augustin Krämer, *Hawaii, Ostmikronesien und Samoa. Meine zweite Südseereise (1897–1899) zum Studium der Atolle und ihrer Bewohner* (Stuttgart: Strecker und Schröder, 1906); and Dietrich Schleip, "Ozeanistische Ethnographie und Koloniale Praxis. Das Beispiel Augustin Krämer," M.A. thesis, Universität Tübingen, 1989. I am especially indebted to Schleip's detailed study, a copy of which is in the library of the Linden Museum, Stuttgart. In addition I have used Krämer's diaries for the years 1894 to 1901, which are in the Linden Museum.

20. Schleip, "Ozeanistische Ethnographie," 13–17; Krämer, *Hawaii, Ostmikronesien und Samoa,* xi.

21. Krämer, diary, vol. 6 (1894), entries for the week of 7–13 May, 29 May, 21 June, and 22 July.

22. Krämer gives the departure date of 17 April 1897, in *Hawaii, Ostmikronesien und Samoa,* 1. Schleip writes that he left Samoa on 25 January 1899, and that the entire trip lasted almost two years ("Ozeanistische Ethnographie," 43).

Chamisso's travel accounts, wrote Krämer, "attentive scientific observation goes hand in hand with innate goodness and purity of intention, exemplary for every researcher and colonizer."[23] One may doubt whether Chamisso was quite so exemplary. He thought Tongan was such childish babble that it hardly deserved to be called a language, and that Hawaiian was still more childish; Krämer researched Pacific cultures more intensively and, compared with this kind of remark, took them more seriously. There was no simple decline from cosmopolitanism to nationalism here. Rather, this kind of hagiographic treatment suggested his ethnography's lineal descent from a more cosmopolitan ancestor. Krämer also, though, slipped an oddly anachronistic note into his eulogy. To link Chamisso's name to colonialism was to anticipate. The *Rurik* had not directly colonized, and Chamisso had had no political or economic errands. The leap from research to colonizing took place in Krämer's imagination as he sought a model for his own adventure in empire building.

The continuities from Chamisso's to Krämer's voyage account went beyond words of praise. The narrative structure of *Hawaii, East Micronesia, and Samoa* resembled Chamisso's travelogue in its movement from the entrepôt corrupted by Western contact to the pure Oceanic paradise. Deeply disturbing to Chamisso was the rapid commercialization of Hawaiian society, symbolized by the open, widespread prostitution, beginning with the women who swam out to their ship as it docked in Honolulu.[24] By the time Krämer arrived there, Hawaii had been sanitized and modernized. On first arriving in Honolulu he saw handsome streets, impressive houses, streetcars, buses—and no natives. Krämer's account presents his native servant-guide, Mahelone (provided by the German consul) like a sit-com version of a subversive servant, infallibly late, lazy, and misinformed. That Mahelone may have been preserving his "culture" by tripping up his master was not an insight that occurred to Krämer. On a trip to Maui Krämer

---

23. Krämer, *Hawaii, Ostmikronesien und Samoa*, 209.

24. *Sämtliche Werke*, 2:224–25. "Diesem Volke der Lust und der Freude—o könnt ich doch mit einem Atemzuge dieser lauen würzigen Luft, mit einem Blicke unter diesem licht- und farbreichen Himmel euch lehren, was Wollust des Daseins ist!—diesem Volke, sage ich, war die Keuschheit als eine Tugend fremd; wir haben Hab- und Gewinnsucht ihm eingeimpft, und die Scham von ihm abgestreift" (225). Not the sensuous freedom of the Hawaiians, but its inclusion in a European commercial nexus angered Chamisso. On the place of "sensuality" in traditional Hawaiian life, see Marshall Sahlins, "Supplement to the Voyage of Cook; or *le calcul sauvage*," in *Islands of History* (Chicago: University of Chicago Press, 1985), chap. 1.

asked Mahelone to arrange for him to see a hula dance—and set in motion an adventure that ended in an embarrassing striptease, with Mahelone asking for an extra tip, the four girls giggling over their fopped German admirer, and Krämer screaming in helpless rage.[25] Even in retrospect, he could not—in contrast to Chamisso in similar situations—give up his self-righteous anger.

Both Chamisso and Krämer found Micronesia more satisfying. The *Rurik* voyagers were possibly the first Europeans to visit the Marshall Island groups Ratak and Ralik. Chamisso found a purity and simplicity that contrasted with the corruption, although also with the robustness, of the Hawaiians.[26] Krämer too (despite his caveats about the tyrannical behavior of the chiefs) was charmed by the Marshall Islanders. He admired their graciousness, their craft skills, their famous boats, and their navigating skills. By the time he arrived, however, one of the evils feared by Chamisso had set in: the islands were ravaged by venereal disease. While critical in some respects of the *Rurik* voyagers, Krämer pronounced the voyage artist Louis Choris's pictures to be remarkably accurate (especially in his rendition of the Micronesian tattoo patterns).[27] His view of Chamisso and his companions was patronizing as well: if good-hearted Chamisso had somewhat sentimentalized the "natives," it was a forgivable corrective to the inhumanity of earlier European travelers around the world. Krämer portrays himself as building on but improving Chamisso's narrative. He is humane in the tradition of Chamisso, but surpasses his "classic" predecessor by replacing naive literary art with skeptical scientific research.

The people of Ralik and Ratak were too few and too far away to attract more than passing attention on this voyage. There was a place, though, where traditional Oceanian culture had survived down to the end of the century. Krämer directed his readers to Samoa as the pearl of Polynesia, a place that had survived the waves of beachcombers, missionaries, commerce, and colonizers with its social elite, way of life, and pride intact. This was a touched-up picture of a place that in 1839 had agreed to a code regulating relations with European ships in the

---

25. Krämer, *Hawaii, Ostmikronesien und Samoa*, 126–27.
26. "Ich fand bei ihnen," wrote Chamisso of the Ratak Islanders, "reine, unverderbte Sitten, Anmut, Zierlichkeit und die holde Blüte der Schamhaftigkeit.—an Kräftigkeit und männlichem Selbstvertrauen sind ihnen die O-Waihier weit überlegen" (*Sämtliche Werke*, 2:237).
27. Krämer, *Hawaii, Ostmikronesien und Samoa*, 210.

port town of Apia and in the 1850s became a German trade center.[28] In the well-trodden plot of travel literature, Krämer made his way past the realms of disillusionment and disappointment to his Samoan Bali-Hi, the place where Polynesia once again became paradise.[29]

It was paradise in the service of empire. Krämer's second voyage to the Samoan islands coincided with the moment when the rivalry between Britain, Germany, and the United States for control of them was entering its crisis.[30] All three countries had commercial interests in the islands and thought them of strategic significance. At the same time the long-standing jockeying for power among rival Samoan factions invited outside intervention. While neither British nor American policymakers found the prospect of responsibility for the islands enticing, German leaders felt under pressure to satisfy public demand for the acquisition of colonies.[31] The German consul in Samoa, a fanatical nationalist, had long proposed that the Germans adopt the highly popular leader Jose'fo Mata'afa, whom they had exiled to the Marshall Islands, as their candidate. When, by consent of the three great powers, the German warship *Bussard* returned Mata'afa to Tupua in late December 1898, Krämer rushed to greet him first, much to the annoyance of the British and American consuls. Krämer continued to mix in local affairs by taking part in Samoan political councils. He thus had a bit part in steering Samoan politics toward German hegemony, a result ratified in November 1899 in a pact with Britain.[32]

The scientific fruit of Krämer's second voyage, *Die Samoa-Inseln,* is a big, lavish work, with a generous selection of photographs, published

---

28. W. P. Morrell, *Britain in the Pacific Islands* (Oxford: Clarendon, 1960), 67–68, 210–11.

29. On the paradisiacal image of Pacific peoples, with special reference to Bali, see James A. Boon, *Affinities and Extremes: Crisscrossing the Bittersweet Ethnology of East Indies History, Hindu-Balinese Culture, and Indo-European Allure* (Chicago: University of Chicago Press, 1990).

30. The following description is summarized from Paul M. Kennedy, *The Samoan Tangle: A Study in Anglo-German-American Relations, 1878–1900* (New York: Harper and Row, Barnes and Noble, 1974).

31. Kennedy, *The Samoan Tangle,* 240.

32. Ibid., 148–54, 238–39. Other scholars emphasize that Jose'fo Mata'afa and other Samoan leaders accepted German rule only to a limited degree and were quite successful after the turn of the century at maintaining internal political autonomy. See Peter J. Hempenstall, *Pacific Islanders under German Rule: A Study in the Meaning of Colonial Resistance* (Canberra: Australian National University Press, 1978), 31–42; and Hermann Joseph Hiery, *Das Deutsche Reich in der Südsee (1900–1921). Eine Annäherung an die Erfahrungen verschiedener Kulturen* (Göttingen: Vandenhoeck und Ruprecht, 1995), 290–302.

by the German navy.[33] Krämer dedicated it to Jose'fo Mata'afa, whom we see in a distinguished-looking picture.[34] The heart of the first volume is its listing of the *Fa'alupega* (honorifics, or titles of rank), the genealogies of leading families, and the oral traditions for each district and village. Traipsing across the islands, sweet-talking and bribing important individuals with written or oral records to visit him in his house, fending off the intrusions of Samoans who suspected that he was taking down this secret knowledge, trying to get more than one account for each list and story to compare and cross-check, he assembled an important compilation of island political institutions.[35] Samoan original and German translation are laid out in large, full type side by side. A few decades later, according to Margaret Mead, Krämer's was the only remaining record of some of the information he had assembled.[36] As for volume 2, it was a sturdy assemblage of information about pregnancy, childhood and puberty, daily life, medicine, cuisine, fishing, crafts, clothing, decoration, women's work, warfare, and flora and fauna on the islands. The monograph gives most weight to the leading men and their families, but other dimensions of the culture, including women's world, are present too. If salvage anthropology was Krämer's program, then he had proved an able practitioner.[37]

---

33. Augustin Krämer, *Die Samoa-Inseln. Entwurf einer Monographie mit besonderer Berücksichtigung Deutsch-Samoas,* hrsg. mit Unterstützung der Kolonialabteilung des Auswärtigen Amts [published with the support of the colonial department of the secretary of state], vol. 1, *Verfassung, Stammbäume und Überlieferungen;* vol. 2, *Ethnographie* (Stuttgart: E. Schweizerbartsche Verlagsbuchhandlung (E. Naegele), 1902–3).

34. Krämer, *Samoa-Inseln,* vol. 1, dedication, n.p.

35. Krämer, *Samoa-Inseln,* 1:4. Krämer was never shy about using the power at his disposal to get his ethnographic goods. On a later trip to the Caroline Islands, he fired off guns to impress the islanders and possibly incarcerated a troublesome shaman in order to carry out his fieldwork. See Rainer F. Buschmann, "Tobi Captured: Converging Ethnographic and Colonial Visions on a Caroline Island," *Isla* 4, no. 2 (1996): 317–40.

36. Margaret Mead, *The Social Organization of Manua,* rev. ed. (Honolulu: Bishop Museum Press, 1969), 186. Cf. Schleip, "Ozeanistische Ethnographie," 39–40, 149–51.

37. "Ist doch das geistige Eigentum jener Naturvölker viel reicher, als man vielfach anzunehmen geneigt ist! Dasselbe genauer festzulegen, hat man in so vielen Fällen sich kaum die Mühe genommen. Und dabei schwindet es vor unsern Augen dahin! Man rüstet jährlich zoologische Expeditionen aus, um Tiere zu erforschen, die nach Hunderten und Tausenden von Jahren auch noch vorhanden sein werden; man bedenkt nicht, dass im Pacifischen Ocean Völker dahinschwinden vor dem mächtigen Andrang der Civilisation, deren geistigen Schatz wir im Begriffe sind dahinschwinden zu lassen, wie die spanischen Konquistadoren es vor 400 Jahren in Westindien gethan. Sollen wir uns dereinst dieselben Vorwürfe machen lassen? Oder ist denn der Mensch weniger interessant als eine Qualle? Was dereinst Feuer und Schwert gethan—und dies reicht doch fast noch in unsere Zeit herein, wenn man der blutigen Maorikriege und der Entvölkerung Tasmaniens gedenkt—, das thut heute in humanster

Settlers and natives had mixed in Samoa since the 1830s, not without a feisty Samoan appropriation of European education and technology. By the late nineteenth century the islands were a "multi-ethnic community," with resilient native politics and culture, an assertive settler community, and commerce of many kinds between the two.[38] What Krämer "salvaged" was Samoa as an aesthetic totality, monumentalized in genealogies, photographs, and lists of material objects. The reader of his monograph follows the expert through the different parts of the whole, district by district through the islands. Without outside knowledge, one would never guess that Krämer's "Samoa"—so learned, so dedicated to the preservation of native lore—was a product of artful exclusion.

Krämer did call attention to the mixing of peoples and cultures within Polynesia and declared his dissatisfaction with an internal-logic model of culture:

> Above all I have tried to illuminate the ethnographic relation of the Samoans to the Tongans and the Fijians. . . . I believe . . . that one can further the whole only by working in strictly defined boundaries and only studying one archipelago in relation to its nearest neighbor. . . . Thus a monograph on Fiji should include its closest Melanesian neighbors, New Hebrides, in its field of vision as well as Tonga and Samoa, Tonga should include only Fiji, Samoa and Rarotonga, the latter only Tonga, Tubuai, Tahiti, etc. Advancing westward step by step in similar fashion, one would gradually make one's way to Asia.[39]

This vision of overlapping circles of culture, verging on the views of contemporaries like Max Weber, Georg Simmel, and Franz Boas (none of whom Krämer seems to have read), was a momentary insight rather than a formative conception. The circle of culture, which opened up as Krämer considered the commerce of peoples around Fiji, Samoa, and Tonga, closed up again, for part of Krämer's self-appointed salvage mission was to demonstrate the Samoans' racial integrity. He ignored the intermarrying with Europeans that had been taking place for decades, even though, by the late nineteenth century, the children of these marriages were begin-

---

Weise die Civilisation, so dass zwar der verkümmerte Repräsentant der Rasse, aber auch nichts mehr als seine leibliche Person übrig bleibt" (Krämer, *Die Samoa-Inseln,* 1:2).

38. I draw here on the title and theme of R. P. Gilson, *Samoa 1830 to 1900: The Politics of a Multi-cultural Community* (Oxford: Oxford University Press, 1970).

39. Krämer, *Die Samoa-Inseln,* 2:iv.

ning to play a prominent role in Samoan politics and trade.[40] The mixing of peoples he observed within Oceania required more careful assessment: "The relations of the Samoans," he wrote, "are more numerous than one would expect from a people which from time immemorial has inhabited its islands in Pacific isolation. Nonetheless one can still say that on the whole, the race of the Samoan people may be understood as pure."[41] It took all Krämer's skills as medical scientist and avid photographer to distinguish the true Samoan type. With as much care as he put into the compilation of genealogies, he photographed and summarized characteristic hair, height, build, cranial form, skin color, birthmarks, nose, upper lip, teeth, ears, male beard, female breasts, arms, hips, feet, and buttocks, and contrasted them to non-Samoan islanders.[42] The pictures, almost entirely of women, form a racial gallery, an older genre going back to the artists' "galleries" of the early nineteenth century but now given a new scientific authority through the use of photography.[43] They permitted Krämer to distinguish the Samoan from Fijian and Tongan phenotypes.[44] Germans would also be able to understand, he thought, from their situation at home. "It is an old experience which we can have often enough with the blond Germanic race, that Jewish blood often makes its reappearance after generation upon generation."[45] Neither at home nor abroad, in Krämer's telling of the story, had mixing damaged the essential purity of the race, at least for the properly instructed eye. Like Central Europeans, Central Oceanians could maintain their racial unity and their distinctive way of life despite the seepage of foreign influences through the centuries.

Samoa, then, was the chosen land of German colonialism, the place where Krämer could define a "special relationship." The German mission in Samoa was a *cultural* paternalism, in contrast to early-nineteenth-century Britain's political mission in Tahiti and Hawaii. This was what could give the German occupation of Samoa in the crisis of

---

40. See J. W. Davidson, *Samoa Mo Samoa: The Emergence of the Independent State of Western Samoa* (Oxford: Oxford University Press, 1967), 68–69.
41. Krämer, *Die Samoa-Inseln,* 2:35.
42. Ibid., 39.
43. The best-known example is the American Indian paintings of George Catlin. See William H. Truettner, *The Natural Man Observed: A Study of Catlin's Indian Gallery* (Washington, D.C.: Smithsonian Institution Press, 1979); and Bridget L. Goodbody, "George Catlin's Indian Gallery: Art, Science, and Power in the Nineteenth Century," Ph.D. diss., Columbia University, 1996.
44. See, for example, the pictures of Tongan, Fijian, and Samoan "types" in Krämer, *Die Samoa-Inseln,* 1:9–13.
45. Krämer, *Die Samoa-Inseln,* 2:35.

1899 a dignity and meaning that went beyond mere flag-waving or commercial advantage. The attempt to create an affinity between native cultures and German culture, and to set the representatives of *Kultur* (German, Samoan) in opposition to the representatives of material and technological improvement and the peoples despoiled by racial intermixing, was part of a broader movement in nineteenth-century Germans' fascination with exotic peoples. Far from the Pacific, it deeply informed Germany's well-known "special relationship" to North American Indians.[46] Germans reached the prairies too late to create a political order that could define their relationship to "natives." In the Pacific, however, Krämer had found out a site of operation; a place that Germans could actually occupy and shelter, a colony that could act as an expansion and island experiment in their version of how the world should work.

In this grand narrative of German colonialism, Chamisso's role was to serve as its notable from the great age of German cosmopolitanism. By recalling Chamisso, Krämer could make his own voyage to the Pacific something more than just an eccentric excursion among "savages"; he could link it to the great flowering of German culture in the late eighteenth and early nineteenth centuries, now to be refurbished and put forward as the heritage of the newly created nation-state. Looking back to Chamisso gave special definition to German colonialism. If they did their work right, Germans could set an example of sensitivity to native cultures that would contrast with the destructive policies of their imperial rivals. Chamisso's limitations, too, were useful for Krämer's colonial narrative. The poet-scientist represented not just prenational Germany's idealism, but also its immaturity; he had the freshness but also the illusions of intellectual adolescence. His was the poignant last moment of innocence before Germany's coming of age in the Pacific. This contrast between youth and maturity, naïveté and experience, was widespread in Germany's educated elite at the turn of the twentieth century. Krämer shared in the widespread anticipation of great responsibilities for the young nation-state; he embodied a mood of wistful last look backward to an easier, untroubled age, and a leap forward to the responsibilities of world empire.[47]

---

46. See Harry Liebersohn, *Aristocratic Encounters: European Travelers and North American Indians* (Cambridge: Cambridge University Press, 1998).
47. Max Weber captured this mood in his Freiburg inaugural lecture, "Der Nationalstaat und die Volkswirtschaftspolitik" (1895), in *Gesammelte politische Schriften,* ed. Johannes Winckelmann (Tübingen: Mohr/Siebeck, 1980), 1–25.

Völkerpsychologie and German-Jewish Emancipation

MATTI BUNZL

In April 1852, the linguist and philologist Heymann Steinthal sent a long letter to his friend and future brother-in-law, the philosopher and psychologist Moritz Lazarus. Composed over a period of several days, it contained Steinthal's initial proposition to cofound a journal of "psychological ethnology" [psychische Ethnologie]. While Steinthal thought that few collaborators would be needed, since "most of it we will have to do ourselves," he was concerned that the periodical reach as wide an audience as possible. To that end, he suggested that the journal's title could carry an addend, "something like: with special attention to languages."[1]

As it turned out, the letter was an important promissory note in the history of German anthropology. For a few years later, Steinthal and Lazarus did in fact collaborate in the founding of the *Zeitschrift für Völkerpsychologie und Sprachwissenschaft* (Journal of folk psychology and linguistics) of which they edited twenty volumes between 1860 and 1890.[2] In the pages of the journal, Steinthal and Lazarus sought to cre-

---
For their helpful comments on this essay, I would like to thank Glenn Penny, Mitchell Ash, Adam Sutcliffe, Dan Diner, John Bunzl, and Billy Vaughn.

1. Ingrid Belke, ed., *Moritz Lazarus und Heymann Steinthal: Die Begründer der Völkerpsychologie in ihren Briefen* (Tübingen: J. C. B. Mohr, 1971), 255.

2. While the *Zeitschrift für Völkerpsychologie und Sprachwissenschaft* continued to list both Lazarus and Steinthal as editors, Steinthal did the bulk of the editorial work for most of the journal's existence. In the final volume of the periodical, Ulrich Jahn is listed as a contributing editor.

ate, delineate, and advance the discipline of *Völkerpsychologie* (folk psychology), a distinct mode of inquiry designed to elucidate the world's *Volksgeister* (geniuses of peoples) in their various forms of development.[3]

In Steinthal's originary letter, however, there is little inkling of the theoretical and conceptual debates that would dominate the pages of the *Zeitschrift*. Even the journal's proposition seems rather incidental in the context of the letter's overall concern, which centered on the composition of a Sabbath sermon. Steinthal was scheduled to deliver the speech to the Jewish congregation of his native Gröbzig (Anhalt) on Saturday, 10 April 1852; and the letter came to chronicle the sermon's gradual development. On Wednesday, 7 April, Steinthal reported his perusal of various midrashic commentaries in search of inspiration.[4] But by Thursday afternoon, he had settled on didactic Hebrew poetry as the basis for his talk, particularly the Book of Proverbs. In approaching the text, Steinthal applied the philological methods championed by proponents of the recently developed *Wissenschaft des Judentums* (science of Judaism). After careful study, he found himself in disagreement with a reigning interpretation that placed the book in the postexilic period. In contrast, he held that the text's "sensual opulence" and "charming lasciviousness" were markers of the pristine time of the kingdom. Steinthal found further support for his interpretation in the book's "purely moral tendency," which stood in opposition to the "national-religious views" he ascribed to later periods of Jewish history.[5] Steinthal's universalist interpretation of the

---

3. *Völkerpsychologie* is a notoriously difficult term to translate. The most literal, albeit clumsy, rendition would be "psychology of peoples." Other terms used in the secondary literature include *ethnopsychology, ethnic psychology,* and *cultural psychology.* For the present essay, I have opted for *folk psychology,* mainly because it is the gloss Franz Boas used to introduce the discipline into the American anthropological canon. See, for example, Boas, "The History of Anthropology," *Science* 20 (1904): 513–24, reprinted in *A Franz Boas Reader: The Shaping of American Anthropology, 1883–1911,* ed. George W. Stocking (Chicago: University of Chicago Press), 23–36. The term *Volksgeist,* much like any other permutation of *Geist,* presents an even greater problem of translation. While I offer "genius of a people" as the most appropriate translation, I tend to use the term in its German original to preserve such additional valences as intellect, mind, and spirit.

4. Belke, *Moritz Lazarus und Heymann Steinthal,* 254. Midrash is a form of biblical interpretation that seeks to derive moral principles, explain theological ideas, or explicate law. The rules for deriving midrash were formulated between the first and the twelfth century C.E., and several influential treatises were composed during the period.

5. Ibid., 256–57.

Book of Proverbs found its expression in the eventual sermon. Conceived by Steinthal as broadly "ethical," the speech was divided into four parts that he rendered to Lazarus in Latin: *de servitute humana* (on the slavery of man), *de libertate humana* (on the freedom of man), *de educatione* (on education), and *de natura libertatis* (on the nature of freedom).[6]

While Steinthal's missive to Lazarus closed on a happy note that told of the sermon's great success, the letter was not without a hint of bitterness.[7] On 7 April, Steinthal had complained about the Jewish community of his hometown. Confronted with an older generation blindly adhering to unreconstructed tradition and a younger group that had lost its religious anchoring without embracing affirmative substitutes, Steinthal had felt alienated. His comfort only returned in the morning of 8 April, when, over coffee, he had immersed himself in the correspondence between Schiller and Goethe. In the writings of these "noble characters" whose "poetic powers" were matched by an uncanny "facility for reflection," Steinthal detected a "total theory."[8] It was in a segue from these thoughts that Steinthal made the original proposition for the founding of the *Zeitschrift für Völkerpsychologie und Sprachwissenschaft.*

Steinthal's letter to Lazarus represents a fascinating document of German-Jewish history. In its fusion of Jewish religious reflection with quintessential images of German *Bildung,* it traces the contours of German-Jewish emancipation in axiomatic fashion. In the context of the present volume, however, the letter's significance extends far beyond the generalities of nineteenth-century German-Jewish existence. For what Steinthal's originary missive to Lazarus begins to suggest, and what this essay is designed to elucidate, is the degree to which the development of *Völkerpsychologie* was predicated on German-Jewish cultural constellations.

As such, this essay functions as both supplement and corrective to the available historiography of German anthropology, whose treatment of *Völkerpsychologie,* if not altogether neglectful of the work of Steinthal and Lazarus, fails to address the Jewish dimension of the dis-

---

6. Ibid., 257.
7. The letter was completed on Sunday, 11 April 1852. Honoring Jewish law, Steinthal had waited until after the end of the Sabbath to finish it (ibid., 258–59).
8. Ibid., 254–55.

cipline they founded.[9] In part, this failure is due to a pervasive figuration of German anthropology's history as inherently free of Jews, a function, in turn, of a certain preoccupation with anthropology's trajectory during the Third Reich. To be sure, the fate of Jewish scholars in Nazi Germany is frequently lamented; but such mournful nostalgia rarely prompts systematic inquiries into German anthropology's Jewish pasts. As a consequence, the *Völkerpsychologie* of Lazarus and Steinthal has remained on the margins of disciplinary histories.

Historians of German anthropology, however, have not been alone in their inattention to *Völkerpsychologie's* Jewish origins. Even as careful and accomplished a scholar as Ingrid Belke, who has edited the correspondence of Steinthal and Lazarus in exemplary fashion, fails to appreciate the centrality of German-Jewish cultural formations in the creation of the discipline.[10] This is not to say that Jewish questions fall outside the purview of Belke's considerations. Quite on the contrary, in her comprehensive biographical introduction to Steinthal and Lazarus's

---

9. In his survey of the cultural sciences in late-nineteenth-century Germany, *Politics and the Sciences of Culture in Germany, 1840–1920* (Oxford: Oxford University Press, 1991), Woodruff Smith fails to mention Lazarus and Steinthal even as he devotes an entire chapter to the discipline of *Völkerpsychologie*. Such radical acts of omission are rare, however. More typically, scholars do mention Lazarus and Steinthal; but they often do so only in passing and without paying any attention to their Jewish identities. See, for example, James Whitman, "From Philology to Anthropology in Mid-Nineteenth-Century Germany," in *Functionalism Historicized: Essays on British Anthropology*, ed. George W. Stocking Jr. (Madison: University of Wisconsin Press, 1984), 214–29; Matti Bunzl, "Franz Boas and the Humboldtian Tradition: From *Volksgeist* and *Nationalcharakter* to an Anthropological Concept of Culture," in *Volksgeist as Method and Ethic: Essays on Boasian Ethnography and the German Anthropological Tradition*, ed. George W. Stocking Jr. (Madison: University of Wisconsin Press, 1996), 17–78; Thomas Hauschild, "Christians, Jews, and the Other in German Anthropology," *American Anthropologist* 99, no. 4 (1997): 746–53; Andrew Zimmerman, "Anthropology and the Place of Knowledge in Imperial Berlin," Ph.D. diss., University of California, San Diego, 1998; Kurt Danziger, "Origins and Basic Principles of Wundt's *Völkerpsychologie*," *British Journal of Social Psychology* 22 (1983): 303–13; Berthold Oelze, *Wilhelm Wundt: Die Konzeption der Völkerpsychologie* (Münster: Waxmann, 1991), Wilhelm Mühlman, *Geschichte der Anthropologie* (Wiesbaden: AULA-Verlag, 1984). An exception to this historiographical situation is Ivan Kalmar, "The *Völkerpsychologie* of Lazarus and Steinthal and the Modern Concept of Culture," *Journal of the History of Ideas* 48 (1987): 671–90. In the essay, which argues that Boas's conception of culture was a restatement of Lazarus and Steinthal's *Volksgeist*, Kalmar devotes some space to a discussion of the folk psychologists' Jewishness. Unfortunately, the analysis remains at a rather superficial level, focusing on Lazarus's and Steinthal's latter-day efforts in the struggle against anti-Semitism, while failing to appreciate the degree to which *Völkerpsychologie's* overall design was a product of the culture of German-Jewish emancipation.

10. The published correspondence comprises three volumes. Complementing the initial publication of 1971, parts 1 and 2 of volume 2 were respectively published in 1983 and 1986.

correspondence, Belke emphasizes the scholars' respective involvement in Jewish affairs.[11] In this regard, she discusses Steinthal's copious writings on Jewish matters and stresses Lazarus's prominent activities in late-nineteenth-century German-Jewish politics—activities that ranged from his presidency at the first and second synods of the Reform Movement (held in 1869 and 1871) to his position as head of the board of trustees of the Hochschule für die Wissenschaft des Judentums (College of Jewish Studies). But Belke regards these involvements in Jewish affairs as wholly unrelated to the design of *Völkerpsychologie.* In the case of Lazarus, she disconnects the scholar's Jewish political commitments from his intellectual concerns; in the case of Steinthal, she argues for a belated return to Jewish interests in the last decades of the nineteenth century.[12] As a result, she treats the creation and codification of *Völkerpsychologie* in the 1850s and 1860s outside a specifically Jewish context. Belke, in fact, forcefully brackets any Jewish intellectual influences when she opens her introduction with the assertion that the "conception of *Völkerpsychologie*" was a "consequence" of the "idea of the nation-state *(Nationalstaatsidee),*" in particular the "vision of a homogeneous and culturally defined German nation *(einheitliche deutsche Kulturnation)*" with the "Prussian state as the core of the nation-state."[13]

While Belke is certainly correct in pointing to German political developments as central elements in the genealogy of *Völkerpsychologie,* the failure to address the Jewish dimensions of the discipline's origin creates a starkly impoverished picture. For as a closer examination of *Völkerpsychologie's* intellectual trajectory reveals, the discipline's conception at once reflected and reproduced the cultural ideology of German-Jewish emancipation. In this manner, the emergence of folk psychology was not only predicated on the historical transformations that had brought Jews like Steinthal and Lazarus into the German republic of letters, but its deployment functioned as an intellectual device designed to promote and safeguard the ongoing process of Jewish integration into German society.

---

11. Ingrid Belke, introduction to *Moritz Lazarus und Heymann Steinthal: Die Begründer der Völkerpsychologie in ihren Briefen,* ed. Belke (Tübingen: J. C. B. Mohr, 1971), xiii–cxlii, esp. lxi–lxxx and cxxiv–cxxxvi. For a presentation that follows the same logic as Belke, see the introduction to Georg Eckardt, ed., *Völkerpsychologie: Versuch einer Neuentdeckung* (Weinheim: Beltz, 1997), 7–123.

12. Belke, introduction, xxxvi, cxxiv.

13. Ibid., xiii.

Steinthal and Lazarus's project expired at a moment when this process began to lose steam—an early harbinger of liberalism's demise across the human sciences and German society at large. The echoes of *Völkerpsychologie*, however, lingered on, especially in the American context. There, the German-Jewish émigré Franz Boas codified an anthropology steadfastly committed to the liberal principles of cosmopolitan humanism. Closely following the design of Steinthal and Lazarus's *Völkerpsychologie*, modern American anthropology thus emerged from a German-Jewish project—the most enduring legacy of German anthropology's long nineteenth century.

The Program of *Völkerpsychologie*

Steinthal and Lazarus codified the discipline of *Völkerpsychologie* in the jointly authored introduction to the first volume of the *Zeitschrift für Völkerpsychologie und Sprachwissenschaft*.[14] An ambitious text whose analytic thrust constituted the programmatic anchor of all later endeavors, it sought to set forth and clarify the concept of *Volksgeist* (genius of a people). The term, Steinthal and Lazarus argued, was widely used in such disciplines as history, anthropology, philosophy, and law, but it had not been treated in a truly "scientific manner."[15] As a result, confusion reigned over the precise nature of the *Volksgeist*, both as a phenomenon at large and in regard to its various specific manifestations. Folk psychology promised to change this situation; the new discipline would not only explicate the concept, but would put the *Volksgeist* itself center stage. In this manner, *Völkerpsychologie* would be the "Wissenschaft vom Volksgeiste."[16]

In their introduction, Steinthal and Lazarus were particularly concerned to distinguish their new discipline from its closest neighbors. In the first instance, there was psychology, which Steinthal and Lazarus regarded in the idealist conception of its originary codification as the

---

14. M. Lazarus and H. Steinthal, "Einleitende Gedanken über Völkerpsychologie, als Einladung zu einer Zeitschrift für Völkerpsychologie und Sprachwissenschaft," *Zeitschrift für Völkerpsychologie und Sprachwissenschaft (ZfV)* 1 (1860): 1–73. Lazarus had begun to sketch out his conception of *Völkerpsychologie* as early as 1851, when he published an essay "Über den Begriff und die Möglichkeit einer Völkerpsychologie," *Deutsches Museum: Zeitschrift für Literatur, Kunst und öffentliches Leben* 1 (1851): 113–26.
15. Lazarus and Steinthal, "Einleitende Gedanken," 2.
16. Ibid., 7.

"Wissenschaft des Geistes."[17] On a basic level, folk psychology was a simple extension of psychology. Both disciplines were concerned with the elucidation of *Geist,* but while the latter defined its object in strictly individualistic terms, the former recognized its collective dimension. Folk psychology would thus be the "psychology of the social human being or of human society."[18] But the discipline had more than an auxiliary role to play in regard to psychology. Given that individual consciousness was predicated on social interaction, Steinthal and Lazarus asserted that all forms of *Geist* were ultimately rooted in collective realities. Since "*Geist* is the social product of human society," not even the most "valuable and powerful personality" could be understood outside a "specific place" and a "specific moment in time."[19] As a result, *Völkerpsychologie* occupied a privileged position vis-à-vis psychology in that inquiries into individuals needed to be premised on folk psychological considerations. These, in turn, always centered around the conceptual category of the *Volk,* since the "separation into *Völker*" was the organizing principle of humanity.[20] While Steinthal and Lazarus suggested that such entities as *Familien-Geist* and *Standes-Geist* (genius of family and class) were also agents of personality formation, they foundationally privileged the *Volksgeist* as the crucial link between individuals and larger historical formations. Since "the development of humanity is tied to the diversity of peoples,"[21] the ultimate questions about the nature of *Geist* could only be answered through attention to the world's various *Volksgeister.*

This global interest in human diversity brought *Völkerpsychologie* into close proximity with the discipline of anthropology; but there too, Steinthal and Lazarus were careful to demarcate a clear boundary. While anthropology, under which they subsumed both physical anthropology and ethnology, was concerned with the "difference in the characters of peoples,"[22] its explanatory framework paid insufficient attention to the inner workings of *Geist.* Anthropologists, Steinthal and Lazarus argued, had neglected the core of human existence by explaining human diversity through external factors like environment

---

17. Ibid., 3.
18. Ibid., 5.
19. Ibid., 3–4.
20. Ibid., 5.
21. Ibid., 7.
22. Ibid., 11.

and descent. The *Völkerpsychologen* vigorously opposed this materialist approach, noting that human beings, due to their "capacity for *Vergeistigung* [intellectualization]," were by "nature more than animals."[23] Assuming with Hegel the near infinite capacity of genius for world historical development, Steinthal and Lazarus regarded anthropological concerns for climate and physiology as analytically misguided. Such material constraints would never "provide sufficient grounds for explaining the *Volksgeist* along with all its psychological manifestations."[24] In the final analysis, only the "inner drive" [innere Antrieb] whose "*geistige* nature" was wholly "independent of externals" could account for the "development of humanity, its peoples and states."[25]

Having carved out a niche for *Völkerpsychologie* as the comparative study of collective genius across space and time, Steinthal and Lazarus proceeded to outline the specific program of the discipline. According to this scheme, folk psychology would fall into two parts. The first, which Steinthal and Lazarus termed "world-historical psychology" [völkergeschichtliche Psychologie] would be "abstract and general." It would explicate the "condition and laws" of the *Volksgeist* and uncover the processes of its "formation and development." At issue in this project was the conceptualization of humanity as one people ("Menschheit als Volk"), whose common traits, such as language and religion, ultimately revealed the presence of a general *Menschengeist* (genius of humanity).[26] In contrast to this theoretical exploration of the *Volksgeist* as a universal category, the second part of *Völkerpsychologie* was "concrete." Under the heading "psychological ethnology" [psychische Ethnologie], it would "treat the actually existing *Volksgeister*" in monographic fashion, "characterizing individual peoples" by paying particular attention to their "specific forms of development."[27]

The empirical domains of Steinthal and Lazarus's inquiry were directly related to this project of charting the trajectories of individual *Volksgeister*. First and foremost, the folk psychologists were concerned with language. More than any other feature of communal exis-

---

23. Ibid., 13.
24. Ibid., 12.
25. Ibid., 14.
26. Ibid., 26–27.
27. Ibid.

tence, it appeared as the unifying psychological essence of a people and hence as a direct expression of the *Volksgeist*. As Steinthal and Lazarus noted, language was the original manifestation of a group's collective psychology, the "first *geistige* product"; and as such it was synonymous with the "awakening of the *Volksgeist*" itself.[28] But if a people's language thus constituted "a complete representation" of its *Volksgeist*, Steinthal and Lazarus conceived the relationship between language and *Volksgeist* in dialectical terms.[29] In this manner, language was not just seen as a passive entity, a mere linguistic screen for the projection of collective genius. Rather, language itself appeared as a formative agent, affecting the *Volksgeist* at every turn. The folk psychologists explicated the relationship in the following terms: "Since everything that has once been created by *Geist* determines, fosters, and limits future creations, so language has a constitutive influence on the innermost peculiarities of the *Volksgeist*."[30] In this conception, language not only appeared as the most immediate representation of a *Volksgeist* at any given moment, but it also seemed to contain the essence of that *Geist*'s prior and future developments.

In the folk psychological project, the investigation of language was intimately related to the study of other shared mental phenomena. Like languages, such collective representations as myths and religions were seen as expressions of particular *Volksgeister*, rendering them part of *Völkerpsychologie's* analytic domain. Here, as well, Steinthal and Lazarus thought dialectically, viewing particular belief systems as both products and producers of a people's historical trajectory. Even more important, however, were their status as testaments to a group's intellectual creativity. A creative *Volksgeist*, Steinthal and Lazarus posited, would produce imaginative religious ideas whose power might exert influence far beyond their originary confines.[31]

The same concern for creativity extended the field of folk psychological inquiry to the realm of literature. Folklore functioned as the crucial link, with the ancient epics appearing as pinnacles of collective achievement as well as the "beginnings of poetry."[32] In this context, *Volksdichtung* (folk poetry) occupied a privileged position for Steinthal

---

28. Ibid., 40.
29. Ibid.
30. Ibid.
31. Ibid., 44–49.
32. Ibid., 49.

and Lazarus, since its systematic treatment would allow the "comparison of the *Volksgeister*" that had found their unique expressions in the respective texts. But if the "character of each individual people"[33] could be ascertained through its popular stories, the products of individual creativity also needed to be understood in folk psychological perspective. After all, no piece of literature could be produced outside the common psychological space of language; and since all mental achievements were ultimately conditioned by the *Volksgeist*, the products of individual genius were another form of its expression. A creative *Volksgeist* would thus produce great authors; while great authors would, in turn, serve as evidence of a vibrant *Volksgeist*.

In devising their folk psychological program, Steinthal and Lazarus drew on various strands of eighteenth- and early-nineteenth-century German social thought.[34] Particularly central to the introduction of the *Zeitschrift für Völkerpsychologie und Sprachwissenschaft*, however, were the figures of Johann Friedrich Herbart and Wilhelm von Humboldt. Respectively, the two thinkers had been the dominant intellectual influences on Lazarus and Steinthal for quite some time.

For the philosopher and psychologist Lazarus, Herbart provided the conceptual framework for an empirically grounded collective psychology. Herbart is remembered today mainly for his development of a mathematical psychology that followed the leads of Leibniz, Wolff, and Kant in the attempt to fashion a Newtonian science of the human mind. Less than Herbart's concern with quantification, however, it was his model of the human mind as an apperceptive mass that influenced Lazarus decisively. Herbart conceived the mind as a series of "representations" whose ongoing reconfiguration in light of various stimuli accounted for psychological developments. Herbart himself suggested that this individual model could also account for collective psychological processes; but it was Lazarus who made this proposition the building block of his scholarly project. Positing a collective mental essence as an irreducible site of psychological inquiry, Lazarus conceived the

---

33. Ibid., 50.
34. In her presentation of *Völkerpsychologie's* intellectual origins, Belke discusses Hegel's philosophy of history, English and French positivism, the emerging disciplines of cultural history, ethnology, legal history, and philology, as well as the psychology of Johann Friedrich Herbart (introduction, xliii–xlvi). Belke's discussion is insightful, but it fails to address the crucial dimension of German-Jewish culture and its operative concept of *Bildung* in the formation of *Völkerpsychologie*.

Volksgeist as a vehicle of dynamic apperception, a notion that allowed its treatment according to the principles of Herbartian psychology.[35]

While Herbart's work thus pointed to the overall conception of folk psychology, Humboldt had articulated the foundational dialectic between language and *Volksgeist*. As part of his program of comparative linguistics, he had proposed that each language contained the truths of the *Geist* that produced it; at the same time, he had argued that individual genius could, in turn, act upon language and, by implication, *Volksgeist*.[36] As a linguist and philologist, Steinthal adapted and built on Humboldt's linguistic hermeneutics and its attempt to elucidate national characters through the investigation of grammatical structures. Indeed, for Steinthal (and Lazarus), the introduction of the *Zeitschrift für Völkerpsychologie und Sprachwissenschaft* was an invitation to follow in "Humboldt's footsteps" by demonstrating that "languages are the representations of particular *Volksgeister*."[37]

The post-Kantian positivist Herbart and the post-Herderian humanist Humboldt constituted a somewhat incongruous pair of guiding lights for the nascent discipline. That *Völkerpsychologie* nevertheless took shape in the 1850s and 1860s was a function of an overarching concern Steinthal and Lazarus shared with both Herbart and Humboldt. That concern was for *Bildung,* the German Enlightenment concept denoting individual and collective self-formation based on intrinsic principles.[38] Herbart, while breaking with the dominant mode

---

35. On Herbart, see David Leary, "The Historical Foundation of Herbart's Mathematization of Psychology," *Journal of the History of the Behavioral Sciences* 16 (1980): 150–63; Harold Dunkel, *Herbart and Herbartianism: An Educational Ghost Story* (Chicago: University of Chicago Press, 1970); Katherine Arens, *Structures of Knowing: Psychologies of the Nineteenth Century* (Dordrecht: Kluwer Academic Publishers, 1989), chap. 3.

36. On Humboldt's anthropology, see Bunzl, "Boas and Humboldtian Tradition," 19–36. See also Jürgen Trabant, *Traditionen Humboldts* (Frankfurt am Main: Suhrkamp, 1990), esp. chap. 3.

37. Lazarus and Steinthal, "Einleitende Gedanken," 41. By the time the first issue of the *Zeitschrift für Völkerpsychologie und Sprachwissenschaft* appeared, Humboldt's work in the field of comparative linguistics had been nearly forgotten, eclipsed as it was by the success of a historical linguistics solely concerned with the reconstruction of Indo-European languages. Steinthal was one of few scholars committed to the Humboldtian project, and he became its most prominent champion in the latter half of the nineteenth century. Steinthal, *Die Sprachwissenschaft Wilh. v. Humboldt's und die Hegel'sche Philosophie* (Berlin: Ferdinand Dümmler, 1848); Steinthal, ed., *Die sprachphilosophischen Werke Wilhelm's von Humboldt* (Berlin: Ferdinand Dümmler, 1883). See also Trabant, *Traditionen Humboldts,* 60–67.

38. On the concept of *Bildung,* see David Sorkin, "Wilhelm von Humboldt: The Theory and Practice of Self-Formation *(Bildung),* 1791–1810," *Journal of the History of Ideas* 44

of idealist philosophy, never abandoned that tradition's preoccupation with *Bildung*. Quite on the contrary, he presented his model of the apperceptive mind as a means to further individual *Bildung*, which could be improved if its cognitive mechanisms were better known and understood.[39]

Humboldt, for his part, was even more dedicated to the cause of *Bildung*, which he advanced both as a theoretician and as a Prussian politician.[40] In the latter capacity, he organized the University of Berlin as a space of communal scholarly enterprise and reformed the Prussian *Gymnasium* according to humanistic principles. Even more relevant in the present context, however, were his copious writings on the question of *Bildung*. As early as 1795, Humboldt had sought to develop a general theory of *Bildung* that would encompass both individual and collective dimensions; and in regard to the latter, he composed a programmatic essay titled "Plan for a Comparative Anthropology."[41] There, Humboldt proposed that each *Volk* had a distinct *Nationalcharakter* (national character), which was embodied in the totality of its mental manifestations—language, religion, traditions, and art foremost among them. These in turn revealed the degree of *Bildung* attained by a given people. While Humboldt asserted that the achievements of any *Volk* were a function of its intrinsic qualities and therefore worthy of respect, he held that some peoples—Germans, English, French, Italians, and ancient Greeks—had optimized their innate potentialities and reached particularly high levels of self-realization. In this light, he proposed to focus his comparative anthropology on those *Völker*, since they might serve as models by which other groups could learn to maximize their own potential. In studying the historical trajectories of the great peoples, Humboldt thus hoped to arrive at objective guidelines for national *Bildung* whose realization among individual groups would, in turn, enhance humanity at large. Humboldt never undertook his comparative anthropology and his programmatic essay remained unpublished until the first years of the twentieth century. But its ideas suffused all of Humboldt's later work,

---

(1983), 55–73; Sorkin, *The Transformation of German Jewry, 1780–1840* (Oxford: Oxford University Press, 1987); Walter Bruford, *The German Tradition of Self-Cultivation* (London: Cambridge University Press, 1975); Ernst Lichtenstein, *Zur Entwicklung des Bildungsbegriffes von Meister Eckhart bis Hegel* (Heidelberg: Quelle und Meyer, 1966).
39. See Dunkel, *Herbart and Herbartianism.*
40. Sorkin, "Wilhelm von Humboldt."
41. Bunzl, "Boas and Humboldtian Tradition," 21–22.

especially his comparative linguistics, which he conceived as a systematic exploration of the world's national characters.[42]

The *Völkerpsychologie* of Steinthal and Lazarus promised to realize Humboldt's plan for a comparative anthropology more than any other project of nineteenth-century German scholarship.[43] Folk psychology's overall design as an empirical survey of peoples' mental achievements greatly resembled Humboldt's scheme, especially in regard to its conception of *Bildung*. Like Humboldt before them, Steinthal and Lazarus expected to chart peoples' "degree of *Bildung*," the specific "forms and levels of self-consciousness attained by each *Volk*."[44] Such a comparative study of collective self-realization would allow the folk psychologists to trace the development of each group from the "lowest level of incoherence" to the "pure consciousness of science, particularly philosophy."[45]

In the introduction to the *Zeitschrift für Völkerpsychologie und Sprachwissenschaft,* Steinthal and Lazarus illustrated this design with quintessential examples. They praised the unsurpassed quality of ancient Greek poetry and argued that modern prose owed its creation to the French rather than the Italians. In a similar vein, they reflected on the world's dramatic repertoires, concluding that, "with the exception of the Athenians," only "four modern *Völker* had created dramatical forms of genuine importance for world literature."[46] On the one hand, these comments anticipated the enduring concern of Steinthal and Lazarus to document and assess each group's *Bildung* in terms of its contribution to humanity at large. On the other hand, they gestured to an optimistic program of cultural improvement. Much like Humboldt, Steinthal and Lazarus expected their efforts to yield tangible results. Folk psychology, they asserted, would "penetrate into the

---

42. Wilhelm von Humboldt, "Plan einer vergleichenden Anthropologie," in *Wilhelm von Humboldt—Werke in fünf Bänden,* ed. Andreas Flitner and Klaus Giel, vol. 1 (Stuttgart: Cotta'sche Buchhandlung, 1980), 337–75. See also Bunzl, "Boas and Humboldtian Tradition," 21–24.

43. It is possible, although not very likely, that Steinthal had read Humboldt's "Plan einer vergleichenden Anthropologie" by the time he and Lazarus codified the discipline of *Völkerpsychologie.* Humboldt's manuscripts were in the care of his assistant Johann Buschmann. After his death in 1880, they were incorporated into the Royal Library in Berlin, where Steinthal consulted them to undertake his 1883 edition of Humboldt's writings on language. See Belke, introduction, ci.

44. Lazarus and Steinthal, "Einleitende Gedanken," 4, 38.

45. Ibid., 38.

46. The four peoples were the French, Italians, English, and Germans (ibid., 53).

Geist of nations past and present" to achieve one principal goal: "to help them along on the right path."[47]

This confidence in *Völkerpsychologie's* ability to effect collective *Bildung* was ultimately grounded in Steinthal and Lazarus's conception of the *Volksgeist* as a historically malleable entity. While it represented the unifying psychological essence of a people, its trajectory was always conditioned by specific historical circumstances. As Steinthal and Lazarus put it, "*Volksgeister* are not something static . . . they change in the course of history."[48] This meant that a *Volksgeist* might be artistically productive in one historical period and creatively dormant in another. As *Geist,* however, it could always soar to great heights if it utilized its full potential—a process that could be aided by contact with other peoples and their *Volksgeister*. Such contacts could introduce new "*Bildungsstoff* [stuff of *Bildung*] and *Bildungsfähigkeit* [capability for *Bildung*],"[49] thereby raising any given *Volksgeist* to new levels of excellence. In the final analysis, this plasticity of the *Volksgeist* stood at the core of folk psychology's analytic program of collective *Bildung*.

The Ideology of Bildung in Two German-Jewish Biographies

The social history of *Bildung* extends back to the early phases of the German Enlightenment.[50] Originally, the concept arose in opposition to external models for self-development, such as those presented in religious systems. In their stead, *Bildung* provided a completely self-referential mode of personhood, grounded in an individual's intrinsic qualities. In the course of the eighteenth century, the cause of *Bildung* was taken up by parts of the emerging bourgeoisie—civil servants, pastors, and professors—who could wield its meritocratic ideology against aristocratic privileges. Into an estate society, the *Gebildeten* (those with *Bildung*) thus introduced a notion of individuality that regarded self-realization as its principal moral goal. As champions of individual self-formation, the *Gebildeten* were also the progenitors of German liberalism, redefining the role of the state as the defender of individual freedom. By the first decade of the nineteenth century, and

---
47. Ibid., 72.
48. Ibid., 63.
49. Ibid., 66.
50. The following discussion draws on the sources listed in note 38, particularly Sorkin, *Transformation of German Jewry,* chap. 1.

following the Napoleonic upheavals, *Bildung* emerged as the organizing principle for the modernization of German society. Most prominently, this was the case in Prussia, where Humboldt instituted his pedagogical reforms in an effort to develop an educational system entirely devoted to individual improvement.

The ideology of *Bildung* was also central to the protracted process of German-Jewish emancipation.[51] For the *Gebildeten,* who envisioned a society based on education and merit, the social status of German Jews presented a challenge. For centuries, Jews had existed in a quasi-separate realm marked by religious and cultural alterity. But if the Jews' religious difference had rendered them outsiders vis-à-vis the old regime, the secularized *Gebildeten* imagined them as potential citizens of the modern state. Full emancipation, however, remained in the future, contingent, as it was, on the Jews' successful transformation according to the principles of *Bildung.* As David Sorkin has explained,

> The *Gebildeten* transmuted the Christian assumption that Judaism was theologically inferior into a secular, moral inferiority. The Jews were potentially men but not yet equals. Because of that alleged inferiority the *Gebildeten* saw the Jews' emancipation first and foremost as a question of education. They conceived emancipation as a quid pro quo in which the Jews were to be regenerated in exchange for rights.[52]

Throughout the nineteenth century, this principle characterized the process of German-Jewish emancipation, which, in the course of several decades, brought legal equality for the Jews of the German lands.

Jews, for their part, took an active role in this development. Throughout the eighteenth century, some members of the elites had already attempted to alter the situation of German Jews. And when the

---

51. On the history of German-Jewish emancipation, see Sorkin, *Transformation of German Jewry;* Jacob Katz, *Out of the Ghetto: The Social Background of Jewish Emancipation, 1770–1870* (New York: Schocken, 1973); Michael Meyer, *The Origins of the Modern Jew: Jewish Identity and European Culture in Germany, 1749–1824* (Detroit: Wayne State University Press, 1967); Michael Meyer and Michael Brenner, eds., *German-Jewish History in Modern Times,* vol. 2, *Emancipation and Acculturation: 1780–1871* (New York: Columbia University Press, 1997); Jehuda Reinharz and Walter Schatzberg, eds., *The Jewish Response to German Culture: From the Enlightenment to the Second World War* (Hanover, N.H.: University Press of New England, 1985); Shulamit Magnus, *Jewish Emancipation in a German City: Cologne, 1798–1871* (Stanford: Stanford University Press, 1997).

52. Sorkin, *Transformation of German Jewry,* 20.

ideology of *Bildung* signaled German interest in the Jews' social and civic improvement, upwardly mobile Jews embraced it wholeheartedly. Berlin became the center of the movement. There, the proponents of the Haskala, the Jewish enlightenment, gathered around the philosopher Moses Mendelssohn, who emerged, far beyond his lifetime, as the symbol of German Jewry's *Bildung*. In many ways, the proponents of the Haskala adopted the analysis of Jewish society offered by the *Gebildeten*. They, too, came to see contemporary Judaism as defective, debilitated by centuries of rabbinic solipsism and the harsh life of the ghetto. Confined to immoral professions, subject to atavistic superstitions, and generally depraved, Jews were in desperate need of improvement in both manners and morals. *Bildung* was required, the proponents of the Haskala asserted, and German culture would serve as the model for the transformative regeneration.

The cultural program of German-Jewish emancipation followed from these premises. Throughout the nineteenth century, it was a project of cultural normalization, centered first and foremost on the question of language. For centuries, the Jews of the German lands had spoken Judendeutsch (Judeo-German, a variant of Yiddish). But in the context of the Haskala, the language came to be seen as the embarrassing remnant of an ignominious past. Instead, Mendelssohn and his followers urged Jews to speak proper German, which soon emerged as the principal sign of cultural improvement. Mendelssohn's German translation of the Bible, completed between 1780 and 1783 and printed in Hebrew characters, was conceived in this very vein. Designed as a medium for the transition from Hebrew/Yiddish to German literacy, it quickly came to function as the principal tool for German Jews' acquisition of Hochdeutsch.

Equally important for the *Bildung* of German Jews were the sweeping reforms introduced into Jewish schooling. Prior to the Haskala, Jews were educated in the *Heder* (literally "room"), with the main goal of achieving proficiency in the recitation of Hebrew. While intellectually gifted students received additional instruction in Bible and often attended a Yeshiva, the traditional educational path, which prepared men for the lifelong ritual study of Talmud, essentially bracketed all secular subjects. All this changed when, beginning at the end of the eighteenth century, numerous institutions were founded to reorient Jewish education according to the modern principles of the Haskala. Committed to *Bildung,* and using German as the language of instruction, the new Jewish schools were characterized by a dedication to moral regeneration and the creation of productive citizens. These notions were a gloss for the promotion of secular subjects that would bring about the Jews' occupational restructuring. Jews, the proponents of the Haskala hoped, would no longer be concentrated in the trading professions, but branch out across a whole range of civic occupations. It was in this context of educational secularization and occupational reform that more and more Jews entered German *Gymnasien* and subsequently universities, resulting, in turn, in the emergence of a class of Jewish *Gebildeten* firmly rooted in the conceptual environs of German culture.

In keeping with the overall goal of cultural normalization, the pedagogical reforms championed by the Haskala were accompanied by transformations in the religious realm.[53] Reflecting broader trends in the formation of modern society, Judaism was reconceptualized as a private confession. In the process, Judaism's public articulation was de-emphasized along with those ritual aspects necessitating a separate communal existence. In consequence, the religion's outward manifestations came to resemble those of protestantism. The function of rabbi changed from that of a legal expert concerned with Talmudic intricacies to a position resembling that of a pastor or *Seelsorger;* and morally uplifting sermons, delivered in German, became a central component of synagogue services. No longer concerned with Judaism's ritual domains, the Jewish *Gebildeten* focused on the religion's essence, its ethical and moral contents. And in line with German Enlightenment conceptions, these came to be seen as consistent with universalist, rationalist principles. Jews still adhered to a different religion, but this fact no longer prevented them from being fully human and fully German.

Heymann Steinthal and Moritz Lazarus were paradigmatic products of the culture of German-Jewish emancipation. Born in the 1820s in small towns on the German periphery, they were members of the first generation exposed to the radical program of Jewish reform emanating from Berlin. Both were the children of merchants who spoke Judendeutsch and who lived traditional Jewish lives quite apart from their German neighbors. Steinthal, who was born in 1823, first experienced German Jewry's cultural transformation when, in 1830, he

---

53. On the history of religious reform in nineteenth-century Germany, see Michael Meyer, *Response to Modernity: A History of the Reform Movement in Judaism* (Oxford: Oxford University Press, 1988).

started attending the newly organized Jewish elementary school in his hometown of Gröbzig.[54] Baruch Herzfeld—a graduate of the famous Jewish Franz School in Dessau, founded in 1799—had just been sent to Gröbzig to instruct the children of the small community, which counted some 150 Jews. In the elementary school, Steinthal was taught German grammar and writing, mathematics, geography, and history, as well as Hebrew. The students were expected to speak only High German (*reines Deutsch*), which Steinthal later recalled as a difficult task given the children's strong dialect *(mauscheln)*. Herzfeld also initiated religious reforms in Gröbzig. Instead of the traditional Bar mitzvah, Steinthal underwent a confirmation at the age of thirteen. For reformers like Herzfeld, the traditional ritual merely signified the technical competence of reciting prayer; a confirmation, in contrast, suggested a student's mastery of Judaism's moral precepts.[55]

In 1836, Steinthal moved to Bernburg, the capital of Anhalt-Bernburg, to attend the *Gymnasium*. Even though he needed remedial tutoring in Greek and Latin, neither of which had been part of his previous education, he managed to graduate on schedule in 1842. Throughout his time in Bernburg, Steinthal also continued his Jewish education, receiving private lessons in Bible and Talmud from the provincial rabbi. By the time of his *Abitur*, however, he had already decided to continue on the path of secular *Bildung*. To this end, he enrolled in 1843 at the University of Berlin, where he studied a great variety of subjects, ranging from philosophy and theology to geography and botany. But it was linguistics and philology that occupied him most. He was strongly influenced by the classical philologist August Böckh, the Indo-Germanist Franz Bopp, and the philosophically inclined linguist Carl Heyse. Early on in his studies, he was also introduced to the writings of Wilhelm von Humboldt—an encounter that led to Steinthal's lifelong engagement with his work. In 1847, Steinthal received his doctorate for a dissertation on relative pronouns; and only two years later, he completed his *Habilitation* (the second doctorate), submitting a treatise on Humboldt's linguistics in light of Hegel's phi-

---

54. On Steinthal's youth, see his short pieces "Aus den Jugenderinnerungen Steinthals," "Die jüdische Volksschule in Anhalt von 1830–1840," and "Aus der Synagoge: Eine Jugenderinnerung," all reprinted in Belke, *Lazarus und Steinthal,* 372–76, 377–84, 385–93. See also Belke, introduction, lxxxi–lxxxiv.

55. On reforms in the practice of confirmations, see Sorkin, *Transformation of German Jewry*, chap. 6.

losophy. By the age of twenty-six, Steinthal had moved from the traditional Jewish environs of his native Gröbzig to the cosmopolitan space of Berlin. Ready to embark on a professional career of *Bildung,* he remained in the center of German learning for most of the rest of his life.

Whereas Steinthal's path to German *Bildung* was relatively straightforward, Lazarus took a more circuitous route.[56] Born in 1824 in Filehne, Posen—a small town of three thousand people, a third of them Jews—he attended the state-sponsored elementary school that had opened its doors to Jews in 1833. Alongside this secular education, he received traditional instruction in Hebrew, Bible, and Talmud. While a promising student intent on furthering his *Bildung,* Lazarus could not attend a *Gymnasium* on account of financial constraints; so at age sixteen, he joined a local Jewish trading company, continuing the regular study of Talmud with his employer. At night, however, he immersed himself in the German classics; Herder and Schleiermacher were a particular inspiration.[57]

At the age of nineteen, he happened upon an opportunity to receive formal German *Bildung* after all. A stipend to study Talmud allowed him to move to Braunschweig, where he would also attend the local *Gymnasium.* Once there, Lazarus had to work hard at improving his speech, his "dialect" having been "so bad";[58] but he reveled in the educational opportunities afforded by his new situation. Even more importantly perhaps, he found among the "*gebildeten* Jews" of Braunschweig "the first glance of purely Germanic being" [den ersten Hauch rein germanischen Wesens].[59] One of those models was the local rabbi, who instructed him in Talmud. L. Herzfeld was not only the first German preacher in Braunschweig, but also a national figure in Jewish debates over religious reform.[60]

Lazarus graduated from the *Gymnasium* in 1846; and the same year, he moved to Berlin to attend university. Having left Braunschweig

---

56. On Lazarus's youth, see *Aus meiner Jugend: Autobiographie von M. Lazarus,* ed. Nahida Lazarus (Frankfurt am Main: J. Kauffmann, 1913); *Moritz Lazarus' Lebenserinnerungen,* ed. Nahida Lazarus and Alfred Leicht (Berlin: Georg Reimer, 1906). See also Belke, introduction, xiv–xix.
57. Lazarus, *Aus meiner Jugend,* 44.
58. Ibid., 22.
59. Ibid., 70–71.
60. Ibid., 67.

without a trace of "intellectual or linguistic dialect" [geistig wie sprachlich dialektfrei],[61] he planned to study philosophy. In Braunschweig, he had already been introduced to the writings of Johann Friedrich Herbart by his student and friend Friedrich Grienpenkerl, who taught at the *Gymnasium*. In Berlin, Lazarus continued his engagement with Herbart's system, negotiating it in light of the reigning philosophical orientation, Hegelianism. To complement his studies, he also heard the historian Leopold von Ranke, as well as Böckh and Heyse. In 1849, Lazarus received his doctorate for a dissertation on aesthetic education.

Throughout his student years at the University of Berlin, Lazarus continued his reading of Thora and Talmud. But his engagement with Judaism extended beyond the realm of ritual study. He was closely acquainted with Leopold Zunz, a pioneer of the *Wissenschaft des Judentums*.[62] The origin of *Wissenschaft* dated back to the late 1810s, when members of the first generation of university-educated Jews sought to apply the developing methods of critical textual and historical scholarship to the Jewish tradition. In 1819, Zunz had been instrumental in the founding of the Association for Culture and the Scholarly Study of the Jews; and in 1822, he became the editor of its short-lived journal, the first scholarly Jewish periodical. In his conception of the *Wissenschaft des Judentums,* Zunz was strongly influenced by his teachers at the University of Berlin, the philologists Böckh and Friedrich August Wolf. In analogy with their treatment of the cultures of antiquity, and in line with the Romantic turn in social thought, Zunz came to understand the historical trajectory of Judaism as the function of a unique Jewish *Volksgeist*. Through recourse to the objective means of science, *Wissenschaft* would at once reconstruct that historical path and identify the elements that truly characterized the Jewish *Volksgeist*. In articulating this program, Zunz followed the logic of German-Jewish emancipation. Believing, much like other followers of the Haskala, that contemporary Judaism was degraded, he advocated regeneration by way of connection to Judaism's pure and glorious past. Documenting this past through scientific means would not only allow reform in accordance with intrinsic Jewish principles, but would also raise respect for Jews in non-Jewish circles. In this spirit, Zunz, for

---

61. Ibid., 112.
62. On the *Wissenschaft des Judentums,* see Meyer, *Origins,* chap. 6; Sinai Ucko, "Geistesgeschichtliche Grundlagen der Wissenschaft des Judentums," in *Wissenschaft des Judentums im deutschen Sprachbereich,* ed. Kurt Wilhelm (Tübingen: J. C. B. Mohr, 1967), 315–53.

example, demonstrated that morally uplifting sermons, so central to the project of German-Jewish *Bildung,* were not a recent invention, but the continuation of a venerable Jewish tradition. Lazarus, who had known Zunz since his time at the Braunschweig *Gymnasium,* thought that he alone had captured the "vastness of Israel's history," his "interpretation of the people's spirit" having "uncovered" its "soul."[63] When Lazarus began to pursue the critical study of the Bible as a first sustained venture into the reform-oriented scientific engagement with Judaism, he was directly inspired by his encounter with Zunz and his scholarship.[64]

Even more crucial for the development of *Völkerpsychologie,* Lazarus and Steinthal actually met at the University of Berlin. They were introduced in 1849 by their mutual teacher Heyse, who noticed that the two young Jews shared many intellectual preoccupations. Indeed, when Lazarus and Steinthal came together, the former's Herbartian concern with the mechanisms of collective psychology amalgamated with the latter's Humboldtian interest in language and national character to form a project centered on the comparative elucidation of *Geist*. In terms of intellectual history, Lazarus and Steinthal merged two strands of late-eighteenth- and early-nineteenth-century German social thought. But in doing so, they developed a formal system whose conceptual basis was rooted in their common experience as assimilating German Jews. We can begin to glean the connection in an account by Lazarus, who—in a later recollection—projected the discipline's origin into his initial encounter with German *Bildung:*

> I was trying to really understand antiquity, and fortunately, I was not lacking an opportunity. I had a pretty big yardstick with me, the Jewish *Geist* and its development, which I knew quite well for my age. I was familiar with the legal system from the Pentateuch to the Shulhan Arukh[65] along with its most recent interpreters. The poetic creations of the Jews, from the blessings of Jacob and Moses to the most recent, delicious translations of *Die Glocke* by Schiller, were known to me, at least in regard to the most significant products of each epoch. . . . Only in this manner did I

---

63. *Lazarus' Lebenserinnerungen,* 492–98.
64. Lazarus, *Aus meiner Jugend,* 111.
65. The Shulhan Arukh is the Code of Jewish Law written by Joseph Caro. It summarizes the commandments governing everyday life, as well as civil and criminal law. It was amended by Moses Isserles and first published in 1565.

want to delve into the *Geist* of the classic peoples, and finally comprehend and experience that of the German nation. . . . Back then, without me being at all aware of it, my inner workings prepared the ground for *Völkerpsychologie*.[66]

The Jews of *Völkerpsychologie*

Jews were never the exclusive focus of *Völkerpsychologie*. True to its original design, the pages of Steinthal and Lazarus's *Zeitschrift* featured a diverse set of topics and peoples. Contributions to the first volumes of the new forum included empirical essays on Italian folklore, French drama, ancient Greek mythology, and the Hungarian language, along with more theoretical pieces on such topics as phonology, etymology, the origin of mores, and the relation between the individual and the collectivity. Showcasing a number of different scholars while maintaining the authorial dominance of Lazarus and especially Steinthal, it was an eclectic mixture that came to characterize all twenty volumes of the *Zeitschrift für Völkerpsychologie und Sprachwissenschaft*.[67]

In this larger comparative framework, however, the Jewish people did occupy a rather prominent place, particularly in the many pieces authored by Steinthal. As early as the first volume of the *Zeitschrift*, he took a recent publication by Ernest Renan as the occasion for an extended reflection on the characteristics of the Semitic peoples.[68] The

---

66. Lazarus, *Aus meiner Jugend*, 91–92. At another point of his memoirs, Lazarus suggested that the experiences of his childhood in Filehne foretold the development of *Völkerpsychologie*. The three thousand occupants of the town were divided into three equal parts of Polish Catholics, German Protestants, and Jews. In retrospect, Lazarus noted, "As the three religious communities in the town . . . were of different descent and spoke different languages, every lonely thought and every search that was prompted by obvious appearances might have become the root of *Völkerpsychologie*, just as the continuous observation of the three populations' different manners in nearly all aspects of life contained the personal beginnings of a comparative psychology" (*Aus meiner Jugend*, 32).

67. The twentieth and final volume of the *Zeitschrift für Völkerpsychologie und Sprachwissenschaft* contains an index for the periodical's entire run. The table documents Steinthal's intellectual domination of the journal. Of the fourteen pages listing contributions by individual authors, Steinthal's pieces take up a full five pages. Alfred Leicht, "Register zu Band I–XX: A. Autorenverzeichnis," *ZfV* 20 (1890): 373–86.

68. H. Steinthal, "Zur Charakteristik der semitischen Völker," *ZfV* 1 (1860): 328–45. The essay was reprinted under the same title in H. Steinthal, *Über Juden und Judentum: Vorträge und Aufsätze, herausgegeben vom Gustav Karpeles* (Berlin: Poppelauer, 1906), 91–104. For a similar argument, see Steinthal's review of A. Geiger, *Das Judenthum und seine Geschichte* (Breslau: Schletter'sche Buchhandlung, 1865), *ZfV* 4 (1866): 225–34.

essay set the tone for all folk psychological engagements with the Jewish question, seeking to document Judaism's historical achievements in a broadly comparative framework. Only this global context—the mode of analysis implied in opposition to the more focused *Wissenschaft des Judentums*—could reveal the genuine character of the Jewish *Volksgeist* and thereby allow the objective assessment of the Jews' contribution to the *Bildung* of humanity at large. At issue in Steinthal's essay was the question of monotheism. Renan had argued that monotheism was the characteristic feature of all Semitic peoples, conditioned by a primitive religious instinct derived in turn from their nomadic character. The argument implied that all the world's monotheistic religions were based on an immutably primitive source, thereby undermining the status of Christianity, as well as that of Islam and Judaism. Steinthal objected on two grounds. On the one hand, he asserted a foundational principle of folk psychology, suggesting that religious ideas, much like the *Geister* that produced them, were never static, but subject to historical transformation. It would thus be false to reduce monotheism to its supposedly primitive beginnings, since it emerged in new forms at every historical juncture. On the other hand, and even more importantly, Steinthal questioned Renan's genealogy of monotheism. Rather than the original primitive religion of all Semites, he identified it as the achievement of one specific people: the Israelites. Steinthal arrived at this conclusion—which rendered the Jewish *Volksgeist* as the historical creator of the world's dominant religious systems—by way of a folk psychological comparison. This analysis revealed an original Semitic polytheism, not unlike that of the Indo-European peoples. But while "Sanskritic polytheism" could never conceive the idea of a single God, the Semitic variant already contained the kernel of the monotheistic idea.[69] It fell upon the "Israelite *Volksgeist*" to realize that potential, not, as Steinthal was quick to note, because the Jews had "superior talents" or "greater mental power *(Geisteskraft)*" than other peoples, but because their *Geist* followed "another direction."[70] As Steinthal explicated, monotheism owed its creation to the ancient Israelites' "prophetic consciousness," which did not "conserve" an already existent primitive monotheism, but rather "created" the theological form "alone and on its own power."[71] In Steinthal's argument, which paralleled that of other nineteenth-cen-

---

69. Steinthal, "Zur Charakteristik der semitischen Völker," 342.
70. Ibid., 343.
71. Ibid.

tury German-Jewish authors, the Jews thus emerged as the original bearers of monotheism, its global triumph at once proving the idea's world historical stature and testifying to the seminal accomplishments of its creators.

If the assessment of the Jews' world historical contributions rested on ancient religious achievements, Steinthal also mobilized folk psychology to address contemporary Jewish concerns. He did so in the tenth volume of the *Zeitschrift*, where he published a sixty-page review of recent works by Bruno Bauer.[72] In the essay, which covered such topics as the work of the ancient Jewish philosopher Philo and Bauer's hypothesis about the Greco-Roman origin of Christianity, Steinthal criticized Bauer's tendency to explain contemporary phenomena as the function of unchanging characteristics. Concretely, Steinthal took exception to Bauer's suggestion that the Jews' proclivity for trade and their concomitant distaste for agriculture were intrinsic to the Jewish *Volksgeist*. Mustering evidence from the Old Testament, which he read as the ancient Jews' epic poetry, Steinthal documented a Jewish preoccupation with agricultural issues and the absence of any concern with trade. Since the "literature of a people shows us its *Geist*," Steinthal concluded that Jews' involvement in commerce was not intrinsic to the Jewish *Volksgeist*, but constituted a "change from the old national ways."[73] Steinthal's response to Bauer, however, was not a defense of his Jewish contemporaries. Quite on the contrary, like other proponents of German-Jewish emancipation, he was worried about the concentration of Jews in trade. In the context of folk psychology's theoretical apparatus, however, this phenomenon did not emerge as the function of an essential depravity, but as the historical consequence of the Jews' diasporic trajectory. Beyond safeguarding the ancient Israelites' reputation, Steinthal's position thus implied that contemporary Jews could improve themselves by overcoming their economic reliance on commerce. The logic of German-Jewish *Bildung* had demanded the Jews' social and cultural transformation; and Steinthal's efforts provided a conceptual framework for this process through the identification of genuine Jewish traits and achievements that could serve as a model for the intended regeneration.

---

72. H. Steinthal, review of Bruno Bauer's *Philo, Strauß und Renan und das Urchristentum* (Berlin: Gustav Hempel, 1874) and *Christus und die Cäsaren: Der Ursprung des Christentums aus dem römischen Griechentum* (Berlin: Eugen Grosser, 1877), *ZfV* 10 (1878): 409–69. The essay was reprinted under the title "Bruno Bauer," in *Über Juden und Judentum*, 148–94.

73. Steinthal, review of Bauer, 422, 425.

Nowhere was the German-Jewish logic in *Völkerpsychologie's* design more evident, however, than in Lazarus's efforts to foster religious reform. Having risen to some prominence in the course of the 1860s, he was invited in 1869 to serve as president of the first Jewish synod. Held in Leipzig to effect theological and cultural unity under the banner of liberal and progressive Judaism, the meeting, which brought together rabbis, scholars, and lay leaders from sixty German communities, was intended to ensure the preservation of Judaism in the contemporary world. In its concern to codify reform according to rational principles, the synod was one of the most potent expressions of German-Jewish *Bildung,* as well as a seminal moment in the history of the Reform Movement in Judaism.[74]

In his presidential speech to the synod, Lazarus developed a folk psychological argument, for both the continued relevance of Judaism and the necessity for its reform.[75] Contrasting Judaism with the religions of ancient Greece and Rome, he argued that a religion could only persist if it continued to be articulated by its originary *Volksgeist.* This had not been the case in Greece and Rome, where moral and philosophical insights had superseded and thereby undermined belief in the original polytheistic system. Lazarus implied that this disjuncture contributed to the eventual downfall of the Greco-Roman religion—a fate he contrasted with the history of Judaism. That history, he argued, was characterized by the unbroken adherence of a people to its authentic religion. "Judaism lives," Lazarus told the synod, because its "old *Geist,* renewed from generation to generation" always had "unity and continuity."[76] The "innermost being" [innerstes Wesen] of Judaism had not changed because the "original sources" were still the "sources of our contemporary insights."[77] Despite this continuity of *Geist,* however, the level of Jewish *Bildung* had been uneven throughout the historical epochs. Jews had adhered faithfully to their original religious precepts; but they resembled Greeks, Romans, and Germans in their

---

74. On the synod, see Meyer, *Response to Modernity,* 187–91. Lazarus is mentioned prominently in Meyer's discussion, but only in conjunction with his official role as president of the synod. The relationship between Lazarus's political/religious commitment and his *Völkerpsychologie* is not explored.

75. M. Lazarus, "Rede zum Schluß der ersten Synode," in *Treu und Frei: Gesammelte Reden und Vorträge über Juden und Judentum* (Leipzig: Winter'sche Verlagshandlung, 1887), 1–17.

76. Ibid., 6.

77. Ibid., 7.

inability to maintain the "same heights" of religious and cultural achievement throughout their long existence.[78] In accordance with the logic of German-Jewish emancipation, Lazarus interpreted the previous centuries as a period of particularly low accomplishments, necessitating the present efforts of regeneration. In the fashion of German-Jewish *Bildung,* Lazarus located these in the religious and pedagogical realm, linking the "rejuvenation of Judaism" to "reforms" in synagogue life and youth education.[79]

Such reforms, Lazarus believed, would bring about a deepening of spiritual commitment, a refocusing on the essence of Jewish *Geist*. Elevated through this self-realization and stripped of its gratuitous ritualistic aspects, a reformed Judaism would revive the religion's world historical mission. In ancient times, Lazarus believed (as did Steinthal and other German-Jewish authors), that mission had been the development and cultivation of the monotheistic idea. In the modern age, Judaism was still the principal "bearer of belief in a single god";[80] but it also emerged as the religious archetype of universal humanity. Invoking his authority as a *Völkerpsychologe,* Lazarus commented that Jews were the only people who asserted the "unity of mankind" in their origin myth. All other *Völker* merely recounted the creation of their "own ancestors," but the first book of Moses spoke of the "creation of man in general" [die Schöpfung des Menschen überhaupt].[81] In the context of the synod, the implications of this folk psychological assessment were clear. Only the reform-oriented elevation of contemporary Judaism could ensure its preservation as the historical bearer of a global religious truth—a truth, moreover, whose conceptual anchoring of universal humanity enabled Jews' entrance into modern German society. Jews thus occupied a privileged, if peculiar, position. Through their ongoing assimilation into the dominant culture, they embodied the principles of cosmopolitan universalism. To continue to do so, however, they needed to retain their religious difference. In this manner, Lazarus provided a raison d'être for Judaism in the modern world. In his folk psychological gloss on German-Jewish *Bildung,* Jews needed to assimilate to German culture in order to express the theological principle and cultural reality of universal humanity.

Lazarus and Steinthal continued to champion the project of Ger-

---

78. Ibid.
79. Ibid., 8–9.
80. Ibid., 11.
81. Ibid.

man-Jewish *Bildung* until the end of their lives. In fact, their efforts to deploy folk psychological insights to advance the state of contemporary Jewry actually intensified in the last decades of the nineteenth century. In this manner, Lazarus and Steinthal sought to react to the emergent anti-Semitic movement that was about to strike the most devastating blow to the cultural logic of German-Jewish emancipation since its original articulation. In an unprecedented attempt to mobilize Jew-hatred for political ends, the court preacher Adolf Stöcker had initiated the anti-Semitic agitation in 1878.[82] Arising in the context of economic depression and Bismarck's alignment with Christian-conservative forces, the anti-Semitic movement came as a shock to Germany's assimilating Jews, especially when, in 1880, it began collecting signatures for a petition demanding the restriction of Jewish immigration from Eastern Europe and the containment of Jewish participation in the professions. Even more devastating for men like Lazarus and Steinthal, however, was the fact that some German *Gebildete* took up the anti-Semitic cause. Foremost among them was the historian Heinrich von Treitschke, professor at the University of Berlin. In 1879–80, Treitschke published a number of essays, asserting the incompatibility of Germans and Jews on account of the latter's invariable alterity and intrinsic depravity. The ensuing debate, the so-called *Berliner Antisemitismusstreit* (anti-Semitism dispute), called forth some of Germany's leading Jewish intellectuals in an attempt to defend the accomplishments and safeguard the future of German-Jewish emancipation.[83]

The fallout of the new political situation could also be gleaned in the pages of the *Zeitschrift für Völkerpsychologie und Sprachwissenschaft*. There, Steinthal pursued a two-pronged strategy that reiterated folk psychology's approach to the Jewish question with renewed urgency. On the one hand, he sought to document the achievements of the Jewish *Volksgeist* with even greater fervor; on the other hand, he vigorously asserted the necessity and success of German-Jewish *Bildung*.

In regard to the former, it was a series of essays on the fifth book of Moses that was designed to showcase the literary accomplishments of the Jewish *Volksgeist*. As early as 1875, Steinthal had complained in

---

82. On the history of the anti-Semitic movement, see Peter Pulzer, *The Rise of Political Anti-Semitism in Germany and Austria* (New York: John Wiley and Sons, 1964); Albert Lichtblau, *Antisemitismus und soziale Spannung in Berlin und Wien, 1867–1914* (Berlin: Metropol, 1994).

83. See Walter Boehlich, ed., *Der Berliner Antisemitismusstreit* (Frankfurt am Main: Insel Verlag, 1965).

the *Zeitschrift* that anti-Jewish scholars undercut the creative achievements of the ancient Israelites by refusing to accept the Pentateuch as the Jewish variant of epic poetry, dismissing it instead as myth and fairy tale.[84] In the three pieces published between 1880 and 1890, Steinthal sought to overturn this damning verdict through extensive readings of Deuteronomy, designed to showcase the Old Testament's literary qualities.[85] In effusive language that rendered the essays a passionate defense of Jewish accomplishments, Steinthal documented that the fifth book of Moses contained poetic motives that were unique among all the world's literatures. Even more importantly, he asserted that the material transmitted in the Old Testament was but a small portion of the "old and rich literature" produced by the ancient Israelites.[86] By further demonstrating that the fifth book of Moses was the work of more than one author, he concluded that the Pentateuch was part of a rich literature created by the Jewish *Volksgeist*. Rather than a form of primitive myth, the Hebrew Bible thus emerged as an unmatched example of folk poetry whose relevance throughout the ages evidenced the cultural prowess of its originators.

In regard to the latter question of German-Jewish *Bildung,* Steinthal presented his folk psychological contribution in the context of a book review on the subject of the Jewish sermon.[87] Steinthal agreed with the author, the reform rabbi Sigmund Maybaum, that morally uplifting sermons in the local vernacular had been an intrinsic part of ancient Jewish religious life, and that Jews had, in fact, invented the practice. But in contrast to the book's focus on ancient times, Steinthal devoted most of his review to the function of the sermon in recent German-Jewish history. Noting that the level of Jewish cultural achievement has always depended on the Jews' ability to take part in the cultural life of their surroundings, Steinthal identified the time before the Haskala as a dark age of enforced separation. During that time, the practice of vernacular sermons was lost, along with other venerable aspects of

---

84. Steinthal, "Der Semitismus, mit Rücksicht auf: Eberhard Schrader, *Die Höllenfahrt der Istar: Ein altbabylonisches Epos* (Giessen: Ricker'sche Buchhandlung, 1874)," *ZfV* 8 (1875): 339–50.

85. H. Steinthal, "Das fünfte Buch Mose: Ein Beitrag zur epischen Frage," *ZfV* 11 (1880): 1–28; "Die erzählenden Stücke im fünften Buch Mose I," *ZfV* 12 (1881): 253–89; "Die erzählenden Stücke im fünften Buch Mose II," *ZfV* 20 (1890): 47–87.

86. Steinthal, "Das fünfte Buch Mose," 2.

87. Steinthal, review of S. Maybaum, *Jüdische Homiletik, nebst einer Auswahl von Texten und Themen* (Berlin: Ferdinand Dümmlers Verlagsbuchhandlung, 1890), *ZfV* 20 (1890): 359–70.

ancient Jewish tradition. Reintroduced in the late eighteenth century by "people whose *Geist* and sensibility had already been nourished by German literature," the sermon thus functioned as a cipher for the Jews' regeneration through the "acceptance of German culture."[88] For Steinthal, the folk psychologist concerned with the trajectory of the Jewish *Volksgeist,* the revival of the vernacular moral sermon symbolized the success of German-Jewish *Bildung;* and much like other recent transformations, it was an achievement that needed to be defended in light of rising anti-Semitism.

While Steinthal reacted to the anti-Semitic threat in the scholarly pages of the *Zeitschrift,* Lazarus emerged as a public defender of Germany's Jews. This role was fitting for one of the most prominent Jewish intellectuals of the late nineteenth century. Indeed, Lazarus's reputation as a leading representative of German-Jewish *Bildung* had steadily increased since the synod of 1869 and was further cemented when, a year later, he took the lead in the founding of the Hochschule für die Wissenschaft des Judentums (College of Jewish Studies). The college, devoted to the scientific study of Judaism according to critical methods, became the intellectual center of liberal Judaism and the principal training ground for reform-oriented rabbis. From its inception, Lazarus served as the head of the institution's board of trustees.[89] In 1879, shortly after the publication of Treitschke's initial anti-Jewish tract, Lazarus took the occasion of the *Hochschule's* annual board meeting to deliver a long lecture that refuted the new anti-Semitic viewpoint on folk psychological grounds.[90] Published immediately and widely read, Lazarus's text was a central contribution to the *Antisemitismusstreit;* and more than any other treatise, it captured the dilemma of both German-Jewish emancipation and folk psychology in the face of exclusionary nationalism.

In "Was heißt national?" (What does national mean?), Lazarus posed the Jewish question in terms of nationality. Were the Jews different? And if so, did they belong to a separate nation? To answer these questions, Lazarus called for the conceptual clarification of the term *nation.* Treating it as a synonym for *Volk,* Lazarus referred his audience to the early issues of the *Zeitschrift für Völkerpsychologie und*

---

88. Steinthal, review of Maybaum, 368, 370.
89. On Lazarus's involvement with the Hochschule für die Wissenschaft des Judentums, see Meyer, *Response to Modernity,* 191. Steinthal, for his part, taught at the *Hochschule* during the last decades of his life (Belke, introduction, xcix).
90. M. Lazarus, "Was heißt national?" in *Treu und Frei,* 53–113.

Sprachwissenschaft, particularly the introduction to the first volume and an essay by the statistician Richard Böckh that had appeared in volume 4.[91] Lazarus quoted the pieces at great length to establish that national belonging was independent of such categories as citizenship, territory, religion, and descent. Asserting folk psychology's foundational presupposition, he argued instead that common nationality could only be established through the principal entity of collective *Geist:* language. As Lazarus put it, "Language was the unmistakable band that tied all elements of a nation into one *geistige* community";[92] and in consequence, it was now possible to answer the question of German Jews' nationality. "We are Germans, nothing but Germans," Lazarus asserted in light of the linguistic and cultural realities in the wake of German-Jewish emancipation; "when we speak of nationality, we only belong to one nation, the German nation."[93] After all, "the scholarship that educates us, the *Bildung* that enlightens us, the art that elevates us, they are all German."[94]

Anti-Semitic agitators sought to negate this *geistige* development; but to Lazarus, their "whole blood and race theory" was nothing but a "refuse of coarse materialism."[95] This is not to say that Lazarus rejected the Jews' racial designation. On the contrary, he accepted that "our descent is not German."[96] But the fact that "as Jews, we are Semites" had no implication for the question of national belonging.[97] "Blood means bloody little to me," Lazarus proclaimed, while "*Geist* and its historical development means nearly everything, especially when one deals with the value and dignity of man *(Mensch),* as an individual or as a people."[98] Against the anti-Semitic notion of racial purity, Lazarus thus asserted the cosmopolitan plasticity of *Geist* and

---

91. Richard Böckh, "Die statistische Bedeutung der Volkssprache als Kennzeichen der Nationalität," *ZfV* 4 (1866): 259–402. Richard Böckh was the son of August Böckh, the philologist who had taught both Lazarus and Steinthal at the University of Berlin.
92. Lazarus, "Was heißt national?" 62.
93. Ibid., 70.
94. Ibid., 71. To be sure, Jews were the bearers of a different religion. But this was entirely unrelated to the question of nationality, since there were no national religions. Christianity was just as French, English, Italian, or German; and in the same manner, Judaism could appear in any particular national guise. Judaism, moreover, was an entirely private confession, and since it made no demands that conflicted with national interests, Lazarus determined that "Judaism is German in the same sense that Christianity is German" (76–77).
95. Ibid., 73.
96. Ibid., 71.
97. Ibid.
98. Ibid., 74.

its realization in the plenitude of universal humanity. In this context, he reaffirmed an original tenet of *Völkerpsychologie:* "Every *Volk* can learn from every other one"—an idea he now redeployed in the specific context of German-Jewish realities.[99] Noting that the *Völker* possessing unsurpassed "cultural energy and historical wealth" had been the ones that "mixed the most,"[100] he identified Germans and Jews as agents in a mutual process of collective improvement. In this framework, Lazarus, once again, redefined the Jews' world historical mission. Emphasizing their diasporic nature, he argued that Jews were responsible for infusing the world's peoples with the vigor of *geistige* diversity. The German nation was particularly receptive in this regard because of the unique "power and depth of its *Geist.*"[101] This quality allowed the absorption of the Jewish into the German *Volksgeist,* thereby ensuring the "ongoing enrichment that comes with the Jews' participation in the *Geister* of other nations."[102] In making this argument, Lazarus had come full circle from the introduction to the *Zeitschrift für Völkerpsychologie und Sprachwissenschaft,* where he and Steinthal had already commented that the Germans were more "suited and willing to recognize and incorporate the foreign" than any other modern nation.[103] Now, in the face of the anti-Semitic movement, Lazarus could only appeal to uphold this "true Germandom *(Deutschtum)*" that was not characterized by "lowly envy and petty ill-will," but by "high-mindedness" and "generosity."[104]

But "Was heißt national?" reiterated the original conception of *Völkerpsychologie* far beyond an appeal to German Enlightenment universalism. In focusing on the constitutive role of language in the formation of national entities, rejecting racial explanations, and positing malleable *Volksgeister* as collective agents of interactive *Bildung,* the essay affirmed the analytic design Lazarus and Steinthal had advanced in the introduction to the *Zeitschrift*. More than any other text, it also revealed the degree to which this design retraced the cultural contours of German-Jewish emancipation. In its assertion of the Jews' membership in the German nation, its critique of anti-Semitic presuppositions, and its explanation of the mutual benefits of Ger-

---

99. Ibid., 95.
100. Ibid., 91.
101. Ibid., 89.
102. Ibid., 94.
103. Lazarus and Steinthal, "Einleitende Gedanken," 66.
104. Lazarus, "Was heißt national?" 89.

man/Jewish coexistence, the piece spoke about the folk psychologists' immediate lifeworld. *Völkerpsychologie* may have sought to account for the comparative development of the world's *Volksgeister;* but in its most powerful form, it remained a theory and defense of German-Jewish emancipation. Like the folk psychology from which it emerged, that project ultimately depended on an open conception of *Volksgeist* and nation and a belief in the universal project of individual and collective improvement; and as these notions began to recede from German consciousness, *Völkerpsychologie* was about to loose its struggle for German-Jewish *Bildung.*

Ends and Beginnings

Lazarus and Steinthal continued to publish widely, reiterating the axioms of their *Völkerpsychologie,* as well as their position on the Jewish question.[105] More and more, however, they were preaching to the converted: other German Jews who shared their fundamental viewpoint and could identify with Steinthal's bitter assessment, advanced in 1892, that "in us [Jews], the German *Geist* shone brighter and more powerfully than in the millions who brag with their Germandom."[106] But as Steinthal and Lazarus emerged as public defenders of German-Jewish emancipation, their interventions went largely unheard in the wider world of German letters. In part, this was a function of their institutional position. While both men carried the title *Professor,* as Jews, neither was ever offered a German *Ordinariat,* the full professorship that provided institutional prestige and financial security.[107] Lacking the infrastructure that fashioned successful university careers, the

---

105. Steinthal advanced his position in an extended series of popular articles published in the *Allgemeine Zeitung des Judentums* from 1890 until his death in 1899. These essays, along with a number of others, were later collected in *Über Juden und Judentum.* Lazarus, for his part, spent his last years working on a grand project on the ethics of Judaism. In 1898, the first volume appeared under the title *Die Ethik des Judentums* (Frankfurt am Main: J. Kauffmann); the second volume followed in 1911. In the wake of Lazarus's death in 1903, it had been compiled by J. Winter and August Wünsche on the basis of handwritten manuscripts.
106. H. Steinthal, "Judentum und Patriotismus," in *Über Juden und Judentum,* 69.
107. Steinthal attained the (unsalaried) position of *außerordentlicher Professor* (associate professor) at the University of Berlin. Lazarus held the title of *ordentlicher Honorarprofessor* (full honorary professor) at the same institution; that position was not salaried either. It should be noted, though, that Lazarus did occupy a full professorship at the University of Bern from 1859 to 1866. He apparently left the position in hopes of attaining a full professorship in Germany, which never materialized. See Belke, introduction, xcix, xl.

Jewish voices of *Völkerpsychologie* remained marginal in the German academy.

Beyond the vicissitudes of the academy's anti-Semitic policies, Lazarus and Steinthal, however, were also losing their battle on intellectual grounds. In codifying *Völkerpsychologie* in the 1850s and 1860s, they had attempted to fashion a modern scholarly discipline on already dated principles; and by the 1870s and 1880s, their humanist insistence on *Geist* and its various manifestations as the central site of comparative research into the world's peoples seemed positively antiquarian, especially in the context of contemporary anthropological theories. As German ethnology professionalized in the last decades of the nineteenth century, more and more scholars rejected the hermeneutics of textual exegesis in favor of a natural science of physical objects. The latter was the model advanced by Adolf Bastian and the contributors of his *Zeitschrift für Ethnologie*. Founded in 1869, the periodical quickly emerged as the principal vehicle of German anthropological thought, establishing Bastian's *Ethnologie,* rather than Lazarus and Steinthal's *Völkerpsychologie,* as the reigning paradigm for the study of human diversity.

Steinthal protested the subordination of linguistics and philology in Bastian's journal; but his interventions merely solidified an approach that regarded language and literature as an unreliable source for the investigation of the world's peoples.[108] For Bastian, a group's language was too volatile to indicate its true character. Peoples, after all, adopted new languages quickly, both in the context of subjugation and cultural assimilation; and it was in this light that Bastian championed the study of enduring entities, such as material artifacts, as the privileged vehicle of ethnology. Underlying this debate between Steinthal (and Lazarus) and Bastian was a larger distinction that isolated *Völkerpsychologie* from the emergent approaches to the human sciences. While Bastian and other scholars working in a modern vein provided a conceptual apparatus that potentially reified differences between ethnic groups by emphasizing their enduring characteristics, Steinthal and Lazarus championed a project that figured human collectivities as supremely malleable. In light of the argument advanced in this essay, this latter commitment emerges as a direct reflection of Steinthal and Lazarus's position as assimilating German Jews. As such, they were

---

108. The argument developed in this paragraph owes much to Zimmerman, "Place of Knowledge," esp. 155–67.

members of a social group that, more than any other faction in late-nineteenth-century Germany, was invested in preserving a social model grounded in the ideology of *Bildung* and its affirmative theory of cultural transformation. When Bastian's materialist ethnology emerged as the dominant approach to the question of human diversity, *Völkerpsychologie* was about to lose its chance to define the terms of intellectual debate. Bastian still combined his emphasis on cultural materiality with a genuine commitment to liberal humanism. But by the time a new generation of ethnologists came to the fore at the turn of the century, his discipline was about to emerge as a defender of German ethnic purity. In concert with the new racial anthropology that made its appearance at the same time, the intellectual project of Germany's human sciences became antithetical to the humanist principles of German-Jewish emancipation.[109] In its ethnic and biological fatalism, the new approach was diametrically opposed to the folk psychological axiom of subordinating the material limitations of the body to the inner freedom of *Geist*.

Intellectually isolated outside the German-Jewish community, Lazarus and Steinthal discontinued their editorship of the *Zeitschrift für Völkerpsychologie und Sprachwissenschaften* in 1890. Publication resumed in 1891, but the journal was reoriented intellectually and issued henceforth as the *Zeitschrift des Vereins für Volkskunde* (Journal of the Folklore Association). The publication Lazarus and Steinthal had founded to celebrate the diverse accomplishments of the world's *Volksgeister* came to serve a discipline, *Volkskunde,* that was about to abandon the cosmopolitanism of its early Romantic articulation in favor of an exclusionary nationalism.[110]

Völkerpsychologie, however, did find a champion after the *Zeitschrift für Völkerpsychologie und Sprachwissenschaft* ceased publication. But when the psychologist and philosopher Wilhelm Wundt took up the discipline in the late 1890s, it hardly resembled the original

---

109. On the shift toward a racialized anthropology, see Benoit Massin, "From Virchow to Fischer: Physical Anthropology and 'Modern Race Theories' in Wilhelmine Germany," in Stocking, *Volksgeist,* 79–154. See also Robert Proctor, "From *Anthropologie* to *Rassenkunde* in the German Anthropological Tradition," in *Bones, Bodies, Behavior: Essays on Biological Anthropology,* ed. George W. Stocking (Madison: University of Wisconsin Press, 1988), 138–79.

110. See Wolfgang Jacobei, Hannjost Lixfeld, and Olaf Bockhorn, eds., *Völkische Wissenschaft: Gestalten und Tendenzen der deutschen und österreichischen Volkskunde in der ersten Hälfte des 20. Jahrhunderts* (Vienna: Böhlau, 1994).

design. Wundt, with whom folk psychology is most commonly associated today, had criticized Lazarus and Steinthal's conception as early as 1863; and when he published his multivolume *Völkerpsychologie* in the first decades of the twentieth century, he significantly narrowed the scope of the field.[111] Rather than a comparative project designed to elucidate levels of communal *Bildung,* Wundt understood folk psychology to be a vehicle for the investigation of universal mental processes.[112] In this context, linguistic and ethnographic data was not deployed to account for the historical trajectories of individual peoples. Quite on the contrary, Wundt's *Völkerpsychologie* was resolutely ahistorical, seeking to provide a general model of collective psychological development. Much like Lazarus and Steinthal, Wundt focused on such phenomena as language, myth, and custom; but in regarding them as the mental products of culturally indistinct forms of sociability, he investigated them apart from specific times and places. According to Wundt, the limits of *Völkerpsychologie* were reached precisely at the moment of individual and cultural differentiation; and it was in that sense that he rejected the concept of *Volksgeist* as part of his folk psychological apparatus. In his attempt to establish a science of general collective psychology, Wundt may have prolonged the existence of *Völkerpsychologie.* But the approach he championed bore little resemblance to the discipline codified by Lazarus and Steinthal; and when Wundt's more narrowly scientific version of *Völkerpsychologie* found no adherents in the intellectual climate of the 1920s and 1930s, the last traces of their efforts to establish a comparative inquiry into the world's *Volksgeister* were eclipsed from the German world of letters.

But as the gradual transition from *Anthropologie* and *Ethnologie* to *Rassenkunde* consigned the *Völkerpsychologie* of Lazarus and Steinthal to obscurity in their native land, the German-Jewish spirit of their discipline found a decisive articulation in the work of Franz Boas. On a basic biographical level, the mythical founder of American anthropology shared Lazarus and Steinthal's cultural background. He, too, was a German Jew, a mere generation removed from the transitional moment of German-Jewish emancipation. Like the folk psychologists, Boas was deeply committed to liberal humanism, *Bildung,*

---

111. Wilhelm Wundt, *Völkerpsychologie,* 10 vols. (Leipzig: Engelmann, 1900–1920).

112. Danziger, "Origins and Basic Principles of Wundt's *Völkerpsychologie,*" 308. See also Belke, introduction, cxvi–cxxii.

and the German nation, which he conceived in the universalist terms of late-nineteenth-century German Jewry.[113]

But there are more specific connections between Boas and the *Völkerpsychologen*. Boas not only met Steinthal on at least one occasion and studied with one of his few students, the philosopher Benno Erdmann,[114] he also invoked the discipline of folk psychology and its founders on several prominent occasions. In his first theoretical piece on anthropology, for example, he spoke of the "study of folk psychology" as an integral part of the ethnological project;[115] and in his famous essay on the history of anthropology, he identified Steinthal and "Völker-psychologie" as predecessors in the social analysis of "psychic actions."[116] Even more importantly, Boas saw his linguistic work in the tradition of *Völkerpsychologie*. In 1904, he noted that "the intimate ties between language and ethnic psychology were expressed by no one more clearly than by Steinthal";[117] and he made the influence even more explicit in a later letter to Robert Lowie, where he remarked that his own work on language had always followed "Steinthal's principles."[118]

But even beyond the domain of language, Boas's anthropology closely resembled the *Völkerpsychologie* of Lazarus and Steinthal. Much like them, he discounted race as a determinant of human behavior, explained human diversity in terms of psychological and historical processes, and focused his empirical work on the products of *Geist*—language, mythology, and art foremost among them. In doing so, Boas hoped to create collections of materials that were "more or less direct

---

113. See Douglas Cole, *Franz Boas: The Early Years, 1858–1906* (Seattle: University of Washington Press, 1999), esp. chaps. 1–3. See also Julia Liss, "German Culture and German Science in the *Bildung* of Franz Boas," in Stocking, *Volksgeist*, 155–84; Liss, "The Cosmopolitan Imagination: Franz Boas and the Development of American Anthropology," Ph.D. diss., Department of History, University of California, Berkeley, 1990.

114. George W. Stocking, "The Boas Plan for the Study of American Indian Languages," in *The Ethnographer's Magic and Other Essays in the History of Anthropology* (Madison: University of Wisconsin Press, 1992), 64; Cole, *Franz Boas*, 53–54.

115. Franz Boas, "The Aims of Ethnology," lecture given in 1888 before the Deutscher-Gesellig-Wissenschaftlicher Verein, New York, in Boas, *Race, Language, and Culture* (New York: Macmillan, 1940), 634.

116. Boas, "The History of Anthropology," 31.

117. Ibid., 28.

118. Robert Lowie, "The Progress of Science: Franz Boas, Anthropologist," *Scientific Monthly* 56 (1943): 184.

expressions of the 'genius of a people.'"[119] These would, in turn, allow anthropologists to undertake the humanistic scholarship characteristic of European philology. Boas's anthropology was thus an extension of Lazarus and Steinthal's *Völkerpsychologie*.[120] In broadening their philological project of comparative *Bildung* to encompass nonliterate groups, he sought to actualize folk psychology's universalist underpinnings.

This overarching universalism, which was shared by Lazarus, Steinthal, and Boas, saw common humanity expressed through its highly malleable cultural constituents. Reflecting the logic of German-Jewish emancipation, it was a conception that, in contrast to Wundt's, emphasized cultural diversity while, at the same time, seeking to avoid the reification of difference. For Lazarus, Steinthal, and Boas, the peoples of the world were radically distinct; but their alterity did not reside in such external domains as geography and biology. Rather, difference was a function of the realm of *Geist*—a realm in which the cultural transformation of *Bildung* was a constant possibility. It was in this sense that Lazarus, Steinthal, and Boas continuously stressed the phenomena of diffusion and acculturation that accounted for the processes by which human groups, from German Jews to African Americans, could overcome their difference. Much like the *Völkerpsy-*

---

119. George W. Stocking, "The Aims of Boasian Ethnography: Creating the Materials for Traditional Humanistic Scholarship," *History of Anthropology Newsletter* 4, no. 2 (1977): 4–5.

120. This interpretation in no way seeks to minimize the well-established link between Boas's approach and the liberal anthropology pioneered by his teachers Bastian and Virchow (see, e.g., the contribution by Glenn Penny in the present volume; cf. George W. Stocking, *Race, Culture, and Evolution: Essays in the History of Anthropology* [Chicago: University of Chicago Press, 1968]; Bunzl, "Franz Boas and the Humboldtian Tradition"). But it does suggest a new appreciation for the different aspects of Boasian anthropology. One way to think about the issue is in relation to the four-field approach Boas pioneered in the American anthropological tradition. Three of the four fields (biological anthropology, sociocultural anthropology, and archaeology, to use today's terms) are congruent with the constituents of Bastian and Virchow's Gesellschaft für Anthropologie, Ethnologie und Urgeschichte. The fourth one, linguistic anthropology in contemporary parlance, however, gestures to a different genealogy. As a philological enterprise concerned with the elucidation of peoples' geniuses, it reintroduced a hermeneutic dimension excluded from Bastian and Virchow's more scientific approach. In a somewhat formulaic gloss, this situation suggests that Boas's four-field vision fused the three fields of Bastian and Virchow's scientific design with the humanist field pioneered by Lazarus and Steinthal; and if Boas's lifelong predilection for linguistic and philological work is any indication, it would seem that it was the text-based project of *Völkerpsychologie* that occupied the position of ultimate privilege.

chologie of Lazarus and Steinthal, the anthropology of Boas was an assimilationist project rooted in the universalist desire of German-Jewish *Bildung*.

But if *Völkerpsychologie* thus clearly emerges as a precursor of Boas's anthropology, it is crucial to attend to the differences between them. This is all the more important in light of recent accounts that see central aspects of Boas's approach in direct derivation from folk psychological principles. In this regard, Ivan Kalmar has taken the strongest position, arguing that the Boasian concept of culture is a mere restatement of Lazarus and Steinthal's notion of *Volksgeist*.[121] Linking the concepts on account of their symbolic dimension and shared pluralism, Kalmar has done much to establish the significance of Lazarus and Steinthal in the larger history of anthropology.[122] But in doing so, he has overstated his case. George Stocking has identified the five components of the Boasian culture concept as historicity, plurality, behavioral determinism, integration, and relativism;[123] and while the *Volksgeist* of Lazarus and Steinthal combined the first four elements to form a crucial antecedent of Boasian culture, it was not until the latter's intervention that relativism became a foundational aspect of anthropological theorizing.

To be sure, *Völkerpsychologie* was committed to pluralism; but it was hardly relativistic. For Lazarus and Steinthal, the unequal achievements of the world's *Volksgeister* were never in doubt. While each *Volk* needed to be understood on its own terms, some people were simply more accomplished than others. Lazarus and Steinthal, of course, were particularly interested in those *Volksgeister* that had accomplished the most, since other peoples would be able to learn from them. In this light, nonliterate peoples made an infrequent appearance in the writings of Lazarus and Steinthal; but when they did, they were judged harshly and assigned their place in the normative hierarchy of *Bildung*. Steinthal, for example, prefaced his book-length treatment of

---

121. Kalmar, "The *Völkerpsychologie*." For an account that traces the intellectual continuities between Lazarus's and Steinthal's concept of *Volksgeist* and Boas's notion of culture without asserting their identity, see Bunzl, "Boas and Humboldtian Tradition."

122. In turn, Kalmar links the pluralism of Lazarus and Steinthal's *Volksgeist* and Boas's culture to their respective originators' marginal status as German Jews. Without any explication of the contours of German-Jewish culture, however, the argument fails to link the ideas of Lazarus, Steinthal, and Boas in a convincing manner. See also the comments in note 9.

123. George W. Stocking, "Franz Boas and the Culture Concept in Historical Perspective," in Stocking, *Race, Culture, and Evolution*, 230.

Africa's Mande languages by commenting on their "highly incomplete organization," which proved their "low status." In true humanist fashion, however, he expressed his confidence that the "negroes were capable of *Bildung*" and implied that his treatise would further that project.[124] Such assessments were hardly surprising in the context of nineteenth-century social thought. If anything, Steinthal's optimism about the possibility of cultural improvement was a progressive position; but it was in no way relativistic.

Boas may have taken the design of *Völkerpsychologie* as a model for his anthropology; and the many intellectual and cultural convergences suggest as much. But he broke with folk psychology and other nineteenth-century projects in his constant insistence on the relativity of cultural values. For Boas, all languages were equally functional, all customs equally irrational, and all myths equally notable as historical products of human *Geist*. Lazarus and Steinthal saw the task of *Völkerpsychologie* in the cultural improvement of the world's peoples. Boas realized that all *Völker* were already fully cultured. In the final analysis, it was this relativistic insight that transformed the *Volksgeist* of German-Jewish *Bildung* into the culture of modern American anthropology.

---

124. As Steinthal put it, "Nothing else can be the duty of the happier and more civilized peoples than to convey *Bildung* to their unhappy brethren." H. Steinthal, *Die Mande-Neger-Sprachen: Psychologisch und phonetisch betrachtet* (Berlin: Ferdinand Dümmler's Verlagsbuchhandlung, 1867), xiv–xv.

Bastian's Museum: On the Limits of Empiricism and the Transformation of German Ethnology

H. GLENN PENNY

In 1900, when visitors arrived in Berlin's Museum für Völkerkunde, they entered an institution that was quickly descending into chaos. As one visitor recalled, the vestibule was dominated by "the strange combination of a gigantic Japanese god" and the "sacrificial alters and architectural remains of ancient Mexican cultures." The central courtyard was filled with a mishmash of gigantic objects: "dugout canoes," "gateways to Peruvian temples," North American totems, "Damascian wax dolls," and an assortment of other odds and ends.[1] Indeed, arrangements throughout the museum showed the degree to which its geographical organization had broken down. Much of the ground floor was filled with either prehistoric pottery from Prussia or Heinrich Schliemann's famous collections from Troy; but an adjacent hall also contained a combination of Persian metal work, fur clothing from the Amur region, and Incan mummies. The situation only worsened as visitors made their way up the stairs. In the gallery on the second floor they found Papuan idols next to a collection of Benin bronzes and urns from pre-Columbian Argentina. If they continued their journey through this floor with artifacts from Africa, they would soon encounter items from the South Seas, stumble without explanation from the New Guinea collections to objects from Tierra del Fuego, and discover Asians, Eskimos, Mexicans, and Chileans presented like

---

1. *Vossische Zeitung,* 26 June 1900.

neighbors in the final "American" hall. On the third floor, collections from Indonesia, China, India, and Japan cluttered the walls, overwhelmed the display cabinets, and pressed into the walkways and stairwells. Only the heartiest of visitors made it to the fourth floor, where American plaster castings and the collections of the Berlin Anthropological Society were crammed into corners.

The museum's condition at the turn of the century is particularly surprising in light of the tremendous fanfare that accompanied its opening only fourteen years earlier. The opening ceremonies in 1886 had been fitting for the world's first free-standing ethnographic museum—an institution that would quickly become the envy of ethnologists and museum directors across Europe and the United States. As dignitaries arrived at the festive occasion, they entered a large, carefully organized space that was meant to capture the breadth of the German ethnographic project. At the back of the entrance hall stood a spectacular, ancient Indian gateway carved out of stone, and its base was a carpeted podium awaiting the royalty and state officials who would open the museum. A veritable jungle of palms and other tropical plants framed the scene, stretching out from either side of the gateway. A statue of a Siamese king set against a fantastically painted banner from a temple in Laos glared through its center. An Indian god was nestled in the plants to the right and to the left of the gateway, and two Javanese gods—Siwa and his wife—were set on either side of the podium. Hanging from the walkway above the green vegetation were four bright yellow Chinese banners. Suspended above the entire room, an enormous flag boasting the Prussian double-headed eagle dominated this otherwise "exotic" scene.[2]

After the guests were assembled, Cultural Minister Gustav von Gossler gave an eloquent speech lauding Adolf Bastian, the museum's director. Gossler celebrated Bastian's persistence and his contributions to science. He portrayed the institution as the material articulation of Bastian's vision, and he called the new museum building a "milestone" for the sciences of anthropology, ethnology, and prehistory. Referring to the array of meticulously ordered displays assembled throughout the building, Gossler emphasized that Bastian and his associates had transformed the museum's collections from "piles of 'rarities' and 'curiosities'" into a solid "base for scientific disciplines." In this manner, the new institution would provide ethnologists with "indispens-

---

2. *Deutscher Reichs- und Königlich-Preußischer Staatsanzeiger,* 18 December 1886.

able aid in their scientific work" by finally giving them a space in which they could engage in the "complete comparison" of material culture from across the globe. This, he emphasized, would afford them critical insights into the fundamental nature of humanity and, perhaps even more importantly, "the basis of [their own] humble past."[3] As Gossler made clear, this ambitious program was made possible by the Berlin museum's Humboldtian design. Reflecting Bastian's empiricist commitments, the museum contained a vast, geographically arranged collection of material culture from all over the world. Unparalleled in size and scope by any other museum, the collections Bastian and his assistants were gathering were meant to lead them toward fundamental truths about humanity—truths that they believed would give them a better understanding of their society and themselves. The universalist character of Bastian's ethnographic project thus expressed the cosmopolitan conviction shared by many German ethnologists that the key to understanding themselves lay in a comprehensive exploration of humanity at large.[4]

Gossler's remarks captured the essence of Bastian's vision, along with the liberal, humanist, empiricist, and cosmopolitan convictions that drove it. In turn, it is the longer and more turbulent history of the museum that reveals the trajectory of the liberal ethnographic project from its optimistic establishment to its gradual decline and ultimate fall. Indeed, I argue in this essay that Bastian's museum—by far the largest and most important of Germany's ethnographic museums—was not simply a by-product of German ethnology. It was a constitutive site for its development, a spatial and institutional cipher for the history of German anthropology, as well as a motor for its subsequent evolution.

During the first decade of the twentieth century, as a younger generation of ethnologists came into institutional power, German ethnology underwent a fundamental transformation that removed it from Bastian's empirical project and its Humboldtian design. In light of the chaos that accompanied the rapid growth of Bastian's museum, a younger generation of scientists abandoned his project and sought out alternative visions. This transformation was caused by a number of historical developments that intersected in German ethnographic

---

3. *Vossische Zeitung,* 19 December 1886.
4. H. Glenn Penny III, "Cosmopolitan Visions and Municipal Displays: Museums, Markets, and the Ethnographic Project in Germany, 1868–1914," Ph.D. diss., University of Illinois, 1999.

museums: the changing character of Germany's public sphere at the turn of the century, the democratization of science that accompanied it, the changing interests and needs of the civic associations and municipal governments that supported ethnologists and their institutions, and the desire of many younger ethnologists to provide more serviceable answers to questions about human history.

A number of scholars have pointed to the marked generational shift that took place in German ethnology and anthropology during the first decade of the twentieth century. Some have focused on the turn toward racial theories among physical anthropologists following the death of Rudolf Virchow in 1902.[5] Others have concentrated on the rise of diffusionist theories in German ethnology and explored some of their political implications.[6] But not enough attention has been paid to the ways in which these transformations stemmed from a more fundamental epistemological shift in the relationship between the universal and the particular in the German cultural sciences. Nor has there been a recognition that this shift was linked to a more general dissatisfaction with the founding generation's devotion to empirical induction.

I argue in this essay that the turn-of-the-century move toward diffusionist theories was secondary to a more basic transformation in ethnology as a science. This transformation entailed a younger generation's abandonment of their predecessors' most essential methodological principles and of the search for the fundamental elements of the human mind. In consequence of this development, empirical induction and the earlier emphasis on human psychology fell by the wayside in favor of more limited and mechanical efforts to locate and compare distinct cultural groups and their respective histories. This move, I shall suggest, had radical implications for the field: it helped to alter the meaning of human difference at the most basic level

---

5. Benoit Massin, "From Virchow to Fischer: Physical Anthropology and 'Modern Race Theories' in Wilhelmine Germany," in *Volksgeist as Method and Ethic: Essays on Boasian Ethnography and the German Anthropological Tradition*, ed. George W. Stocking Jr. (Madison: University of Wisconsin Press, 1996), 79–154; Robert Proctor, "From *Anthropologie* to *Rassenkunde* in the German Anthropological Tradition," in *Bones, Bodies, Behavior: Essays on Biological Anthropology*, ed. George W. Stocking Jr. (Madison: University of Wisconsin Press, 1985), 138–79.

6. Suzanne Marchand, "Leo Frobenius and the Revolt against the West," *Journal of Contemporary History* 32, no. 2 (1997): 153–70; Woodruff D. Smith, "The Social and Political Origins of German Diffusionist Ethnology," *Journal of the History of the Behavioral Sciences* 14 (1978): 103–12, and Smith, *Politics and the Sciences of Culture in Germany, 1840–1920* (Oxford: Oxford University Press, 1991).

and transformed German ethnology into a discipline that was much more politically malleable than the science their predecessors had pursued.

In what follows, I use the rise and fall of Bastian's museum to help explain the transformation that took place in German ethnology around the turn of the century. I begin by sketching out Bastian's vision, contrasting it to the Anglo-American tradition, and showing the ways in which it was governed by a fundamental belief in a unitary humanity and the search for self-knowledge. I stress Bastian's commitment to empiricism and inductive science, and I use the fate of his museum to illustrate how his ethnographic project faltered as it reached its physical and material limits. For Bastian's contemporaries, the failure of the Berlin museum opened a discursive space for rethinking German ethnology's fundamental goals, and I contend that it led to an essential reconceptualization of the discipline's most basic methodological principles. External pressures further contributed to this transformation: popular demands, institutional limitations, and professional pressures convinced a younger generation of ethnologists to embrace change, to rework their open, experimental exhibits into didactic displays, and to shift their focus from building an empirical base for the study of a unitary humanity to crafting pointed representations of human difference. Ultimately, I argue below that institutional and professional contexts are critical for explaining the multiple trajectories of nineteenth-century German ethnology, not only in regard to such diffusionists as Bernard Ankermann, Fritz Graebner, and Willy Foy, who remained in Germany, but also Franz Boas, who emigrated to the United States.

Bastian's Vision and the Search for Self

Soon after arriving in the United States in 1886, Franz Boas became involved in a heated, public debate with Otis T. Mason, the curator of ethnography at the U.S. National Museum. The story of this confrontation is well known in Boasian lore; scholars have repeatedly used it to illustrate that Boas's ideas about the goals of ethnology and the purpose of ethnographic museums were fundamentally different than those of the leading figures in late-nineteenth-century American anthropology.[7] But they have seldom stressed the broader implica-

---

7. Matti Bunzl, "Franz Boas and the Humboldtian Tradition: From *Volksgeist* and *Nationalcharakter* to an Anthropological Concept of Culture," in Stocking, *Volksgeist,*

tions: that German ethnology in general differed in striking ways from its Anglo-American counterpart.

Boas's actions in the United States throw the particularities of the German ethnographic project into stark relief. As his biographer Douglas Cole has argued, Boas was very much the product of the liberal German cultural sciences championed by such figures as Bastian and the German pathologist and anthropologist Rudolf Virchow. We can see this in his commitment to liberal humanism, the ways in which he was "driven by his Bildung," and the fact that his historicism "discarded any teleological ingredient."[8] We can see it as well in his commitment to empirical induction, his cultural relativism, his refusal to link race to human faculty, the emphasis he placed on mental processes, his penchant for massive empirical projects, and the fact that he was first and foremost an emphatic methodologist.[9] Boas, Cole reminds us, "was consciously and ineradicably German," and many of his actions and experiences in America can help us to understand the character of Bastian's liberal vision, as well as its ultimate demise.[10]

Having worked for several years as an assistant in Berlin's *Völkerkunde* museum before traveling to the United States, Boas was deeply invested in the historicism, empiricism, and inductive approach underlying Bastian's geographical provinces.[11] As a result, he was taken aback by Mason's displays at the National Museum, which grouped artifacts not in regard to their origins, but according to type, arranging them in developmental sequences governed by a priori, biological categories. Boas echoed Bastian's vision when he wrote a trenchant critique of Mason's evolutionary arrangements in the pages of *Science* in 1887. There, he declared that the central assumption informing Mason's schemes—that "like causes produce like effects"—was at best "a vague hypothesis." Recalling Bastian and Virchow's methodological criticisms of evolutionary theories, Boas argued that this

---

56–58; Curtis M. Hinsley Jr., *Savages and Scientists: The Smithsonian Institution and the Development of American Anthropology, 1846–1910* (Washington, D.C.: Smithsonian Institution Press, 1981), 98–100; Ira Jacknis, "Franz Boas and Exhibits: On the Limitations of the Museum Method of Anthropology," in *Objects and Others: Essays on Museums and Material Culture,* ed. George W. Stocking Jr. (Madison: University of Wisconsin Press, 1985), 75–111, and Stocking, *Race, Culture, and Evolution: Essays in the History of Anthropology* (Chicago: University of Chicago Press, 1982).

8. Douglas Cole, *Franz Boas: The Early Years, 1858–1906* (Seattle: University of Washington Press, 1999), 277.

9. Ibid., 123, 125–28, 132, 168, 261, 266, 272, 277.

10. Ibid., 280.

11. Stocking, *Race, Culture, and Evolution,* 207.

assumption revealed the weakness of the deductive method—which Boas stressed was the "foundation of most errors of the human mind" and thus "not fit for scientific research."[12]

The young Boas was quickly put in his place by sharp rebuttals issued by Mason and John Wesley Powell, the director of the Bureau of Ethnology in Washington D.C. While Mason conceded that Boas's ideas had some merit,[13] Powell made it clear that an arrangement by "ethnographic districts" and governed by the recognition that "our ideas and conceptions" are "relative rather than absolute" was impractical, indeed impossible, given the mobility of the Native American tribes.[14] Moreover, Powell argued that the diverse audience of the National Museum—soldiers, potters, musicians, artists, and others— wanted to see artifacts in juxtaposition, a point, Powell noted, Boas needed to bear in mind.[15] In the face of opposition from the most powerful members of American anthropology, Boas withdrew from the argument until he was well enough established in the profession to launch a more systematic critique.[16]

Even more to the point, the debate revealed the fundamental differences between the goals of ethnology and the function of ethnographic museums in the Anglo-American and German contexts. While Powell and Mason stressed the importance of education and the needs and desires of their visitors, Boas followed Bastian in conceiving of museums first and foremost as research institutions. Bastian's plan was to create an institution that would facilitate a vast empirical inquiry into human character and history, one in which lay audiences were expected to play little or no role. Arrangements in American museums during the 1880s were evolutionist, deductive, and created in an effort to help *articulate* the natural laws that governed human progress. Those in Germany, in contrast, were historicist, inductive, and

---

12. Boas, "The Occurrence of Similar Inventions in Areas Widely Apart," *Science* 9 (1887): 485–87, and Boas, "Museums of Ethnology and Their Classification," *Science* 9 (1887): 587–89.

13. Mason, in fact, was already thinking of moving toward life groupings and cultural displays by this time (Hinsley, *Savages and Scientists,* 100).

14. Otis T. Mason, "The Occurrence of Similar Inventions in Areas Widely Apart," *Science* 9 (1887): 534; John Wesley Powell, "Museums of Ethnology and Their Classification," *Science* 9 (1887): 612–14.

15. Hinsley, *Savages and Scientists,* 100; Jacknis, "Franz Boas and Exhibits," 82.

16. Franz Boas, "The Limitations of the Comparative Method in Anthropology," *Science* 4 (1896): 901–8; cf. Bunzl, "Boas and Humboldtian Tradition," 57–58.

designed to help ethnologists *locate* the empirical laws[17] that would explain the multiplicity of humanity. Identifying the universal characteristics shared by all human beings was a critical, even central motivation behind Bastian's ethnographic project, but so was understanding their particular manifestations. The precise nature of universals could therefore never be assumed. Moreover, while the displays in most British and American museums provided visitors with representational justifications for their positions vis-à-vis their colonial "others," Bastian prescribed museums that eschewed narrative modes of display. In their stead, he envisioned open-ended institutions that facilitated the comparative analysis of other cultures; these analyses were meant to lead to the discovery of fundamental truths about the character of human beings, and thereby also aid in a search for self.

As these remarks begin to make clear, Bastian's ethnology was governed less by an overarching theory than by a set of methodological and political convictions. Like his intellectual hero Alexander von Humboldt, he drew on inductive and empirical methods to avoid the classification of data according to predetermined categories, consistently regarding schemes of classification as works in progress rather than definitive models. In consequence, Bastian and his German counterparts were reluctant to speak in terms of hierarchies or scales of "progress"; they were unwilling to include any teleological component in their historicism, and they were reticent about viewing the differences among people as more than variations on a theme of a unitary humanity.

This methodological commitment to careful, empirical research over "speculative theorizing" prompted Bastian and Virchow to shun Darwinian schemes and isolate themselves from the race debate.[18] Virchow did argue publicly that Darwinism was dangerous because of its possible association with Social Democracy; but his chief criticism always targeted Darwinism's speculative nature.[19] Bastian took the same position. While he admired Darwin's travels, he lamented the lack of "factual evidence" that might support his conclusions; and he

---

17. By empirical laws I mean laws that develop a posteriori through the analysis of empirical data.
18. Massin, "From Virchow to Fischer."
19. Andreas W. Daum, *Wissenschaftspopularisierung im 19. Jahrhundert: Bürgerliche Kultur, naturwissenschaftliche Bildung und die deutsche Öffentlichkeit, 1848–1914* (Munich: R. Oldenbourg, 1998), 66–71.

compared Darwin's postulates about the "genealogy of mankind" to "fantasies" from the "dreams of mid-day naps."[20] But he regarded Ernst Haeckel's efforts to popularize these ideas as particularly offensive. In his public debates with Haeckel—Germany's leading Darwinian—Bastian denounced these efforts as "unscientific forgery," lacking a sufficient empirical base for responsible presentation. As he noted, "Nothing is further from my intentions than popularization, because I know that my newly born science of ethnology is still too young for such a daring deed." While Haeckel strove "above all and with reckless abandon toward popularization," Bastian believed that only theories based on solid empirical evidence should be used to explain complex phenomena to laymen.[21]

Such well-defined ethnological theories, however, would be long in coming from Bastian. His reading of Humboldt's *Cosmos* had convinced him that the creation of universal theories about human history were secondary to the accumulation of knowledge about its particulars. "All systems-construction," he argued during his speech in honor of Alexander von Humboldt in 1869, "remains mere metaphysical illusion unless knowledge of the details has been accumulated." For this reason, Humboldt had posited no great theory, no general explanatory system in his *Cosmos;* nor, as far as Bastian was concerned, was one necessary. Such "systems," Bastian argued, "are ephemeral by their nature," but Humboldt's method—the development of a vast synthesis based on empirical induction—was "everlasting" and would eventually lead to scientific truths.[22] In short: Alexander von Humboldt's efforts to fashion a total empirical and harmonic picture of the world had a tremendous impact on Bastian and inspired his efforts to unite all knowledge of human history—ethnological, philosophical, psychological, anthropological, and historical—into a huge synthesis while abstaining from tentative explanatory theories.[23]

In lieu of a definitive ethnological theory, Bastian had a set of

---

20. Bastian, "Darwin, *The Descent of Man,* 1871," *Zeitschrift für Ethnologie* 3 (1871): 138.

21. Bastian, *Offner Brief an Prof. Dr. E. Haeckel, Verfasser der "Natürlichen Schöpfungsgeschichte,"* Berlin 1874, 8. Cf. Annemarie Fiedermutz-Laun, "Aus der Wissenschaftsgeschichte: Adolf Bastian und die Deszendenztheorie," *Paideuma* 16 (1970): 1–26.

22. Bastian, *Alexander von Humboldt. Festrede* (Berlin: Wiegend und Hempel, 1869), 23–25.

23. Bastian's *Mensch in der Geschichte,* which was dedicated to Humboldt, was the beginning of the project and set out the goals from which he never wavered.

specific convictions and a three-part plan of action. World history for Bastian was the history of the human mind. With a strong monogenicist bent stemming largely from his worldwide travels, he argued that "human nature is uniform all over the globe" and that "if there are laws in the universe, their rules and harmonies should also be in the thought processes of man."[24] Thus Bastian's first task was a vast comparative analysis of these thought processes. This procedure would pave the way for the second object: the emergence of empirical laws. Once these laws were revealed, Bastian believed that they could in turn be applied to his ultimate end—the effort of Europeans to better understand themselves.

As Bastian wrote in 1877, "the physical unity of the species man [has already] been anthropologically established." In consequence, his project was focused on locating "the psychic unity of social thought [that] underlies the basic elements of the body social." The best way to do this, he contended, was not through subjective self-reflection on European cultural history, but by bringing together and examining the physical traces of human thought. In the material culture produced by peoples everywhere, Bastian thus expected to find the "monotonous sub-stratum of identical elementary ideas" that could exfoliate the more general history of the human mind.[25]

Bastian stressed that every group of people shared these "elementary ideas," or *Elementargedanken,* even though they were never directly observable. Having an "innate propensity to change,"[26] they always materialized in the form of unique patterns of thought, or *Völkergedanken,* reflecting the interaction of peoples with their environments, as well as their contacts with other groups. *Elementargedanken* were thus hidden behind humanity's cultural diversity—a diversity that was historically and geographically contingent. Understanding the unique contexts in which each culture took shape, Bastian stressed, was thus critical for gaining insight into the universal character of

---

24. Bastian, *Alexander von Humboldt,* 23–25.
25. Adolf Bastian, "Ethnologische Erörterung," *Zeitschrift für Ethnologie* 19 (1877): 183, excerpted and translated in Klaus-Peter Koepping, *Adolf Bastian and the Psychic Unity of Mankind: The Foundations of Anthropology in Nineteenth Century Germany* (London: Queensland Press, 1983), 176.
26. Klaus-Peter Koepping, "Enlightenment and Romanticism in the Work of Adolf Bastian: The Historical Roots of Anthropology in the Nineteenth Century," in *Fieldwork and Footnotes: Studies in the History of European Anthropology,* ed. Han F. Vermeulen and Arturo Alvarez Roldán (New York: Routledge, 1995), 86.

"the" human being.[27] Indeed, it was largely Bastian's interest in identifying these contexts that led Fritz Graebner to term Bastian the *Naturvölkers* "Erwecker zu historischem Leben," quite literally, the one who brought natural peoples (or ostensibly primitive peoples) into history.[28]

In addition to Bastian's notion of *Elementargedanken* and *Völkergedanken,* it was the idea of geographical provinces that formed the core of his thought.[29] For Bastian, the *Völkergedanken* that characterized different groups of people emerged within identifiable zones where geographical and historical influences shaped specific cultures. Unique *Völkergedanken,* like "actual organisms," fit within these particular geographical provinces, shifting and changing as they came into contact with others. This interaction, Bastian emphasized, was the basis of all historical development, and it could be observed most readily in certain geographical areas: on rivers, coastlines, and mountain passes, which he referred to as "Völkertore."[30]

In Bastian's ethnology, human difference played a critical role. On a basic level, humanity could be divided into two major categories, the *Naturvölker* (natural peoples) and the *Kulturvölker* (cultural peoples).[31] Having achieved literacy, the latter had a recorded past that historians and philologists could explore. This did not mean, however, that the former were without history or culture. Quite the contrary, Bastian believed that there were "essentially next to no peoples left on earth who were without historical influences."[32] The historical and cul-

---

27. Bastian, *Die Rechtsverhältnisse bei verschiedenen Völkern der Erde. Ein Beitrag zur vergleichenden Ethnologie* (Berlin, 1872).

28. F. Graebner, "Adolf Bastians 100. Geburtstag," *Ethnologica* 3 (1927): x.

29. Bastian, *Zur Lehre von den geographischen Provinzen. Aufgenommen in die Controversen* (Berlin, 1886). His conception of the geographical provinces was well recognized during his lifetime as a seminal part of his thought, and it was sketched out in a number of his obituaries. See, inter alia, Karl von den Steinen, "Gedächtnisrede auf Adolf Bastian," *Zeitschrift für Ethnologie* 37, no. 2 (1905): 236–49; and Edward B. Tylor, "Professor Adolf Bastian," *Man* 75–76 (1905): 138–43.

30. Bastian, *Geographische und ethnologische Bilder* (Jena, 1873), 324. Cf. Annemarie Fiedermutz-Laun, *Der Kulturhistorische Gedanke bei Adolf Bastian: Systematisierung und Darstellung der Theorie und Methode mit dem Versuch einer Bewertung des Kulturhistorischen Gehaltes auf dieser Grundlage* (Wiesbaden: Franz Steiner Verlag, 1970), 147–93.

31. The term *Halbkulturvölker* (half-cultured peoples) was also posited as a term for people who had no written language but possessed "a distinct and highly developed culture." However, this was a term Bastian seldom employed (Fiedermutz-Laun, *Kulturhistorische Gedanke bei Bastian,* 114).

32. Ibid., 114 n. 36. A similar comment was made almost a century earlier by Franz Heger during the celebration in honor of Bastian's seventieth birthday in 1896, when he

tural trajectories among the world's *Naturvölker* were in fact at the heart of Bastian's ethnological project. Indeed, what Bastian sought to explain were not so much the coincidences between conceptions among natural peoples, but the specific differences. It was these differences that held the key to historical development through the emergence of *Völkergedanken*.

To account for the general development of *Völkergedanken*, Bastian recommended investigations of the most isolated and simple societies. While "European cultural history" was "almost unmanageable due to its complex bifurcations," the cultures of simple societies could be readily contextualized. Using a botanical analogy, Bastian likened Europe to a "tree that grew for hundreds and thousands of years." Simple societies, in contrast, were similar to small plants. They "grow according to the same laws as the mighty tree," but their "growth and decline are easier to observe, since we are looking at a limited field of observation which could be compared to an experiment in a laboratory."[33]

Bastian did not believe that this analysis of simple societies would allow ethnologists to locate a normative sequence of cultural achievement of the kind proposed by British anthropologist Edward B. Tylor.[34] Rather than using ethnographic data to construct putative hierarchies, Bastian believed that a broad, comparative analysis of *Naturvölker* would help him identify a "set of seminal ideas from which every civilization had grown." This set of seminal ideas would in turn become the "methodological tool for unraveling more complex civilizations." Allowing the formulation of empirical laws regarding the effects of physiological, psychological, and social conditions of the human mind, Bastian's ethnographic insights could later be applied to Europeans.[35]

In short, Bastian's quest to unveil the inner workings of simple soci-

---

reminded ethnologists that according to Bastian's vision, there were essentially no people without history or culture. Franz Heger, "Die Zukunft der ethnographischen Museen," in *Festschrift für A. Bastian zu seinem 70. Geburtstag, 26. Juni 1896* (Berlin: Reimer, 1896), 585–93.

33. Bastian, *Alexander von Humboldt*, 15–16; translations based on Koepping, *Adolf Bastian*, 161.

34. Edward. B. Tylor, *Primitive Culture: Researches into the Development of Mythology, Philosophy, Religion, Language, Art, and Custom*, 2 vols. (London: John Murray, 1873). Boas made the differences between Bastian's and Tylor's conceptions of "the psychic unity of mankind" explicit in several cases. See, for example, Boas, "The Methods of Ethnology," *American Anthropologist*, n.s. 22 (1920): 311–22, and Boas, "Limitations of the Comparative Method." Cf. Fiedermutz-Laun, *Kulturhistorischen Gedanken bei Bastian*, 120, 143.

35. Bastian, *Alexander von Humboldt*, translated in Koepping, *Adolf Bastian*, 161.

eties was part of a conscious effort to help Europeans better understand themselves. In the final analysis, these introspective possibilities provided the central stimulus for Bastian's interest in ethnology and his desire to erect a monumental ethnographic museum. Such an institution, he argued, would allow ethnologists to assemble the broadest possible collections of material culture, thereby facilitating the most effective comparative analysis. As Bastian envisioned it in the early 1870s, the ideal ethnographic museum would contain material culture from all areas of the world and all periods of history. But it would not be constructed to articulate pointed narratives. Bastian favored open collections in which objects were arranged in cabinets made of glass and steel, flooded by natural light from large windows and glass ceilings, and positioned in such a way that scientists could move easily through the geographically organized displays, gain an overview of the objects from entire regions, and make mental connections between the material cultures of people living in different times and places. This design differed markedly from art museums, natural history museums, or even the colonial museums and exhibitions that gained popularity later in the century.[36] No particular object, grouping, or arrangement was supposed to stand out, or be emphasized; there was no developmental series of artifacts of the kind found in the evolutionary arrangements of many British and American museums; and the museum's goal was not explicitly pedagogical. Bastian's displays were meant to function as tools of induction and comparative analysis. They were expected to facilitate the location and exploration of the elementary characteristics of a unitary humanity—the fundamental nature of "the" human being.

Bastian sketched out this vision in his earliest writings on the museum,[37] and he continued to press the position throughout his lifetime. In one of the first guidebooks to the Berlin museum, he stressed that the institution was designed to "bring before our eyes the vivid embodiment of the growth process of an intellectual organism" that "blooms" in the "thought processes of humanity."[38] And shortly

---

36. See, inter alia, Tony Bennett, "The Exhibitionary Complex," *New Formations* 4 (1988): 73–102; Robert W. Rydell, *All the World's a Fair: Visions of Empire at American International Expositions, 1876–1916* (Chicago: University of Chicago Press, 1984).

37. Adolf Bastian, *Führer durch die Ethnographische Abtheilung* (Berlin: W. Spemann, 1877), 3.

38. Königliche Museen zu Berlin, *Führer durch das Museum für Völkerkunde,* 2d ed. (Berlin: W. Spemann, 1887), 7.

Fig. 1. A view into the vestibule of Bastian's Museum für Völkerkunde in Berlin. The combination of artifacts that made up this initial encounter with the museum's collections—ranging from the large statue of Buddha, the pieces of a Central American temple, the Indian gateway behind them, and the boats, vases, totem poles, teepees, and other objects arranged in the interior courtyard—captured Bastian's efforts to take in the entire world. The mosaic on the vestibule's ceiling representing familiar aspects of European life and classical humanism, as well as the prehistorical collections from Europe contained in the museum, reminded visitors that European culture was only one part of this larger whole. (Reproduced courtesy of the Staatliche Museen zu Berlin, Ethnologisches Museum.)

Fig. 2. Tall glass cases in Bastian's museum, arranged parallel to each other. These arrangements were supposed to facilitate a comparative analysis of the museum's contents. (Reproduced courtesy of the Staatliche Museen zu Berlin, Ethnologisches Museum.)

before his death in 1905, he reiterated that ethnographic museums should not only function as archives and libraries, but must also serve as laboratories in which ethnologists worked to "decipher ornamental and allegorical symbols from their hieroglyphics into readable text."[39] Museums, he repeatedly argued, were the only places where the diversity of humanity could be reassembled for observation and comparison, and where scientists could test the latest ethnological theories

By the early 1880s, Bastian's ethnographic vision was widely embraced throughout Germany. This situation can perhaps best be gleaned from a memorandum issued in 1883 by the directorial committee of the Leipzig *Völkerkunde* museum:

> It is clear that as soon as one enters the way of inductive research in order to progress from the singular to the general, and as soon as one recognizes that a system will first emerge only as particularities are brought together, then one must also realize that museums are a *conditio sine qua non,* and must be there from the beginning.[40]

In a little over a decade, museums had generally been accepted as *the* critical tool for ethnographic studies, the key institutions for the exploration of "human cultures," and the sites at which to make sense of human diversity. Great expectations were tied to the creation of ethnographic museums. German ethnologists and their supporters expected their museums to become the new libraries of "mankind," the central resources for the study and analysis of human history, and a primary means for understanding the European "self." They envisioned ethnographic museums as the perfect research tools of the future, the places where all new and old information could be gathered, sorted and, finally, put to use. In short, Bastian and his counterparts believed that the study of all aspects of humanity might find its ultimate expression in ethnographic museums.

---

39. Cited in Sigrid Westphal-Hellbusch, "Zur Geschichte des Museums," in *Hundert Jahre Museum für Völkerkunde Berlin,* ed. K. Krieger and G. Koch (Berlin: Reimer, 1973), 4.

40. "Über die Bedeutung ethnographischer Museen: mit besonderer Beziehung auf die vor zehn Jahren erfolgte Gründung eines solchen in Leipzig," dated 23 May 1883 and issued by Geh. Reg-Rath von Seckendorff als Vorsitzender des Aufsichtsrathes des Verein des Museum für Völkerkunde in Leipzig, Stadt Archiv Leipzig (LSA), Kap. 31, no. 12, vol. 1 (1873–95), 160–61.

The Perplexing Nature of Collecting and Display

As Prussian Cultural Minister von Gossler emphasized in his opening-day speech, and as the directorial committee of Leipzig's ethnographic museum confirmed, Bastian's ethnographic vision was widely accepted. This was due, in part, to Bastian's tremendous success in expanding his collections. By 1880, the museum's collections comprised over forty thousand artifacts, more than five times their initial size in 1873;[41] and by the time the new building was opened in 1886, Bastian had four directorial assistants working under him, each supervising a different geographical section of the museum.[42] By opening day, Bastian and his associates appeared to have, as Gossler put it, transformed the museum's collections from "piles of 'rarities' and 'curiosities'" into a solid "base for scientific disciplines," and Bastian's great success at building acquisition networks promised the continuous expansion of that base. Indeed, during the next decade, Berlin's collections grew so rapidly as to quickly leave other European and American museums behind. And by the turn of the century, British ethnologists were complaining that the collections in the Berlin museum were six, seven, or even "ten times as extensive" as those in London.[43]

Yet the perplexing thing about German ethnologists' unprecedented success was how quickly it revealed their ultimate failure: the inability to contain the rapidly growing collections. Indeed, as these collections sprawled out of bounds, they exposed the limits of Bastian's ethnographic project; and by the turn of the century, Berlin's ethnologists were engaged in an urgent discussion about reforms. Bastian and his assistants were concerned with the overcrowding in their rooms, halls,

---

41. The ethnographic material had been separated from the rest of the Royal Collections in 1870, and the Museum für Völkerkunde had been founded officially in 1873. Bastian gave the following figures for acquisitions and holdings in 1884: When the museum was divided off from the other Royal Collections in 1870, it contained seven thousand items. The collections grew to fifteen thousand by 1875, and to fifty thousand by 1883, and he expected to continue to acquire a further ten thousand per year. Bastian to the General Administration of the Royal Museums (GVKM), 24 July 1884, in the archive of the Berlin Museum für Völkerkunde (MfVB), "Die Gründung des Museums," Vol., 27/85.

42. Albert Voss (1876) Albert Grünwedel (1883), Wilhelm Grube (1885), and Felix von Luschan (1886). Eduard Krause was also working with him as a curator by 1884 (Sigrid Westphal-Hellbusch, "Zur Geschichte des Museums," 12–13).

43. O. M. Dalton, *Report on Ethnographic Museums in Germany* (London: Her Majesty's Stationary Office, 1898); Northcote W. Thomas, foreword to Alice Werner, *The Natives of British Central Africa* (London: Archibald Constable and Company, 1906).

and display cases, distressed that they had been forced to close out entire collections and cancel public tours, and dismayed that they were unable to maintain the geographic organization of their artifacts. Moreover, German and non-German visitors alike were beginning to assail them with criticism. As conditions continued to degenerate while the collections grew and grew, Berlin's ethnologists were faced with the realization that their internationally acclaimed scientific institution was quickly becoming unmanageable.

The central problem was that by the turn of the century collecting had evolved from a means to an end. Possession, of course, had been at the heart of German ethnology from the very beginning. Berlin's ethnologists had set out to acquire the broadest possible collections in order to compile what Bastian termed a *Gedankenstatistik*—"a statistical tabulation of ideas" that would include all of the world's *Völkergedanken*.[44] These efforts, which paralleled the activities of their counterparts in other German cities, were driven by a conviction that the *Naturvölker* were rapidly disappearing in the wake of European expansion. Consequently, the goal was to acquire as much empirical evidence as possible in the shortest amount of time. This salvage mentality, along with the empirical need for material objects, led ethnologists to privilege collecting over everything else, including the itemizing, cataloging, and ordering of artifacts. This situation was further exacerbated by a keen sense of competition that led British ethnologists to protest that they were not keeping up with the Germans (or ethnologists in Leipzig to complain that they were falling behind their counterparts in Hamburg or Berlin). Professional, municipal, and even national reputations were linked to acquisitions, as was a museum's level of funding. For all of these reasons, an overriding passion for possession dominated ethnology by the turn of the century, and the disorderly displays ethnologists had been tolerating as a temporary inconvenience eventually became a permanent condition.[45]

The results of this situation were stark. Just a little over a decade after the grand opening, Bastian and his assistants declared conditions in their museum "unbearable." As they complained to the Royal Museums, they simply could not fit all their collections into the cabi-

---

44. Adolph Bastian, *Controversen in der Ethnologie* (Berlin: Weidmannsche Verlagsbuchhandlung, 1893–94), 172.

45. This passion for possession can be found repeatedly in their publications and private correspondence across the period 1860–1918, and it was never limited to Bastian's generation (Penny, "Cosmopolitan Visions").

nets at their disposal, or fit all the cabinets they needed into their hallways and rooms.[46] In response to the administration's 1899 request for reports on the museum's collections, Felix von Luschan, the directorial assistant in charge of Africa and Oceania, noted that his section had contained 14,676 items in seventy-three cabinets when it was opened in 1886. By 1899 the number of artifacts had quadrupled and sixty cabinets had been added to the display areas, but the size of the rooms had remained the same.[47] Similarly, Albert Grünwedel explained that despite the run on acquisitions, "no oriental collections had been unpacked and put on display since moving [into the new building] in 1885."[48] Complaining that the conditions in the Indian section were simply "impossible," he argued that an "orderly display of the Indian collections" would require the "entire floor" as well as the stairways leading to it;[49] Grünwedel, however, shared his floor with collections from China and Indonesia.

In the face of these problems, Berlin's ethnologists found themselves increasingly forced to close different sections of the museum, mix their various collections, or remove entire collections altogether. Indeed, many of the artifacts that were meant to become part of Bastian's *Gedankenstatistik* remained packed away in boxes, while others never made it into the museum at all.[50] A European section, for example, was included in the museum's initial plans, but it was never created due to space constraints.[51] Similarly, a section devoted to physical anthropology was anticipated in the museum's guidebook in 1881; promised to visitors in 1888 and again in 1892, it was still "in process" in 1911.[52]

---

46. Bastian to GVKM, 12 July 1899, in MfVB, "Erweiterungsbau des Königlichen Museums für Völkerkunde," vol. 1, 712/99 and 1134/99.

47. Official reports from all the section leaders were submitted to the GVKM along with Bastian's. Bastian to GVKM, 31 October 1899, in MfVB, "Erweiterungsbau des Königlichen Museums für Völkerkunde" vol. 1, 1134/99.

48. Grünwedel to GVKM, 10 July 1903, in MfVB, "Erweiterungsbau," vol. 2, 878/03.

49. Grünwedel to GVKM, 18 October 1899, in MfVB, "Erweiterungsbau," vol. 1, 1134/99.

50. Bastian to Wirklichen Geheimen Rat, Geheimen Kabinet Rat Seiner Majestät des Kaisers und Königs, Kapitular des Domstifts Merseburg, Herrn Dr. jur. u. med. v. Lucanus, 25 November 1903, in GSA Rep. 89 H, 20491: 49–51.

51. Königliche Museen zu Berlin, *Führer durch das Museum für Völkerkunde,* 7th ed. (Berlin: W. Spemann, 1898), 199.

52. There was a very small physical anthropology collection belonging to the Berlin Anthropological Society on the fourth floor, but this was not the section promised in the guides.

Not only were entire collections consistently excluded from the museum, but the existing displays were often shuffled around, thereby undermining the museum's geographical arrangement. By the mid-1890s, in fact, Berlin's guidebooks commonly included apologies for the state of the collections, noting that although the displays "were [meant to be] geographically ordered," the "continual" and "strong growth" of the collections had not always permitted their proper distribution.[53] By 1906 the museum's ethnologists had given up on this goal altogether. Their new guidebooks no longer even attempted to maintain the pretense of a geographic arrangement. Since artifacts from any given region were no longer grouped together or displayed in their proper locations, the guidebooks simply listed geographical areas and explained where different parts of various collections could be found.[54]

By the first decade of the twentieth century, Berlin's ethnographic museum—once the envy of the ethnological world—had acquired an ambivalent reputation. The institution's ability to accumulate tremendous numbers of artifacts continued to be praised and admired across Europe and the United States, but the state of its displays was deplored by staff and visitors alike. Berlin's ethnologists regularly complained that the conditions in their museum "made respectable scientific endeavors all but impossible," and an array of disgruntled visitors heartily agreed.[55] The director of the Chicago Field Museum, for example, remarked to Bastian in 1899 that, while Berlin's collections were quite probably "the most complete in the world," the "crowded conditions of the cases" were a "great hindrance to study in this museum." "A majority of the collections," he continued, "can leave only a feeling of confusion in the mind of even the most casual observer."[56]

This sense was clearly shared by a "public" that had become aware

---

53. Königliche Museen zu Berlin, *Museum für Völkerkunde,* 7th ed., 61–62. Cf. Königlichen Museen zu Berlin, *Führer durch das Museum für Völkerkunde,* 6th ed. (Berlin: W. Spemann, 1895), 192.

54. Königlichen Museen zu Berlin, *Führer durch das Museum für Völkerkunde,* 13th ed. (Berlin: W. Spemann, 1906).

55. Paul Hambruch to Georg Thilenius, 2 June 1908, in Hamburger Staatsarchiv 361–5 I, HW I. C II, a 12, vol. 2.

56. Cited by Bastian in an undated letter from 1899 to the GVKM, in MfVB, "Erweiterungsbau," vol. 1, 1134/99.

of the "deplorable conditions" in this (and other) ethnographic museums.[57] Public debate about the state of the Berlin museum in fact broke out in the city's newspapers in 1900. The reports revealed a museum much closer to old-style curiosity cabinets than the premier scientific institution invoked in Gossler's opening-day speech. Critics wrote that they were "flabbergasted" by the "strange combination" of objects wedged into the vestibule, "astonished" and "amused" by the assemblage of different things in the courtyard, and "distressed" by the general state of the institution. As one commentator put it, the museum's "unheard of riches" and "costly rarities" were "set so close to, next to, behind, before, and above each other that one almost began to hate them."[58] In little more than fourteen years, the calculated aesthetics of the museum's opening ceremonies had degenerated into an impressionistic chaos: a scene completely devoid of order or logical arrangement.[59]

Bastian had foreseen many of the museum's problems, and for this reason he proposed a new kind of building on several occasions. More than once, for example, he suggested the creation of a museum of glass and steel, much like London's famous Crystal Palace, that could be expanded along with its collections.[60] But even if Bastian's proposal for an expandable building had been accepted, he realized that the task of collecting and ordering the vast numbers of objects was simply impossible to complete. Indeed, as early as 1881 he noted that, while ethnologists had been "enticed" and even "entranced" by the promises of their new discipline, the "daring intentions soon began to crumble to

---

57. In Leipzig, for example, their museum was also suffering under strong public criticism, with one observer remarking that conditions within the museum had made "the careful contemplation of any given area of human activity" a "totally desperate" endeavor (*Leipziger Tageblatt*, 25 July 1909).

58. Karl Scheffler, *Berliner Museumskrieg* (Berlin: Cassirer, 1921), 21–22.

59. *Vossische Zeitung*, 26 June 1900.

60. Bastian was credited with this idea by Otto Georgi, the Oberbürgermeister of Leipzig in Georgi, *Vortrag das Grassi-Museums betreffend.*, 11 April 1884, in LSA, Kap. 31, no. 14: 40–63. See also Bastian to GVKM, 24 July 1884 in MfVB, "Die Gründung des Museums," Vol. 1, 27/85; Cf. Hans-Christian Mannschatz, "Mit Grassi auf dem Dach und Klinger im Hof—100 Jahre Wilhelm-Leuscher-Platz 10/11: Die Geschichte eines Hauses," 1996 (unpublished paper in the Leipzig Staatsbibliothek), 13. This proposal was revisited in the *Vossische Zeitung*, 24 January 1901, cited in Andrew Zimmerman, "Anthropology and the Place of Knowledge in Imperial Berlin," Ph.D. diss., University of California, San Diego, 1998, 181.

Fig. 3. Museum chaos. The cabinets in Bastian's museum were almost immediately overfilled; the sheer volume of artifacts overwhelmed scientists and laymen alike. (Reproduced courtesy of the Staatliche Museen zu Berlin, Ethnologisches Museum.)

Fig. 4. Cabinets in Bastian's museum. (Reproduced courtesy of the Staatliche Museen zu Berlin, Ethnologisches Museum.)

dust as we looked into the more intricate depths of the materials so copiously accumulated, as the mountain of publications [and collections] grew to an awesome height." Consequently, he argued that ethnologists "must abandon the aim, indeed the very idea, of achieving one comprehensive and comprehensible whole from all the materials thus far presented to us." Instead, they should continue to focus on collecting, and leave the task of ordering the acquisitions to a future generation.[61]

What Bastian had failed to anticipate in 1881, however, and what he failed to realize as his collections rapidly grew out of control, was that the next generation would refuse his patrimony. By 1900, a dramatic generational shift was already under way in German ethnology and anthropology, and by 1907 it was essentially complete. The transition was spurred by the deaths of the discipline's towering figures (Virchow died in 1902, Bastian and Friedrich Ratzel in 1905) along with a range of lesser-known individuals who had helped safeguard the institutional hegemony of their intellectual project. In the wake of these passings, Germany's leading ethnological museums gained new directors in very short order—Hamburg in 1904, Berlin in 1905, Leipzig in 1907, and Munich in 1907.[62] In each case, the previous directors were succeeded by much younger individuals who were professionally trained, had multiple university degrees, and, because they had grown up in an age of aggressive nationalism and colonialism, were not nearly as adverse to the nation's imperialist goals. Nor, for that matter, were they any longer interested in placing the accumulation of empirical data above and beyond everything else, as Willy Foy, the young director of the new ethnographic museum that opened in Cologne in 1906, made clear.[63] In general, the new generation was driven less by a desire to fulfill Bastian's project than by the often contradictory demands of professionalism, the pressures to democratize science, and the larger transformations in the consumption of science. These new contexts

---

61. Adolf Bastian, *Die heilige Sage der Polynesier*, excerpted and translated in Koepping, *Adolf Bastian*, 216–17.

62. The directors of these museums were replaced by younger men who had completed both a doctoral degree and a *Habilitation*. Each was also closely connected to the local university (or in the case of Hamburg the Colonial Institute once it was opened, and then the university when it was founded in 1919). None of the earlier directors had been *habilitiert*, only two had honorary Ph.D.s, and consequently only Bastian was connected in any significant way to a university. See Penny, "Cosmopolitan Visions."

63. Foy made this explicit in his foreword to F. Graebner, *Methode der Ethnologie* (Heidelberg: Carl Winter, 1911), xv–xvi.

changed everything. In the emerging world of professional ethnology, Bastian's project quickly became obsolete. In place of their predecessors' interest in painstakingly building up an empirical basis from which they might later locate elusive universal human characteristics, the new generation embraced a more practical project, centered around the quickly satisfying identification of differences among people. In the context of the colonial heyday, this shift in orientation not only promised greater public resonance, but also more successful careers.

The Transformation of German Ethnology

The transformation of German ethnology during the first decade of the twentieth century was publicly signaled by what Woodruff Smith has termed the diffusionist revolt.[64] At the 1904 meeting of the Berlin Society for Anthropology, Ethnology, and Prehistory, Fritz Graebner and Bernard Ankermann issued the revolt's originary declarations. Presenting papers on the *Kulturkreise* (cultural areas) and *Kulturschichten* (cultural layers) of Oceania and Africa, the young assistants from Berlin's *Völkerkunde* museum challenged the ways in which Germans had been pursuing their ethnographic project for decades. Diffusionism, of course, was nothing new in 1904. George Stocking has termed it "one of the ur-forms of anthropological speculation in the Western-European intellectual tradition,"[65] present even in late-nineteenth-century British anthropology, the dominance of Edward B. Tylor's evolutionism notwithstanding.[66] German ethnologists such as Leo Frobenius and Friedrich Ratzel, moreover, had been advocating diffusionist theories for decades before Graebner and Ankermann spoke out.[67] What was new, however, was the willingness of these young ethnologists to oppose Bastian's vision publicly. As such, their actions reflected a radical transformation that was under way in German eth-

---

64. Bernard Ankermann, "Kulturkreise und Kulturschichten in Afrika," *Zeitschrift für Ethnologie* 37 (1905): 54–84; and Fritz Graebner, "Kulturkreise und Kulturschichten in Ozeanien," *Zeitschrift für Ethnologie* 37 (1905): 28–53; cf. Smith, *Politics,* 140–61.
65. George W. Stocking Jr., *After Tylor: British Social Anthropology, 1888–1951* (Madison: University of Wisconsin Press, 1995), 180.
66. Ibid., 11, 183.
67. See especially Graebner's own discussion of this intellectual trajectory (*Methode der Ethnologie,* 92–94, 104). On Frobenius and his place in German ethnology see, inter alia, Eike Haberland, ed., *Leo Frobenius: An Anthology* (Wiesbaden: F. Steiner, 1973).

nology—one that consisted of much more than the move toward diffusionist theories.

Much like Ratzel before them, Graebner, Ankermann, and especially Foy not only situated themselves in opposition to Tylor's evolutionary schemes, they also consciously opposed Bastian's vision.[68] In their intellectual practice, evolutionary theories were their preferred target. But they also took repeated issue with the German ethnological tradition, arguing for a shift from psychology and the human mind to the analysis of groups, their behavior, and their "cultural traits."[69] These "traits," which might range from the kinds of weapons a group preferred (e.g., spears over bows) to the kinds of monuments they built, could be used to sketch out particular *Kulturkreise,* or cultural areas.[70] As sites of distinct cultural traits, the diffusionists' *Kulturkreise* resembled Bastian's geographical provinces;[71] in the final analysis, however, they were much more rigid and distinct.[72] Diffusionism was based on an assumption that similarities of culture "could only be explained by direct transmission from one people to another," an assumption that Bastian refuted as too absolute. The diffusionists championed this principle to set themselves apart from evolutionary theorists, and in their determination to do so, diffusionists sometimes even argued for the influence of a single culture over regions that were separated by great distances.[73]

---

68. Indeed, some diffusionists such as Friedrich Ratzel and Willy Foy eagerly misrepresented Bastian's position in order to strengthen their own. Others, such as Graebner and Ankermann, were more circumspect (Smith, *Politics,* 113). For one example of rather aggressive rhetoric see W. Foy, "Ethnologie und Kulturgeschichte," *Petermanns Geographische Mitteilungen* 1, no. 3 (1911): 230–33.

69. Foy and Graebner in Graebner, *Methode der Ethnologie,* v. cf. Smith, *Politics,* 156.

70. Smith, *Politics,* 149.

71. Indeed, even his critics recognized this point. Graebner argued that "it is incorrect when one so often speaks of a new theory from Ratzel, in opposition to Bastian." Graebner, *Methode der Ethnologie,* 94. And Ankermann stressed that the concepts of *Völkergedanken* and *Kulturkreise* were "obviously both the same thing, the *Völkergedanken* seen from the psychological side and the *Kulturkreise* from the ethnographic." The difference between Bastian and diffusionist like himself, he argued, was simply one of method and priorities. Bastian refused to place diffusionist theories at the center of his project. Bernard Ankermann, "Die Entwicklung der Ethnologie seit Adolf Bastian," *Zeitschrift für Ethnologie* 58 (1926): 229. See also Paul Honigsheim, "Adolf Bastian und die Entwicklung der ethnologischen Soziologie," *Kölner Vierteljahrshefte für Soziologie* 6, no. 1 (1926): 59–76; and Robert H. Lowie, *The History of Ethnological Theory* (New York: Farrar and Rinehart, 1937), 36.

72. Frobenius took this rigidity to perhaps the greatest extreme.

73. Stocking, *After Tylor,* 180. It is difficult to define diffusionism more precisely, because as Smith notes, it was "a theoretical pattern rather than a coherent theory," and in many cases the details of their approaches "varied substantially" (*Politics,* 155).

Diffusionists like Graebner regarded their emphasis on cultural interactions and the dissemination of "traits" as explicitly antievolutionary.[74] Ironically, however, the triumph of their methodology actually brought German ethnology closer to Tylor than ever before. Graebner's diffusionism, much like Tylor's evolutionism, was a totalizing method that assumed the existence of certain patterns and ordered the world according to them. This mode contrasted with Bastian's approach, which foresaw the discovery of those patterns as the end result of a careful process of induction. Indeed, Boas made precisely this point in his 1911 critique of Graebner's work.[75] Neither evolutionism nor diffusionism, Boas stressed throughout his career, could prove that their respective interpretations were "justifiable."[76] From Bastian's vantage point, both Graebner's diffusionism and Tylor's evolutionism disregarded the most basic principles of inductive science.[77]

Diffusionism and evolutionism also shared another quality, one that had very real political implications in regard to questions of human differences: a conception of progress that allowed for easy classification of cultural areas or individual groups according to hierarchical scales.[78] This was particularly evident in the arrangements and displays created by Foy and Graebner in Cologne's new ethnographic museum. There was a tremendous amount of open space in Cologne's display rooms, hardly any crowding in the display cabinets, and a rather limited number of objects in the entire museum (only 23,400 by 1909). Here, indeed, were orderly displays. Unlike Berlin, Europeans and a number of Asian *Kulturvölker* were intentionally excluded, not just from the museum, but from the realm of *Völkerkunde* altogether.[79]

---

74. Graebner, *Methode der Ethnologie*, 77–80.

75. Franz Boas, review of Graebner, *Methode der Ethnologie*, in *Science*, n.s. 34 (1911): 804–10, reprinted in Franz Boas, *Race, Language, and Culture* (Chicago: University of Chicago Press, 1982), 295–304, here 297.

76. Boas, "The Methods of Ethnology," 282.

77. While most German ethnologists took the diffusionist route, there were isolated voices that questioned the epistemological basis of the new approach. See especially the critique by Michael Haberlandt, who argued, "It appears that the inductive character of ethnology has been thrown into oblivion by the representatives [of diffusionism] and that determined deduction has trumped it again." "Zur Kritik der Lehre von den Kulturschichten und Kulturkreisen," *Petermanns Geographische Mitteilungen* 1, no. 3 (1911): 118. Haberlandt's criticism set off a debate in this journal, and was revisited at the Heilbronner conference later that year.

78. Smith, *Politics*, 142.

79. W. Foy, *Führer durch das Rautenstrauch-Joest-Museum der Stadt Cöln* (Cöln: M. Dumont Schauberg, 1906), 16.

Foy, moreover, made excessive use of the term *race* in his museum guidebooks, a modern concept noticeably absent from Bastian's museum.[80] In further contrast to Bastian, who had stressed the scientific goals of his museum in the introduction of his guidebooks, Foy prefaced his guide with explicit discussions of the practical uses of ethnology for colonialists. "Planters, traders, officials, and missionaries" who planned to go abroad were thus invited to make use of the museum. After all, "Knowledge of foreign peoples often protects against misunderstandings or mistakes in one's own behavior. Thus it is especially ethnology that provides colonial commerce with an essential service and offers the basis for colonial success."[81] Such rhetoric, while increasingly common in ethnologists' grant proposals and journals by the turn of the century, was unthinkable in the context of Bastian's museum of ethnological science.

The most striking contrast between the museums in Berlin and Cologne, however, lay in the treatment of the general public. While Bastian refused to compromise his scientific vision by making his exhibits more accessible to visitors, Foy introduced an explicit narrative for their consumption. Foy's narrative was governed by his *Kulturkreismethode* and articulated by displays that were arranged according to a clear-cut hierarchy.[82] For Foy, the *Naturvölker* were not just "simple societies," they were indeed "primitive." They "stood closer to the *Urstande* [primal state of humanity] than did the Kulturvölker," and they had "stagnated in their development."[83] For Foy, these were scientific facts. In contrast to Bastian and later Felix von Luschan in Berlin, who both felt that the general public had little interest in what concerned specialists, Foy hoped to teach his facts to the museum's visitors.[84]

To this end, he organized his museum in an explicitly developmental fashion. The public would begin their journey through the "cultures of non-European peoples" with Australia, "because on that continent, the lowest cultural forms remained protected," affording Europeans

---

80. Ibid., especially 22–23, and 35.

81. Ibid., 19.

82. The most fundamental change to Foy's guidebook in its second edition was the insertion of new paragraphs with greater explication of the *Kulturkreismethode*. See, for example, W. Foy, *Führer durch das Rautenstrauch-Joest-Museum der Stadt Cöln,* 2d ed. (Cöln: M. Dumont Schauberg, 1908), 19.

83. Foy, *Rautenstrauch-Joest-Museum* (1906), 29–32.

84. Willy Foy, "Das städtische Rautenstrauch-Joest-Museum für Völkerkunde in Cöln," *Ethnologia* 1 (1909): 47 n. 1.

an uncomprised view of primitive society. From this starting point, Foy directed his visitors to his collections from New Guinea, where they would not only find "considerable development from the oldest cultural forms," but should be able to "ascertain a number of Western influences." On the second floor of the museum, the public would encounter the collections from Micronesia and Polynesia. Those, Foy explained, were characterized by "higher cultural forms" than the ones found in New Guinea, due undoubtedly to a "strong and commensurately young flow of people and culture from the West." Further along on the second floor, the visitors were introduced to the collections from Greenland and North America, where they found peoples who had begun using metals. In America, Foy noted, one could find "many higher cultural forms," even as they often "retained very primitive properties" and "surprising similarities" to the materials from the South Seas. As the visitors' ascent in the building continued to mimic the progress of mankind, they arrived on the museum's third floor to find Foy's collections from Africa, the Near East, India, and Indonesia, all of which contained evidence of what Foy termed the "blooming iron culture." This level of achievement notwithstanding, Foy continued to stress "older, and in part very primitive cultural forms" that had persisted throughout these geographical areas. Finally, visitors were directed down the back stairwell to a collection from East Asia. With this last collection, Foy explained, "we come into the land of an idiosyncratic high culture, one that stands on an equal plane with the European, and which makes a fitting end to our tour of the cultures of non-European peoples."[85] From the most primitive cultures, to the somewhat stagnated, to those benefiting from Western influence, and finally to those which Foy deemed the equal of the Europeans—this was Foy's cultural tour of the world.

By the time of Bastian's death in 1905, the dominant trend in German ethnology had shifted away from his emphasis on exploring a universalized self. Bastian's ethnological vision was replaced by a focus on characterizing and defining particularized Others, as the positive reception of Ankermann and Graebner's papers, the triumph of diffusionist ideas, and the design of Foy's museum make clear.[86] Even the

---

85. Foy, *Rautenstrauch-Joest-Museum* (1906), 45–46.
86. Of course this did not happen immediately and did not encompass everyone. Some, such as Max Buchner in Munich or Ratzel in Leipzig, had never agreed with Bastian's method or goals, and there were many holdouts from the older generations who had shared Bastian's convictions, such as Paul Ehrenreich and Karl von den Steinen. But the general transformation is clear. Cf. Zimmerman, "Place of Knowledge," 334–35 n. 101.

Blick in den Afrika-Saal

Fig. 5. A view into the African Hall of the Rautenstrauch-Joest Museum für Völkerkunde in Cologne after Foy opened it to the public. Note the amount of empty space, the small number of representative objects, and the dividers within each case meant to confine the observer's view to a limited number of objects. (Source: W. Foy, *Führer durch das Rautenstrauch-Joest-Museum [Museum für Völkerkunde] der Stadt Cöln*, 2d ed. [Cöln: Druck der Kölner Verlagsanstalt A. G., 1908].)

Fig. 6. A view into the American Hall of the Cologne museum. (Source: W. Foy, *Führer durch das Rautenstrauch-Joest-Museum [Museum für Völkerkunde] der Stadt Cöln*, 2d ed. [Cöln: Druck der Kölner Verlagsanstalt A. G., 1908].)

Mittelsaal des I. Obergeschosses

Fig. 7. A view into the central hall of the second floor of the Cologne museum. (Source: W. Foy, *Führer durch das Rautenstrauch-Joest-Museum [Museum für Völkerkunde] der Stadt Cöln*, 2d ed. [Cöln: Druck der Kölner Verlagsanstalt A. G., 1908].)

young ethnologists trained in Bastian's museum had lost their interest in using the particularities of different peoples to create a global *Gedankenstatistik,* and they, too, began studying human differences for their own sake. As a result, they posited more stringent boundaries between peoples than Bastian had been willing to recognize; and they argued that progress arose from the mixing of different peoples until one group dominated.[87] They also became involved in categorizing groups of people based on their most significant "traits," mapping

---

87. Graebner, *Methode der Ethnologie,* 132–33.

these out in cartographic volumes and thereby creating ideal types around conceptions of abstract individuals such as "the Polynesian."[88] This new emphasis on the particular over the universal increased ethnologists' willingness to consider rigid discussions of progress and cultural hierarchy, as Foy had done in his museum. It also made their science much more compatible with contemporary interests in nation and empire than Bastian's vision had ever been.[89] In this respect, it made little difference that few ethnologists became politically engaged, or that many couched their theories in reminders that Europeans should respect primitive cultures.[90] Ultimately, their hierarchies and rhetoric were easily seized and put to use by others to support neo-Darwinian and racial-biological schemes.[91] In an ironic twist, German ethnologists' departure from Bastian's commitment to cultural pluralism occurred at the very moment Franz Boas was beginning to lead American anthropologists in just that direction.[92] The "diffusionist revolt," in other words, was more a result than a cause of ethnologists' increasing willingness to abandon the search for a universalized self.

Recently, Benoit Massin has argued that German physical anthropology experienced a similar transformation after 1895. He has shown that the discipline was radically transmuted from an essentially "antiracist" science under the dominant leadership of Rudolf Virchow to a science that was primarily racial and Darwinian in orientation. According to Massin, this transformation took place largely because Virchow's physical anthropology (much like Bastian's ethnographic project) ran out of steam conceptually, methodologically, and epistemologically. While Virchow's personal and institutional power kept race theorists at bay from 1895 until his death in 1902, the first decade of the twentieth century witnessed a radical shift toward "a biological and selectionist materialism more concerned with the inequalities of evolution than the universal brotherhood or spiritual unity of humankind."[93] What Massin does not explain, however, is why German anthropologists, many of whom had been trained by Virchow,

---

88. Smith, *Politics*, 159–60.
89. Joan Vincent, *Anthropology and Politics: Visions, Traditions, and Trends* (Tucson: University of Arizona Press, 1990), 122.
90. Foy, *Rautenstrauch-Joest-Museum* (1906), 32.
91. Smith, *Politics*, 160–61.
92. On the nascent cultural pluralism in German ethnology see especially Ivan Kalmar, "The *Völkerpsychologie* of Lazarus and Steinthal and the Modern Concept of Culture," *Journal of the History of Ideas* 48 (1987): 671–90.
93. Massin, "From Virchow to Fischer," 80, 100.

Bastian, or one of their students, were so willing to abandon their liberal humanism. Nor does he explain the sudden shift in their most fundamental positions about what constitutes good science, or their new willingness to move toward an easy coexistence with colonialist goals and theories of race.

To a large degree, the explanation lies in ethnologists' tenuous professional positions, particularly in relation to a changing public sphere. Indeed, external forces as much as theoretical concerns dictated the direction they would go.[94] Within the increasingly professional discipline of ethnology, the fervent competition for jobs and funding combined with ethnologists' salvage agenda to produce a frantic flight forward that intensified from about the mid-1880s.[95] Driven by a desire to enhance their professional and institutional standing, ethnologists felt increasingly pressured by their patrons, supporters, and each other to cast their nets wider, acquire the rarest and most coveted artifacts, gain the largest and most comprehensive collections, and lead the biggest and best-equipped expeditions into the field. As the fate of the Berlin museum documents, this emphasis on acquisition over everything else led to the daunting growth of their collections and increased frustration with their museums. By the turn of the century, however, ethnologists had become too invested in these institutions to abandon them. While the directors of Germany's leading museums became affiliated with the universities in their respective cities by 1907, museums remained their primary source of institutional stability, professional credibility, and financial support. Indeed, it is worth bearing in mind that both Graebner and Ankermann had been trained in museums and continued to work in them throughout their careers. Far from positing a set of theories that would encourage ethnologists to abandon museums for universities, diffusionists ultimately provided themselves with a theoretical justification for making their museums more "useful" and publicly appealing—something ethnologists' supporters in municipal and regional governments were calling for at precisely that time.

I do not mean to cast doubt on the diffusionists' genuine efforts to make sense of the masses of materials in their museums; nor do I argue

---

94. See Penny, "Cosmopolitan Visions." For considerations of how external forces affected the trajectory of British anthropology as well, see Henrika Kuklick, *The Savage Within: The Social History of British Anthropology* (Cambridge: Cambridge University Press, 1991).

95. For a similar consideration of professionalization and geography see Cornelia Essner, *Deutsche Afrikareisende im neunzehnten Jahrhundert: Zur Sozialgeschichte des Reisens* (Stuttgart: Steiner Verlag, 1985).

that theoretical considerations played no role in the transformation of German ethnology. But I do want to stress the ways in which ethnographic museums were tied into the prestige politics of their respective municipalities. Municipal governments and local elites had invested considerable sums in these institutions in the hopes of gaining the cultural capital associated with them.[96] And when the museums became increasingly chaotic by the turn of the century, city governments were eager and able to influence the direction Germany's ethnologists would turn.

The directors of these museums had always been faced with a Faustian dilemma. They were consistently forced to accept the input and influence of individuals and groups who underwrote and safeguarded the existence of their museums. But by the turn of the century, their supporters' interests had undergone a fundamental transformation. In the 1870s and 1880s, both the museums and their audiences were relatively small, and the educated elites who supported and frequented them generally accepted ethnologists' convictions that their museums should function primarily as scientific tools. Thus before the turn of the century, Germany's leading ethnographic museums rarely faced open criticism by their constituencies. This is not to say that ethnologists operated free of public influence during these decades; their supporters had after all demanded a "useful" science. But in the 1870s and 1880s, the presence of scientific institutions alone had provided a service, endowing the cities that housed them with the fame that came with participating in an internationally recognized science. By the turn of the century, however, the municipal bodies that supported these institutions became increasingly interested in public education, and when museums in general embraced pedagogy during this period, ethnographic museums were expected to conform—a task to which Foy, for instance, adapted very well.[97]

The trend toward the accommodation and education of an increasingly large and socially diverse public did meet some opposition from Germany's ethnological community. Bastian predictably argued that ethnographic museums were first and foremost tools of scientific

---

96. Penny, "Cosmopolitan Visions."

97. This was an international movement toward education that stemmed to a large degree from the United States. It encompassed all kinds of museums but did not affect them all simultaneously. For a general discussion of the "New Museum Idea" and its implications see Tony Bennett, *The Birth of the Museum: History, Theory, Politics* (London: Routledge, 1995).

exploration and research. As such, they were never meant to function like colonial museums or the displays at international exhibitions that were geared toward pointed instruction and spectacular entertainment. To reorganize ethnographic museums as tools of instruction, Bastian warned in 1900, would undermine the most fundamental principles of ethnology as a science.[98] Bastian might have regarded Foy's instructional displays as unscientific and remedial; but to the growing audience of ethnographic museums, they appeared much more orderly, scientific, and legitimate than the sprawling cabinets in the Berlin museum. By the turn of the century, the scientific reputation of the Berlin museum began to suffer, and the new orientation toward popular education became a means for ethnologists to protect their scientific legitimacy and their professional positions.

The trajectory of Leipzig's museum provides dramatic evidence for a transition toward popular pedagogy. In this case, the shift was initiated by Karl Weule, who turned to the newer, broader audience for direction when he became the director of Leipzig's ethnographic museum in 1907. Unsatisfied with his museum's geographical arrangements and overwhelming collections, he began to experiment with different kinds of comparative displays. When those cabinets met with enthusiastic responses from visitors, he set up a series of temporary exhibits focused on particular themes such as methods of transportation and modes of industry among primitive cultures.[99] Weule paid careful attention to public responses, discussed his methodology with his visitors, and used this information as a guide to refine his methods. In a 1909 report to the local government, he noted that the desire for the entire museum to be reorganized along the lines of the temporary exhibits "ran like a red thread through each of these private discussions."[100]

Weule also emphasized that the attendance at his new exhibits grew "greater and stronger with each day," becoming "just enormous" in the last weeks, and he went to great lengths to account for the various

---

98. Bastian to GVKM, 17 November 1900, in MfVB, "Erweiterungsbau des Königlichen Museums für Völkerkunde," vol. 1, 985/1900.

99. *Führer durch die Sonderausstellung über die Wirtschaft der Naturvölker* (Leipzig, June 1909); *Illustrierter Führer durch die Sonderausstellung über Transport- und Verkehrsmittel der Naturvölker und der außereuropäischen Kulturvölker* (Leipzig, summer 1910).

100. Karl Weule, "Bericht über die Spezialausstellung über die Wirtschaft der Naturvölker und aussereuropäischen Kulturvölker im Juni und Juli 1909," 22 July 1909, in LSA, Kap. 31, no. 12, vol. 6: 79–80; *Leipziger Tageblatt,* 25 July 1909.

constituencies present among his visitors. In particular, he stressed the "unexpectedly large" number of schoolchildren whose attendance had to be restricted, because it was simply impossible to "fit any more classes in the exhibition hall."[101] While reporting on the lecture series that followed, Weule included tables that listed the numbers of visitors according to social classes,[102] arguing that "the composition of listeners from all circles of the population, from the most simple worker to the highest official, [wa]s the best indication of the necessity of [these] courses."[103]

To Weule, the social breadth and sheer number of his visitors clearly validated his project; and he and his assistants wrote to Leipzig's city fathers, with a clear sense of satisfaction about the staggering audience response.[104] This aspect of Weule's correspondence with the city is particularly revealing; it shows a keen awareness that his own legitimacy and professional integrity were contingent on his museum serving agendas that were local and educational as well as international and scientific. Prior to the turn of the century, such concerns had been wholly absent from the correspondence of German museum directors; after 1900, they became commonplace.[105]

But Weule's success not only pleased his employers; it also impressed his peers. At the 1910 meeting of the German Anthropological Society, he spoke to them about his experimental exhibits. He explained that he and his associates had "recognized what our museum was lacking" by observing the "great enthusiasm" with which the

---

101. Weule, "Bericht über die Spezialausstellung," 79–80.

102. 22 percent teachers, 17 percent university students, 28 percent businessmen, 4 percent bureaucratic officials, 6 percent schoolchildren, 18 percent workers, 5 percent private persons. Weule to the Leipzig city council, "Bericht über die Museumskurse 1909/1910," 3 March 1910, in LSA, Kap. 31, no. 12, vol. 6.

103. Two lecture series organized under the title "The Essentials of Völkerkunde, and Instructions for a Useful Visit to the Völkerkundemuseum" were held in the winter of 1909–10. Weule's report on these lectures reflected his strong interest in reaching, and showing that he had reached, a broad public.

104. In his report to the city council on the temporary exhibit in 1910, Weule's assistant Fritz Krause noted that 386 school classes, four hundred teachers, and a total of 13,400 students attended in only forty-two days. Krause, "Bericht über die Sonderausstellung über Verkehrs- und Transportmittel im Museum für Völkerkunde," 24 September 1910, in LSA, Kap. 31, no. 12, vol. 6: 185–86.

105. As Hamburg set out to build a new building for their Völkerkunde museum in 1904, for example, there was a general consensus that its "primary goal" would be to serve the "education of the general population." "Mitteilungen des Senats an die Bürgerschaft," no. 109, in HSA, CIIa, no. 16, vol. 1.

"public" studied the new displays. Reporting that his audience had "shown [him] the direction [ethnologists] should take," Weule posited the combination of a broad, geographically organized permanent exhibit, with rotating comparative exhibitions and lecture series as the best means for communicating with a range of different publics.[106] Weule's talk generated a wave of excitement among ethnologists, and some even visited his museum in the hopes of learning from his efforts.[107]

There was, of course, resistance. Some of Berlin's ethnologists called Weule's efforts "dilettantish"[108] and continued to champion Bastian's principles. But while Berlin's unique financial security allowed them to resist the democratization of their elite science somewhat longer than their colleagues at other institutions, even Berlin's ethnologists were beginning to take the needs of the "uneducated public" seriously. Efforts along those lines had been under way since about 1900;[109] and by 1905, Felix von Luschan, who became director of the museum following Bastian's death, made the methods for these efforts public. Berlin's ethnologists were only prevented from following Weule's lead in 1910 by the state of their museum and their focus on designing a new museum building—a project that was not completed until after World War I.[110] Despite Berlin ethnologists' commitments to "scientific arrangements," any strong position against displays aimed at an "uneducated public," became essentially untenable by 1914; and after the war, a return to the more "scientific" collections and comprehensive displays was unthinkable.[111] In Berlin's new museum building—their own resentment of the situation notwithstanding[112]—exhaustive displays would be replaced by representative objects. Berlin too was

---

106. Weule, "Der volkserzieherische Wert des Leipziger Völkermuseums," *Leipziger Tageblatt,* 5 August 1910.

107. Arrangements made by Berlin following Weule's talk, for example, were noted by Krause, "Bericht über die Sonderausstellung."

108. Zimmerman, "Place of Knowledge," 336–37.

109. Cf. Königlichen Museen zu Berlin, *Führer durch das Museum für Völkerkunde,* 2d ed. (Berlin: W. Spemann, 1887), and 8th ed. (Berlin: W. Spemann, 1900).

110. Indeed, the displays were not actually reorganized until 1924. See "Die Neuordnung des Museums für Völkerkunde," in *Berliner Tageblatt,* 26 October 1924.

111. Following the 1918 revolutions, the "elite" focus of Prussian museums came under heavy attack (Scheffler, *Berliner Museumskrieg,* 22).

112. Indeed, even in 1927 during the new opening, the enthusiasm of the Prussian minister for science and education for the new *Schausammlung* was not mirrored in comments by F. W. K Müller and the other ethnologists running the museum. Ferdinand Lehmann-Haupt, "Adolf Bastian und das Berliner Museum für Völkerkunde," *Klio* 21 (1927): 193.

forced to conform, and the search for self was replaced by the characterization of others.

Of Institutions and Legacies

The transformation of German ethnology that took place around the turn of the century not only reveals a shift in the cultural capital of science, but highlights some of the limitations accompanying its institutionalization and professionalization. In providing a space for the creation of a liberal humanist *Gedankenstatistik,* museums allowed Bastian and his German counterparts to pursue their ethnographic project in ways that would have been impossible in other institutions. But these museums also tied German ethnologists to a public realm that would continue to shift and change, thereby reconfiguring the cultural functions both of their institutions and their science. As John Wesley Powell explained to Boas in 1887, museums were ultimately public institutions, and the people who funded and visited them had their own interests and desires. They wanted the museum's artifacts juxtaposed in ways that would illustrate the differences among people; and they demanded easily digestible, pedagogical displays that could be taken in at a glance rather than through a contemplative, protracted gaze. Boas resisted this notion because of his association with the German liberal sciences and his conviction that ethnographic museums should be places for self-actualization and self-improvement, that is, *Bildung,* rather than *Erziehung* through the uncritical distribution of concepts and ideas.

Because of the cultural capital of elite science in nineteenth-century Germany, Bastian and the directors of Germany's other large ethnographic museums were initially able to use their museums in pursuit of their scientific goals. But as Bastian's project proved untenable and Germany's leading museum was overcome by chaotic disorder, his successors were increasingly pressured by their patrons to follow Anglo-American trends in public education. At the same time, humanism went disciplinary in the late nineteenth century, and in the wake of that professionalization Humboldtian projects fell out of favor. By the turn of the century, a younger generation of ethnologists was dissatisfied with Bastian's chaotic efforts to achieve a vast synthesis; and they moved—for professional as much as intellectual reasons—away from Bastian's methodological convictions and toward more mechanical, theory-driven projects that would dovetail with popular interests. In the process, they abandoned the focus on the particular as a means to better understand the universal, replacing it with a search for human differences for their own sake.

Franz Boas had been confronted with the popularization of ethnology somewhat earlier than his fellow German scientists; and upon his immigration to the United States, he chafed under the debilitating power of public patronage in New York City and Washington, D.C. Eventually, however, he was able to retreat into the institutional setting of the American academy.[113] The flexibility of that institutional framework allowed Boas to stay much more focused on Bastian's initial goals than his German counterparts. At Columbia University, Boas developed and extended Bastian's vision beyond material culture. But while he freed it from the limitations of the museum setting, his commitment to inductive empiricism never wavered. In opposition to the new trends in German ethnology, Boas continued to argue that "safe progress" could only be found in the "patient unraveling of the mental processes that may be observed among primitive and civilized peoples, and that express the actual conditions under which cultural forms develop." Only after careful analysis of these "mental processes" was it possible to "proceed gradually to the more difficult problems of the cultural relations between isolated areas that exhibit peculiar similarities." For Boas, gaining a sense of the particular remained a prerequisite for understanding the universal, much as it had been for Bastian.[114] For this reason, Boas also maintained Bastian's salvage mentality; and extending it beyond peoples' "things," he placed at least as much emphasis on "recording" their cultures.[115] In essence, Boas's anthropology can be regarded as a continuation of the humanistic project that guided nineteenth-century German ethnographic museums.

Nineteenth-century German ethnology, however, had multiple trajectories, and the changing character of Germany's institutional landscape helps to explain why Bastian's tradition could not survive in Germany the way it did in the United States. Given the rigidity of Germany's institutions and the degree to which professional ethnology

---

113. Cole, *Franz Boas,* 243–49.
114. Franz Boas, review of Graebner, 810.
115. On Boas and his penchant for practicing salvage anthropology see Boas, "The Methods of Ethnology." Cf. Akhil Gupta and James Ferguson, "Discipline and Practice: 'The Field' as Site, Method, and Location in Anthropology," in *Anthropological Locations: Boundaries and Grounds of a Field Science,* ed. Gupta and Ferguson (Berkeley and Los Angeles: University of California Press, 1997), 1–46.

was wedded to museums, German ethnologists were simply unable to follow Boas's lead. Indeed, it is clear that Boas himself could not have pursued his project in Germany. The need to maintain his professional position in the context of the changing cultural functions of German ethnographic museums would have made it impossible.

With the loss of Bastian's greater ethnographic project the goal, indeed even the possibility, of pursuing self-knowledge through mass-scale ethnological comparison was also lost. That ambition was replaced by the much easier goal of defining and displaying Germans' multiple others.[116] This new task was not only divorced from the liberal and methodological convictions of an older generation, it was also more politically malleable. Ultimately, the construction of teleological theories of human history and the explicit articulation of cultural hierarchies were much more compatible with both romantic notions of *Volk* and the increasingly popular theories of race. This new and dangerous focus on difference for its own sake was first articulated in ethnologists' museum displays at the turn of the century; but it was taken to its natural extension in the decades that followed.

116. Massin, "From Virchow to Fischer," 106.

Spectacles of (Human) Nature: Commercial Ethnography between Leisure, Learning, and *Schaulust*

SIERRA A. BRUCKNER

> They are recurring educational establishments in the best sense. Not only do they serve the specialist, who can examine the offerings with his expert eye. Rather, they are also for the general public. . . . Each display is a vivid, extremely useful book that reads itself, so to speak, to the visitor . . . the evident instruction contained [in the displays] is combined with a wealth of amusement.
> —"Sehenswürdigkeiten der Ausstellungen 1896," *Die Gartenlaube*

The fervor of scientific discovery and the excitement of confronting an exotic unknown pervaded most of nineteenth-century European society. By the turn of the century, such enthusiasms were not restricted to the realm of fantasy but rather were a prominent feature of German popular culture. A Berlin journalist writing in 1898 described the urbanite's voyage to the exotic:

> Nowadays, we don't need to travel in order to learn about [foreign] people and places. Not only do travel writings attempt to provide us with accurate knowledge. Some enterprising men also bring natives from other regions of the world to our own country.

Special thanks to Rudolf Kräuter, Catherine Rymph, Michael Hau, and the editors of this volume, Matti Bunzl and H. Glenn Penny, for their helpful comments on earlier drafts of this essay.

Thus, with ease—and without strenuous toil—we can acquaint ourselves with a variety of human specimens.[1]

In this case, "a variety of human specimens" was on display in 1898 in Berlin's Feenpalast, an entertainment locale that catered to a middle-class audience. Here, Africans representing the Ashanti people were presented as a *Völkerschau*—a living ethnographic collection. During their stay in Europe, these men, women, and children lived in fenced-off kraals and engaged in "ethnographic activities." Like other cultural performers on tour in Europe, they dressed in traditional clothing, ate what was supposed to be a European equivalent of their diet, coexisted with indigenous animals that had also been transported from overseas, and offered a full program of indigenous songs, dances, rituals, and war games. Touring through major European cities, this group of approximately one hundred Africans lived and appeared in these reconstructed settings, sometimes for months at a time. Throughout the course of their day, hundreds of European men, women, and children strolled by the "natives," observing and studying them in their "natural" setting.

Völkerschauen or "commercial ethnographic exhibitions" emphasized both edification and entertainment and were a regular feature of popular culture in the 1870s and 1880s. During this period, commercial ethnography emerged as a sphere in which bourgeois interests and values, especially those of self-cultivation and national improvement, could be expressed. For the educated middle classes, the *Völkerschauen* served as a site of study and research in the anthropological sciences. Visitors to the exhibitions could gain firsthand knowledge of non-Europeans without venturing abroad, while at the same time publicly presenting themselves as armchair scientists engaged in "scholarly practice."[2] Show organizers recognized this appeal and unreservedly

---

1. "Nach exotischen Ländern," *Berliner Fremdenblatt*, 3 March 1898, Nachlaß Rudolf Virchow, Archiv der Berlin-Brandenburgischen Akademie der Wissenschaften, Berlin (hereafter NRV), Zeitungsauschnitt-Sammlung, 3017.

2. Lothar Gall, "Zur politischen und gesellschaftlichen Rolle der Wissenschaften in Deutschland um 1900," in *Wissenschaftsgeschichte seit 1900,* ed. Helmut Coing et al. (Frankfurt am Main: Suhrkamp Taschenbuch Verlag, 1992), 9–28; Jutta Kolkenbrock-Netz, "Wissenschaft als nationaler Mythos: Anmerkungen zur Haeckel-Virchow-Kontroverse auf der 50. Jahresversammlung deutscher Naturforscher und Ärzte in München (1877)," in *Nationale Mythen und Symbole in der zweiten Hälfte des 19. Jahrhunderts: Strukturen und Funktionen von Konzepten nationaler Identität,* ed. Jürgen Link and Wulf Wülfing (Stuttgart: Klett-Cotta, 1991), 212–36.

linked their efforts to the values of the *Bildungsbürgertum,* envisioning their business as an educational venture that provided the audience with an opportunity to partake in a form of civic culture.[3]

The very participatory quality of this site of learning, however, also led to its eventual rejection by many individuals who identified with the values of an educated middle class. Around the turn of the century, as the *Völkerschau* came to be more pointedly associated with a wide range of social groups, the meaning assigned to these events began to change. The lines that separated the traditional middle classes from both the "new middle classes" *(neuer Mittelstand)* and workers blurred at these shows, and concerns about class and group integrity took a prominent place in the rhetoric surrounding them.[4] Critics of commercial ethnography pointed out that lower-class crowds had also become part of a spectacle, and they lamented the symbolic ruin of the sphere of commercial ethnography. According to these critics, *Völkerschauen* were increasingly dictated by the demands of mass culture and shaped by a crowd that they consistently described in gendered terms.

Their criticisms, however, also exposed deeper middle-class fears regarding their loss of cultural capital, a specifically bourgeois gaze that constituted public comportment and thus embodied social and cultural identity. In their eyes, the "objective" way of seeing of the cultivated German seemed to be giving way to *Schaulust,* the untutored "lust to look" and undisciplined behavior of gawking spectators. Indeed, from the construction of museum displays to the disordered gaze of the spectator, the ways that the public "looked" *(schauen)* was

---

3. Studies in the history of science that examine science as a cultural phenomenon are few. Examples include Andreas Daum, *Wissenschaftspopularisierung im 19. Jahrhundert: Bürgerliche Kultur, naturwissenschaftliche Bildung und die deutsche Öffentlichkeit, 1848–1914* (Munich: R. Oldenbourg, 1998); Lynn K. Nyhart, "Civic and Economic Zoology in Nineteenth-Century Germany: The 'Living Communities' of Karl Möbius," *Isis* 89 (1998): 605–30; Kathryn Olesko, "Civic Culture and Calling in the Königsberg Period," in *Universalgenie Helmholtz: Rückblick nach 100 Jahren,* ed. Lorenz Krüger (Berlin: Akademie Verlag, 1994), 22–42.

4. Regarding the leisure culture of the new middle classes, see Heinz-Gerhard Haupt and Geoffrey Crossick, *Die Kleinbürger: Eine europäische Sozialgeschichte des 19. Jahrhunderts* (Munich: C. H. Beck, 1998), esp. 254–84. On leisure in working-class culture, see Lynn Abrams, *Workers' Culture in Imperial Germany: Leisure and Recreation in the Rhineland and Westphalia* (London: Routledge 1992); Dietrich Mühlberg, *Arbeiterleben um 1900,* 2d ed. (Berlin: Dietz Verlag, 1985). See also the overviews on German leisure culture by Kaspar Maase, *Grenzenloses Vergnügen: Der Aufstieg der Massenkultur 1850–1970* (Frankfurt am Main: Fischer Taschenbuch Verlag, 1997); and Gerhard Huck, *Sozialgeschichte der Freizeit: Untersuchungen zum Wandel der Alltagskultur in Deutschland* (Wuppertal: Hammer, 1980).

consistently at the center of the discourse of ethnography. It is ultimately this tension between edification and recreation, scientific practice and commercialism that makes German popular anthropology a subject rich with issues of class and national identity in the context of cultural modernity.

The *Völkerschau:* A Site between Entertainment and Science

In commercial ethnography "scientific displays" were combined with theatrical narrative and the popular mass medium of panoramic display. Despite the often spectacular nature of these shows, edification as much as entertainment was at the heart of commercial ethnography's appeal. As part of an exhibitionary tradition common in the second half of the nineteenth century, the shows replicated visual encyclopedias in which ethnographic artifacts and cultural performers were presented in museological form (figs. 1 and 2). This style of display, in which cultures were collected and exhibited as though in a showroom, was most evident in large-scale productions like the 1896 German Colonial Exhibition, which featured an array of villages populated by German East Africans, Togolese, Herero, and Pacific Islanders (figs. 3, 4, and 5).[5] But even the smaller ventures of commercial ethnography emphasized an encyclopedic quality.[6]

The commercial and scientific display of "natural peoples" took many forms during the *Kaiserreich*. The impresarios who organized commercial ethnographic exhibitions were astute businessmen who recognized that the growing commercialization of the entertainment

---

5. Gustav Meinecke, ed., *Deutschland und seine Kolonien im Jahre 1896* (Berlin: Dietrich Reimer, 1897). Other examples of these large exhibitions that replicated grand-scale museum galleries include the 1897 Transvaal Exhibition, which displayed adjacent to one another a variety of ethnic groups from southern Africa; the 1902 Industry and Trade Exhibition in Düsseldorf, which featured both a "Nubian Village" and a "Cairo Village" replete with the respective indigenous populations; and the 1904 International Art, Art History, and Horticulture Exposition, also in Düsseldorf, which presented East Indian and Japanese cultural performances as an attraction. See *Officieller Führer durch die Transvaal-Ausstellung am Kurfürstendamm und Stadtbahnhof "Savigny Platz" 1897* (Berlin: Weylandt und Bauchwitz, 1897); Karl Markus Kreis Private Collection, Völkerschau-Sammlung. For an analysis of the organization of the 1896 German Colonial Exhibition, see Sierra A. Bruckner, "The Tingle-Tangle of Modernity: Popular Anthropology and the Cultural Politics of Identity in Imperial Germany," Ph.D. diss., University of Iowa, 1999, 1:134–222.

6. For a chronological overview of commercial ethnographic exhibitions in Germany between 1870 and 1914, see the appendix in Bruckner, "Tingle-Tangle of Modernity," 2:472–506.

Spectacles of (Human) Nature 131

Fig. 1. "Chief's Hut in Abyssinian Village" at the 1907 Mannheim Anniversary Exhibition. (Source: Karl Markus Kreis Private Collection.)

industry as well as the increasing cultural value of scientific education and research served as the contexts in which they could best market their products. Changing appetites for the sensational, the exceptional, and the eccentric usually determined the content of commercial ethnography. Thus, the size and ethnic composition of the performing troupes as well as the featured ethnographic programs and dramatized presentations varied greatly. As exhibition organizers responded to changing trends in the entertainment industry, for example, large-scale ethnographic displays with their replicated villages and imported animals grew in importance, overshadowing smaller traveling shows that featured only a handful of individuals.[7] Similarly, impresarios were

---

7. The *Völkerschauen* circuit was focused on large cities where entrepreneurs knew that a substantial audience eagerly anticipated the most recent offering of the amusement industry. However, Wolfgang Haberland's thorough study of the Bella Coola show in 1885 and 1886 shows that the northwestern Native Americans traveled to a number of midsized and small cities in the provinces of Saxony and Thuringia. Wolfgang Haberland, "Nine Bella Coolas in Germany," in *Indians and Europe: An Interdisciplinary Collection of Essays,* ed. Christian F. Feest (Aachen: Rader Verlag, 1987), 344.

Fig. 2. "The Tunisians" in Carl Marquardt's 1904 *Völkerschau*. (Source: Karl Markus Kreis Private Collection.)

mindful of the larger political situation and the public curiosity it might arouse. When Cameroon became a German colony in 1884, for example, the Hagenbeck family in Hamburg "did not pass up the opportunity to take advantage of the good circumstances" that might draw a crowd eager to learn more about their new colonial subjects. The following year, the Hagenbeck brothers together with Fritz Angerer similarly produced a successful show of Dualla from

Fig. 3. "Group from Cameroon" at the 1896 German Colonial Exhibition. (Source: Meinecke, *Deutschland und seine Kolonien,* 150.)

Fig. 4. "Togo Negroes in Dance Costumes" at the 1896 German Colonial Exhibition. (Source: Meinecke, *Deutschland und seine Kolonien,* 39.)

Fig. 5. "Massai Cooking Meat at the Campfire" at the 1896 German Colonial Exhibition. (Source: Meinecke, *Deutschland und seine Kolonien,* 28.)

Cameroon featuring "Prince Dido," the brother-in-law of the ruling Bismarck Bell.[8]

While very little information exists that would shed light on the impresarios as a social group, a few conclusions can be made from the available evidence. Collectively, impresarios were jacks-of-all-trades, wildly adventuresome, connected to a multinational European colonial community, fluent in ethnological concepts, and known as keen businessmen. Encouraged by research expeditionists and often recognized travelers themselves, they tended to specialize in a geographical area and ethnic group. Joseph Menges (who focused on troupes from North Africa and the Sudan), Fritz Angerer (a businessman on the Gold Coast and organizer of a Cameroonian show), Carl Marquardt (who showed primarily Samoans, but also organized three shows of African people), Eduard Gehring (an organizer of exhibitions of various nomadic groups from Russia), and John Hagenbeck (a specialist of East Indian productions) all carved a geographic and economic niche

---

8. John Hagenbeck, *Fünfundzwanzig Jahre Ceylon: Erlebnisse und Abenteuer im Tropenparadies* (Dresden: Deutsche Buchwerkstätten, 1922), 9–10.

for themselves that was recognized by the international entertainment industry as well as scholarly circles.

If a characterization of the impresarios as a social group poses challenges, the attempt to typify the eclectic group of cultural performers appearing in commercial ethnographic displays is even more difficult. Those individuals and troupes that traveled to Germany during the Wilhelminian period came from a myriad of cultures and continents and thus had drastically different experiences as cultural performers. The Eskimo, Bella Coola, or Tierra del Fuegians, all *Völkerschau* participants who lived in relatively remote and sparsely inhabited regions, arrived in Germany quite naive about European customs. They were usually at the mercy of the whims of their impresarios and often suffered from severe homesickness as well as diseases that sometimes even ended in death. In contrast, people from parts of northern Africa (the Somali or individuals in the innumerable "Bedouin caravans"), the coastal regions of West Africa (the Togolanders and Ashanti, for example), and British India were well versed in European conventions.

The individuals who joined *Völkerschau* troupes were motivated by a variety of reasons. Many *Völkerschau* performers were as entrepreneurial in spirit, as their impresarios and took advantage of what their experiences in Europe had to offer them. The most significant motivating factor for cultural performers, however, was the opportunity to earn relatively large sums of money that could not be procured in indigenous or colonial economies. Troupe members, in fact, had a very clear sense of the market value of their ethnographic skills and would not engage in shows at just any price. Performers in the 1896 German Colonial Exhibition even bartered with impresarios over fair salaries for the troupe, and German contemporaries often commented—usually with disapproval—on the entrepreneurial abilities of the cultural performers.[9] In a few instances, indigenous elites who agreed to perform in commercial ethnographic exhibitions did so in order to support their travel to Germany for diplomatic reasons. Such was the case in 1896 for the Herero chief Samuel Maherero, who met with Kaiser Wilhelm to discuss the fragile balance of power in German Southwest Africa. Other individuals joined traveling shows to establish contacts

---

9. For example, Köhler to Hohenlohe-Schillingsfürst, 14 November 1895, Bundesarchiv Potsdam R1001 (hereafter BAP), 6349, pp. 24–27. For a more detailed discussion of the market values for ethnographic performance, see Bruckner, "Tingle-Tangle of Modernity," 1:332–34.

Fig. 6. J. C. Bruce (center) with his troupe of Togolanders, probably 1900–1903. (Source: Meinecke, *Deutschland und seine Kolonien*, 28.)

in Germany, where they hoped to acquire an apprenticeship in a trade, and a few even went on to function as *Völkerschau* impresarios themselves, like the Somali Hersi Ergeh Gorseh and the Togolander J. C. Bruce (see fig. 6).[10]

The impresarios who brought these individuals together were interested in more than just entertainment and profit. Indeed, they took their task as scientific popularizers quite seriously and figured themselves as part of the educated world. Because the teachings of evolution were disallowed in classrooms, popularizers were able to fill a vacuum in German scientific and political discourse.[11] Newspapers regularly

---

10. Regarding Hersi Ergeh Gorseh, see Hilke Thode-Arora, "'Characteristische Gestalten des Volkslebens': Die Hagenbeckschen Südasien-, Orient-, und Afrika-Völkerschauen," in *Fremde Erfahrungen: Asiaten und Afrikaner in Deutschland, Österreich und in der Schweiz bis 1945*, ed. Gerhard Höpp (Berlin: Das Arabische Buch, 1996), 125–26; Musa Haji Ismael Galaal, "Germany and the First Somali Technical Trainee," *Somali News*, 26 October 1962; Lothar Dittrich and Annelore Rieke-Müller, eds., *Carl Hagenbeck (1844–1913): Tierhandel und Schaustellungen im Deutschen Kaiserreich* (Frankfurt am Main: Peter Lang, 1998), 172. Regarding J. C. Bruce, see "Eine Unterhaltung mit einem Togo-Häuptling," *Kölnische Zeitung*, 11 October 1896; BAP, 6350 and 4457/8; Hans-Werner Debrunner, *Presence and Prestige: Africans in Europe—A History of Africans in Europe before 1918* (Basel: Basler Afrike-Bibliographie, 1979), 364.

11. Daum, *Wissenschaftspopularisierung*, 82–83; Alfred Kelly, *The Descent of Darwin: The Popularization of Darwinism in Germany, 1860–1914* (Chapel Hill: University of North Carolina Press, 1981), 74.

reported on the *Völkerschauen,* often presenting popular theories of Darwinist evolution and debunking myths about so-called missing links. Furthermore, many impresarios participated in learned societies or published monographs on their regions of specialty. Some produced narratives about their experiences as collectors of artifacts and organizers of ethnographic exhibitions, tracts that frequently read like travelogues. While most scientists were not convinced that impresarios had the skills of ethnographers, the show promoters' reputations as travelers and men of the world did impart a kind of scientific legitimacy to the early *Völkerschauen.* Indeed, travel experience served as an alternative to formal education and a kind of symbolic capital that some anthropologists did not have. Impresarios applauded themselves for bringing "populations from all parts of the world closer to Europeans" and presenting to the German public those "human races that still remained in their development in childhood."[12]

Up until the late 1890s, such well-known scientists as Rudolf Virchow and Franz Stuhlmann endorsed the *Völkerschauen,* publicly praising impresarios for providing the opportunity for scientists and lay public alike to view people never before seen in Europe. Members of local scientific associations like the Berliner Gesellschaft für Anthropologie, Ethnologie, und Urgeschichte (BGAEU)—which included both professional and amateur scientists—regularly visited public displays of indigenous people. Especially in the 1870s and 1880s, commercial ethnography provided access to "research material" otherwise difficult to obtain. The presence of the *Naturvölker* in German cities allowed scientists to directly observe their subjects, therefore reducing scholars' reliance on the inadequate accounts of untrained travelers and eliminating arduous journeys to the respective "natural habitat."

Impresarios were proud when members of learned societies mingled in the sphere of the *Völkerschau.* Newspaper accounts and brochures often reported visits by prominent scientists, reinforcing the notion that these events deserved the attention of all those who considered themselves educated. For the organizers of commercial ethnographic presentations, acknowledgment by the scientific community was also crucial for the positive reception of their businesses in the eyes of their middle-class audience as well as for their own professional identity. Moreover, endorsements from scientists were essential to the enter-

---

12. *Deutsch-Afrika: Carl Hagenbeck's Kamerun-Expedition* (Munich, 1886), Nachlaß Adrian Jacobsen, Archiv des Museums für Völkerkunde, Hamburg, Sonderdrucke.

prise of commercial ethnography. Scholars were among those who could certify that a production served "scientific" purposes, thus enabling impresarios to circumvent a federal ordinance that interdicted potentially "immoral" displays for the purpose of sheer entertainment.[13] For example, Rudolf Virchow, one of the most prominent advocates of commercial ethnography at the time, issued a certificate lauding the 1889 presentation of Dinkas in the Charlottenburger Flora, a park in an upscale region of Berlin. Brought to Germany by the impresarios Willy Möller and Fritz von Schirp, the Dinkas belonged to the "purest Nigritians that have ever been presented to us" and therefore "deserve . . . a lot of attention."[14] While Virchow's endorsement ensured him future access to other potentially interesting ethnic groups, his public attestation was crucial for the impresarios. Indeed, scientists were as much a part of the show as the exotic people on display; the presence of specialists observing, measuring, and quantifying the bodies and behavior of the "natives," frequently in front of onlookers, helped legitimate the *Völkerschauen* in the eyes of the public.[15] Furthermore, scholars contributed to the spectacle by taking notes on language, recording songs and proverbs, and measuring skulls and limbs. Indeed, this interaction between scientists and per-

---

13. The paragraphs that affected impresarios were 32 and 33 in the *Reichs-Gesetzblatt* (Berlin, 1883), 160. Regarding the commercial laws that ethnographic exhibitions were subject to see Wolfgang Jansen, *Das Varieté: Die glanzvolle Geschichte einer unterhaltenden Kunst* (Berlin: Edition Hentrich, 1990), 63–70.

14. *Deutsches Tageblatt*, 27 June 1889, NRV, Zeitungsausschnitt-Sammlung, 3002. Regarding an 1889 Ceylonese show and an 1896 Samoan show, see respectively *Berliner Fremdenblatt*, 21 July 1889, and *Frankfurter Zeitung*, 24 June 1896, NRV, Zeitungsausschnitt-Sammlung, 3016. Virchow's importance to impresarios was expressed in his obituary in *Der Komet*, a journal of the entertainment industry: "Giants and midgets, skeleton people and snake people, desensitized fakirs and beings with a variety of unusual bodily and physical capabilities, even all types of savages and members of interesting racial tribes from the most distant regions were presented to and scientifically examined by Virchow" (13 December 1902, 2). Regarding the mutual relationship between scientists and impresarios, see also Felix von Luschan's reluctant support in von Luschan to Marquardt, 31 December 1895, BAP, 5576, p. 14.

15. For example, see the comments by the organizers of the Cairo Exhibition in *Berlin und seine Arbeit: Amtlicher Bericht der Berliner Gewerbe-Ausstellung 1896* (Berlin: Dietrich Reimer, 1898), 870. Some of these public episodes of recording, measuring, and classifying were later published as reports, for example, in Felix von Luschan's anthropological account of the 1896 colonial exhibition. See Luschan, *Beiträge zur Völkerkunde der deutschen Schutzgebiete: Erweiterte Sonderausgabe aus dem "Amtlichen Bericht über die Erste Deutsche Kolonial-Ausstellung" in Treptow 1896* (Berlin: Dietrich Reimer, 1897).

formers symbolized the power of the industrializing world, and impresarios made sure to market this as part of the show.

In the most idealistic sense, commercial ethnography was a site that taught the public how to "see." As one author of an exhibition brochure explained, the public could learn to practice a positivistic gaze similar to that of contemporary scholars by observing scientists at work at the *Völkerschau*.[16] Alongside anthropologists, spectators observed with their own eyes the peculiarities of the people from "dark Africa," the gracious nature of the indigenous of the South Seas, or the rugged qualities of individuals from the icy north. Advocates of commercial ethnography hailed the significance of firsthand experience as the most effective method of learning:

> The customs and habits of people provide the best information about their cultural progress.... With wonder, the *Kulturmensch* observes a Botokude family with wooden pieces in their earlobes and lower lips or a caravan of Wittu Negroes with their *pelele* and their exposed lower jaws. These are all rare pleasures for the *Kulturmensch* who is becoming ever more distanced from nature.[17]

Skin color, facial features, hair structure, muscle tone, scars, and filed teeth constituted some of the physical characteristics that the exhibition visitor learned to observe through popular anthropological literature. Show organizers also provided small brochures with background information that would further prepare the viewer to cast a "scientific" eye on the living ethnographic exhibitions and analyze them for him- or herself.[18] Commercial ethnography thus functioned as a site in which the public was encouraged to acquire and practice the measured and rational gaze of the educated.

---

16. Johannes Flemming, *Völkerschau am Nil* (Hamburg, 1912), Hagenbeck-Archiv, Hamburg, Völkerschau-Sammlung.

17. "Anthropologische Ausstellungen und deren Schauwert," *Der Komet*, 17 January 1903.

18. Often written by the impresarios themselves or writers whom they commissioned, the pamphlets, which usually cost about one-fifth of the ticket price, provided information about the geography of the land, including the natural resources and climate, and offered the reader physical anthropological descriptions as well as the cultural historical development of the people onstage. After the late 1880s, many of the brochures included a colonial historical account and often described the most recent expedition in which the indigenous were "discovered" or contracted to travel to Germany.

Debating the Pleasures of the Metropolis

By the mid-1890s, the scientific support of ethnographic shows had reached its peak. This level of approval began to disintegrate thereafter, as professional and social distinctions between scientists and entertainment entrepreneurs became magnified.[19] As cultural scientists acquired more professional recognition, they became wary of associating their scientific practice with the spectacle of the *Völkerschau*. Despite his continued interests in commercial ethnography as a potential source for new subjects to examine, Virchow, along with other scholars, voiced his reservations and began more and more to examine his subjects in private. At the same time, scholars, the educated public, and the press became more vocal in their criticisms of ethnographic performances, decrying the commercial character of these undertakings. Popular ethnography came to be associated not with a cultivated milieu, but rather one in which bourgeois behavior had ceased to exist. Whether the composition of the public attending *Völkerschauen* actually changed is difficult to assess. But clearly the crowds of spectators—much like the scientists—came to be perceived as an element of the show. Indeed, by the turn of the century, middle-class critics increasingly focused on the crowds and characterized them as an uneducated, *schaulustige* proletariat.

Although *Völkerschauen* continued sporadically into the 1920s (and a few even took place in the 1930s), a transformation in the cultural meaning of commercial ethnography occurred around the turn of the century. This shift was marked by the debate that emerged in 1899 and that resulted in a 1901 prohibition of the appearance of Germany's colonial subjects in ethnographic shows. Initiated by members of the German Colonial Society, formerly an important proponent of commercial ethnography, the discussion addressed concerns about the exploitative, unethical, and politically precarious character of the exhibitions. Most importantly, however, the debate, which involved colonial propagandists, overseas administrators, missionaries, scientists, and entertainment producers, engaged issues of class and status that were provoked by the increasingly proletarian behavior of the *Völkerschau* audience.[20]

---

19. Bogden notes a similar development in the American amusement industries. Robert Bogden, *Freak Show: Presenting Human Oddities for Amusement and Profit* (Chicago: University of Chicago Press, 1988), 62–68.

20. "Bericht über die ordentliche Hauptversammlung der Deutschen Kolonialgesellschaft im Saale des Görresbaues zu Koblenz am 1. und 2. 1900," BAP, 6686, p. 171.

At the German Colonial Society's annual meeting in 1898, Paul Kayser, director of the association, addressed the social concerns engendered by commercial ethnography:

> Exhibitions of natives arouse a feeling of embarrassment in all of us. The way in which the European conducts himself at the exhibitions does not help to dismiss these doubts. Instead of European culture, the people [performers] take the opposite with them when they go home.[21]

For Kayser, "European culture" was clearly synonymous with *bürgerliche* German culture. He and his contemporaries feared that the influence of working-class culture—specifically the behaviors associated with promiscuity, alcoholism, and social democratic ideas—might affect individuals in the colonies.

Concerns about commercial ethnography's potential challenge to bourgeois norms were not entirely new in 1900. The Colonial Society described the general distress associated with an occurrence in 1879 in which "not only women of the lower classes" but also others engaged in behavior that "relinquished all sense of shame."[22] In this incident the performing Nubians and Dinkas had to be escorted by the local police in order to protect them from the hands of their female fans. Other critics focused on the possible political ramifications of commercial ethnography. In 1892, one overseas missionary, for example, argued that Africans in Germany might be susceptible to the influence of "social-democratically minded people" who might introduce them to "the low life of the pub."[23] By the turn of the century, however, the criticisms had become much more pointed. Writing in 1901, the governor of Togo, August Köhler, claimed the colonial subjects were endangered by "the throngs of a *schaulustiges* public." He explained that the "native in his homeland recognizes and respects the ranking of our social and bureaucratic ladder."[24] At commercial ethnographic exhibi-

---

21. Ibid.

22. "Denkschrift über die Frage der Ausfuhr von Eingeborenen aus den deutschen Kolonien zum Zwecke der Schaustellung," 6 June 1900, BAP, 5576, p. 5. In 1898, Köhler also complained about the "undignified advances" and "the curiosity of uneducated and educated whites in regard to sexual issues having to do with the coloreds" (Köhler to Foreign Ministry Colonial Office, 1 June 1901, BAP, 6343, pp. 22–23).

23. Böhner to von Zimmerer, May 1892, BAP, 5571, p. 141; The Catholic prefect Pieter also complained that indigenous people who had been in Germany were "treated . . . as something special, like princes even." *National-Zeitung,* 25 August 1898, BAP, 5575.

24. Köhler to Foreign Ministry Colonial Office, 1 June 1901, BAP, 6343, pp. 22–23.

tions, however, spectators did not exhibit the manner of comportment colonial Germans usually displayed in front of Africans. For Köhler, the crowd—working-class in behavior and social-democratic in ideology—was thus a danger to government authority, the social order, and effective colonial administration.

For outspoken critics of the *Völkerschau*, the transformation of commercial ethnography's audience went hand in hand with impresarios' attempts to sensationalize their product. In a memorandum issued in 1900, the colonial association criticized this practice:

> The attraction of just observing indigenous people in their typical dress and customary jewelry surrounded by their weapons and tools, or even [the presentation of their] native dances is not enough to draw the spectator anymore. Therefore, one turns to methods that are geared to titillate the masses to attend [the exhibitions]. The indigenous are dressed up so that they laugh at themselves and the gullible spectator, they are taught dances that they never knew before, and thus they deceive the public and simultaneously become corrupted.[25]

The memorandum pointed to the German Colonial Society's fear that the virtuous motive of scientific edification had been swept up by a quest for profit. As one opponent of the *Völkerschau* put it, "The impresarios undoubtedly do not intend to disseminate ethnological and anthropological knowledge in Europe, but rather have the desire to earn money. It is purely a slave trade."[26] Others argued that consumer demands and the desire for novelty had obstructed scientific authenticity in the exhibitions. In their view, the sphere of the *Völkerschau* had lost its function as a laboratory of research, inquiry, and learning.

Rudolf Virchow had pointed to the dangers of this development as early as 1890:

> The introduction of wild natives from various lands has not stopped. This year we have seen Somali, Wakamba, Samoans, and finally "the Amazons of the Kingdom of Dahomey." But real faith and confidence in the accounts of their tribal affiliation has

---

25. "Denkschrift," 4.
26. "Bericht über die ordentliche Hauptversammlung," 171.

been quite shaken, since the reliable entrepreneurs like Herr Carl Hagenbeck have reduced their ventures. A sense of shrewdness is increasingly necessary in order to distinguish between authenticity and inauthenticity, and even the knowledge of older travelers has proven insufficient in light of the enigmas produced by the various competing troupe leaders.[27]

Virchow underscored the conundrum in which learned individuals found themselves when they examined their research subjects in a sphere of popular entertainment. As respectable showmen like Carl Hagenbeck cut back on producing *Völkerschauen,* scientists and the middle-class public were left with spurious presentations in which the individuals on display frequently represented ethnicities not truly their own.[28] As commercial ethnographic displays proliferated in the course of the 1890s, members of the BGAEU often spent their meetings trying to assess the true ethnic and racial typology of the people on display.[29] By the turn of the century, Virchow and his fellow anthropologists no longer viewed the *Völkerschau* as an ethnographic laboratory. For them, the *Völkerschau* had degenerated into an exotic sideshow that was no longer an adequate or useful arena for the scientific community.

In this context of rising anxieties about the scientific authenticity of commercial ethnography and the potential threat to colonial authority, the German Colonial Society pushed through a resolution prohibiting the export of indigenous people from the German colonies for the purpose of exhibition.[30] In the wake of the Federal Council's resolution passed in 1901, representatives of the *Bildungsbürgertum* signaled their disassociation from the sphere of the *Völkerschau*. By the turn of the century, neither respectable scientists nor members of the

---

27. *Verhandlungen der Berliner Gesellschaft für Anthropologie, Ethnologie und Urkunde* 22 (1890): 589–90.

28. Between the years 1890 and 1907, Carl Hagenbeck virtually pulled out of the *Völkerschau* business, although his motives for this are not clear. Exceptions are the 1895 Somali Show at the Crystal Palace in which he partially sponsored the impresario Joseph Menges, and the 1896 Berlin Industrial Fair, in which he hired two Eskimo to take care of the bears in his polar bear show.

29. *Die Post,* 23 May 1892, NRV, Zeitungsausschnitt-Sammlung, 3008.

30. "Denkschrift." See also Harald Sippel, "Rassismus, Protektionismus oder Humanität? Die gesetzlichen Verbot der Anwerbung von 'Eingeborenen' zu Schaustellungszwecken in den deutschen Kolonien," in *Kolonialausstellungen—Begegnung mit Afrika?* ed. Robert Debusmann and János Riesz (Frankfurt am Main: IKO, Verlag für Interkulturelle Kommunikation, 1995), 43–64.

colonial movement's upper echelons regarded commercial ethnography as a site of civic education. In their view, the integrity of rational contemplation had been compromised. Instead, commercial ethnography had come to represent *Schaulust,* an undisciplined voyeurism that contradicted the characteristics of the gaze of the educated. As is evidenced by the 1901 resolution, the *Bildungsbürgertum* publicly associated the *Völkerschau* as an arena of proletarian culture in which sensationalism and theatricality overshadowed bourgeois sentiments. Indeed, the rhetoric surrounding a notorious incident in 1907 exposes the manner in which the middle-class press used the *Völkerschau* as a means to raise concerns about shifting class and gender relations as well as issues of nation and empire.

The Damuka "Uprising"

On 11 June 1907, the Berlin press announced that a "revolt" had taken place in the "Negro village of Damuka."[31] The scandalous "flight of the Blacks out of 'Africa,'" however, was not an escape from the African continent, but from "Wild Africa"—a *Völkerschau* held in the imaginary territory of "Damuka," the acronym for the German Army, Marine, and Navy Exhibition (Deutsche Armee-, Marine- und Kolonial-Ausstellung).[32] Hired for an ethnographic presentation that featured "Negroes from the Sudan, [and] Arabians from the steppes of Tunisia and Morocco," the performers left the exhibition enclosure where they were required by contract to remain during their four-month stay in Berlin.[33]

> Agitated by the unfamiliar consumption of prohibited alcohol ... a number of blacks could not withstand the temptation to have a look at the splendors of the exhibition. They pushed the guard ... aside, left their compound, and [roamed] around in ... the neighboring streets. Of course, they were quickly surrounded by a large crowd.[34]

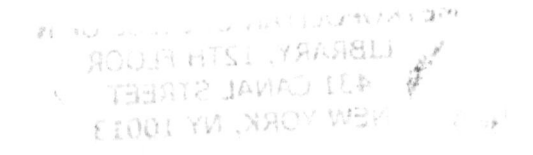

---

31. *Berliner Lokal-Anzeiger,* no. 292, 12 June 1907, and no. 293, 12 June 1907.
32. *Tägliche Rundschau* no. 272, 13 June 1907, Geheimes Staatsarchiv Preußischer Kulturbesitz, Berlin (GSPK), Rep 120 E XVI.2. 13Ag Adh.
33. "Deutsche Armee-, Marine- und Kolonial-Ausstellung Berlin 1907. Sonderausstellung: Afrika," 1, Archiv des Berliner Missionswerks (ABerM), Ausstellungen I.12.24a 1906/7.
34. Ibid.

The escapade incited a frenzied search for the African performers on the part of both the exhibition security and the Berlin police. By midnight, the police had managed to retrieve only fourteen of the eighteen men who had illicitly left the exhibition grounds. The remaining four did not turn up until the next morning, apparently having enjoyed the pubs and nightlife of Berlin. In addition to cries of outrage about the bumbling Berlin police, the heterogeneous middle-class press also highlighted the problems associated with this rubric of popular entertainment.[35]

The 1907 German Army, Marine, and Navy Exhibition was organized by radical nationalist business leaders representing the military, heavy industry, and colonial interests.[36] Although a *Völkerschau* of colonial performers would have been a logical part of an exhibit highlighting the government's imperial might, the 1901 prohibition prevented the Damuka organizers from showcasing German colonial subjects. Acknowledging this situation, the organizers were quick to announce that "because of corruption, demoralization, and brutalization [of the natives], the transportation of natives from *our* colonies was not ever considered." Instead, the organizing committee sought out a promoter of commercial ethnography "who could offer anthropological and ethnographic presentations from *non*-German regions in Africa."[37] Having thus avoided a conflict with the Reich government, the Damuka organizers commissioned the experienced *Völkerschau* impresarios Felix and Carl Marquardt. Asked to represent the "dark parts of the world," the Marquardt brothers formed "Wild Africa," a troop comprised of Sudanese, Moroccan, and Tunisian men and women who lived in reconstructions of their native north African villages, dressed in their traditional clothing, and engaged in their usual daily activities.[38]

Even though "Wild Africa" was primarily comprised of Muslim North Africans, Carl Marquardt claimed that the ethnographic exhibition would offer the public a lesson in colonial issues. Maintaining the

---

35. For criticisms of the Berlin police, see for example, "Modernes Sklavenleben," *BZ am Mittag*, 13 June 1907, GSPK Rep 120 E XVI.2. 13Ag Adh.

36. "Eine werdende Austellung," *Berliner Tageblatt*, no. 109, 1 March 1907, BAP, 6657, p. 173. An overview of colonial exhibitions is provided in Stefan Arnold, "Propaganda mit Menschen aus Übersee—Kolonialausstellungen in Deutschland 1869–1940," in Debusmann and Riesz, *Kolonialausstellungen*, 1–24.

37. "Unterlagen zu einem Bericht an. Se. Durchlaut den Herrn Reichskanzler," undated, BAP, 6657, 40–43.

38. "Deutsche Armee-, Marine- und Kolonial-Ausstellung," 1.

rhetoric of *Bildung,* he insisted that "Wild Africa" provided the "great flock of [people who were] eager for knowledge [with] a sample of lively illustrative lessons that make a deeper and longer-lasting impression than the study of textbooks and travelogues."[39] Furthermore, he claimed, their ethnographic presentation would remind the German public of their colonial responsibility in "the cultural uplifting of our black masses" who were culturally "far lower" on the evolutionary scale than the Muslim performers standing before them.[40] By 1907, however, this argument was no longer believable, and multiple newspaper accounts described the event as, first and foremost, a spectacle intended for entertainment purposes.[41] As one visitor observed, "Even though the weavers and carpet makers were at work on the opening day, the primary attraction was the horseback riders, the dancers, and the motley crew that presented the noisy parade."[42] (See fig. 7.) Whether the audience—after watching the belly dancers, snake handlers, and the dramatized attack of Arab bandits—left the exhibition more informed of North African cultures or aware of their prescribed role in the civilizing mission is questionable.[43]

It is interesting that in the published debate over "Wild Africa," the North African performers were discursively treated as though they were indeed colonial subjects from Germany's overseas empire. The *Berliner Lokal-Anzeiger,* the paper responsible for the initial report of the Damuka "uprising," introduced a rhetoric that toyed with the public's perceptions of the unpredictability of the escaped Africans.[44] Another paper reported: "We have hardly overcome the [Herero-Nama] rebellion in Africa and already the blacks in Damuka have united forces."[45] The chase that ensued was like a "real slave

---

39. "Deutsche Armee-, Marine- und Kolonial-Ausstellung."
40. DAMUKA Cat., 9. According to contemporary ethnological theory, Muslims did not belong to the *Naturvölker*—as did the pagan majority in Germany's colonies—but were more culturally advanced and were thus categorized as *Halbkulturvölker.* For the history of ethnological theory, see Woodruff Smith, *Politics and the Sciences of Culture in Germany, 1840–1920* (Oxford: Oxford University Press, 1991); and Wilhelm E. Mühlmann, *Geschichte der Anthropologie,* 2d ed. (Frankfurt am Main: Enke, 1968).
41. "Damuka," *Das Deutsche Blatt,* 16 May 1907, GSPK, Rep 120 E XVI.2. 13Ag Adh.
42. "Ausstellungswesen," *Der Reichsanzeiger,* 16 May 1907, GSPK, Rep 120 E XVI.2. 13Ag Adh.
43. "Die Deutsche Armee-, Marine- und Kolonial-Ausstellung, II.," uncited newspaper clipping, 30 June 1907, ABerM, Ausstellungen I.12.24a 1906/07.
44. *Berliner Lokal-Anzeiger,* no. 292, 12 June 1907, and no. 293, 12 June 1907.
45. Alfred Scholze, "Verlorene Ideale," *Welt am Montag,* 17 June 1907, GSPK Rep 120 E XVI.2. 13Ag Adh.

Fig. 7. "Caravan Parade at the German Army, Marine, and Navy Exhibition, Special Exhibition 'Africa,'" 1907. (Source: Karl Markus Kreis Private Collection.)

hunt."[46] Other newspapers responded to the metaphor of a "revolt" and "slave hunt" by indicating their level of dissatisfaction with the state's approach to colonial politics—despite the fact that the North Africans had nothing to do with Germany's colonies. "By no means was there a revolt," corrected the *Tägliche Rundschau*.[47] Voicing the concerns of their largely Protestant middle-class readership, the national conservative paper identified what they saw as the real problem behind the scandal: too much schnapps.[48] Because alcohol was considered by advocates of prohibition to be a racial poison, arguments against alcohol combined concerns about public health and morality.[49] The *BZ am Mittag*, however, contradicted the conservative paper's moralism, claiming that drunkenness was not specifically

---

46. Ibid.
47. *Tägliche Rundschau*, 13 June 1907.
48. Ibid.
49. J. S. Roberts, *Drink, Temperance, and the Working-Class in Nineteenth-Century Germany* (Boston: Allen & Unwin, 1984); and Paul Weindling, *Health, Race and German Politics between National Unification and Nazism, 1870–1945* (Cambridge: Cambridge University Press, 1989), 175–77.

148   *Worldly Provincialism*

an African problem since "that supposedly happens to civilized whites as well."[50]

Voicing a socialist critique of colonialism, the *BZ am Mittag* also posed questions about the individual rights of the African performers and focused on the dramatic capture of the North Africans as though they were slaves.[51] "After all," they argued "we do live in a civilized state where it is not generally the practice to forcefully capture someone and bring them back to their employer."[52] Although the performers received salaries, their contract was laden with obligations and responsibilities and "almost no rights."[53] Marquardt's response, that such a strict contract was a necessary measure "due to the difficult character of the natives," found support among proponents of a firm and authoritarian colonial administration.[54] In support of the enclosure and physical regulation of the performers, one paper agreed that "strict discipline and order are absolutely necessary since such people, even when they make a very good impression, do not necessarily qualify as the best of their race."[55]

Questions about the character of the African performers, their rights to move about freely, and the merits of colonial empire indicates the variety of interests surrounding the *Völkerschauen*. But the pressing concerns about the audience, specifically the female spectators who had played a role in the "uprising," are perhaps the most revealing. As it turned out, a number of German women had avidly joined the liberated North Africans in the streets of Berlin. And while the specific conduct of their non-European companions hardly attracted attention in the press, the behavior of these women did. Indeed, the behavior of the "questionable white representatives of the fair sex" became a focal point in the criticism of the Damuka *Völkerschau*, suggesting the degree to which the sphere of commercial ethnography had come to signify the unbridled excesses of the lower classes.[56]

The satirical postcard in figure 8 illustrates this stereotyped coarticulation of gender and class in middle-class discourses about popular anthropology. Produced as a memento for Hagenbeck's park in Ham-

---

50. "Modernes Sklavenleben."
51. Ibid.
52. The report mentions that servant girls and youth were an exception to this rule (ibid.).
53. Ibid.
54. "Modernes Sklavenleben."
55. "Die Deutsche Armee-, Marine- und Kolonial-Ausstellung, II."
56. *Tägliche Rundschau,* 13 June 1907.

Fig. 8. "No Racial Hatred at Hagenbeck's. Who's that Nibbling at my House."
(Source: Karl Markus Kreis Private Collection.)

burg sometime in the first decade of the twentieth century, the caption jestingly claimed that at the *Völkerschau,* one would not find "racial hatred" *(Rassenhaß)* since the "white ladies" did not discriminate in their "attempts to get close to the Bedouin men" who performed there.[57] Female sexuality in the public sphere challenged the norms of bourgeois respectability, and the perceived lapse in female propriety was immediately seen as an enigma of working-class identity. Commodified sites of exoticized mass entertainment became identified with the erosion of appropriate civic and moral conduct. The *Völkerschau* emerged as a space of dangerous working-class sociability, at least in the minds of its middle-class patrons. The gendered dimension of this bourgeois preoccupation was made particularly clear by one of the more expressive (and insulting) writers on the subject of "Wild Africa," the teacher and journalist Alfred Scholz.[58] In the wake of the Damuka "uprising," he composed the following for the newspaper *Welt am Montag:*

---

57. "Annäherungsversuche weißer Damen an die Beduinen bei Hagenbeck." "Kein Rassenhaß bei Hagenbeck," Karl Markus Kreis Private Collection.
58. *Deutscher Biographischer Index,* 2d ed. (Munich: K. G. Saur, 1988), 7:8182.

Natürlich in dem Negerdorf
Gibt's keine weiße Frauen,
Da sind sie alle schwarz wie Torf
und garstig anzuschauen.
Nun hat der Nigger, wie bekannt
App'tit auf weiße Ware;
Die Frauen aber hier zu Land
Lieben pervers das Rare.
Nun ka[u]ern wieder sie vereint
Im Hottentottenkrale
Und unsere Damenwelt beweint:
"Verlorene Ideale."[59]

Scholz drew on contemporary clichés of a corporeal and untamed African sexuality.[60] Dismayed at a budding sexual revolution, scientific research on the nature of women's sexual drive, and the public discourse on prostitution, the patrons of traditional middle-class morality feared the behavior of the local German women in the Damuka "uprising" to be that which would lead to the nation's decline. In the fantasies of writers such as Scholz, the "white representatives of the fair sex" were responsible for seducing African men and colonial subjects. The "women here at home" failed to embody the virtues of the *Bürgertum* and the German nation. In his eyes, these "public" women lacked the middle-class virtues of self-discipline, restraint, and propriety. Indeed, Scholz's commentary can be read as an attack on the growing women's movement, which included female demands for sexual emancipation. While German women might have lamented the "lost ideals" of African masculinity after the men were brought back to the exhibition enclosure, Scholz used the same metaphor to comment on his own perception of the "lost ideals" of bourgeois womanhood.

Complaints about the behavior of women at the 1907 *Völkerschau*

---

59. A verbatim translation of the German poem follows: "Of course, in the Negro village, / There are no White women, / There they are all black as tar, / And loathsome to look at. / But the Nigger, as is known, / Has an appetite for White goods; / The women here however, / Perversely love the rarity. / They crouch again together, / In the Hottentot kraal, / And our ladyhood laments: 'Lost ideals'" (i.e., beauty and manhood). Alfred Scholz, "Verlorene Ideale," *Welt am Montag,* 17 June 1907, GSPK, Rep 120 E XVI.2. 13Ag Adh.

60. Stereotypes of Africans are discussed in Amadou Booker Sajdi, *Das Bild des Negro-Afrikaners in der deutschen Kolonialliteratur: Ein Beitrag zur literarischen Imagologie Schwarzafrikas* (Berlin: Dietrich Reimer, 1985).

were much shriller than at the turn of the century and were bound up with growing concerns about public behavior and mass culture in general. In the turn-of-the-century discourse, female impropriety was identified first and foremost as a proletarian characteristic. Indeed, it was "the masses" that consumed alcohol, were sexually promiscuous, and were bearers of proletarian—and specifically *unbürgerliche* behavior. However, in 1907, when the sphere of commercial ethnography had supposedly been largely abandoned by the *Bürgertum,* complaints about perverse and decadent sexual tastes addressed the supposed tastes of the "New Woman"—that is, emancipated bourgeois women.[61] Thus, in a confusing slippage of class associations that identified female impropriety as a proletarian characteristic and that simultaneously relied on the rhetoric associated with critics of the middle-class women's movement, the gendered crowd was accused of behaving in ways that contradicted bourgeois norms.[62] For the critics of the *Völkerschau,* the crowd appeared to embrace a proletarian identity in the public sphere. At worst, it behaved instinctually, irrationally, and shamefully, and its comportment could be read as a direct rejection of middle-class norms. Hence, the sphere of commercial ethnography came to be construed as a genuine threat to bourgeois progress and national well-being.

Visual Consumption and the Criticism of *Schaulust*

The Damuka "uprising," emerged as a moment for the middle-class press to express their attitudes and anxieties about social regulation, race relations, and sexuality. The ways in which these criticisms shifted from the performances to German society also reveal that during the

---

61. An extensive analysis of the gendered dimension of the rhetoric of commercial ethnography is beyond the scope of this essay.
62. Regarding the role of the crowd as a means of public articulation, see Mark Harrison, "The Ordering of the Urban Environment: Time, Work, and the Occurrence of the Crowd, 1790–1835," *Past and Present* 110 (1986): 134–68; George Rudé, *The Crowd in History: A Study of Popular Disturbances in France and England, 1730–1848* (New York: Wiley, 1964); Natalie Zemon Davis, "The Rites of Violence: Religious Riot in Sixteenth-Century France," *Past and Present* 59 (1973): 51–91; E. P. Thompson, "The Moral Economy of the English Crowd in the Eighteenth Century," *Past and Present* 50 (1971): 76–136. Works of this kind in German history include Thomas Lindenberger, *Straßenpolitik: Zur Sozialgeschichte der öffentlichen Ordnung in Berlin, 1900–1914* (Bonn: Verlag J. H. W. Dietz Nachfolger, 1995); and Belinda Davis, *Home Fires Burning: Food, Politics, and Everyday Life in World War I Berlin* (Chapel Hill: University of North Carolina Press, 2000).

Völkerschau, society too was on display. Although the growing lower middle classes and the working classes had become the major targets for impresarios, the pricing, press coverage, and character of the special events of Damuka indicate that the entire spectrum of the population converged at the 1907 *Völkerschau.*[63] Despite the established consensus that commercial ethnography belonged to a proletarian milieu after the turn of the century, it nevertheless continued to be frequented by the middle classes and continued to be an arena of concern to the *Bürgertum.* The episode of the "Damuka uprising" thus exposed how the *Völkerschau* functioned as a tenaciously popular site in which the tensions in a changing and modernizing German society continued to flare up.

Nevertheless, a major transformation had taken place in the cultural associations of the *Völkerschau.* While the organizers of the German Colonial Exhibition in 1896, for example, had attempted to articulate the role of ethnography and anthropology in the nation's colonial project, the producers of Damuka made little effort to display the anthropological aspects of Germany's colonial empire. In part, the shift that occurred around the turn of the century can be traced to commercial ethnography's changed style of presentation. After the turn of the century, *Völkerschau* pamphlets no longer featured scientific prose that encouraged an "objective" view, the mode of looking, observing, and gazing associated with bourgeois sensibilities. Instead, the new brochures moved away from an effort at teaching spectators how to see, describing instead what the observer should see, smell, and hear. Spectators were no longer encouraged to participate as critical observers but rather were animated to lose themselves in the event.

Such behavior did not correspond in any way to the class-specific norms of rational and discriminating behavior. It was this shift in visual consumption and spectatorship—a shift that had already been under way during the last part of the nineteenth century—that incurred the wrathful charges that the commercial ethnographic exhibition had become a realm of *Schaulust,* or ogling voyeurism, rather than popular education. Indeed, even members of the entertainment industry admitted that, by the turn of the century, spectators at ethnographic exhibitions "don't notice the variations in the body structure

---

63. Like the fees for the larger "Damuka" exhibition, entrance prices for "Wild Africa" also ranged from fifty pfennigs to 1.50 marks, suggesting that a broad spectrum of the population was able to attend the event (Mühlberg, *Arbeiterleben um 1900,* 123–27).

of the strangers nor the oftentimes greatly differentiated structures of their houses and the like."[64] In fact, they claimed to agree with their critics that one should "keep at bay that element of the public that only goes to such presentations because of their *Schaulust*."[65]

At the heart of the criticisms of commercial ethnography was a middle-class concern about the loss of cultural capital—particularly the definitional control over *schauen* (looking), contemplative observation, and judicious learning. These characteristics of *Bildung* played a significant role in public comportment and symbolic identity in the nineteenth century. It was not just the association with the supposedly proletarian public that tainted the *Völkerschau*, but also the perception that commercial ethnography had come to be marketed to an uncritical and irrational society. Branded a "most extravagant carnival . . . that entailed so much nonsense of the highest order that it will be remembered for years to come as a joke and spectacle," the 1907 exhibition confirmed the worst of its critics' fears.[66] Indeed, criticisms of the unruly behavior of the public and its *Schaulust* underscored middle-class anxieties about the role of mass culture in the transformation of the respectable sphere of popular science. Amid growing concerns regarding crowd behavior and mass culture, Damuka was far from being considered a site of bourgeois edification.

On the contrary, the "Damuka uprising" was seen as just another commercial spectacle—a spectacle that obviously featured the indigenous on show, but also included the gawking and *schaulustiges* public, the agents marketing Damuka and "Wild Africa," and the *bürgerliche* press. Indeed, as evidenced in the case of Damuka, it was not only the *Völkerschau* that provided a dramatized display for the masses. The masses also constructed the spectacle. Thus, another element of commercial ethnography's affiliation with consumerism and the entertainment industry was the changing relationship of the public to the spectacle. Commercial ethnography asserted the theatricality of its performers as well as the role of the spectators—both at the exhibition and through the press—as part of the representation itself.

In conclusion, the sensationalizing of commercial ethnography indicates that the gaze of the educated middle-class had been largely discarded for one that emphasized consumption over contemplation. In

---

64. "Die Schaustellung fremder Völkerschaften," *Der Komet*, no. 867, 2 November 1900.
65. Ibid.
66. *Breslauer Zeitung*, 16 May 1907, GHKP, Rep 120 E XVI.2. 13Ag.

the early years of commercial ethnography, scientists and the general population had intermingled, each had engaged in some sort of "scholarly" endeavor that relied either on methodologies of established scientific institutions or the cultivated gaze of the lay person. As such, *Völkerschauen* had offered a peculiar combination of "field research" and popular entertainment. Here, both scientists and the public could observe their non-European counterparts and draw conclusions about similarities and differences. Up until about the 1890s, commercial ethnography had functioned as an arena in which popular scientific knowledge was produced and in which civic values and social norms were symbolically reproduced. By the turn of the century, however, the *Völkerschau* had come to connote a public of intoxicated workers and sexually promiscuous women. As middle-class commentators complained about the ongoing proletarianization of culture, the *Völkerschau* lost its status as a bourgeois vehicle of leisure and learning. Instead, commercial ethnography came to be associated as a form of "Tingl-Tangl," a term emphasizing the nexus of commerce and display in such amusements as vaudeville, the circus, and the cabaret.[67] While *Völkerschau* impresarios continued to promote their product as a means of edification, its increasing theatricality, both in presentation of scientific material and the comportment of its audience, pushed it outside the cultivated sphere of the *Bildungsbürgertum*.

Once the link between commercial ethnography and middle-class science was broken, however, the *Völkerschau* would never regain the respectability that had rendered it the principal site of popular anthropology in late-nineteenth-century Germany. Thus, turn-of-the-century opponents of the *Völkerschau* argued that consumer taste and not scientific or political edification had moved to the forefront of commercial ethnography. It was not just the association with capitalism and money that tainted the *Völkerschau*. It was also the perception that commercial ethnography had come to be marketed for a proletarian *Schaulust* and a consuming rather than contemplative gaze. One of the

---

67. For a contemporary discussion of the "Tingl-Tangl," see Hans Ostwald, *Großstadt-Dokumente* (Berlin: H. Seeman Nachf., 1905). See Wolfgang Jansen's discussion of "Die Rätsel 'Tingeltangel,'" in *Das Varieté*, 55–62. Also see Abrams, *Workers' Culture*. The literature on consumption and the displays of department stores is extensive. See Rosalind Williams, *Dream Worlds: Mass Consumption in Late Nineteenth-Century France* (Berkeley and Los Angeles: University of California Press, 1982); Rachel Bowlby, *Just Looking: Consumer Culture in Dreiser, Gissing, and Zola* (New York: Methuen, 1985); Michael Miller, *The Bon Marché: Bourgeois Culture and the Department Store, 1869–1920* (Princeton: Princeton University Press, 1981).

most disturbing elements of modern leisure culture for the *Bürgertum* was not simply that class differences blurred as various publics milled about in the same civic sphere. Moreover, preconceived distinctions between the German spectators and their African counterparts onstage were obscured. Reflecting on his participation as part of the *Völkerschau* audience, one observer of "Wild Africa" wrote:

> If you look a little more closely at the faces of these [African] people during their performance, you begin to feel truly uneasy. The superior smile of the Arabian and the sneering grin of the Negro say quite frankly: "What stupid people you Europeans are who take this hocus pocus seriously and even pay money [to see it]."[68]

---

68. "Kolonial-Ausstellung," *Die Freiheit,* no. 6, 27 May 1907, GSPK, Rep 120 E XVI.2. 13Ag Adh.

Adventures in the Skin Trade: German Anthropology and Colonial Corporeality

ANDREW ZIMMERMAN

> Now that we have become a seafaring people and have increased our colonies with great speed, we are compelled to deal with our new compatriots, to bring ourselves into an intellectual *(geistige)* relationship with them, and to learn to appreciate them, at least with respect to their heads and brains.
> —Rudolf Virchow

German physical anthropology was not only a science and an ideology but also one of the practical regimes that sustained, and were sustained by, European colonial rule.[1] Anthropology both created and presupposed certain relationships between colonizing and colonized bodies, constituted by asymmetrical practices of measuring, representing, and collecting.[2] The discipline thus depended upon, and gave meaning to, the

---

The author wishes to thank Glenn Penny and Lora Wildenthal for their comments on earlier drafts of this essay.

1. I use such apparently circular formulations as *sustained/sustained by* to render in narrative what is essentially a nonnarrative, structuralist explanation. I follow, among others, Louis Althusser in regarding chronological accounts of cause and effect as inadequate to the logic of social formations. I am thus interested in how anthropology formed part of a larger imperialist social formation, rather than in determining whether anthropology was a cause or an effect of this formation. The latter I regard as a misleading demand for an answer that can only be a simplification confusing history and chronology. For a detailed theoretical explication of the analysis of social formations, see Louis Althusser and Étienne Balibar, *Reading Capital,* trans. Ben Brewster (London: Verso, 1997).

2. Before the First World War, the disciplinary terminology of German anthropology

institutions of colonial violence, including prisons, battlefields, and concentration camps. The routes by which the bodies of non-Europeans were made accessible to anthropological knowledge in Germany show the practical interdependence of physical anthropology and colonial rule.

Before considering these routes I will describe the basic project of physical anthropology in Germany, with a look at the bodily relations of knowledge in techniques of measurement and representation. The "skin trade" that gives the title to this essay is the political economy of human body parts that supplied anthropologists with data for their empiricist project. The role of physical anthropology in colonial rule can be traced in the campaign to exterminate the Herero of German South West Africa, perhaps the first explicitly genocidal policy ever.[3]

Historians of German anthropology have tended to divide the discipline's history into a liberal phase, associated with Rudolf Virchow, and a racist and imperialist phase, associated with Eugen Fischer.[4] Not

---

was less clear than it is today, when *Anthropologie* refers to what English speakers call physical anthropology and *Ethnologie* refers to what English speakers call cultural or social anthropology. In the nineteenth century there were many competing uses of the terms. *Anthropologie* could mean a philosophical discussion of the general nature of humankind or an anatomical, materialist discussion of the human body. *Ethnologie* referred to a broader study of ethnic groups. Because the best-remembered theorist of German *Ethnologie,* Adolf Bastian, did not pursue craniometry, it is commonly held that *Ethnologie* excluded the physical studies I discuss in this essay. However, Bastian explicitly included what we would today call physical anthropology in his programmatic discussion "Das natürliche System in der Ethnologie," *Zeitschrift für Ethnologie* 1 (1869): 1–23. Indeed, he proclaimed: "Much better the round skull of craniology than some philological tailbone" (2). Although Bastian was personally less interested in bones than in artifacts, he did not wish to restrict his colleagues to following his individual research interests. I will follow the anthropologists of imperial Germany in considering *Anthropologie* as a single discipline, although in this essay I focus on what one might today call "physical anthropology."

3. Robert Gordon connects questions of physical anthropology, notions of race and gender, and the origins of Nazi genocide in "The Rise of the Bushman Penis: Germans, Genitalia and Genocide," *African Studies* 57 (1998): 27–54.

4. For this liberal to racism historiography in physical anthropology, see Benoit Massin, "From Virchow to Fischer: Physical Anthropology and 'Modern Race Theories' in Wilhelmine Germany," in *Volksgeist as Method and Ethic: Essays on Boasian Ethnography and the German Anthropological Tradition,* ed. George W. Stocking Jr. (Madison: University of Wisconsin Press, 1996), 79–154; Robert N. Proctor, "From *Anthropologie* to *Rassenkunde* in the German Anthropological Tradition," in *Bones, Bodies Behavior: Essays on Biological Anthropology,* ed. George W. Stocking Jr. (Madison: University of Wisconsin Press, 1988), 138–79; Paul Weindling, *Health, Race, and German Politics between National Unification and Nazism, 1870–1945* (Cambridge: Cambridge University Press, 1989). For the argument that there was a shift from liberalism to ethnocentric imperialism in German anthropology, see Woodruff D. Smith, *Politics and the Sciences of Culture in Germany, 1840–1920* (Oxford: Oxford University Press, 1991).

only does this scheme propose a misleading opposition between liberalism on the one hand and racism and imperialism on the other, it also ignores the practices of anthropology, as if the discipline were a branch of speculative philosophy.[5] Both colonialism and anthropology tended toward a similar treatment of the colonized as pure body, pure objectivity. Treating the human as pure object was a defining theoretical feature of German anthropology, which considered itself a natural scientific discipline, opposed and superior to humanistic studies of humankind. It was also a feature of colonial politics, which denied non-Europeans full subjectivity and therefore full sovereignty. The heightened state of corporeality to which the colonized were subjected characterized and made possible both physical anthropology as a scientific discipline and colonialism as a form of political rule.[6]

Physical Anthropology as Objective Human Science

Anthropology emerged in Germany as a natural scientific challenge to the academic humanities. As I argued in my *Anthropology and Antihumanism in Imperial Germany,* the anthropological challenge to humanism and the humanities was part of a larger reorientation of German

---

5. For a view of physical anthropology more attentive to practice and less reliant on the liberalism/racism binary opposition, see my "Anti-Semitism as Skill: Rudolf Virchow's *Schulstatistik* and the Racial Composition of Germany," *Central European History* 32, no. 4 (1999): 409–29.

6. The relationship between anthropology and imperialism has received such extensive and varied treatment that no note could adequately summarize it. My own view of this relationship has been shaped primarily by three authors, Talal Asad, Edward Said, and Nicholas Thomas. Asad has cautioned that the relationship between anthropology and colonialism is complex and often contradictory, and is not exhausted merely by understanding the varying opinions anthropologists held about colonial rule. He emphasizes that anthropology must be understood within the larger context of an "unequal power encounter between the West and Third World which goes back to the emergence of bourgeois Europe." Talal Asad, *Anthropology and the Colonial Encounter* (New York: Humanities Press, 1973), 16. While Said's *Orientalism* (New York: Vintage, 1994) has inspired a tradition that reduces the relationship of anthropology and colonialism to a spectral realm of "images" of "others," the author himself has rejected this idealistic misreading of the problem and has called for a treatment of anthropology in the context of the politics of colonial domination and resistance. See especially "Representing the Colonized: Anthropology's Interlocutors," *Critical Inquiry* 15 (1989): 205–25. Finally, Nicholas Thomas has pointed out the importance of relations of exchange and cultures of objects in the construction of cultures and practices of colonialism. See *Entangled Objects: Exchange, Material Culture, and Colonialism in the Pacific* (Cambridge: Harvard University Press, 1991).

society marked by the growth of urban mass culture, ideologically driven natural science, and European imperialism.[7] In this essay I am especially interested in the connection between imperialism and antihumanism. Anthropologists were, for the most part, natural scientists and physicians who regarded conventional humanistic scholarship, above all historiography, as overly "subjective" because of its focus on the philological interpretation of literary documents. Adolf Bastian, the premiere theorist of German anthropology in the last third of the nineteenth century, criticized historians for never rising above self-referentiality, doing no more than interpreting their ancestors' own self-interpretations:

> Since history must constantly orbit in narrow circles around the center of its own national consciousness *(Volksbewusstsein)* it can never escape subjectivity, neither in its subject matter nor in relation to the historian himself.[8]

Because historians interpreted their own past and the documents they interpreted were self-representations of that past, they could never establish a perspective on their subjects that was not already implicated in their own subjectivity. Anthropology would, by contrast, be objective because it would consider "others" held to differ fundamentally from the modern European "self" and consider objects rather than texts. Anthropology, according to Bastian, would thus maintain "a standpoint of pure objective observation, sharply distinguished from history, which cannot rid itself of a subjective coloration, because it is based on 'research into motives.'"[9]

Physical anthropology, more than any other branch of the discipline, allowed anthropologists to construct what they regarded as a natural scientific alternative to subjective historical narratives. The anthropologist Robert Hartmann warned against a "blind preference for 'historical method'" since the documents on which historians based their accounts often contained self-congratulatory exaggerations or even lies. As a more secure source of knowledge about the human past

---

7. Andrew Zimmerman, *Anthropology and Antihumanism in Imperial Germany* (Chicago: University of Chicago Press, 2001).

8. Adolf Bastian, *Ethnologie und Geschichte in ihren Berührungspunkten unter Bezugnahme auf Indien,* vol. 2 of *Ideale Welten in Wort und Bild* (Berlin: Emil Felber, 1892), 21.

9. Ibid., 27.

Hartmann recommended "the examination of the physical properties of humans."[10] Anthropologists thought that characterizations of human groups based on physical traits, especially skull form, would allow them to reconstruct the historical relations among various populations independently from those societies' own self-representations in historical documents.[11] (They made similar assertions about their use of artifacts, a method that became especially important after the development of diffusionism in the early twentieth century.) Anthropologists based this objective study not on analyses of supposedly typical or representative objects but rather on massive collections that they endeavored to assemble in Germany. Hartmann thus mocked the lone scholar who takes "this or that cranium" and "measures, describes, draws, and with childish joy catalogs it in one of the usual craniological categories."[12] While today we might imagine that anthropology consists of empathetic interpretations of individual social groups, for the discipline's nineteenth-century German practitioners the science was based on what were regarded as objective observations of centralized collections.

Anthropologists' attempts to grasp the people they studied as natural scientific objects paralleled the ideological move fundamental to every colonial project, the attempt to deny full subjectivity to the indigenous inhabitants of the colony. At the most basic level, colonial sovereignty presupposed that the inhabitants of the colonies were not legislative agents in the same sense as inhabitants of the metropole. Whereas European subjects were subjected to the disciplinary human sciences so brilliantly characterized by Foucault as "biopower"—the power over life rather than over death—the colonized were subjected to less humanistic forms of administration. In contrast to European subjects, the colonized were routinely denied the "soul" that would become, in Foucault's phrase, a "prison of the body."[13] This refusal to

---

10. Robert Hartmann, "Untersuchungen über die Völkerschaften Nord-Ost-Afrikas," *Zeitschrift für Ethnologie (ZfE)* 1 (1869): 31–32.

11. For an example of this type of inquiry, see the Berlin Anthropological Society's discussion of the origin of the inhabitants of the Sudan in *Verhandlungen der Berliner Gesellschaft für Anthropologie, Ethnologie und Urgeschichte (VBGAEU)* 10 (1878): 333–55, 387–407.

12. Hartmann, "Untersuchungen über die Völkerschaften Nord-Ost-Afrikas," 33.

13. Michel Foucault, *Discipline and Punish: The Birth of the Prison,* trans. Alan Sheridan (New York: Vintage Books, 1977), 30. On this productive disjuncture between Foucault's analysis and European colonialism, see Megan Vaughan, *Curing Their Ills: Colonial Power and African Illness* (Cambridge: Polity Press, 1991). See also Ann Laura Stoler, *Race and the Education of Desire: Foucault's History of Sexuality and the Colonial Order of Things* (Durham: Duke University Press, 1995).

grant political subjectivity was invariably overlaid with, and legitimated by, an ethnocentrism that denied non-Europeans full humanity. German anthropology advanced one of the most blatant forms such denial could take: the indigenous inhabitants of sub-Saharan Africa, the Pacific islands, and the Americas were regarded as "natural peoples" *(Naturvölker)*, societies without history or civilization *(Kultur)*.[14] This differed from, for example, British notions of primitive culture, which represented the colonized as a very early stage of a universal process of development. For Germans, the "natural peoples" were out of history entirely. In this context, change did not mean development but rather that the "natural peoples" would, in the words of Adolf Bastian, "succumb to a quick physical decline and die out."[15] Anthropologists' methodological critique of humanist historicism was sustained by an imperialist project that denied full humanity to colonized societies.

Problems of the Flesh: Photographs, Calipers, and Plaster Casts

For German anthropologists, the task of transforming the colonized subject into a natural scientific object was a real, technical problem of their discipline. It was this problem of scientific methodology rather than its ideological connotations that inspired anthropologists to work out the practices of what I am calling colonial corporeality. The paradox of anthropology as a natural science of humanity was that its attempts to grasp historical human subjects as ahistorical, natural objects depended upon numerous intersubjective negotiations and historical interventions. At least in the nineteenth and early twentieth centuries, the physical anthropological object was a coproduction of colonizers and colonized, enabled by the history of European imperialism. The most common—and, for anthropologists, least satisfactory—physical anthropological objects were representations such as pho-

---

14. Anthropologists did also study and display in museums the artifacts of what they regarded as the *Kulturvölker* of India, China, and ancient South and Central America. They included these societies, they explained, because they were traditionally ignored by academic humanists and expected that one day they would be recognized as disciplines separate from anthropology. See Wilhelm Grübe (directoral assistant in the East Asian section of the Berlin museum), memo, 24 March 1888, Archiv des Museums für Völkerkunde, Berlin (MfV), VII, vol. 1., 129/88; Eduard Seler (directorial assistant in the ancient American section of the Berlin museum and professor at the University of Berlin) to the Philosophical Faculty, 7 November 1911, HU, Phil. Fak., 196, Promotionen, Bl. 299.

15. Reported in Richard Schöne to Wilhelm von Gossler, 23 May 1885, GStA PK, I. HA, Rep. 76Ve, Cultusministerium, Sekt. 15, Abt. XI, Nr. 2, Bd. 6, Bl. 32–33 (M).

tographs, anthropometric measurements, and plaster casts of living individuals.

Photographs provided anthropologists with a fairly easily obtainable, and apparently objective, representation of the people they studied. Late-nineteenth-century anthropologists were themselves often accomplished photographers and viewed the camera as a way to check the "artistic hand" that had made earlier anthropological drawings unreliable sources of knowledge.[16] Despite their wide use of photography, however, anthropologists were anything but naive realists and were particularly concerned that the optical distortions of the camera made it impossible to take accurate anthropometric measurements from photographs.[17] Furthermore, photography presented anthropologists with a difficulty endemic to their discipline: grasping humans as objects required negotiations with human subjects. Even if a photographer could persuade an individual to be photographed, the subject often refused to remove his or her clothing, which obscured the anthropometric dimensions. Thus, on a trip to South Africa, Gustav Fritsch, perhaps the greatest proponent of anthropological photography, found that even those people he could convince to stand before his camera were not always willing to undress:

> The desired goal regarding disrobing could not always be reached, in that various circumstances imposed themselves on the process. In very few cases was it the feeling of shame that one had to combat, but rather, especially among the chiefs and the students of the mission schools, extraordinary pride in the rags that civilization had hung on them, and those who are clothed often appear in European dress.[18]

Fritsch, like many anthropologists, had to rely on colonial prisons, mission schools, and the farmhands of a local European to get most, if not all, of the subjects for his study.[19]

---

16. Gustav Fritsch, review of *Anthropologisch-ethnologisches Album in Photographien Herausgegeben mit Unterstützung aus der Sammlung der Berliner Anthropologischen Gesellschaft,* by C. Dammann, *ZfE* 6 (1874): 67–69.

17. On the problem of photography and visual representation in anthropology, see my "Looking beyond History: The Optics of German Anthropology and the Critique of Humanism," *Studies in History and Philosophy of Biological and Biomedical Sciences* 32 (2001): 385–411.

18. Gustav Fritsch, *Die Eingeborenen Süd-Afrika's* (Breslau: Ferdinand Hirt, Königliche Universitäts- und Verlags-Buchhandlung, 1872), 4.

19. See Fritsch's descriptions of the subjects of the photographs in *Die Eingeborenen Süd-Afrika's.*

Anthropologists had no access to individuals outside the ordinary channels of colonial government. For example, when the anthropologist Felix von Luschan traveled to South Africa in 1905, he visited a prison where he found "perhaps a greater number of Bushmen, Hottentots and Griqua . . . than had ever before been placed at the comfortable disposal of a scientific traveler."[20] Colonial prison hospitals provided frequent occasions for measuring and collecting, and Virchow and other professors of medicine who were interested in anthropology steered their students toward the colonial service to take advantage of this opportunity.[21] The photography collection of the Berlin Anthropological Society contains a number of photographs of prostitutes, presumably because there were preexisting routines for viewing them without clothing.[22] However, even individuals already subjected to European power did not always willingly cooperate with anthropologists, even for the relatively painless process of photography.

Anthropometric measurements, provided they were taken by a trustworthy individual, gave anthropologists more useful data than photography. Measurements of a living individual obviously did not present the same problems of distorted proportions that photography did. However, it was difficult to convince people to submit to the lengthy and often uncomfortable procedures associated with anthropometric investigations. Anthropologists wanted measurements reflecting the dimensions of the skeleton exclusive of the flesh, since the amount of flesh on a body resulted from eating habits and other apparently individual and subjective factors. Thus to take measurements on the living, one had to tighten the calipers until the flesh was pinched to a negligible thinness.[23] In his attempts to measure Africans and Pacific

---

20. Luschan, "Bericht über eine im Sommer 1905 ausgeführte Reise in Süd Afrika," in Bundesarchiv Potsdam (BAP), Auswärtiges Amt, 37582, Bl. 109. See the similar comments on taking measurements from colonial chain gangs in a letter of Adolf Bastian (in Batavia) to Rudolf Virchow, 19 November 1873, NL Virchow 117, Bl. 3–4 (part 1).

21. In the period before Germany took colonies, Bastian discussed sending medical students to the Dutch colonial service in a letter to Virchow of September 1879 and November 1879, Nachlaß Rudolf Virchows, Akademie der Wissenschaften, Berlin (NL Virchow), 117 (part 1). Virchow's colleague in the medical faculty of the University of Berlin, Wilhelm Waldeyer, writes of former students currently in the military in German East Africa who wish to collect for him in a letter to the Foreign Office, 2 January 1892, BAP, Reichskolonialamt, 6109, Bl. 52.

22. "Aktstudien von Rasse Typen meist aufgenommen durch Prof. Gustav Fritsch," box in Archiv der Berliner Gesellschaft für Anthropologie, Ethnologie und Urgeschichte.

23. Felix von Luschan, "Anthropologie, Ethnologie und Urgeschichte," in Anleitung zu Wissenschaftlichen Beobachtungen Auf Reisen in Einzel-Abhandlungen, ed. Georg von Neumayer, 3d ed. (Hannover: Dr. Max Jänecke, Verlagsbuchhandlung, 1906), 37–38.

Islanders performing at the 1896 Colonial Exhibition, Felix von Luschan found that "a general difficulty... lay in the great aversion of most people to letting themselves be measured, and in the complete impossibility of exercising any coercion over them."[24] He felt that very good measurements could only be gotten from slaves, who had no choice but to accept the pain of accurate measurement, or from corpses.[25] However, most anthropometric investigators did not have the luxury of dealing only with slaves and corpses, and they therefore had to make compromises with subjects. For example, Luschan recommended avoiding measurements that required subjects to remove all of their clothes, since many people refused to be measured if they had to be naked.[26] He advised his contacts abroad to measure the strength of people in addition to their physical dimensions, because people often submitted to a whole battery of procedures so they could also test their strength on a dynamometer.[27]

One of the more novel solutions to transforming people from around the world into anthropological data was to take a plaster cast of their face, hands, and feet, or even of their whole body.[28] The technique was apparently pioneered by the traveler Hermann von Schlagintweit, who found that "such plastic models are especially good for comparisons, because they are totally objective" and eliminate the facial distortions that photography provoked "through the strong

---

24. Felix von Luschan, *Beiträge zur Völkerkunde der Deutschen Schutzgebiete. Erweiterte Sonderausgabe aus dem "Amtlichen Bericht über die Erste Deutsche Kolonial-Austellung" in Treptow 1896* (Berlin: Dietrich Reimer, 1897), 9.
25. Luschan, "Anthropologie, Ethnologie und Urgeschichte," 38.
26. Ibid., 5.
27. Luschan, "Anthropologie, Ethnologie und Urgeschichte," 31–32. One of Luschan's students noted about the dynamometer: "It is the only [measurement] that gives the subjects any joy and attracts them to measurement. They are driven by curiosity about their strength to submit willingly to the entire procedure of anthropological evaluation. That, more than its scientific value, is the significance of the dynamometer." Krum Drontschilow, *Beiträge zur Anthropologie der Bulgaren* (Braunschweig: Vieweg, 1914), 25. This dissertation is located in the archive of the Humboldt University, Philosophische Fakultät, Promotionsvorgänge, Nr. 553, Bl. 224–79.
28. On anthropological interest in hands and feet, see S. Weissenberg, "Über die Formen der Hand und des Fusses," *ZfE* 27 (1895): 82–111; Alexander Ecker, "Einige Bemerkungen über einen schwankenden Charakter in der Hand des Menschen," *Archiv für Anthropologie* 8 (1878): 67–74; Hans Virchow, "Graphische und plastische Aufnahme des Fusses," *VBGAEU* 18 (1886): 118–24; Eugen Zintgraff, "Kopfmessungen, Fussumrisse und photographische Aufnahmen in Kamerun, vorzugsweise von Wei- und Kru-Negern," *VBGAEU* 21 (1889): 85–98.

stimulation of the light or the customary request 'to remain completely still.'"[29] At the University of Berlin, Luschan taught this technique to students—many of whom were bound for German colonial service— by having visiting Africans and Pacific Islanders sit for a cast in his anthropology courses.[30] Making a plaster cast of a face took about forty minutes, during which time even pure gypsum plaster often began to irritate the skin. If the plaster was adulterated with lime, as it occasionally was, the process could cause serious burns.[31] Some anthropologists favored putting pieces of straw or rubber tubes in the nose of the subject to assist breathing, although others thought that this was not necessary and distorted the face too much.[32] It is not surprising that Otto Finsch, perhaps the most famous anthropological plaster caster, found that "in general a strong dislike prevails against the process of having a cast taken," making it expensive and occasionally dangerous for the collector.[33] Plaster casts gave anthropologists a virtual human body, which, once taken, could be studied without having to deal with a resistant subject. However, plaster casts, like photographs, were difficult to measure usefully, since they provided dimensions of flesh rather than skeletal structures.

Anthropological data not only relied upon, but also legitimized, the unequal power relations of colonialism. This may help explain the enthusiastic participation of the German navy in anthropology. Beginning as early as 1872, over a decade before Germany took its first colonies, and continuing into the twentieth century, the Admiralty welcomed requests for assistance in anthropological observation and collection. Albrecht von Stosch, the chief of the Admiralty, applauded "scientific activity" as a leisure-time pursuit for sailors.[34] This both

---

29. Hermann von Schlagintweit to Rudolf Virchow, 13 May 1873, in *Briefe an Rudolf Virchow* (Berlin: Litteraturarchiv-Gesellschaft, 1921), 47–48. Original in NL Virchow.
30. On the plaster casts Luschan made in his classes, see Luschan, memo, 6 June 1901, MfV, IB 39, vol. 1, 613/1900. On the makeup of one of Luschan's courses, see Luschan to the General Museum Administration, 27 December 1892, MfV, XIIa, vol. 1, 1560/92.
31. See Luschan, "Anthropologie, Ethnologie und Urgeschichte," 6–7.
32. See Franz Boas and Ales Hrdlicka, "Facial Casts," *American Anthropologist,* n.s. 7 (1905): 169; and Luschan, "Anthropologie, Ethnologie und Urgeschichte," 6.
33. Otto Finsch, *Gesichtsmasken von Völkertypen der Südsee und dem malayischen Archipel nach Leben abgegossen in den Jahren 1879–1882* (Bremen: Homeyer and Meyer, 1887), 2.
34. Stosch (Chief of the Admiralty) to the Board of Directors of the Berlin Anthropological Society, 19 August 1872, *ZfE* 4 (1872): 4.

encouraged officers to behave virtuously and distinguished them from ordinary sailors, who had a reputation for wanton rowdiness.[35] Still, the kind of intimacy born of extreme power differences that found expression in sexual exploits had a kind of equivalent among officers and doctors conducting anthropological inquiries. At the conclusion of a physical anthropological questionnaire written by the Berlin Anthropological Society for the navy, which mostly called for precise numerical measurements, the investigator was requested to give unspecified "information" about "the ears, the nose, the mouth, the breasts or chest, the belly, the external genitals, the buttocks, the form of the hands, calves, feet."[36] Berlin anthropologists appear to have drawn on a navy tradition much older than their own science. Anthropology may have found such enthusiastic cooperation in the navy because it gave a certain dignity to forms of colonial corporeality already practiced by sailors.

Photography, the measurement of living subjects, and plaster casting all sought to render human subjects as objects. Anthropologists relied on colonial relations of domination and subordination to obtain this objective data from subjects who often resisted, for example by refusing to stand naked before the camera, defying anthropometric calipers, and rebuffing attempts to take casts of their faces. These representational techniques also lacked the precision anthropologists desired, for none of them gave access to skeletal dimensions. Body parts taken from individuals in the colonies and shipped to Germany, or from Africans and Pacific Islanders visiting Europe, thus provided the most important anthropological evidence. The dead could not resist anthropology, and their bodies presented a kind of direct access to objective humanity, unmediated by any representational technique.

The Skin Trade

The corpse was in many ways a perfection of anthropological evidence voided of subjectivity. It was not simply that corpses did not resist anthropologists' investigations, but also that they could be measured

---

35. This impression informed, for example, A. B. Meyer, an anthropologist traveling in New Guinea in the 1870s, who wrote to Virchow that he was disappointed to find that "the Papuas live under such strict moral laws that one can not even consider orgies such as those celebrated in the South Seas between sailors of whalers and warships etc. and the local girls." Adolf Bernhard Meyer to Rudolf Virchow, 22 October 1873, NL Virchow, 1429.

36. Virchow, Bastian, et al., "Ratschläge für anthropologische Untersuchung auf Expeditionen der Marine," *ZfE* 4 (1872): 325–56.

and collected in ways that living humans could not. As we have seen, human flesh represented a form of subjectivity that anthropologists rejected from their studies. Anthropologists tightened their measuring calipers as much as possible to get to the dimensions of bones, but the pain of accurate measurement limited the extent to which this technique could be employed. Corpses, on the other hand, could be stripped of flesh, a process that regularly occurred in the laboratories of the Berlin Museum of Ethnology.[37] Furthermore, these supposedly objective skulls or skeletons could be assembled into massive collections, presenting a comparative, centralized overview of the world's "races" that no individual studying living humans could ever have obtained. However, as with the techniques discussed in the previous section, anthropologists had to deal extensively with subjective, historical circumstances to obtain their objective, natural scientific data. In this "skin trade" anthropologists further participated in the bodily relations of colonialism. It was not simply that colonialism made anthropology possible, but rather that both colonial rule and anthropology worked together to create a corporeality that was fundamental to each.[38]

Anthropologists were interested in a wide range of body parts, although they strongly favored skulls. Rudolf Virchow, the head of the German and the Berlin Anthropological Societies, and Felix von Luschan, the curator of the African and Oceanic collections of the Berlin Museum of Ethnology, were the two most important collectors of physical anthropological objects in Germany. Their collections have been united in the Museum für Naturkunde in Berlin and today number more than six thousand skulls, as well as skeletons, hair samples, and at least one scalp. Virchow requested that travelers get fresh severed heads and mail them to Berlin in zinc containers filled with alcohol.[39] Otherwise anthropologists recommended a removal of most of the flesh before shipping, although this sometimes proved impossible

---

37. See Felix von Luschan to Sergeant Pietsch (German East Africa), 30 March 1907, MfV, IB 39, vol. 2, 64/97.

38. A corporeality that was also fundamental to medicine. See Ruth Richardson, *Death, Dissection, and the Destitute* (Chicago: University of Chicago Press, 2000). It was no accident that the majority of anthropologists were medical doctors. On the connection between anthropology, medicine, race, and genocide, see Weindling, *Health, Race;* and Robert N. Proctor, *Racial Hygiene: Medicine under the Nazis* (Cambridge: Harvard University Press, 1988).

39. Rudolf Virchow, "Anthropologie und prähistorische Forschungen," in *Anleitung zu Wissenschaftlichen Beobachtungen Auf Reisen,* ed. Georg von Neumayer (Berlin: Verlag von Robert Oppenheimer, 1875), 582–83.

and led to decomposing body parts being mailed to Germany.[40] Virchow also suggested collecting skin, hands, and feet at executions, hospitals, and battlefields; they could then be dried, salted, or preserved in sprits.[41] Hair was the easiest body part to collect and ship because it could be acquired from the living and did not decompose. In the collection of the Berlin Anthropological Society there were envelopes, test tubes, and cigar boxes full of hair, all labeled according to origin.[42]

The simplest way to acquire body parts for anthropological collections was through grave robbery. This was a common practice among travelers collecting for anthropological purposes, who often covertly exhumed corpses and shipped them to Berlin. In an article about the Coroados of Brazil, for example, the anthropologist Rheinhold Hensel expressed regret that he could only collect the skulls, but not the entire skeletons, from graves that he opened. "There was no time to collect the skeletons as well," he explained, "since I was afraid I would be surprised by the Indians."[43] The traveler and later museum director A. B. Meyer attempted to purchase skulls from the inhabitants of areas he visited. When he could not buy them, he stole them.[44] Often, depending upon local circumstances, anthropological collectors could hire indigenous laborers to rob graves. Luschan, for example, commented that in parts of German East Africa one could get a skeleton dug up for "a bright cloth or a piece of soap," but that in other regions grave robbers required a full day's wages or even "quite considerable sums of cash to appease any scruples."[45] Grave robbing thus often involved the cooperation of indigenous groups, who were thus also sometimes able to successfully deny anthropologists the corpses of their compatriots.

---

40. See Felix von Luschan to Sergeant Pietsch, German East Africa, 30 March 1907, MfV, IB 39, vol. 2, 64/97. For examples in which decomposing heads and bodies were mailed to Berlin, see Anneli Yaam to Luschan, 29 February 1904, MfV, IB 39, vol. 1, 461/01; Yaam to Luschan, 7 April 1904, MfV, IB 39, vol. 1, 657/04; Luschan to Yaam, 11 May 1904, MfV, IB 39, vol. 1, 579/04.

41. Virchow, "Anthropologie und prähistorische Forschungen."

42. A number of these hair samples are in the Museum für Naturkunde in Berlin. While working with Virchow's literary remains in the archive of the Academy of Sciences in Berlin I was also surprised by item 2693, "head hair samples, 7 bundles (no date)."

43. Reinhold Hensel, "Die Schädel der Corados," *Zeitschrift für Ethnologie* 2 (1870): 195–203.

44. Thus when writing of the 150 skulls he purchased in New Guinea, Meyer commented, "Here I did not have to steal them, as I did in the Philippines." A. B. Meyer to Rudolf Virchow, 22 October 1873, NL Virchow 1429.

45. Luschan to Herr Biallowons, German East Africa, 3 January 1907, MfV, IB 39, vol. 2, 2330/06.

Fig. 1. Rudolf Virchow with skull, by Hans Fechner, 1891. (Source: Tilmann Buddensieg et al., eds., *Wisenschaften in Berlin, Objekte* [Berlin: Begri. Mann Verlag, 1987], 109.)

For example, in 1911 residents of German Samoa learned that a number of their skulls had been stolen for anthropology collections in Berlin. They claimed this would cause them misfortune, so when a dysentery outbreak occurred among them they blamed it on the German official who took the skulls. The official asked Luschan to return the skulls so they could be reinterred. Luschan did so, but warned that the official should inquire first about what skulls they thought were

170   *Worldly Provincialism*

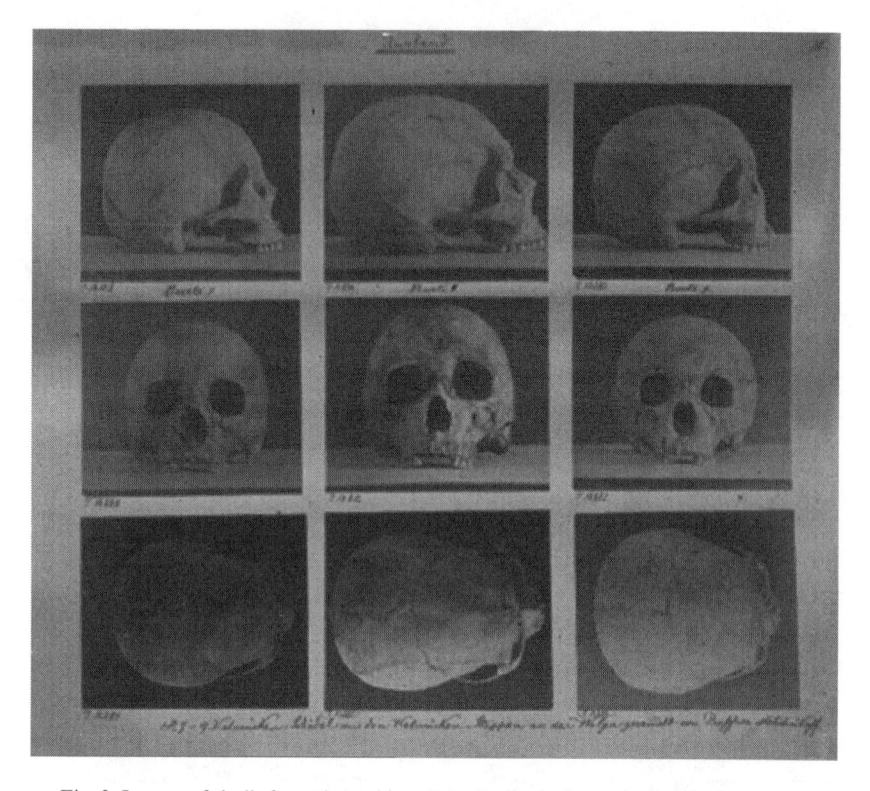

Fig. 2. Images of skulls from the archive of the Berlin Anthropological Society. Photo by Andrew Zimmerman.

missing, since if more were returned than the Samoans believed to have been stolen in the first place, they might become suspicious.[46]

Despite this cavalier attitude toward the bodies of the colonized, Luschan always sought to preserve an appearance of legality. He often worried that his requests for skulls would encourage enthusiastic collectors to murder individuals for their corpses. During a 1905 trip to South Africa on the occasion of a meeting of the British Association for the Advancement of Science, Luschan encouraged so many doctors and police officers to collect "Bushman" skeletons "that finally someone drew to my attention that it would be no wonder if in the next

---

46. Luschan to Dr. E. Schulz, Imperial Judge, Apia, Samoa, 30 January 1911; Schulz to Luschan, 22 March 1911 and 17 May 1911; Luschan to Shulz, 22 July 1911, MfV, IB 39, vol. 4, 168/11.

years a few Bushmen died before they became sick. The collection of tattooed and mummified heads in New Zealand, for example, did in fact lead to a series of quite cruel murders."[47] Luschan began specifying in letters to his contacts in the colonies that he only wanted body parts that could be obtained "in a loyal way" and without "giving offense."[48]

Individuals who died in prison or were executed, as well as those killed in battle, were fair game for anthropological collecting. For example, the traveler and collector Fedor Jagor mailed forty-one skulls exhumed from a prison cemetery in Rangoon to Rudolf Virchow. Jagor also persuaded the prison doctor to send Virchow additional bones and bodies and provided duty-free spirits in which to preserve and ship prisoners' brains.[49] In 1910 Luschan purchased 250 skulls of Chinese and Malaysian prisoners executed in Singapore.[50] Anthropologists also regularly received skulls taken from soldiers killed in battle with Germans soldiers.[51] While anthropologists clearly did not object to taking bodies against the will of the colonized, the extent to which they endeavored to operate within the institutions of colonial legality is remarkable.

Legality, in fact, played a similar role to that of science in justifying German colonial rule. Colonial law closely paralleled colonial science in its treatment of the indigenous inhabitant not as a self-legislating subject, but rather as an object of law. Indeed, as late as 1909 colonial reformers debated whether indigenous subjects should be allowed to give legal testimony under oath.[52] Presenting colonial interventions as

---

47. Luschan to Waldeyer, 10 May 1906, MfV, IB 39, vol. 1, 849/06.
48. See, for example, Luschan to Dr. G. Gadow, Cape Colony, 21 June 1906, MfV, IB 39, vol. 1, 849/06; Luschan to Dr. Dempwolf, German East Africa, 1 February 1907, MfV, IB 39, vol. 2, 1288/06; Luschan to Edgar Walden, 29 May 1908, MfV, IB71, vol. 2, 1136/08; Luschan to P. Schumacher, Rwanda, German East Africa, 7 September 1910, MfV, IB 39, vol. 4, 1719/10.
49. Fedor Jagor to Rudolf Virchow, 16 July 1875, NL Virchow, 1009.
50. H. Trebing to Luschan, 12 March 1910, Luschan to the General Museum Administration, 11 April 1910, MfV, IB 39, vol. 4, 1910–14, 522/10.
51. See, for example, Rudolf Virchow, "Zur Frankfurter Verständigung," XXII Versammlung der DAG, Danzig, CBDAG 22 (1891), 122. See also the correspondence about the bodies of East Africans slain during the Maji Maji uprising, Luschan to the Government of German East Africa, 31 March 1906, MfV, IB 39, vol. 1, 589/06; Luschan to the Government of German East Africa, 11 July 1906, MfV, IB 39, vol. 2, 1240/06; Government of German East Africa to Luschan, 3 October 1906, MfV, IB 39, vol. 2, 1240/06.
52. Christian von Bornhaupt, "Die Vereidung von Eingebornen in den deutschen Schutzgebieten," *Koloniale Rundschau* 1 (1909): 427–32.

scientific suggested that they involved the systematic application of universal norms rather than simple, arbitrary brutality.[53] Colonial Secretary Bernhard Dernburg formulated the role of science in German colonial ideology in 1907, when he contrasted an older colonialism based on "means of destruction" with a newer "scientific colonization" based on "means of preservation, that is, advanced theoretical and applied sciences in all areas."[54] By presenting colonialism as a contribution to science, its denial of full sovereignty to a large portion of the earth's inhabitants appeared to be part of a universal discourse rather than an arbitrary asymmetry of power.[55] Luschan's concern that the science legitimizing colonial rule itself be legitimate according to ethical and legal standards—"in a loyal way," in his often used formulation—is a kind of unintentional reference to the circularity of this argument. Physical anthropology—like colonial law—was at once parasitical upon the corporeal relations of colonizer and colonized and a means of legitimizing those very relations. Colonial corporeality, including both colonial law and the anthropological skin trade, was in fact a kind of foundational violence that provided a practical ground for later rationalizations of colonial rule.[56]

Genocide and the Natural Science of Humanity

The genocidal campaign against the Herero of German South West Africa, which began in 1904, represents an extreme case, and a logical end, of the corporeality that made up both anthropology and imperialism.[57] South West Africa was unique among German colonies

---

53. See Michael Taussig's related argument in *Shamanism, Colonialism, and the Wild Man: A Study in Terror and Healing* (Chicago: University of Chicago Press, 1987).
54. Bernhard Dernburg, *Zielpunkte des Deutschen Kolonialwesens* (Berlin: Ernst Siegfried Mittler und Sohn, 1907), 9.
55. The same could be said of earlier universal discourses, such as Christianity, or later universalisms, such as human rights. That all of these discourses amount to "exterminate the brutes!" was, of course, the central point of Joseph Conrad's critique of colonialism in *Heart of Darkness*.
56. My notion of foundational violence comes from Walter Benjamin, "Critique of Violence," in *Reflections*, trans., Edmund Jephcott (New York: Schocken, 1978), 277–300; and Emmanuel Levinas, "The Temptation of Temptation," in *Nine Talmudic Readings*, trans. Annette Aronowicz (Bloomington: Indiana University Press, 1990), 30–50.
57. The best and the most extensively researched account of the period of German colonization in Namibia is Jan-Bart Gewald, *Herero Heroes: A Socio-Political History of the Herero of Namibia, 1890–1923* (Oxford: James Currey, 1999). Other very good accounts include Helmut Bley, *South-West Africa under German Rule 1894–1914*, trans. Hugh Ridley

because it was based on German ranchers rather than on the exploitation of indigenous economies. In this sense German colonialism in South West Africa resembled American westward expansion more than it did German rule elsewhere in Africa or in the Pacific. The dominant society in South West Africa was the Herero, a group whose primary economic activity was cattle herding. The Germans had solidified their power in South West Africa by allying with the Herero against their major rivals, the Nama, as well as by involving themselves in a political struggle within Herero society. European settlers in the colony, however, competed with the Herero for cattle and land. When an 1897 cattle plague epidemic decimated the Herero herds, settlers were able to use the ensuing economic crisis to purchase land from Herero leaders and persuade large numbers of Hereros to work on European farms. This further weakened Herero economic and political power and subjected the Herero to the brutal treatment of European masters.

In January 1904 these depredations finally led to open military conflict between the Herero and Germans.[58] German troops were able to surround the Herero, at which point General Lothar von Trotha was brought in to pursue an even more aggressive policy than Governor Theodor Leutwein, who had sought to negotiate with the Herero. Trotha's strategy against the Herero was not simply to defeat them militarily, but to exterminate them as a people.[59] The Herero were driven into the desert and kept from sources of water, and Trotha ordered soldiers to shoot every Herero man, woman, or child not fleeing into the desert. The Hereros' former rivals, the Nama, also rose against the Germans and led a successful guerila war for years. In the end, how-

---

(Evanston, Ill.: Northwestern University Press, 1971); Jon M. Bridgman, *The Revolt of the Hereros* (Berkeley and Los Angeles: University of California Press, 1981); and Horst Drechsler, *"Let Us Die Fighting": The Struggle of the Herero and Nama against German Imperialism (1884–1915)*, trans. Bernd Zöllner (London: Zed Press, 1980).

58. The standard account of the war is that it began with Herero attacks on German settlers. However, Gewald has marshaled significant evidence suggesting that German troops, fearful of a Herero attack, fired the first shots in panic. See *Herero Heroes,* chap. 5, *"Ovita Ovia Zürn:* Zürn's War, 1904–1908."

59. There has been some dispute about whether Trotha's strategy actually amounted to a self-conscious plan of genocide. Even the best arguments against the genocidal interpretation of the war against the Herero rest, I believe, on exaggerated readings of a limited range of documents. See Brigitte Lau, "Uncertain Certainties—the Herero-German War of 1904," in *History and Historiography* (Windhoek: Discourse/MSORP, 1995); and Gunter Spraul, "Der 'Völkermord' an den Herero: Untersuchungen zu einer neuen Kontinuitatsthese," *Geschichte in Wissenschaft und Unterricht* 39 (1988): 713–39.

ever, they met a fate similar to the Herero. While Trotha was soon recalled and his orders overturned by the government in Berlin, his campaign was brutally effective. By the time the state of war ended in 1907 there were less than twenty thousand Herero surviving from an original population of between sixty and eighty thousand. The Germans had also killed more than half of the Nama, who had numbered twenty thousand before the war. The Germans took all collective property of the Herero and Nama and dissolved their political organizations. Those who surrendered or who could be captured were forced into concentration camps, were they continued to die in great numbers from typhus and other diseases.[60]

In April 1905, over a year after the war began, Luschan contacted Lieutenant Ralf Zürn, the district chief of Okahandja, whose paranoia and aggressive behavior toward the Herero had incited the first shots of the war. Zürn was back in Germany facing the possibility of court martial proceedings on account of his provocative behavior.[61] Luschan was interested in a Herero skull that Zürn was rumored to have brought back with him from Africa. The anthropologist persuaded the lieutenant to donate the skull to the museum, which soon prompted a further request:

> The skull you gave us corresponds so little to the picture of the Herero skull type that we have thus far been able to make from our insufficient and inferior material, that it would be desirable to secure as soon as possible a larger collection of Herero skulls for scientific investigation.[62]

Perhaps Luschan was thinking of the genocidal policy pursued in South West Africa, or perhaps he simply hoped that the ordinary course of colonial war would make additional Herero bodies available, when he asked Zürn "if you are aware of any possible way that we might acquire a larger number of Herero skulls." Luschan was so enthusiastic that, in his initial draft of the letter, he forgot to insert his customary qualification that his request for skulls only be filled "in a

---

60. At the time of this writing, the Herero are attempting to get reparations from the German government. See Roger Boyes, "Germany Apologises for 1904 Slaughter of Africans," *Times* (London), 9 June 1998.
61. See Gewald, *Herero Heroes*, chap. 5.
62. Luschan to Oberleutnant Zürn, 15 April 1905, 21 June 1905, MfV, IB 39, vol. 1, 775/05.

loyal way"—a phrase he inserted in the final draft of the letter.[63] Loyal or not, Zürn was optimistic about meeting Luschan's demands through a contact still serving in the German army near Swakopmund:

> I hope that my requests will have success, since in the concentration camps taking and preserving the skulls of Herero prisoners of war will be more readily possible than in the country, where there is always a danger of offending the ritual feelings of the natives.[64]

Zürn was correct in his assessment, and anthropologists were able to obtain a number of Herero corpses and skulls from the concentration camps. Germans involved in this process reported that, to prepare the skulls to be shipped to Berlin, they forced imprisoned Herero women to remove the flesh from the severed heads of their countrymen with shards of broken glass.[65] The zoologist Leonard Schultze, who happened to be on a collecting trip in South West Africa when the war broke out, also found new opportunities for physical anthropology. While the fighting made the collection and preservation of animals difficult, he reported, "I could make use of the victims of the war and take parts from fresh native corpses, which made a welcome addition to the study of the living body (imprisoned Hottentots [Nama] were often available to me)."[66] The military doctors Dansauer, Jungels, Mayer, and Zöllner in South West Africa also collected Herero body

---

63. Luschan to Zürn, 21 June 1905.
64. Luschan to Zürn, 21 June 1905, Oberleutnant Zürn to Felix von Luschan, 25 June 1905, MfV, IB 39, vol. 1, 775/05.
65. See Gewald, *Herero Heroes,* 189–90 n. 256. Gewald's information comes from a letter of 31 July 1908 from German Colonial Secretary to the Governor of Southwest Africa in the Namibian National Archives in Windhoek, Zentralbureau 2027, SAWW.II.d.8. He also cites a photograph in *Meine Kriegs-Erlebnisse in Deutsch-Südwest-Afrika, Von Einem Offizier Der Schutztruppe* (Mindenm, 1907), 114 with the following caption: "A chest of Herero skulls was recently sent by troops from German South West Africa to the pathological institute in Berlin, where they will be subjected to scientific measurements. The Skulls, from which Herero women have removed the flesh with the aid of glass shards . . ."
66. Leonard Schultze, *Zoologische und anthropologische Ergebnisse einer Forschungsreise im westlichen und zentralen Südafrika ausgeführt in den Jahren 1903–1905* (Jena: Gustav Fischer, 1908), viii. Schultze is cited in Gewald, *Herero Heroes,* 189 n. 256. See also H. von Eggeling, "Anatomische Untersuchungen an Den Köpfen von vier Hereros, Einem Herero- Und Einem Hottentottenkind," in *Zoologische und anthropologische Ergebnisse einer Forschungsreise im westlichen und zentralen Südafrika Ausgeführt in den Jahren 1903–1905,* ed. Leonard Schultze (Jena: Gustav Fischer, 1909), 322–48.

parts in the concentration camps and shipped them to Berlin, where they were studied by the anthropologist Wilhelm Waldeyer and his students.[67] The collection of body parts in concentration camps, a practice familiar to students of the Holocaust, was no exclusively Nazi monstrosity, but rather part of a much longer tradition of colonial corporeality.[68]

German colonialism, however, was not a monolithic entity. Even though it was wholly consistent with the "scientific colonization" fashionable in colonial circles after the turn of the century, the collection of body parts in concentration camps for anthropological study was a controversial practice. Although headed by Bernhard Dernburg, the great advocate of science as a means of colonization, the Colonial Office did not support the anthropological skin trade to the extent that Luschan would have liked. The Colonial Office denied a direct request from Luschan for bodies from the pacification efforts following the war, because of the unrest this might cause among the indigenous population:

> Attention to political calm in the protectorate must be the first priority of the administration, even if this is regrettable for the interests of science in the current situation.[69]

Undeterred, Luschan continued to solicit corpses and body parts from local administrators throughout South West Africa. There he had much greater success, noting in the margins of a letter in which the gov-

---

67. See Wilhelm Waldeyer, foreword to Sergio Sergi, "Cerebra Hererica" and Sergio Sergi, "Cerebra Hererica," in Schultze, *Zoologische und Anthropologische Ergebnisse*, 1–321.

68. The most infamous anthropological research and collecting in concentration camps was, of course, that of Josef Mengele. On doctors in Nazi death camps, see Robert Jay Lifton, *The Nazi Doctors: Medical Killing and the Psychology of Genocide* (New York: Basic Books, 1986). On Mengele's anthropological research, see 284–87, 337–83. See also Weindling, *Health, Race*, 552–64; and Benno Müller-Hill, *Murderous Science: Elimination by Scientific Selection of Jews, Gypsies, and Others in Germany, 1933–1945*, trans. George R. Fraser (Plainview, N.Y.: Cold Springs Harbor Laboratory Press, 1998), 71–94. Whether other European colonial powers engaged in similar practices is not a question that can be answered without research in the archives of all the European colonial powers. If the colonial corporeality I describe here were indeed common to all European powers, it would lend empirical weight to Aimé Césaire's promising hypothesis that Nazism amounted to European colonial practices unleashed in Europe. See *Discourse on Colonialism* (New York: Monthly Review Press, 1972).

69. Imperial Colonial Office to Felix von Luschan, 1 June 1908, MfV, IB 39, vol. 3, 1057/08.

ernor himself promised three skeletons: "cf. the unfriendly response of the Imperial Colonial Office in the same affair!!"[70] Luschan was also able to acquire skeletons from local officials, whose general crackdown on the Herero facilitated the acquisition of body parts. For example, Luschan received a skeleton in 1910 from a Major Maerker who had served in South West Africa. Maerker had acquired the body of an individual who had been shot by a police officer after attempting to steal cattle. The major had apparently brought the skeleton with him when he was reassigned to Posen, and only then mailed it to Luschan.[71] Although for Dernburg and the new colonial advocates in Berlin science was ultimately subordinate to goals of colonial pacification, colonists in the field were quite eager to ship bodies to Luschan. That men like Lieutenant Zürn and Major Maerker actually brought body parts with them from their tour of duty indicated a relation to colonized bodies fundamentally different from the niceties of peace with which Dernburg concerned himself. By donating to "science" the body parts they perhaps originally took as trophies, Zürn, Maerker, and others perhaps sought to exculpate their own barbarism.

The relation of physical anthropology to colonialism, however, involved more than an ideological cover for brutality. Physical anthropology certainly legitimated the colonial project, and likely eased the burden of conscience for men like Zürn and Maerker, transforming acts of colonial brutality into contributions to science. More importantly, the basic gestures of physical anthropology in particular, and German anthropology more generally, were the very stuff of which colonialism was made. The critique of academic humanism as "subjective" and the creation of an "objective" human science rested on the real voiding of subjectivity in the colonial situation. Human subjects were transformed into objective data through procedures that depended upon the limitations of individual sovereignty. Photographing individuals in ways they did not welcome—as anthropological nudes rather than as individual portraits—as well as taking plaster casts of individuals and subjecting them to the discomfort of accurate, objective measurement all depended upon unequal power relations.

---

70. Luschan, Marginalia, in Imperial Governor to the Berlin Museum of Ethnology, 2 November 1908, MfV, IB 39, vol. 3, 2064/08.
71. Maerker to Luschan, 2 July 1910, MfV, IB 39, vol. 4, 1560/10. Maerker is likely the Ludwig Rudolf Georg Maerker who went on to lead a Free Corps in the Weimar Republic. See L. H. Gann and Peter Duignan, *The Rulers of German Africa, 1884–1914* (Stanford: Stanford University Press, 1977), 232–33, 254.

Such relations do not, of course, require a colonial context.[72] However, colonial politics rendered non-Europeans—in both ideology and in practice—as merely partial subjects. Anthropologists grasped colonial subjects as pure bodies, repressing the subject both as source of resistance and as category of human scientific analysis. The most radical form of this ideology—one whose lineage can be traced perhaps to Aristotle's theory of slavery in the *Politics*—is the argument that the ruled is pure body, body without subjectivity. The perfect anthropological subject—that is, the subject without subjectivity—was, as anthropologists themselves realized, a corpse. The empiricism that led anthropologists to desire a complete collection, to constantly want more, meant that the discipline found its ideal and practical realization in genocide. This colonial corporeality, the specific relation of European to non-European bodies, both produced and was produced by a regime of colonial practices that included the anthropological skin trade.

---

72. Indeed, such physical anthropological studies have been carried out on European soldiers and prisoners, as well as, more famously and recently, on undergraduates at Yale and other elite U.S. universities. The significant difference is, of course, that the Ivy League anthropological nudes have been destroyed to protect their subjects, while similar photographs of Africans and Pacific Islanders are readily available in numerous publications and public archives. See Ron Rosenbaum, "The Great Ivy League Nude Posture Photo Scandal," *New York Times Magazine,* 15 January 1995.

Turning Native? Anthropology, German Colonialism, and the Paradoxes of the "Acclimatization Question," 1885–1914

PASCAL GROSSE

As early as the end of the eighteenth century, the question of human acclimatization had become a hotly debated topic in Western Europe's scholarly circles, especially those of France, Great Britain, and Germany. German philosophers, such as Immanuel Kant,[1] as well as medical anthropologists, such as Johann Friedrich Blumenbach, speculated on human evolution, in particular the extent to which the biological and cultural variability of mankind could be attributed to migration.[2] These early academic forays embedded the topic of human acclimatization in a general academic discourse that involved the

---

Translated by Tom Lampert and Jeffrey Schneider
I would like to thank Jeffrey Schneider for his thoughtful and constructive response to earlier drafts of this essay.

    1. See especially Immanuel Kant, "Von den verschiedenen Rassen der Menschen zur Ankündigung der Vorlesungen der physischen Geogaphie im Sommerhalbenjahre 1775," in *Schriften zur Anthropologie, Geschichtphilosophie, Politik und Pädagogik,* vol. 1, ed. Wilhelm Weischedel (Frankfurt am Main: Suhrkamp, 1996), 11–30.

    2. For the British and French perspectives see especially David N. Livingston, "Human Acclimatization: Perspectives on a Contested Field of Inquiry in Science, Medicine, and Geography," *History of Science* 25 (1987): 359–94; Michael A. Osborne, *Nature, the Exotic, and the Science of French Colonialism* (Bloomington: Indiana University Press, 1994); and Warwick Anderson, "Climates of Opinion: Acclimatization in Nineteenth-Century France and England," *Victorian Studies* 35 (1992): 135–57.

acclimatization of plants and animals. By the nineteenth century, the topic of human acclimatization had extended beyond the realm of speculative philosophy and, having been adopted by medical doctors, anthropologists, bureaucrats, and the general public, took on strongly defined biological contours. In these early stages, the issue of acclimatization also reached beyond the horizon of the human sciences to include geography and climatology, thereby establishing something akin to a comprehensive ecology. In the field of anthropology,[3] the "acclimatization question" provoked a range of debates spanning the origin of mankind, the question of biological determinism, and the social relevance of racial difference. As such, acclimatization became the touchstone for the most fundamental problem of nineteenth-century biological and cultural anthropology: the variability or constancy of the biological characteristics of racially defined collectives. Theorists of acclimatization oriented the discussion along the dual axes of geographical climate zones and anthropological taxonomy, that is, the classification of humans according to "race."

Toward the end of the nineteenth century, the agenda for the study of physical and cultural anthropology shifted yet again. European imperialism created a need for the production of scientific knowledge on the colonial subject. As Germany entered the circle of European colonial powers in 1884–85 with the annexation of Togo, Cameroon, German East Africa, German South West Africa, German New Guinea, and some Pacific islands, German anthropology's development as a scholarly discipline became intimately linked to colonial politics. Historians of German and European colonialism have focused almost exclusively on the "colonial other" in order to explain how the concept of race came to dominate European colonial thought; but the issue of race actually dominated the intellectual horizon much closer to home, that is, as an anthropological question of European biological and cultural identity. In short, the growing settlement of white European colonists throughout the nineteenth century forced anthropology

---

3. The term *anthropology* in Germany differs markedly from its use in England and the United States. Since the mid–nineteenth century, the German term has referred mainly to physical anthropology, which can be understood as an extension of human anatomy devoted specifically to racial traits. In Germany, the predominant Anglo-Saxon notion of anthropology is denoted by the term *Ethnologie,* which encompasses cultural and social approaches to the study of ethnic differences. In this essay I will use the term *anthropology* in the German sense, thus stressing the biological foundation of the field and its intimate relation to biological concepts of culture and society.

to consider acclimatization as a "white problem," in particular, whether, biologically, whites could exist in tropical regions at all. Until the advent of emigration to the colonies, science had considered the tropics biologically hostile to European whites, even seeing them as a possible death sentence for Europeans taking up residence there. But the establishment of permanent colonies called for a new, stable, and stringent racial politics of "white supremacy" in order to justify colonial practices vis-à-vis indigenous populations. While a number of German anthropologists, such as Rudolf Virchow, argued vehemently against European colonialism on both political and scientific grounds, many procolonialist anthropologists took up the task of providing scientific evidence that white settlers could at once survive in tropical conditions and preserve a biologically derived "white identity." In the context of European colonial history, the biological and cultural self-definition of European colonialists as white formed the essential—if often unarticulated and even disavowed—core of the acclimatization question. Indeed, I want to suggest that the acclimatization question became a self-reflexive code for the racial and cultural identification of white Europeans *as whites* in colonial societies.

The epistemological pressure placed on whiteness needs to be seen as the result of an intellectual and political paradox in the scientific narrative of race and European colonialism up to this point. On the one hand, overseas expansion occurred in the name of the cultural and biological superiority of the "white race," which enabled its claims to rule in the name of "white supremacy." On the other hand, the dogma of acclimatization—handed down from acclimatization doctrines of the eighteenth century—held that Europeans, as whites, had to adapt to their natural environment in order to secure their own biological survival. In other words, to be able to survive in the tropics, whites would have to lose their biological characteristics as whites. Though this paradox remained in tension throughout the history of colonialism, German anthropologists "resolved" the dilemma to the extent that they introduced the category of gender into the colonial equation. Until the end of the nineteenth century, colonial expansion appears as an exclusively male project, since the acclimatization doctrines of the period only granted men the, albeit limited, ability to survive in the tropics. According to the premises of a biologically defined colonial racial politics, however, an exclusively male colonial rule could not assure the biological reproduction of white society in the tropics. Thus, the settlement of European women in Africa and Asia became the touchstone of colonial racial politics by the end of the nineteenth century. Since women had long been seen as incapable of surviving in the tropics, their inclusion in the colonial equation represented a decisive intellectual turn in the acclimatization debate. As it became evident after the turn of the century that the acclimatization problem could not be "solved" within a purely white male colonial society, the locus of "white racial identity" was transferred onto white women and their biological and cultural reproductive capacity. Thus, a new discourse on the biology of white women in the tropics eventually replaced the classic equation between manliness and colonial expansion. At the heart of this transformation was a eugenicist conception with the bourgeois white family at its core.[4] Indeed, by the end of the nineteenth century the shift marked the injection of eugenicist ideas into colonial racial politics.

With its particular emphasis on biological issues, German anthropology set the international pace for the conceptualization of colonial politics on biological grounds and its link to eugenic policies.[5] This particular stress on the biological foundation of culture and society represented the continuation of a specific German intellectual interest in the study of mankind and its varieties. Moreover, the biological orientation of German anthropology meant that, unlike in Britain or in the United States, anthropologists in Germany were almost exclusively medical doctors (Rudolf Virchow is perhaps the most important example), and that physicians in general played a significant role in shaping the discourse and domain of anthropology. As a result, the close and overlapping relationship between German anthropology and eugenics—another late-nineteenth-century political offshoot of medical science—seems to have been almost inevitable.[6] Whereas anthropologists

---

4. For the broader perspectives of colonialism and eugenics see Pascal Grosse, *Kolonialismus, Eugenik und bürgerliche Gesellschaft in Deutschland, 1850–1914* (Frankfurt am Main: Campus, 2000).

5. The more common term in German to denote "eugenics" was *racial hygiene.*

6. The term *eugenics,* as it will be used in this essay, does not refer to a circumscribed disciplinary field or group of individuals. It is rather a particular string within the set of biologistic interpretations of society at the end of the nineteenth and the early twentieth centuries. Thus, there is no clear-cut group that can be labeled "eugenicists." On the one hand, a core group of people such as Alfred Ploetz, Richard Thurnwald, and Wilhelm Schallmayer, among many others, promoted eugenicist ideas in Germany and helped to institutionalize eugenics through the foundation of the German Racial Hygiene Society and the journal *Archiv für Rassen- und Gesellschaftsbiologie* (Archive for racial and social biology). On the other hand, eugenicist ideas were so widespread within the academic world and governmental administration as to make it questionable to localize eugenic thinking in just one influential group.

were engaged in a theoretical field of research, exploring the biological differences between racially defined collectives, eugenicists understood themselves as practical (medical) therapists of collective social illnesses that resulted, they contended, from racial degeneration.[7] The ultimate goal of eugenics was to "heal society" by selectively controlling biological reproduction—that is, sexuality—along racial and social lines in an effort to promote the breeding of a better race.

But German colonialist thought did not represent an a priori *Sonderweg*. Since the beginning of German colonialism in the mid-1880s, the German discussion of human acclimatization was closely tied to international scholarly debates on the subject. Furthermore, as I stress later on, the primary strains of Germanic anthropological thinking on race often had uncertain or even paradoxical implications for the project of colonialism—implications, moreover, that could not always be derived from the scientific claims made on behalf of anthropology. Germany was nonetheless the site of a unique coarticulation of anthropology, eugenics, and colonial thought. Germany's attempt to use colonialism to stem the tide of emigration to the Americas, for example, placed greater intellectual pressure on a defense of permanent white populations in the colonies than was the case among other colonial powers. If eugenicist conceptions of colonial politics thus reacted to population pressures, they also reflected the general "eugenicist consensus"[8] in German science and society at the end of the nineteenth century. Ultimately, German anthropology's contribution to colonialism represented an important stage in the development of anthropology's disciplinary domain. It also resulted in the emergence of race as a central concept in Imperial Germany's scientific and political discourse, thereby also laying some of the intellectual groundwork for the subsequent scientific legitimization of National Socialism's racist expansionism, particularly in its reaffirmation of the link between race and (geographical) space *(Rasse* und *Raum)*. Whereas the traditional anthropology of the nineteenth century explicitly contended that the white race could not expand beyond its natural biological borders, the colonial anthropology of the early twentieth century ultimately chal-

---

7. For a comprehensive study of eugenics in Germany see Paul Weindling, *Health, Race, and German Politics between National Unification and Nazism, 1870–1945* (Cambridge: Cambridge University Press, 1989).

8. Geoff Eley, "Die deutsche Geschichte und die Widersprüche der Moderne," in *Zivilisation und Barbarei. Die Widersprüchlichen Potentiale der Moderne,* ed. F. Bajohr, W. Johe, and U. Lohalm (Hamburg: Christians, 1991), 54.

lenged this doctrine. With the Nazi drive to establish settlements outside the German borders to accommodate the *Volk ohne Raum,* the acclimatization question remained crucial for German anthropology not only in regard to overseas colonial politics, but also with respect to German expansion in Eastern Europe.[9]

Acclimatization and Colonialism

The transfer of plants and animals from the Old to the New World (and vice versa) provided the basis for the early intellectual models of acclimatization during the sixteenth and seventeenth centuries. Soon thereafter, botanical and zoological gardens emerged as institutions, making various acclimatization experiments visible to the general public. By the eighteenth century, acclimatization became a topic for speculative philosophers probing nature's design according to the Enlightenment episteme of natural history. The first systematic acclimatization theories developed at this time, incorporating philosophical, anthropological, zoological, botanical, medical, astronomical, geological, and economic knowledge in an effort to scrutinize the overall order of the living and nonliving world. In these ecological analyses, migration and transplantation—that is, the developmental possibilities of humans, animals, and plants in a natural environment that was new and unusual for them—became focal points.

By the early nineteenth century, acclimatization was attuned to the limited presence of Europeans in the tropics. At this time, the proverbial "white man's grave" lay in Africa. If Europeans didn't die there, then at least they felt ill. Among the most common physical ailments reported by Europeans in the tropics were a general lack of energy and the sensation of physical weakness. Others, however, asserted the very opposite, claiming to experience greater physical stimulation when in the tropics. This so-called tropical nervousness or tropical neurasthenia often developed into a condition of overstimulation and the com-

---

9. German expansionism in Eastern Europe had a twofold relation to the problem of acclimatization. In the first instance, the question of acclimatization of Germans in eastern Europe resembled analogous discussions regarding the tropics. In the second instance, those anthropologists and medical experts who were pessimistic that Europeans could settle permanently in the tropics, such as, for example, Ferdinand Hueppe, suggested after the turn of the century that Germany should establish settlements in "the East." See Ferdinand Hueppe, "Über die modernen Kolonisationsbestrebungen und die Anpassungsmöglichkeiten der Europäer in den Tropen," *Berliner klinische Wochenschrift* 38 (1901): 7–12, 46–51.

plete eruptive loss of control—a condition subsumed under the pseudomedical construction "tropical rage" *(Tropenkoller)*. Furthermore, Europeans registered specific heat-related bodily phenomena such as sunstroke, heat rash, the sensation of increased body temperature, even persistent fever. Anthropological conceptions at the time attributed the physical discomfort experienced by Europeans in the tropics to their biological "whiteness," which was believed to render them unsuited for such a climate. Thus, the acclimatization debate laid down the supposed physical and psychic limits of Europeans according to two presumably stable variables: the natural environment and race-specific biology.

In the course of the nineteenth century, however, the continued presence of whites in the tropics put pressure on such acclimatization theories, leading to their eventual rearticulation. On the one hand, colonialism came to use the acclimatization problem as the basis for its own narrative of masculine achievement. Until the middle of the twentieth century, European expansion in Africa, Asia, and the Americas produced countless stories of brave and sensible European men: inquisitive adventurers, efficient businessmen, rugged soldiers, circumspect administrators, robust settlers, and charitable missionaries. The florid imagery of European colonial literature clung to these stereotypes of "omnipotent supermen" bred in dangerous colonial laboratories. To some extent, European colonialism staged itself as the white man's battle against the perils of tropical climates—a battle, in other words, between Western technological culture and an originary, unforgiving environment that Europeans entered against their own nature as whites. European expansion became an expression of the will to meet the environmentally conditioned perils of the non-European world. Of course, this expansion called for the development of technical rationality in order to overcome nature, but it primarily symbolized virility, expressed above all in an adventurousness that defied both nature and climate. The acclimatization prognosis of certain death only increased and exaggerated the transcendent, omnipotent masculinity of colonialism.

On the other hand, the acclimatization debate also needed to account for the success of many colonial adventurers in the tropics. The scientific treatment of the acclimatization problem systematized individual experiences of European men living in the colonies in order to arrive at natural laws. Physicians of the eighteenth and nineteenth centuries had attributed most of the psychic and physical phenomena associated with the tropics to such general climatic and meteorological factors as temperature, which was held responsible for both under- and overstimulation of the nervous system.[10] It was not until the 1880s that acclimatization research began to focus on the individual and collective requirements necessary for adaptation to foreign environments. As acclimatization researchers augmented eighteenth- and nineteenth-century travel reports and medical treatises with numerous empirical investigations, they also began to apply new laboratory methods to investigate human variations in temperature regulation, metabolism, and skin pigmention.[11]

By the end of the nineteenth century, this systematization localized entirely around race. Enlightenment natural history had postulated a biological-geographical determinism in response to the unexplained biodiversity of the living world. According to this framework, each living species corresponded to a specific climatic or geographic territory which alone could ensure its biological existence. In human ecology, variations in the physical appearance of ethnic groups thus represented an adaptation to a specific set of natural conditions. For researchers of human migration, the most symbolic materialization of this biological-geographical determinism was the skin of "whites" and "colored" people. In the late nineteenth century, anatomical and physiological research reinforced this nexus even further by documenting that skin reflected physical influences in such forms as differences in the number of sweat glands or the amount of melanin across skin types. Thus, human skin—in many ways the very foundation of anthropological classification—came to symbolize a specific version of selective biological-geographical determinism. According to this determinism, humanity could not exist equally in all geographical or climatic regions of the world. Since geographic and biological determinism conditioned each other reciprocally, adherents of biological determinism postulated a constancy of the color of the human skin, and hence of different races. Rudolf Virchow, Germany's most celebrated medical scientist and a leading anthropologist in the second half of the nineteenth

---

10. While physicians also alluded to other factors, such as minimal seasonal differences and lack of variation in the length of daylight over the course of the year, they, of course, were never able on this basis to develop the necessary strategies for avoiding or overcoming all of the health dangers of the tropics. Only at the end of the nineteenth century with the identification of microorganisms as a cause of illnesses, did a distinction between climate-related infectious diseases and strictly climatic illnesses follow.

11. Dutch research in the Dutch Indies took the lead in exploring physiology under extreme conditions.

century, summarized this differentialized anthropological conception when he noted that "no one has ever observed one race transform into another. No one has ever seen a white population that has settled in the tropics become black. No one has observed that Negro population that has moved to the polar region or at least to Canada become white."[12] On the basis of this logic, Virchow excluded the possibility of permanent acclimatization of any racial group migrating from its "natural" environment to a new one.

But the growing significance of the acclimatization question after the mid–nineteenth century cannot be reduced to its role in a "normal science," where each piece of new research clarified misconceptions, and thereby helped to move anthropological knowledge forward. Rather, acclimatization debates were also inextricably tied to the internal organization of colonial social systems and European emigration politics. Concretely, the acclimatization question split into two separate problems, each of which had its own relevance for European expansionist politics. First, the transition from the eighteenth to the nineteenth century brought with it a new type of colonial territorial rule by European nation-states. This form of colonial rule differed both from the predominant settler colonialism in the New World and the system of base colonies in Africa and Asia.[13] The prototypical model of colonial social organization was established in British India at the end of the eighteenth century: a social organization aimed at territorial rule through the intervention of the nation-state. In this model, which pointed the way for the nineteenth-century colonization in Asia, Africa, and Oceania, European nation-states coupled colonial politics with their—temporally limited—military and administrative presence. In this colonial system, acclimatization focused on where and according to what conditions Europeans could *individually* adapt to tropical climates. Pragmatically, this matter revolved around questions of Europeans' performance as administrators, settlers, or soldiers. Ultimately, the gradual transition from an informal colonialism based on commercial ventures by privileged charter societies to a formal state colonialism increased the importance of acclimatization debates, as

---

12. Rudolf Virchow, "Vortrag vor der Versammlung deutscher Naturforscher und Ärzte," *Tageblatt der 58. Versammlung deutscher Naturforscher und Ärzte in Strassburg, 18–23 September 1885*, Strasbourg, 1885, 540–52.

13. Up to the twentieth century, all of these organizational forms of European colonial expansion coexisted next to one another, often in the same colony.

colonialism itself became more tightly aligned with questions of national security and welfare.

The second historical context for the increasing significance of the acclimatization question in the nineteenth century lay in the immigration movements resulting from population pressures back in Europe. In the course of the century, Canada, Australia, New Zealand, and South Africa had all developed into supplementary national settler-territories for Great Britain, much as Algeria had for France.[14] Colonial formations of this type attained their ultimate national-political significance only with the division of Africa, Southeast Asia, and the Pacific region after 1880. In the rhetoric of colonial propaganda, they were then no longer merely of interest as national settler-territories, but also as strategic military and commercial bases. As a result of these developments, migration to the colonies began to hold a value for European nation-states seeking to tie them politically, socially, and culturally to the motherland. In this context, the acclimatization debate expanded from a concern with work performance to the question of Europeans' biological reproduction in the tropics. The task at hand was to determine which biological-anthropological course facilitated the establishment of a permanent European territorial hegemony overseas.

As colonialism played an increasingly important role in the broad spectrum of European imperialism, German colonialist politics provided the most fertile ground for the virulent development of acclimatization theory. This development resulted from the perceived benefits colonies offered in light of the dual narration of Germany's population "crisis." First, certain imperialist segments in the political public sphere imagined Germany as a "people without [enough] space" (*Volk ohne Raum*). Thus, while the founding of neo-European nation-states ruled by a minority white settler regime—British Rhodesia or French Algeria, for example—remained the exception after 1880,[15] only Imperial Germany consistently attempted to connect emigration and colonial politics by establishing permanent colonies in South West and

---

14. As emigration destinations, these territories competed with the United States and the countries of South America—without, however, ever possessing their potential for the absorption of immigrants.

15. Jürgen Osterhammel, *Kolonialismus. Geschichte-Formen-Folgen* (Munich: C. H. Beck, 1995), 12.

East Africa.[16] This drive for an emigration-based colonialism even persisted after the turn of the century, when relevant emigration movements no longer existed. Second, throughout the nineteenth century, Germany sent waves of immigrants to the United States, where they were subject to great assimilatory pressures that rendered them lost resources to the newly united German nation-state. Thus, the national-political rhetoric of this era sought to establish overseas colonial rule in order to channel the mass emigration of Germans away from the United States and toward German settler territories, where emigrants could preserve their cultural identity as Germans. Since German colonial-political aspirations thus had a strong settler impetus, German debates on colonialism focused on the prospective acclimatization of greater settlement communities.

The ensuing debate among German anthropologists fractured along three different acclimatization-colonialism axes. First, the group of traditionally liberal members of Berlin's Anthropological Society, with Rudolf Virchow, August Hirsch, and Adolf Bastian at its core, postulated the unchangeability of human races. Virchow derived the reasons for Europeans' poor acclimatization prospects in the tropics from a nexus of racial and gender anthropology. Evaluating the degree of acclimatization in Europeans according to gender-specific criteria, he measured the degree of male acclimatization in terms of work ability, while defining that of female acclimatization according to biological reproduction, that is, marital fertility. Since Virchow flatly rejected—as did the majority of acclimatization researchers—the idea that women could acclimatize in the tropics, he argued that full racial acclimatization would never occur there. Rather, he believed it scientifically proven that "women of the emigrated race become less and less fertile, that they produce increasingly fewer children, which still accord with the mother's race, and that, when the family is strictly limited to marriage, the race will die out."[17] Politically, Virchow, a member of the Free Thinking (Freisinnige) opposition in the Reichstag, used these classical anthropological tenets to oppose Bismarckian colonial politics, denouncing all procolonial rhetoric as the betrayal of

---

16. Neither a traditional colonial power such as Holland, nor the new colonial states of Belgium, Italy, the United States, and Japan sought to establish independent national settler colonies overseas to any substantial degree.

17. Rudolf Virchow, "Akklimatisation," *Verhandlungen der Berliner Gesellschaft für Anthropologie, Ethnologie und Geschichte, Zeitschrift für Ethnologie* 17 (1885): 213.

the German nation. Emigration to the tropical colonies, he argued, did "not merely place our countrymen in the greatest danger," it lead "them in all probability to their certain death as well." If they were not "eaten up" there, they would "find, at best, an honest grave."[18]

Though Bismarck countered Virchow's dogmatic arguments with romantic notions of energetic settlers fleeing civiliation,[19] the most interesting and important opposition to Virchow's view emerged from two mutually antagonistic traditions of anthropological thought: egalitarian cosmopolitanism, centered for the most part in Dutch anthropological circles, and procolonialist propaganda, carried out by German medical and scientific researchers, either based in the colonies or with expertise in tropical medicine (for example, Robert Koch). The so-called cosmopolitans worked from the principle that all humans were equally equipped with a capacity for survival. This idea was particularly widespread within Dutch anthropology, where, around the turn of the century, it led to pathbreaking scholarship in physiology, particularly by Christaan Eijkman, who demonstrated that all humans—regardless of ethnicity and gender—shared elementary biochemical processes.[20] In that same vein, the most prominent member of the cosmopolitans, the Dutch physician Barend Joseph Stokvis, came to the conclusion that humans

---

18. *Stenographische Berichte über die Verhandlungen des Deutschen Reichtages,* vol. 82, pp. 1865ff., from the session held on 16 March 1885. Berlin: Verlag der Buchdruckerei der Norddeutschen Allgemeinen Zeitung, 1871–1900.

19. Bismarck took up the accusation that he would "subject unknowing Germans to the perils of the climate," opposing to this the idea of individual self-realization: after all, "each person forges his own happiness. If a German entrepreneur calls for protection from the German Reich, . . . should he request an examination from the German medical office, of which Herr . . . Virchow is a member, and pose the question: could you provide a medical bulletin?" (*Stenographische Berichte über die Verhandlungen des Deutschen Reichtages,* vol. 82, pp. 1863ff., from the session held on 16 March 1885). Bismarck's standpoint encouraged a romanticized flight from civilization and strengthened an energetic settler mentality, which was in opposition to a scientifically grounded, planned colonial politics. The African researcher Henry Morton Stanley expressed this pragmatic standpoint of a manly, antiscientific adventure as follows: "A little common sense, not the study of scientific geography, would teach them [the whites] how to avoid sunstroke, and how to pass from one street to another without being broiled to death. It is this art of living which we want to teach the young Englishmen who go to Africa, full of so much enthusiasm and ambition." Stanley's contribution at the Sixth International Geographical Congress in London, in *Report of the Sixth International Geographical Congress held in London* (London, 1896), 546.

20. Eijkman's research in the late 1890s focused essentially on the physiology of human metabolism in the tropics. He demonstrated that the regulatory functions of body temperature are essentially the same between the different ethnic groups living in the Dutch Indies.

are able to live and are able to adjust themselves to external conditions everywhere in the world, as long as the necessary conditions for survival are fulfilled. . . . The unity of the human race appears increasingly to be beyond all reservations, in the physical sense as well. All humans are brothers and sisters, creatures of the same origin, the same development.[21]

Though implicitly egalitarian, cosmopolitan anthropology had a colonial flip side. By removing any biological factors preventing whites from succeeding in the tropics, it could have been construed as a theoretical justification for colonial ventures. Though this theoretical framework partly fueled Dutch colonialism in the East and West Indies, it did not prevent the Dutch colonial power from exercising a colonial rule based on traditional notions of racial difference throughout the first half of the twentieth century. In light of its overarching egalitarianism, however, cosmopolitan anthropology found few adherents among German anthropologists.

Cosmopolitan anthropology had countered Virchow's restrictive anticolonial anthropology on a scientific basis. But its ideal of (potential) equality could not legitimate the establishment of a white supremacist culture in the colonies. In this situation, it was essential for the procolonial acclimatization research faction in the German academy to modify the classical one-dimensional concept of acclimatization without, at the same time, encouraging egalitarianism. In this context, unlinking individual and racial acclimatization theories became decisive in formulating a new intellectual compromise. Ratzel's diffusionist anthropo-geography supported this stance as he claimed speculatively in his support for a German colonial engagement that human migration would inevitably lead to the adaptation to the new environment. Individual acclimatization, on the one hand, came to refer to individual humans and the particular biological characteristics they possessed, enabling them to meet the demands of life in the tropics. If particularly fit Europeans were compelled to adapt their form of life to the climatic and cultural requirements of the tropics, it was also possible for them to maintain their identity as whites. This was especially true if they remained in tropical regions only temporarily, for example as soldiers, merchants, or colonial administrators. The individual con-

---

21. Barend Joseph Stokvis, *De invloed von tropische gewesten op den mensch in verband met colonistie en gezondheid. Drei vordrachten* (Haarlem, 1894), pp. 5f.

ception of acclimatization thus hinged on a "suitability for the tropics" *(Tropentauglichkeit)*, which entailed a medical selection process. "Racial acclimatization," on the other hand, denoted the long-term tropical settlement of whites as ethnically closed and culturally autochthonous reproductive communities. The successful acclimatization of Europeans in the tropics formed the biomedical basis for Europe's global political claims—a foundational link suggested by the physician Carl Däubler, a noted German acclimatization researcher:

> Acclimatization by Europeans in tropical lands does not simply mean that those people live in full power and health and maintain their capacity for work as they did in Europe, without any noteworthy increase in mortality. It also means, in particular, the capacity to reproduce in the usual manner and to generate robust offspring in the tropics, without having to bring in either foreign blood or continually new reinforcements of European colonists.[22]

Racial acclimatization thus set a completely new goal, based entirely on the idea of racial difference and ethnic segregation. With a firm belief in the cultural and normative superiority of the white race, procolonial anthropologists and physicians focused on "positive" alterations in the somatic and physical constitution resulting from climatic changes. Paradoxically, in citing such somatic changes as the tanning of white skin, their biological-geographical model—designed to legitimate a global white supremacist culture based on a superiority in adapting to new climes—further established "colored natives" as the norm.

Acclimatization, Gender, and Eugenics

Neither before nor after the turn of the century did acclimatization researchers reach consistent results in deciphering biological regularities in human migration. In light of the consequent failure to develop concrete proposals for colonial politics, a general pessimism about acclimatization research set in at the beginning of the twentieth century. If acclimatization was not yet regarded as completely antiquated internationally, it certainly lost much of the force it had had in the

---

22. Karl Däubler, *Die Grundzüge der Tropenhygiene,* 2d ed. (1st ed. 1985) (Berlin, 1900), 5.

1880s. In Germany, however, it retained a certain currency in the context of a virulent settler-colonialism that came to rearticulate the acclimatization question in eugenic terms. This convergence furthered the installation of acclimatization as an evaluative criterion for German colonial expansion and ultimately underwrote the relatively unique development of deep-seated racialist principles in German anthropological thought. At the same time, the perspective of biological reproduction also modified the monolithic notion of race, refracting it through the category of gender in light of the assumption that life in the tropics affected white men and women differently. For men, the extreme temperatures were thought to produce "increased excitability . . . of sexual life," which meant that tropical existence was marked by the constant "influence of sexual stimuli."[23] For women, in contrast, tropical conditions were seen as the cause for a decline in sexual functions. Thus, as one leading figure charged, the "acclimatization of the European race has often failed because of the sexual unfitness (*Untüchtigkeit*) of women."[24]

For the eugenicists, "pure race" biological reproduction was the key for the future of Germany as well as humanity at large. In terms of colonial politics, this meant a focus on how European colonizers could reproduce themselves as whites. Eugenicists' primary interest in the acclimatization question thus engaged the conventional view of European women as unfit for tropical climates—a situation that rendered colonial societies' long-term survival a virtual impossibility. At the turn of the century, the majority of anthropologists strongly believed that there were gender-specific limits to acclimatization. As the physician Havelburg summarized, tropical life had severe consequences for white European women:

> Those individuals who have hardened their bodies through . . . physical activity are in a more favorable position. This is not the case, however, with females who follow their men into foreign regions as daughters or wives, without strict selection in regard to their physical robustness. Under the climatic influences there . . . they becomes easily nervous. They have menstrual disorders with unusual frequency. . . . These women are not fit for the tasks of

---

23. V. Havelburg, "Klima, Rase und Nationalität in ihrer Bedeutung für die Ehe," in *Krankheiten der Ehe. Darstellung der Beziehung zwischen Gesundheits-Störungen und Ehemgemeinschaft*, ed. H. Senator and S. Kaminer (Munich, 1904), 102.
24. Ibid.

marital life; they have miscarriages more easily. As a rule, young mothers lose their milk. Endometric ailments develop, which lead to all kinds of uteral disorders . . . and end in sterility. In addition to this, the woman's general condition declines, she becomes thin. Her nervous life and her orderly spiritual condition are shaken up. As a result, the marital life which one sees among Europeans is frequently rather strained. While the sexual demands of men in the tropics increases, the robustness of women diminishes.[25]

Anthropologists based the pathologization of European women's entire physical and spiritual existence in the tropics on the ostensible decrease of female sexual functions—an argument that came close to figuring all women as hysterical. Gender-neutral conceptions, such as those of the Berlin anthropologist and physiologist Gustav Fritsch, who in 1885 noted that "white women suffer because they belong to the white race, not because they are women,"[26] remained an exception over the next decades.

The topic of women's acclimatization in the tropics came to the forefront in Germany through the so-called mixed-marriages debate. After 1900, colonial mixed marriages and racial mixing—glosses for the tendency of white male European settlers to have sexual relations with indigenous women—were regarded by politicians and anthropologists alike as the most urgent social problem of German colonial population politics. Up to the turn of the century, the frequent sexual relations between white men and local women had been regarded as socially legitimate, especially given the absence of white women in the tropics. By the early twentieth century, however, mixed marriages had come to be seen as a long-term threat to white supremacy in the colonies. As eugenicists reopened the question of women's acclimatization in order to allow German men to be sexually active in the colonies without endangering the continued existence of the white race, leading colonial bureaucrats attempted to curtail mixed-race sexual relations by introducing special legislation banning mixed marriages. While colonial administrators failed to criminalize all sexual relations between German men and indigenous women before 1914, the legisla-

---

25. Ibid.
26. *Verhandlungen der Berliner Gesellschaft für Anthropologie, Ethnologie und Urgeschichte, Zeitschrift für Ethnologie* 17 (1885): 258.

tion banning mixed marriages did create lasting limits on masculine sexual freedom.

The colonial mixed marriage debate and the renewed attention on women's acclimatization had two important consequences. First, it brought about a gradual reconsideration of female acclimatization to supposedly hostile climates. During the first half of the twentieth century, acclimatization researchers thus began to undertake empirical work on the physiology and pathology of European women's sexual functions in the tropics. Though the fundamental tendencies of this research remained ambivalent and even misogynistic, it produced results that documented European women's ability to acclimatize not only as whites, but also as sexual partners and mothers.[27] This evidence notwithstanding, few experts acknowledged women's capacity for full acclimatization. Instead, anthropologists and colonial officials merely conceded that "the lack of descendents among European families" did not prove "that the European race is incapable of reproducing in the tropics, but rather that European men have not always married European women."[28] With this conclusion, anthropologists abandoned the previously accepted view that women could not sufficiently acclimatize to the tropics. They now left the issue open, thereby suspending any scientific objections to the political project of systematically recruiting German women for the colonies.

Second, the focus on biological reproduction shifted the discourse on acclimatization from virile adventurers to the long-term assimilation of European families in the tropics. Thus, after a period of colonial latency brought on by Germany's loss of its colonies in the First World War, the topic of female acclimatization resurfaced in National Socialism's colonial politics. While the proponents of a restorative German colonialism in Africa reached back to models developed before the war, the fundamental tenor of their work revealed the compatibility of colonial expansion and the establishment of a racial state in the National Socialist sense. During the Third Reich, anthropolo-

---

27. For an overview of the abundant accounts of female acclimatization written by pro-colonial women, see especially Lora Wildenthal, "Colonizers and Citizens: Bourgeois Women and the Woman Question in the German Colonial Movement, 1886–1914," Ph.D. diss., University of Michigan, 1994, esp. 167ff.

28. Bundesarchiv, Bestand Reichskolonialamt Nr. 6278, p. 44, records on the meeting of the Reichsgesundheitsrat—Committee for Marine and Tropical Hygiene on 14 February 1908, contribution by Breger.

gists and colonial physicians attributed renewed significance to the acclimatization problematic, considering the specific acclimatization prospects of white women as a matter of course.[29] As the prominent Nazi anthropologist Ernst Rodenwaldt formulated it, the acclimatization of women was still the linchpin of the colonialist project:

> What must ensure the maintenance of Germanness *(Deutschtum)* in the future, even in a racially foreign environment, and exorcise the danger of the penetration of colored blood into the body of our people *(Volkskörper)* is the connection between the German woman and her own household, and the social ostracization of those who betray their race. . . . Today, the spirit still reigns according to which young civil servants and employees can be brought to fear bringing a German woman with them, because she would ostensibly quickly succumb to the climate and could bear no child, because that child would die there. All of these errors have long since been refuted, but this spirit of the bachelor household in which the female European is seen only as a burdensome watchdog—this racially destructive spirit still exists.[30]

Though writing in 1936, Rodenwaldt rehearsed the colonial mixed-marriage debate. In doing so, he insisted on the need for curtailing male sexual freedom in the name of white racial purity even more forcefully than the previous generation of eugenicists had done. In light of the positive acclimatization prospects of German women, Rodenwaldt envisaged an entirely new synthesis of "race and space," centered on the expansion of a racially pure German empire into foreign—even climatically hostile—lands.

---

29. See, for example, Ernst Rodenwaldt, "Das Geschlechtsleben der europäischen Frau in den Tropen," *Archiv für Rassen- und Gesellschaftsbiologie* 26 (1932): 173–94; Felix von Bormann, "Ist die Gründung einer europäische Familie in den Tropen zulässig?" *Archiv für Rassen- und Gesellschaftsbiologie* 31 (1937): 89–118; Margaret Hasselmann-Kahlert, "Über Menstruationsstörungen bei der gesunden weißen Frau in der Tropen," *Archiv für Schiffs- und Tropenhygiene* 44 (1940): 124–33; Heinrich Werner, "Hygienische Maßnahmen zum Schutze von deutschen und farbigen Frauen und Kindern im tropischen Afrika," *Deutsche medizinische Wochenschrift* 66 (1940): 729–31.

30. Ernst Rodenwaldt, "Wie bewahrt der Deutsche die Reinheit seines Blutes in Ländern mit farbiger Bevölkerung," in *Jahrbuch für auslandsdeutsche Sippenkunde* (Stuttgart, 1936), 67.

Conclusion

By the onset of National Socialism's imperialist politics, German anthropology had abandoned the classical unity of race, space, and culture as the conceptual basis of human ecology. At the beginning of European colonialism, this unity had at once undermined and underwritten the colonial project in the sense that acclimatization seemed both a biological impossibility and the basis for white supremacy. Over the course of the nineteenth century, the discourse on acclimatization succeeded in keeping a cultural imperialist ideology in precarious but fruitful tension with a sense of the biological limits of European expansion. In turn, this tension helped produce the figure of the unattached colonial adventurer who struggled against harsh climates in heroic fashion, thereby legitimating his practice of colonizing others. But as colonialism—especially in Germany—began to dream of permanent settlements forever attached politically, economically, and culturally to the motherland, racial reproduction moved to the fore. With the goal of preserving a white identity in the colonies, the fate of white culture became ineluctably tied to the presence of European women. As a result, colonial racial politics redefined the social role of European men by curtailing the sexual freedom characterizing the unattached adventurer. Eugenically inspired colonial racial politics replaced this stereotype of the heroic man with the "white family." Thus, paradoxically, what began with white male freedom ended with its very control, as the restrictive category of race was no longer applied only to the indigenous population, but ultimately to the (male) colonialists themselves.

Anthropology at War: Racial Studies of POWs during World War I

ANDREW D. EVANS

In the first six months of World War I, 625,000 prisoners of war streamed into holding camps in the German Empire.[1] Anthropologists in Germany took special note of this development, because among the long columns of men marching into German prisoner-of-war camps were thousands of soldiers from the colonial armies of the French and British. Troops from Africa, India, and Asia were of great scientific interest to German anthropologists, who recognized in them the rare opportunity to study non-Europeans on European soil. With growing excitement, they regarded the camps as a "very rich observational area for anthropologists"[2]—an "opportunity for scientific research never present before and never to return."[3] Anthropologists were exultant: "Our enemies have collected such a colorful mixture of peoples around their flags that almost all the races of the world are represented."[4] For the specialist, they argued, "a visit to some of these camps [is] as worth-

---

I would like to thank Glenn Penny, Matti Bunzl, Lydia Murdoch, Tim Pursell, Tim Schmitz, and Jeff Wilson for their generous help with earlier drafts of this essay.

1. Richard B. Speed III, *Prisoners, Diplomats, and the Great War: A Study in the Diplomacy of Captivity* (Westport, Conn.: Greenwood Press, 1990), 7.

2. Georg Buschan, "Krieg und Anthropologie," *Deutsche Medizinische Wochenschrift* 26 (1915): 773.

3. Rudolf Pöch, "Anthropologische Studien an Kriegsgefangenen," *Die Umschau* 20 (1916): 989.

4. Buschan, "Krieg und Anthropologie," 773.

while as a trip around the world."[5] To some, the POW camps represented the ultimate manifestation of the nineteenth-century *Völkerschauen*, the popular exhibitions of non-European "exotics" that had toured Europe in the 1880s and 1890s. As one anthropologist put it, the POW camps simply were "a *Völkerschau* without comparison!"[6]

The overwhelming enthusiasm about the non-European populations in the camps notwithstanding, once the project to study the POWs was under way, it focused as much on Europeans as it did on peoples from Africa, India, and Asia. As the project progressed, it was especially the physical anthropologists who became increasingly interested in European peoples.[7] In the process, the question of "race" among Europeans became a major focus of inquiry.[8] Exploring how and why the POW projects developed into a study of European racial identity sheds light not only on the construction of race in the European context, but also on the effect of war on physical anthropology.

One of the central issues in the recent historiography of German anthropology is the radical break between the liberal and often antiracist anthropological science of the nineteenth century and the illiberal, racist anthropology of the twentieth. Robert Proctor, Benoit Massin, and others have presented convincing arguments that locate the fundamental shift in anthropology between the turn of the century and the 1920s.[9] At the center of these accounts is the rise and fall of a

---

5. Felix von Luschan, *Kriegsgefangene, Ein Beitrag zur Völkerkunde im Weltkriege: Einführung in die Grundzüge der Anthropologie* (Berlin: Dietrich Reimer [Ernst Vohsen], 1917), 1–2.

6. Pöch, "Anthropologische Studien an Kriegsgefangenen," 989.

7. Although both physical anthropologists and ethnologists conducted studies in the camps, this essay is primarily concerned with physical anthropology. Anthropology in German anthropological societies encompassed four basic fields of study: ethnology, physical anthropology, prehistoric archaeology, and linguistics. In the German context, the specific term *Anthropologie* usually referred to physical anthropology, while the terms *Ethnologie* or *Völkerkunde* were used as general equivalents for cultural anthropology.

8. Whenever the term *race* is used in this essay, quotation marks surrounding the word are implied. I refer to race not as a concept with a basis in biological reality, but as a social and ideological construct shaped by the historical circumstances in which it is used.

9. See Robert Proctor, "From *Anthropologie* to *Rassenkunde* in the German Anthropological Tradition," in *Bones, Bodies, Behavior: Essays on Biological Anthropology*, ed. George W. Stocking Jr. (Madison: University of Wisconsin Press, 1988), 138–79; Benoit Massin, "From Virchow to Fischer: Physical Anthropology and Modern Race Theories in Wilhelmine Germany," in *Volksgeist as Method and Ethic: Essays on Boasian Ethnography and the German Anthropological Tradition*, ed. George W. Stocking Jr. (Madison: University of Wisconsin Press, 1996), 79–154. Similar views can be found in the work of Woodruff Smith and Paul Weindling. See Woodruff Smith, *Politics and the Sciences of Culture in Germany,*

liberal brand of anthropology, championed by the renowned pathologist Rudolf Virchow (1821–1902) and his colleagues, such as the Munich anthropologist Johannes Ranke (1836–1916) and the Swiss anatomist Julius Kollmann (1834–1918). In the late nineteenth century, these men maintained that no one race or people was superior to any other. They opposed anti-Semitism, rejected Germanic racial theories, and forcefully argued for the unity of the human species. By the twentieth century, however, this strain of liberal anthropology faded as a younger generation of scholars such as Eugen Fischer (1874–1967) readily accepted biological determinism and *völkisch* racism. By the 1920s, traditional physical anthropology was replaced by racial science or *Rassenkunde,* which sought to link physical characteristics to mental and cultural faculty.[10]

While there is little doubt that such a shift occurred, historians have been at great pains to provide convincing explanations as to how and why it took place. Benoit Massin, whose work was crucial in identifying the contours of the break, looks mainly to events within the anthropological community to account for the change.[11] Specifically, he pins his explanation on the death of Virchow, arguing that the great scientist's passing in 1902 left a vacuum within the discipline that was quickly filled by virulent Darwinism and Germanic racial theories. In Massin's formulation, Nordic racial biology became the norm within anthropology as early as 1910, a mere eight years after Virchow's death. This view, however, not only overlooks the continued presence of liberal ideas in German anthropology, championed during this period by scientists like Johannes Ranke, Felix von Luschan (1854–1924), and Rudolf Martin (1864–1925), but also fails to take extradisciplinary factors and outside events into account. Woodruff D. Smith, for his part, ties his explanation of the change to a teleological variant of the famous *Sonderweg* thesis, arguing that the erosion of "neoliberal" anthropology was related to the wider decline in the salience of German liberalism in the 1880s and 1890s.[12] In this historiographic context, the significance of World War I in the shift has remained unexplored.[13]

1840–1920 (Oxford: Oxford University Press, 1991); Paul Weindling, *Health, Race, and German Politics between National Unification and Nazism, 1870–1945* (Cambridge: Cambridge University Press, 1989).
    10. Proctor, "From *Anthropologie* to *Rassenkunde,*" 148–52.
    11. Massin, "From Virchow to Fischer."
    12. Smith, *Politics.*
    13. In opposing the dominant historiographic trend, Andrew Zimmerman has suggested

This essay suggests that the war played a critical role in the transformation of German anthropology by creating new contexts in which the science could be pursued. In particular, practicing anthropology in the camps helped to reorient German anthropologists toward European subjects in ways that contributed significantly to the erosion of the categories at the heart of the liberal tradition. Since Virchow's heyday, liberal anthropologists had maintained that the categories of race, nation, and *Volk* (translated roughly as "people" or ethnic group) were distinct and unrelated. They sought to identify different physical morphologies or racial types, but argued that these classifications were in no way linked to cultural identities or national groupings, which were determined by language, customs, geography, and politics, rather than physical characteristics. Before the war, the leaders of the German anthropological community had used this principle to emphasize the interrelated nature of the peoples on the European continent, arguing that Germans, Slavs, and other groups were not physically or racially distinct. In contrast to the Germanic racial doctrines of theorists like Houston Stewart Chamberlain, for whom the categories of race, nation, and *Volk* were nearly identical,[14] the leading physical anthropologists insisted that they should not be confused. Even anthropologists who had begun to break with the tenets of liberal anthropology before 1914, such as Gustav Schwalbe (1844–1916) and Eugen Fischer, claimed that race and nation were unrelated.

It was during the Great War that a younger generation of anthropologists began to conflate the concepts of nation and race in their research on the POW population. Working in the camps, they investigated and portrayed the European enemies of the Central Powers as racial "others," assigning distinct racial and biological identities to European peoples and nations in the process. What caused this conflation of nation and race in the camps? This essay utilizes the stories of three scientists—Otto Reche (1879–1966), Egon von Eickstedt (1892–1965), and Rudolf Pöch (1870–1921)—to illustrate three different ways by which anthropologists arrived at the construction of the

---

that no such radical break took place, arguing that in practice there was little difference between the anthropology of the nineteenth century and that of the twentieth. This view overlooks the ideological differences in German anthropology before and after the first decade of the twentieth century. Andrew Zimmerman, "Anti-Semitism as Skill: Rudolf Virchow's Schulstatistik and the Racial Composition of Germany," *Central European History* 32 (1999): 409–29.

14. Geoffrey G. Field, *Evangelist of Race: The Germanic Vision of Houston Stewart Chamberlain* (New York: Columbia University Press, 1981), 223.

European enemy as a racial "other." In each of these cases, this process was driven by two central factors. The first was some form of heightened patriotism that encouraged the anthropologists to view the POWs in national terms and to imbue the category of nation with biological meaning. The second was the particular context, or more accurately, the series of contexts, in which the studies took place, which circumscribed the process of racial investigation. A critical combination of ideology and circumstances, in other words, came together in the camps. On the one hand, the war intensified the nationalism of the participants, thereby creating a dichotomy between allies and enemies; on the other hand, it provided the specific setting in which the studies took place: the POW camp. The camp milieu was a major influence on all three anthropologists. It served to collapse the distinction between European and non-European groups, replacing it with a dynamic that highlighted the differences between captors and prisoners—a situation that encouraged these anthropologists to link nation and race and facilitated the unproblematic refashioning of their national rivals into racial "others."

The story of POW studies thus suggests that the shift in anthropology was not simply a matter of good liberals giving way to a generation of racist nationalists. Rather, the process of conflating nation and race was contingent on the political, personal, and environmental contexts in which the anthropologists did their work—a set of contexts in which even the students of the liberal anthropologist Felix von Luschan felt free to link nation and race. In this regard, the camp projects demonstrate the ways in which experience influenced anthropological discourse and practice reshaped theory. The wartime contexts in which anthropologists worked significantly affected the directions they would take in the postwar period, accelerating certain nationalistic tendencies and leading them away from the tradition of liberal anthropology.

Race, Nation, and *Volk* in Prewar German Anthropology

In the years leading up to World War I, the liberal tradition in German anthropology continued to exert a powerful influence on the discipline. This was particularly true in regard to the distinction between race, nation, and *Volk*. That distinction was the cornerstone of Virchow's anthropological project, suggesting that all Europeans were interrelated and that race had no association with the nation as a unit of cultural or political organization.

Another chief characteristic of liberal anthropology was the refusal to link the concept of race with human faculty or ability. Virchow and others in the liberal tradition considered race a category of physical, rather than cultural or mental, variation. The goal of physical anthropology was the investigation and classification of human types through measurement and quantification. Physical anthropology was thus a statistical endeavor, with the mean or average of bodily measurements forming the basis of classification. Since categories of physical variation were in no way linked to mental ability or levels of cultural achievement, the construction of racial hierarchies was impossible, as no one group could be ranked higher than any other.[15]

Conceiving of race as nothing more than a category of physical variation meant that liberal anthropologists were reluctant to link the concept to language or culture. Groups that shared a common tongue or set of customs did not necessarily share a common physical type, and therefore race, language, and culture were not congruent. This stance was the basis of liberal anthropologists' opposition to "Aryan" or "Teutonic" racial theories.[16] Felix von Luschan, for example, rejected the notion of an Aryan race on the grounds that language and physical categories did not coincide.[17] Even as late as 1916, Rudolf Martin wrote that "Germans, Celts, and Slavs are linguistic terms, and therefore it is as laughable to speak of a Germanic or Celtic race, as it would be to refer to a long-skulled language."[18] In his influential anthropological textbook of 1914, Martin had similarly, if less polemically, argued that race, nation, and *Volk* were unrelated concepts.

---

15. George W. Stocking Jr., *Race, Culture, and Evolution: Essays in the History of Anthropology* (Chicago: University of Chicago Press, 1968), 167. Also see Massin, "From Virchow to Fischer," 87; Weindling, *Health, Race,* 55. After Virchow's death, his former student Franz Boas emphasized the importance of Virchow's argument that the "theromorphic variations of the human body . . . cannot be considered as proof of a low organization of the races. . . . There is no proof that such forms are connected with a low stage of culture of the people among whom they are found." Franz Boas, "Rudolf Virchow's Anthropological Work," in *The Shaping of American Anthropology, 1883–1911: A Franz Boas Reader,* ed. George W. Stocking (New York: Basic Books, 1974), 39–40.

16. Massin, "From Virchow to Fischer," 91–94.

17. Felix von Luschan, "Die anthropologische Stellung der Juden," *Correspondenz-Blatt der Deutschen Anthropologischen Gesellschaft (CBDAG)* 23 (1892): 95.

18. Rudolf Martin, "Germanen, Kelten, und Slaven," *Die Umschau* 20 (1916): 201. The distinction between race, language, and culture in German anthropological circles in the late nineteenth century also influenced the work of Franz Boas, who studied under Virchow and Adolf Bastian (1826–1905) in the 1880s. Echoing his German mentors, Boas maintained throughout his early career that there was no correlation between racial, linguistic, and cultural classifications. Cf. Douglas Cole, *Franz Boas: The Early Years, 1858–1906* (Seattle: University of Washington Press, 1999), 267–68.

The ethnological word *Volk* is to be sharply distinguished from the zoological and anthropological term *variety* or *race*. Whole units of smaller or larger groupings (tribe, clan, *Volk*, nation) are racial aggregates or racial pluralities that have fused into ethnic unions. The deciding factor [in these cases] is not, as with race, morphological agreement, blood relationship, or common ancestry. Rather, what binds the members of a *Volk* together is a common language and culture, a national feeling developed over time, a common government, political boundaries, etc. In anthropology, the term *Volk* has no place.[19]

In no uncertain terms, liberal anthropologists like Virchow and Martin inveighed against investing categories like nation and *Volk* with racial meaning. The anthropological study of physical varieties, or races, had nothing to do with cultural, linguistic, or political classifications.

This position accounted for the views of liberal anthropologists on the peoples of Europe. Virchow considered Europeans to be mixtures of racial elements or varieties. Admittedly, in his famous study of the skin, hair, and eye color of German schoolchildren in the 1870s, he had posited the existence of two basic European types: a blond, long-skulled variety and the brunette, short-skulled sort. As John Efron and Andrew Zimmerman have pointed out, this conceptual methodology reflected assumptions of Jewish and German difference, echoing the persistent popular view of the Jews as a "group apart."[20] Still, the fact remains that Virchow used the studies to show that the national population of Germany was a racial mixture and to argue that this mixture of types was a positive development. Virchow not only concluded that a mere thirty-two percent of Germans were of the blond type, but he also maintained that eleven percent of Jews belonged in that category as well, suggesting, in turn, that his two European types transcended national boundaries.[21]

Virchow, in other words, because of his political and scientific convictions, refused to posit clear-cut physical distinctions between Euro-

---

19. Rudolf Martin, *Lehrbuch der Anthropologie in systematischer Darstellung* (Jena: Gustav Fischer, 1914), 9.

20. John Efron, *Defenders of the Race: Jewish Doctors and Race Science in Fin-de-Siècle Europe* (New Haven: Yale University Press, 1994), 25–26; Zimmerman, "Anti-Semitism as Skill." See also George Mosse, *Towards the Final Solution: A History of European Racism* (Madison: University of Wisconsin Press, 1985), 90–93.

21. Rudolf Virchow, "Gesammtbericht über die Statistik der Farbe der Augen, der Haare, und der Haut der Schulkinder in Deutschland," *CBDAG* 16 (1885): 91.

pean peoples, and, in consequence, he continually maintained that all Europeans were interrelated. Even near the end of his life, Virchow argued that he could not tell any difference between a Germanic and a Slavic skull, and he similarly maintained that there were no clear physical boundaries between Celtic and Germanic peoples.[22] Moreover, his followers more or less retained this stance as well. Although Johannes Ranke used Virchow's study to argue that the blond type was more prominent in Germany than in the rest of central Europe—which rendered northern Germany the "land of the blondes"—he also affirmed that Poles, Finns, Slavs, and other peoples of Eastern Europe exhibited the characteristics of the blond, long-headed type as well.[23] In a similar vein, Julius Kollmann wrote that large national groupings like the French, Germans and Italians, as well as smaller groups like the Finns, Hungarians, and Bavarians, were mixtures of many different races.[24]

In the first decade of the twentieth century, some anthropologists began to break with central tenets of the liberal tradition, but they often continued to uphold the distinctions between race, nation, and *Volk*. The acceptance of Nordic racial typologies, for example, was one avenue along which several prominent anthropologists moved away from the ideas of Virchow and the liberal generation. The concept of the Nordic race, which was associated with the so-called anthroposociological school of Gustav de Lapouge in France and Otto Ammon in Germany, found several prominent adherents in the German anthropological community after 1900, including Gustav Schwalbe in Strasbourg and Eugen Fischer in Freiburg. Proponents of the Nordic race concept argued for the existence of up to six races in Europe, always contrasting a blond and long-skulled type with so-called Mediterranean, Alpine, and Dinaric varieties.[25] More importantly, they often glorified the Nordic race and ascribed nonphysical qualities to it. In 1903, Gustav Schwalbe, for example, argued that the Nordic race pos-

---

22. On Germans and Slavs, see Rudolf Virchow, "Über das Auftreten der Slaven in Deutschland," *CBDAG* 31 (1900): 112. On Celts and Germans, see Rudolf Virchow, "Meinungen und Thatsachen in der Anthropologie," *CBDAG* 30 (1899): 82.

23. Johannes Ranke, *Der Mensch,* vol. 2 (Leipzig: Verlag des Bibliographischen Institutes, 1887), 255, 263.

24. Julius Kollmann, "Die Menschenrassen Europa's und Asien's," *Vortrag gehalten in der zweiten Sitzung der 62. Versammlung Deutscher Naturforscher und Aerzte zu Heidelberg, 21. Sept.* (Heidelberg: Universitäts-Buchdruckerei von J. Hörning, 1889), 7.

25. See Joseph Deniker, *Les Races de l'Europe: L'indice cephalique en Europe* . . . (Paris, 1899). See also William Z. Ripley, *The Races of Europe: A Sociological Study* (New York: D. Appleton, 1899).

sessed a specific psychology that contrasted sharply with that of the Mediterranean race and other European types.[26] Similarly, Eugen Fischer maintained in 1910 that the Nordic race had been the driving force behind the greatest cultural achievements in European history.[27] But even these men, who had begun to consider race as an indicator of cultural and psychological character, were hesitant to equate it directly with nation or *Volk*. Schwalbe, for example, continued to emphasize that race was not related to the political category of nation or the linguistically determined classification of *Volk*.[28] Even Fischer, a staunch supporter of Nordic race typologies, was reluctant to apply the new racial breakdown to the peoples of Europe. In 1910, he warned against "wanting to connect these anthropological types [Nordic, Alpine, Mediterranean, and Dinaric] with peoples *(Völker)*. I consider the attempt to glean exact relationships to Finns, Slavs, Scythians, etc. premature."[29]

Despite the impact of Nordic race theory, the liberal figures in the field continued to view Germans as racially indistinct from other Europeans. As late as the eve of the war, they maintained that European populations did not possess essentialized racial identities linked to national categories. In the summer of 1914, Felix von Luschan, the professor of anthropology and ethnology at the University of Berlin, publicly championed the view that "among the peoples of Europe, there are extreme types and in-between forms, but nowhere firm boundaries."[30] Even the state of Prussia, he argued, was a racial mixture, adding that only "romantics and fanatics dream of physical unity as the single foundation of the highest cultural development."[31]

These views persisted in anthropological circles even after the outbreak of war. Johannes Ranke maintained in 1915 that the idea of "instinctive racial hatred between the 'Germanic' Germans and the

---

26. Gustav Schwalbe, "Über eine umfassende Untersuchung der physisch-anthropologischen Beschaffenheit der jetzigen Bevölkerung des Deutschen Reiches," *CBDAG* 34 (1903): 73–74.

27. Niels C. Lösch, *Rasse als Konstrukt: Leben und Werk Eugen Fischers* (Frankfurt am Main: Peter Lang, 1997), 101.

28. Schwalbe, "Über eine umfassende Untersuchung," 74.

29. See Fischer's comment at the end of E. Tschepourkovsky, "Zwei Haupttypen der Grossrussen, ihre geographische Verbreitung und ethnische Provenienz," *CBDAG* 41 (1910): 85.

30. "Felix von Luschan zum 60. Geburtstag," *Berliner Tageblatt*, 11 August 1914.

31. Felix von Luschan, "Zur Anthropologie der Preußen," *Berliner Tageblatt*, 7 June 1914.

'Celtic' English" was "obvious nonsense," since the Germans and the English were closely related.[32] In 1915, Rudolf Martin advanced a similar position: "To talk about racial hatred on European soil is . . . nonsense, a thoughtless act." Analyzing the peoples of Europe from the French in the west to the Russians in the east, he concluded, once again, that they were interrelated:

> From this examination of the prehistoric and historic relationships in Europe, the indisputable conclusion arises that despite regional variations all the peoples of western and central Europe are racially related to the highest degree as a result of their fusion and mixture stretching back thousands of years. In every one of us rolls the blood of innumerable ancestors; we are carriers of a manifold hereditary construction, and what we are, we are by virtue of this constant mixture and renewal of our blood.[33]

Instead of emphasizing the differences among Europeans, Martin argued that the peoples of Europe—his "we"—were not physically or racially distinct, but rather part of a common hereditary group among whom intermingling was a mark of progress. Despite the circulation of new Nordic racial typologies, Martin, Luschan, and Ranke treated "European" as a category that possessed conceptual unity; and even after the outbreak of the war in 1914, they adhered to the liberal tradition of separating race, nation, and *Volk*. But on the grounds of the POW camps, the liberal distinctions began to erode.

Setting Up the Studies

The POW project was an enormous undertaking that involved the military, a variety of government ministries, and representatives from various academic disciplines. Among the physical anthropologists, the plan to conduct studies in the camps also involved the scholarly communities of two countries, Germany and Austria-Hungary. And as the project took shape, many of the scientists who undertook the work on the ground were younger scholars in the very early stages of professionalization.

The original impetus for the studies in prisoner-of-war camps came

---

32. F. Birkner, "Johannes Ranke," *CBDAG* 47 (1916): 38.
33. Martin, "Germanen, Kelten, und Slaven," 204.

from several sources, chief among them the anthropological community in the Austro-Hungarian Empire. In the summer of 1915, Karl Toldt (1875–1961), the president of the Viennese Anthropological Society, raised the idea of studying the large numbers of captured Russian soldiers streaming into the POW camps of the Habsburg Empire.[34] Stressing the singular opportunity that the camps presented to scholars, the anthropological society of Vienna sought and quickly received approval of the Austro-Hungarian Imperial War Ministry to carry out studies in June 1915.[35] Toldt chose Rudolf Pöch, the professor of anthropology at the University of Vienna, to lead the Austrian POW project; and by the early summer of 1915, Pöch prepared a team for visits to camps in Bohemia.

At the same time, anthropologists and ethnologists in Germany broached the possibility of scientific work in the German camps. The first step was taken by the psychologist Carl Stumpf (1848–1936), a professor at the University of Berlin, who organized support for a "phonographic commission" designed to record the languages and songs of the POWs. Stumpf's idea found an early champion in Wilhelm Doegen (1877–1967), a Gymnasium teacher in Berlin with connections in the government and an interest in languages who soon became the driving force behind the project.[36] Scholars in Hamburg, including the linguist Carl Meinhof (1857–1944) and the ethnologist Paul Hambruch (1882–1933), also expressed interest in joining the project. Under the aegis of the Oriental Seminar in Berlin and the Prussian Cultural Ministry, the Royal Prussian Phonographic Commission was indeed created in 1915.[37] Stumpf was put in charge of the commission; but Doegen, who organized the phonographic recordings and arranged the visits to the camps, became the project's central figure. The high degree of organization and the widespread desire to

---

34. "Sitzungsberichte der Anthropologischen Gesellschaft in Wien: Jahrgang 1915/16," *Mitteilungen der Anthropologischen Gesellschaft Wien (MAGW)* 46 (1916): 10–11.

35. Rudolf Pöch, "I. Bericht über die von der Wiener Anthropolg. Gesellschaft in d. k. u. k. Kriegsgefangenlagern veranlaßten Studien," *MAGW* 45 (1915): 219.

36. Something of a self-promoter, Doegen claimed after the war that the idea of a wartime phonographic commission was more or less his, since he had long dreamed of founding a state language museum that would include "the voices, the languages, and the music of all peoples of earth on gramophone recordings." Wilhelm Doegen, introduction to *Unter Fremden Völkern: Eine neue Völkerkunde* (Berlin: Otto Stohlberg, Verlag für Politik und Wirtschaft, 1925), 9.

37. Meinhof to Bürgermeister von Melle, 9 October 1915, Staatsarchiv der Freien und Hansestadt Hamburg, 361–5 II Hochschulwesen II W a 8, Bl. 1.

participate signaled that that POW project was the most prominent anthropological endeavor of the war years.

Although the commission originated around the study of language, it also included a section for physical anthropology, headed by Felix von Luschan. Luschan's group was to conduct measurement-based studies of bodily characteristics, a project that presented a research opportunity for his students. Luschan quickly chose Egon von Eickstedt, a young anthropologist in search of a dissertation topic, as a central participant. Having served as a doctor in a mobile X-ray unit on the western front for several months, Eickstedt was particularly pleased to secure leave and join the POW project. After an injury on the front, Otto Reche, a physical anthropologist at the ethnographic museum in Hamburg, also joined the project in 1917.

Luschan, who was born and raised near Vienna and retained close ties to anthropologists there, was eager to collaborate with the Austrians. He agreed with Pöch's suggestion that the German and Austrian POW projects adopt standardized methods of measuring prisoners and recording data.[38] Both teams would seek to investigate the physical and racial makeup of prisoners in order to determine the original racial elements that had combined to form the groups under study.[39] In practice, this goal meant that anthropologists investigated a host of physical characteristics by taking measurements of heads and bodies and conducting observations of bodily features ranging from hair color to eye shape. These methods were no different from those of Virchow's generation, but the interpretations that emerged from the camps diverged considerably from the liberal tradition. The shift was fueled not only by wartime nationalism, but also by the surroundings in which the anthropologists conducted their work.

---

38. Pöch to Luschan, 29 August 1915, Nachlaß Felix Luschans, Handschriftenabteilung, Staatsbibliothek zu Berlin—Preußischer Kulturbesitz (NL Luschan), File Pöch. Over the course of the war, Pöch wrote a series of articles that described the standard measurement schema and recording methods that both German and Austrian anthropologists were to use in the camps. See Rudolf Pöch, "I. Bericht . . ." *MAGW* 45 (1915): 219–35; Rudolf Pöch, "II. Bericht über die von der Wiener Anthropologischen Gesellschaft in den k. u. k. Kriegsgefangenenlagern veranlaßten Studien," *MAGW* 46 (1916): 107–31; Rudolf Pöch, "III. Bericht über die von der Wiener Anthropologischen Gesellschaft in den k. u. k. Kriegsgefangenenlagern veranlaßten Studien," 47 (1917): 77–100; Pöch, "IV. Bericht über die von der Wiener Anthropologischen Gesellschaft in d. k. u. k. Kriegsgefangenlagern veranlaßten Studien," *MAGW* 48 (1918): 146–61.

39. Pöch, "III. Bericht," 79.

Encounters in the Camps

Unlike previous anthropological undertakings, the study of POWs took place within a peculiar context in the history of the discipline. The project was defined not only by the realities of a major world war, but also by a specific wartime milieu: the prisoner-of-war camp. The conditions at these sites had a direct impact, both on the studies as scientific practice and on the conclusions drawn from them. As locations for anthropological inquiry, the camps placed Europeans into subject positions that were almost identical to those occupied by many non-Europeans in similar camps created during earlier colonial wars. Indeed, in this prison environment, the distinction between Europeans and non-Europeans quickly collapsed, replaced by a new constellation that sharply contrasted a variety of national and ethnic groups with their captors. Housed together as enemies of the German or Austrian empire, the prisoners were already political "others" by virtue of their affiliations in the European conflict—a division that was further underscored by the difficult physical conditions and military discipline of the camps. Within this world, German anthropologists held positions of significant power and authority, often equaling or even exceeding the dominance they enjoyed in colonial situations. In the camps, anthropologists gained unprecedented access to the bodies of prisoners, non-Europeans and Europeans alike, compelling them to take part in anthropological investigations. The physical circumstances and lopsided power relationships drastically altered the subject position of the European prisoners, highlighting their difference from Germans and thereby allowing new categorizations to emerge.

For the scientists, the POW camps were ideal for anthropological work. The concentration of so many different peoples in one place rendered them veritable laboratories for the study of race. In addition, anthropologists like Pöch were pleased that the camps contained a population in which bodily deformities and abnormalities had been eliminated, as the men had been selected for fitness and health by their respective armies. As he noted, "All the preparations for finding and bringing in those to be measured fall away: the people are there and at our disposal. The [human] material doesn't need to be sifted through first; through the requirements of fitness for service, less useful elements for the study of racial characteristics are shut out."[40] Perhaps

---

40. Pöch, "Anthropologische Studien an Kriegsgefangenen," 989.

Abbildung 1. Kontrollierte vertikale Haltung des Anthropometers.

Fig. 1. Rudolf Pöch's team at work taking measurements in the camps during World War I. Subjects were forced to stand in stiff, fixed positions. (Courtesy of the New York Public Library.)

most importantly, the camps also allowed immediate comparisons of the POWs from diverse racial backgrounds, an undertaking that was normally impossible, even in the colonial context. Pöch wrote that "the prisoner-of-war camps offer a rare opportunity for comparative observations; never before have representatives of the most different human groups been [available] to observe alongside each other under such similar conditions!"[41] In the camps, the European prisoner stood alongside the non-European, both inviting anthropological comparison as racial "others," different, in other words, from Germans.

On a daily basis, the spaces in which the anthropologists lived and moved distinguished them from the prison population. Indeed, the conditions in the camps highlighted the distinction between inmates and captors at the same time as they broke down divisions between European and non-European prisoners. From the very beginning of the war, the German military housed all imprisoned soldiers together. Despite the protests of the Allied powers, inmates were not separated or sorted according to nationality or ethnicity.[42] This policy meant that POWs from Russia, Britain, Belgium, Serbia, and France not only shared living space with each other, but also with colonial soldiers from Africa, India, and other parts of the globe. As a result of this arrangement, the primary institutional distinction in the camps was not between groups of inmates, but between the staff and the peoples under their control. Moreover, the physical conditions in the compounds further served to demarcate the camp personnel from the imprisoned soldiers. Because of the enormous influx of prisoners in the first few months of the war, the camps were often overcrowded and ill equipped.[43] While the prisoners were housed in cramped barracks, the anthropologists resided in separate military quarters that, while by no means luxurious, were certainly more spacious. The scientists also ate with the camp officers and doctors, separate from the inmates.[44]

The military discipline of the camps further distanced the internees from their captors. The POWs were under the martial law of the German army and subject to a battery of rules, ranging from regulations about the washing of clothes to restrictions against smoking in the bar-

---

41. Rudolf Pöch, review of O. Stiehl's "Unsere Feinde," *MAGW* 47 (1917): 122.

42. Speed, *Prisoners, Diplomats,* 65. See also Daniel J. McCarthy, *The Prisoner of War in Germany* (New York: Moffat, Yard, 1917), 45–46.

43. As the war dragged on and shortages gripped the German home front, many of the prisoners suffered from malnutrition and disease (Speed, *Prisoners, Diplomats,* 66). Also see Robert Jackson, *The Prisoners, 1914–18* (New York: Routledge, 1989), 8–54.

44. "Sitzungsberichte der Anthropologischen Gesellschaft," 11.

Kleinrusse aus dem Gouvernement Kijew

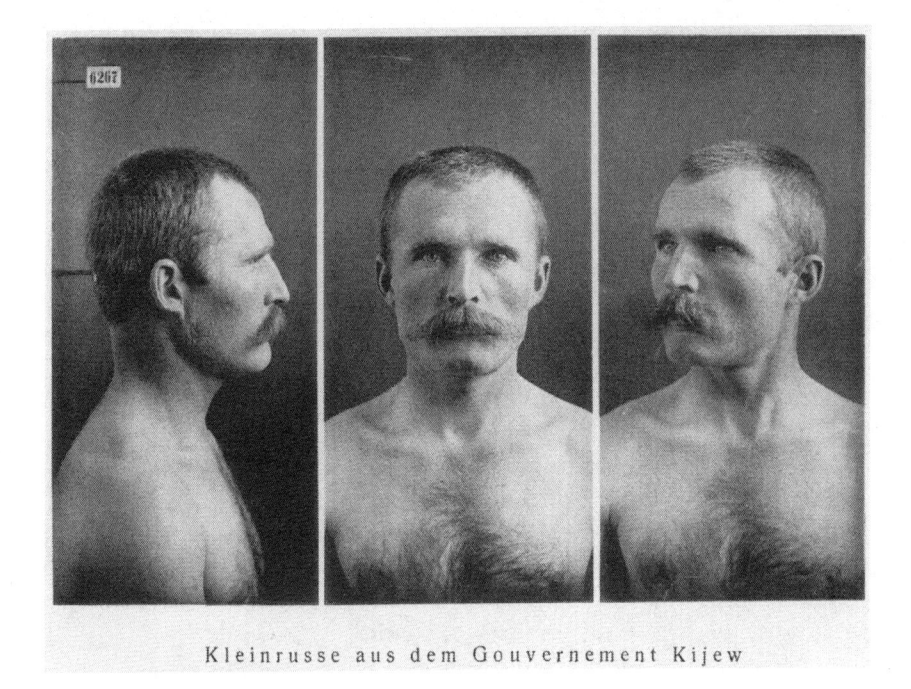

Fig. 2. Photograph of Ukrainian soldier taken by Rudolf Pöch's team in the standard anthropological format of profile, frontal, and three-quarter views, 1917. Subjects were to be photographed naked against blank backgrounds to isolate racial characteristics. (Courtesy of the New York Public Library.)

racks.[45] Although the general level of discipline within the camps varied widely and depended heavily on the camp commander,[46] the prisoners' movements and behaviors were always supervised and monitored: a camp schedule determined the daily routine of prisoners, mail was censored, escape attempts were punished. All aspects of life were conducted in a common space under the singular authority of the German army. Erving Goffman has noted that in institutions controlling the time and space of inmates, a fundamental split occurs between the prisoners and the staff.[47] The organizational dynamic of such a situa-

---

45. McCarthy, *Prisoner of War in Germany,* 281–94.
46. Speed, *Prisoners, Diplomats,* 76.
47. Goffman's model of the "total institution" is problematic because it does not allow for the agency of the inmates, but his description of the interactions between inmates and staff in such institutions as prisons and asylums is useful here. Erving Goffman, *Asylums: Essays on the Social Situations of Mental Patients and Other Inmates* (New York: Anchor, 1961).

tion creates social distance between the two groups, limiting the flow of information and social interaction across the divide. The arrangement of life in the camps similarly accentuated the distance between the prisoners and the staff, further demarcating the anthropologists from the POWs they were to study.

In many ways, the camp dynamic replicated and even heightened the dominance anthropologists enjoyed over their subjects in many colonial contexts. A comparison between the POW projects during World War I and the well-known German South Sea Expedition of 1908–10 is particularly useful in this regard, especially because several anthropologists, including Paul Hambruch and Otto Reche, participated in both enterprises. On the South Sea voyage, ethnological and anthropological study took place in a militarized atmosphere, in which scientists often used weapons and threats of violence to force their subjects to hand over cultural artifacts or participate in measurements.[48] And to this end, scholars often arrived at indigenous villages backed by armed escorts. The situation in the camps was similar. The wartime prison milieu was also militarized, and the anthropologists clearly had the backing of the German army to conduct their studies.

But in several respects, the power of the scientists in POW camps even exceeded that of most colonial undertakings. During the South Sea Expedition, Otto Reche, for example, complained that it was difficult to measure or photograph the indigenous peoples, since they were "afraid of every instrument and [ran] away."[49] In the camps, by contrast, the prisoners could not escape; they were at the disposal of the anthropologists. Rudolf Martin commented in 1915 that the military discipline of the camps made the prisoners more available: "The people are not busy (or only partly), and because they stand under military guard, [they] are more accessible for bodily measurements than they would be in their homeland."[50] Moreover, in the POW camps, the anthropologists felt no danger from their subjects. During the South Sea Expedition, groups of antagonized islanders attacked the anthropologists on several occasions, both on land and on water.[51] In the POW camps, by contrast, the presence of the military rendered the

---

48. Hans Fischer, *Die Hamburger Südsee-Expedition: Über Ethnographie und Kolonialismus* (Frankfurt am Main: Syndikat, 1981), 125–38.
49. Ibid., 98.
50. Rudolf Martin, "Anthropologische Untersuchungen an Kriegsgefangene," *Die Umschau* 19 (1915): 1017.
51. Fischer, *Die Hamburger Südsee-Expedition,* 132.

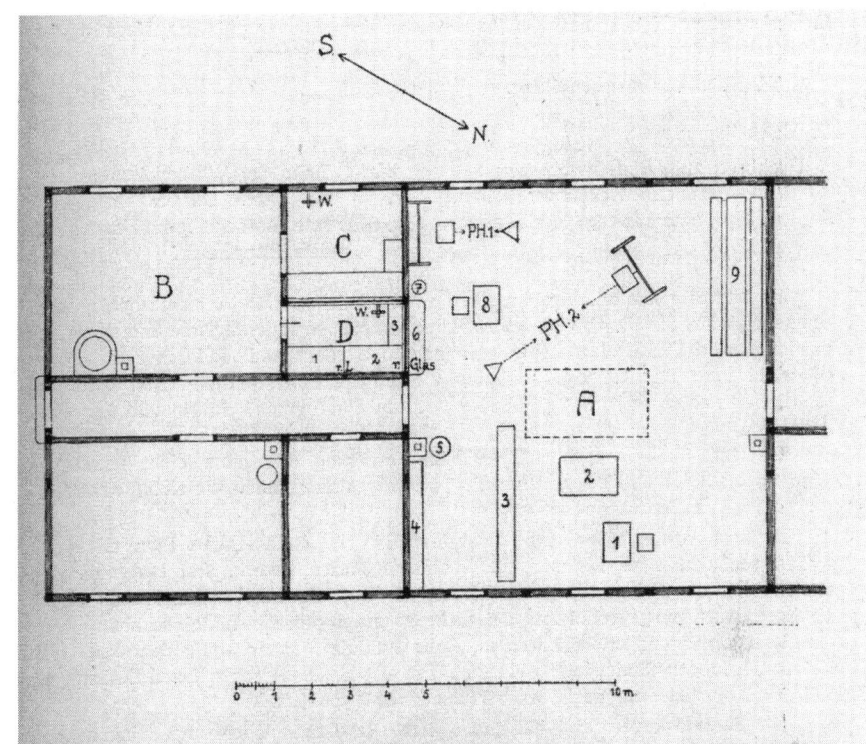

Abb. 2. **Plan der Einrichtung einer Baracke zu anthropologischen Untersuchungen.**

A. Großer, sechsfenstriger Saal zur anthropo-geographischen Aufnahme, Messung, Somatoskopie und Photographie.

1. Tisch des Schreibers;
2. Podium für die Körpermessung;
3. Tisch zum Auflegen der Meßgeräte;
4. Wandgestell zum Trocknen der entwickelten Negative;
5. Ofen;
6. Wandgestell für photographische Kassetten, Metronom u. dgl.;
7. Waschbecken;
8. Tisch zum Somatoskopieren;
9. Bänke und Tisch zur anthropo-geographischen Aufnahme.

PH 1. Aufstellung des photographischen Apparates, Stuhles und Hintergrundes für Gesichtsaufnahmen,

PH 2. Aufstellung des photographischen Apparates, der Fußplatte und des Hintergrundes für Körperaufnahmen.

B. Zweifenstriger Nebenraum zum Gipsformen, gleichzeitig Depotraum für Kisten und Material.

Fig. 3. Pöch's plan for setting up a barracks for anthropological investigations, 1917. The space included a podium for anthropological measurements (2), a table and benches for recording geographical data (9), areas for photography (PH. 1 and 2), and a room for making plaster casts (B). (Courtesy of the New York Public Library.)

encounter with the inmates a nonthreatening venture. Anthropologists like Pöch felt safe and therefore claimed that the camps allowed for a more objective anthropological science: "The investigation can take place in the best possible outer conditions. . . . All hindrances from prejudices fall away, all possible thoughts or fear of the unknown."[52] For the same reason, he described the study of POWs as "work in a laboratory, compared to that of the research trip outside."[53] The lopsided power relations in the camps confirmed the position of the prisoners as subjects of anthropological and racial inquiry, as "others" fundamentally unlike their captors. In this "laboratory," anthropologists could study Europeans and non-Europeans alike.

The resistance of both Europeans and non-Europeans to the studies confirmed the common subject position of the prisoners. Officially, Rudolf Pöch proclaimed that the participants in his studies were volunteers, who enjoyed the investigations as an escape from the crushing boredom of imprisonment.[54] In reality, however, many of the prisoners sought to avoid or even undermine the studies by disrupting or resisting the process of taking bodily measurements, photographs, or plaster moldings. When working in a POW camp near Berlin, for example, Pöch had to rely on the camp commander for help in overcoming prisoners' hesitations regarding the plaster casting process. The commander allowed a molding of his own head to be taken in an attempt to surmount, as Pöch put it, the "persistent shyness of the people toward this procedure."[55] Many prisoners clearly did not wish to undergo the process of having a cast made of their features. Eickstedt, for his part, complained to Luschan about the unwillingness of some prisoners to participate in his investigations: "I have begun to measure the Russian Jews. Most of these find little pleasure in anthropology and seek . . . to get out of my nice [*nett*] measurements in every way possible."[56] Eickstedt's "nice measurements" were clearly unpleasant for these POWs, who were hardly volunteers. Eickstedt also complained that some of the prisoners, such as the Algerians, purposefully tried to "shirk" the studies by misleading him about their ethnic backgrounds and home regions.[57] The French were particularly untrustworthy, he claimed,

---

52. Pöch, "Anthropologische Studien an Kriegsgefangenen," 989.
53. Ibid.
54. Pöch, "Anthropologische Studien an Kriegsgefangenen," 990.
55. Pöch to Luschan, 27 February 1918, NL Luschan, File Pöch.
56. Eickstedt to Luschan, 11–12 January 1916, NL Luschan, File Eickstedt.
57. Eickstedt to Luschan, 18 March 1916, NL Luschan, File Eickstedt.

because they made false statements about their origins; the Tartars, in contrast, were "nice people and don't do this."[58] As subject of anthropological inquiry, the French thus came to occupy the same category as Algerians or Tartars. Located opposite Germans in a difficult and tense power relationship, the POW researchers put these Europeans in the same colonial position as Africans and Asians: disciplined by outside control, their racial background defined by those with power over them.

Nationalism, Race, and the European Enemy

In their work with the POW population, each of the three principal anthropologists in the camps—Eickstedt, Reche, and Pöch—came to conflate the categories of nation and race, thereby departing from the tenets of Virchow's liberal anthropology. In so doing, they also implicitly crafted a new definition of the "European" modeled on the peoples of the Central Powers. There were several different avenues that led to the investigation and portrayal of national enemies as racial "others," as each anthropologist made decisions that, while governed by his ideological convictions, were nevertheless channeled, shaped, and in many ways made possible by conditions and experiences within the camps. Of the three men, Egon von Eickstedt was most influenced by the camp milieu, investigating Europeans on the basis of national citizenship only after several months on the project. Motivated by a brand of expansionist nationalism, Reche, in turn, was more interested in establishing racial connections between Germans and the peoples they might rule over as a result of the war. Rudolf Pöch, for his part, was influenced by his position as a subject of Austria-Hungary. In his work, he avoided the racial investigation of ethnic groups that were part of the Dual Monarchy, assigning non-European racial identities to the Eastern opponents of the Central Powers instead. The common element in each case was the combination of wartime nationalism and the scientific practice of camp studies. In and of themselves, neither the camps nor the nationalist ideologies were enough to cause the conflation of nation and race; but in combination, they greatly facilitated the efforts of these three anthropologists to move away from the sharp distinctions of liberal anthropology.

Egon von Eickstedt's gradual path to the conflation of race and nation demonstrates the dual effects of the camp experience and

---

58. Eickstedt to Luschan, 3 April 1916, NL Luschan, File Eickstedt.

wartime nationalism. At the outset of his project, Eickstedt had been thoroughly uninterested in European prisoners as objects of anthropological inquiry. Following Luschan's advice, he had initially sought to investigate the physical characteristics "of an anthropologically interesting group: Indians, Turks, or inner Asians."[59] Eventually settling on the racial characteristics of the Sikhs as the topic for his dissertation,[60] he, at first, considered camps that contained large concentrations of peoples from Western or Eastern Europe a disappointment. On one of his first visits to a camp near Gross-Brusen, Eickstedt reported to Luschan that Armenians, Georgians, and Tartars were available for study there, but added with a hint of frustration that "otherwise there are only known Europeans."[61] After several months, however, his view changed. His correspondence with Luschan reveals a growing sense that certain European groups did warrant racial investigation; and when faced with a shortage of "foreign" (i.e., non-European) peoples in June 1916, Eickstedt asked permission to expand his focus: "Under these conditions allow me to ask . . . if it would not be appropriate to take on the investigation of peoples like the Scots, Irish, English, Ukrainians, Poles, ethnic Russians, etc."[62] His delay in identifying European peoples as anthropologically interesting suggests that his shift in focus was motivated by more than pure contingency or a shortage of "exotics." Only after he had spent several months in the camps and worked in an atmosphere that helped break down the distinctions between Europeans and non-Europeans did he begin to place Europeans into the new position of anthropological object.

This gradual development of new categorizations was also fueled by Eickstedt's nationalist perspective. He came to consider certain Europeans as racial "others" because of their status as enemies. His letters reveal that he subscribed to a brand of wartime nationalism that imagined Germany as surrounded by hostile opponents. He referred to the allied blockade, for example, as a "boa constrictor set upon us by our enemies." More importantly, he associated the Allies with non-European peoples, speculating that their possible victory would unleash a new "yellow danger" on Europe and signal cultural domination by

---

59. Luschan to Eickstedt, 30 July 1915, NL Luschan, File Eickstedt.
60. See Egon von Eickstedt, "Rassenelemente der Sikh," *Zeitschrift für Ethnologie* 52 (1920–21): 317–94.
61. Eickstedt to Luschan, 31 December 1915, NL Luschan, File Eickstedt.
62. Eickstedt to Luschan, 9 June 1916, NL Luschan, File Eickstedt.

East Asia.⁶³ In the milieu of the camps, it was a short step from a nationalism that coded Germany's enemies as non-European to a view of Europeans as racial others. As overtly nationalist considerations began to drive his selection of subjects, he, for example, wrote to Luschan that he had located a number of Jews, but wanted to change his focus to the "enemy peoples" of Russia: "I would like to ask . . . if I can finish with this group so that I can turn to the generally harder to reach enemy Russian peoples."⁶⁴ His use of the term *enemy* suggests that he considered the peoples of Russia anthropologically interesting not only because they were harder to reach, but also because they were Germany's opponents in the Great War.

In a process of contingent negotiation shaped by the conditions in the camps and his own nationalism, Eickstedt fully abandoned the liberal distinction between nation and race, beginning to select and investigate his subjects on the basis of national citizenship. The organization of Eickstedt's data provided evidence for this process. Before the war, anthropologists usually organized their data according to ethnic group, region, or physical type; but Eickstedt listed the peoples he examined according to national citizenship. A summary of the individuals he examined in 1916 revealed that he had measured hundreds of subjects from Russia and Western Europe, including 743 "Russian citizens," ranging from "Jews from Russia" to "peoples of the Caucasus." And while Eickstedt made a distinction between "colored" soldiers and those of "European descent" in his list of 353 "French citizens," he nonetheless organized sub-Saharan Africans, Moroccans, Corsicans, Basques, and "southern French" under one overall heading. In other words, Eickstedt considered the French soldiers as a coherent racial "other," classing them in a grouping that included troops from Africa and the Near East. Eickstedt also listed 104 "Serbians and British," an odd category that unified only Scots, Serbian Gypsies, and Irish.⁶⁵

Equally telling, however, were the groups Eickstedt did not select for study. For example, he apparently never measured any English POWs, even though he had mentioned them as possible objects of study. Nor did he examine any soldiers from northern France, a region

---

63. Eickstedt Luschan, 8 June 1916, NL Luschan, File Eickstedt.
64. Eickstedt to Luschan, 15 January [1916], NL Luschan, File Eickstedt.
65. Eickstedt to Luschan, 6 December 1916, NL Luschan, File Eickstedt.

whose inhabitants were considered to be closely related to Germans. Most importantly, however, he did not examine Russian POWs of German descent, despite the presence of Volga Germans in the camps.[66] All these groups were linked, however tangentially, to "Germanness"—a fact that precluded their investigation as racial "others." Thus, Eickstedt's implicit category of "European" included the English, northern French, and, at the center, Germans, suggesting that a notion of Germanness functioned as the standard against which racial otherness was judged. By selecting anthropological subjects on the basis of national citizenship, Eickstedt filled the concept of nation with racial meaning. At the same time, he narrowed the category of European, casting many groups as worthy of anthropological attention because of their hypostatized difference from an unstated German norm.

While Eickstedt created new categories of Europeanness based largely on his experience in the POW camps, Otto Reche brought a fully formed nationalist perspective to the project from the very beginning. Before the war, Reche had already signaled his adherence to a brand of Nordic racialism with a 1909 article on the prehistoric peoples of the Stone Age that characterized the Nordic race as "warlike" and "robust."[67] And if anything, Reche's wartime experiences strengthened his nationalist convictions even further. He joined the POW project in 1917 after being injured at the front, where he had served as an infantry officer for three years. Later, during the 1930s, Reche's admirers pointed out that his service during the Great War had been crucial in shaping his nationalist convictions as well as his politically driven anthropology.[68]

In addition to his overtly nationalist motivations, the camp milieu also had an effect on Reche, who did not immediately begin his investigations with the study of Europeans. Luschan initially recommended that he focus on an ethnic group from Central Asia, and Reche briefly

---

66. Doegen's ethnological team collected songs and folktales from Russian soldiers of German descent in German POW camps. Adolf Lane, "Deutsche Bauernkolonien im alten Russland," in *Unter Fremden Völkern: Eine neue Völkerkunde,* ed. Wilhelm Doegen (Berlin: Otto Stollberg Verlag für Politik und Wirtschaft, 1925), 267–74.

67. Otto Reche, "Zur Anthropologie der jüngeren Steinzeit in Schlesien und Böhmen," *Archiv für Anthropologie* 35 (1908): 230.

68. In 1939, Günther Spannus wrote that Reche had "found his way to the *völkisch* movement and with it to political anthropology as an old frontline soldier and nationalist." See Otto Spannus, "Otto Reche als Völkerkundler," in *Kultur und Rasse: Otto Reche zum 60. Geburtstag,* ed. Michael Hesch and Günther Spannaus (Munich: J. F. Lehmann, 1939), 251.

examined Tartars and other Asian groups when he began work on the project.[69] After some weeks, however, his nationalist motivations came to the fore as he shifted his attention to Germany's western European enemies: "I have occupied myself less with the Eastern theater of war—Pöch already has [made a] pleasant series there—and more with our Western enemies, especially those which until now have been the least measured."[70] This process of selection was motivated by more than a shortage of "exotic" subjects, however, as Reche eventually also turned to the investigation of groups from the Eastern Front, such as the peoples of the Baltics.

Motivated by an expansionist vision of the German empire, Reche selected those Europeans for study who might fall under German dominion in the wake of the Great War. In other words, he was primarily interested in determining the racial makeup of the peoples who might be permanently incorporated into the German empire. Reche readily admitted that political considerations drove his selection of subjects. In 1918, his report to his superiors in Hamburg read:

> I devoted my work to the representatives of smaller peoples that until now have been less accessible to anthropology or were completely uninvestigated, and in particular those that *as a result of the war may come into a tighter political connection with us and therefore deserve our special attention.* Therefore I measured Lithuanians, Latvians, Estonians, and especially Flemish, as well as Rumanians, southern French, Bretons, Irish, Scots, and English from a general anthropological point of view and for purposes of comparison.[71]

Writing in a period when German victory still seemed possible, Reche thus paid particular attention to the peoples who lived in territories already occupied by Germany. In 1918, when Reche conducted his investigations, the German empire did indeed control the Baltic, which it was fashioning into a veritable German colony. Likewise, Germany controlled large stretches of Belgium, where the Flemish were a major part of the population. In another report, Reche stated that he also

---

69. Reche to v. Luschan, 2 July 1917, NL Luschan, File Reche.
70. Otto Reche to Felix v. Luschan, 8 January 1918, NL Luschan, File Reche.
71. Emphasis added. Reche to Hamburg Oberschulbehörde, 13 March 1918, StA Hmg 361–5 II Hochschulwesen II W a 8, Bl. 31–32.

investigated POWs from northern France, where Germany had a foothold as well.[72]

Reche's conclusions represented an attempt to legitimize the extension of the German empire on racial terms. Not surprisingly, the peoples Reche envisioned as part of a future Germany were of predominantly Northern European extraction. To these groups, he assigned primary racial characteristics that emphasized their connection to Northern European, that is, Germanic, stock. He reported that "in Estonians, Latvians, and Lithuanians, one finds a quite extraordinarily strong element of Northern European blood." Similarly, he argued that "the Flemish were certainly to be characterized anthropologically as Germans," implying not only that Germans possessed a singular anthropological profile, but that the Flemish matched it.[73] Reche maintained that the Rumanians, under German control when he studied them in 1917, were primarily of Mongolian and Mediterranean extraction; those from the Carpathian Mountains, however, demonstrated a strong strain of Nordic blood and often possessed blond hair and blue eyes.[74] In contrast, the Irish and Bretons, opponents whose eventual inclusion in the German empire was unlikely, demonstrated elements of a "long extinct old European type," ostensibly unrelated to the Nordic race. Conflating race, nation, and *Volk,* such judgments served to assign racial types to the peoples under consideration, at the same time as they identified Germans as possessing a unified anthropological makeup associated with the Nordic race. While Eickstedt cast a selection of Germany's enemies as racial others, Reche, in effect, sought to accomplish the inverse: he portrayed certain European groups as racially related to Germans as a means of legitimizing political expansion and national aggrandizement.

Much like Eickstedt, the Austrian team under Rudolf Pöch concentrated its energies on creating anthropological definitions of the Central Powers' chief opponents. However, in doing so, they avoided national groups represented both in the POW population and the Austro-Hungarian Empire. In the process, Pöch and his assistants primarily focused on the racial identities of Russians and other enemies on the Eastern front. In the multiethnic context of the Habsburg Monarchy, rife with nationalist struggles, the association of the enemy with non-

---

72. Georg Thilenius, "Museum für Völkerkunde: Bericht für das Jahr 1917," Museum für Völkerkunde, Hamburg D 4,44, Bl. 1–5.

73. Reche to Hamburg Oberschulbehörde, 13 March 1918. StA Hmg 361-5 II Hochschulwesen II W a 8, Bl. 31–32.

74. Reche to Oberschulbehörde, 13 March 1918.

European racial elements was an effective means of creating difference between Austria-Hungary and its opponents while maintaining the precarious image of a unified empire. Thus, Pöch's conflation of nation and race was motivated by proimperial patriotism, reflected in the path he took to arrive at his position.

Pöch's patriotic politics combined with his experience in the camps to determine the selection and characterization of his subjects. Like Eickstedt (and Reche to a lesser extent), Pöch and his team found their way to the racial characterization of Austria-Hungary's enemies only after some time in the camps. Initially, they privileged the "exotic," officially targeting peoples from Central Asia as their primary interest. In his first report on the studies, Pöch claimed that his team aimed at investigating "the smaller, anthropologically less well known peoples of the Russian Empire . . . such as the peoples of the Caucasus, Siberia, and the Mongolian tribes in the southeast of European Russia."[75] But despite these official goals, Pöch and his assistants quickly came to focus most of their attention on peoples from the Western parts of the Russian Empire. Pöch's choices demonstrated the dual influence of the camp milieu and his political considerations. Depending on the particular camp, Pöch investigated ethnic Russians, Ukrainians, Bulgarians, Serbs, and other peoples from the Balkans, most of whom were hardly part of a "smaller, less anthropologically known group." In fact, ethnic Russians, Ukrainians, and Serbs made up the bulk of the individuals Pöch investigated.[76]

While this focus reflected the proportions of peoples actually present, as there were few "exotics" from Central Asia in most Austrian camps, political considerations were equally important. Pöch's inclusion of the Serbs, for example, indicated that his project went beyond the boundaries of the Russian empire to encompass all of Austria-Hungary's principal enemies on the Eastern Front. In addition, although he measured some twelve Poles and seven Italians at a camp in 1917, Pöch generally avoided the investigation of ethnic groups that were part of Austria-Hungary, even though many of them were represented in the Russian army.[77] As in Eickstedt's case, it is also

---

75. Pöch, "I. Bericht," 220.
76. Pöch, "III. Bericht," 97–100.
77. Pöch, "IV. Bericht," 147–48. The place of the Italians in Pöch's project was admittedly ambiguous. Pöch measured few Italians in the camps, but he contributed a collection of anthropological photographs to the popular "war exhibit" in Vienna that included several racial portraits of Italian POWs alongside images of the Dual Monarchy's other principal enemies, Serbs and Russians. See "Sitzungsberichte der Anthropologischen Gesellschaft in Wien: Jahrgang 1916/17," *MAGW* 47 (1917): 57.

significant that Russian POWs of German descent never turned up in the lists of subjects. In short, Pöch implicitly refused to consider the peoples of the Austro-Hungarian Empire as racial "others." The chief exception was the Serbs, who warranted racial investigation as one the empire's central enemies, internal and external. His choices suggested that he had the tenuous multinational configuration of the Dual Monarchy in mind when he conducted his studies. Rather than make physical distinctions among the peoples living within the empire, he sought to emphasize its unity through the characterization of its enemies as racially different.

Pöch's blending of race and nation can best be seen in his characterization of the peoples of Russia. Despite examining a huge assortment of ethnic groups from a variety of regions and backgrounds, he produced a portrayal that suggested a unified racial identity associated with Asia rather than Europe. Specifically, Pöch set out to determine the degree of Mongolian influence on the peoples of the Russian Empire; and he spent a great deal of time scrutinizing his subjects' eyes, because they "were the carrier of characteristics that easily gave away a mixture of Mongolian blood."[78] Pöch's emphasis on Mongolian features in the studies of Russian POWs was documented in an article for a popular science journal in 1916, in which he provided a montage of Russian eyes designed to demonstrate the degrees of Mongolian influence in the Russian population.[79] Despite his overall claim that the peoples of the Russian Empire were a racial mixture, Pöch sought to cast his subjects, albeit to widely varying degrees, as Mongolian. Considering the political situation in Europe during World War I, it is hardly surprising that Pöch characterized Russians through racial characteristics traditionally viewed as alien to Central Europe. While he never discussed the history of the Mongols in Europe and avoided popular stereotypes of invading Mongol hordes, his emphasis on the Mongolian makeup of Russians cast Austria-Hungary's eastern enemy as a non-European racial "other." Operating within the multiethnic context of Austria-Hungary, Pöch deemphasized the potentially divisive notion of Germanness; instead, he implicitly contrasted Central Europeans to "Asian" Russians—a characterization that rendered the categories of nation and race fluid and ascribed a racial identity to the enemy.

---

78. Pöch, "I. Bericht," 224.
79. Pöch, "Anthropologische Studien an Kriegsgefangenen," 990.

A similar mode of operation characterized the work of Pöch's chief assistant in the camps, Joseph Weninger. In a lecture before the Viennese anthropological society on the POW studies, Weninger argued that Serbs and Albanians exhibited "Near Eastern" racial characteristics. In this case, the Serbs—a principal antagonist of Austria-Hungary on the eastern front and the group blamed for the outbreak of the war—received a distinctly non-European racial identity:

> In the middle of the [Balkan] peninsula as well as in the north with the Serbs and in the west with the Albanians the [physical] elements classify themselves as closely related to the Near Eastern. Yes indeed, these racial elements contribute a great deal to the makeup of the physical characteristics of the peoples who oppose us there today.[80]

The message was clear: the enemies of the Central Powers on the Eastern Front, particularly the Serbs, were not of European origin. Moreover, by linking the Serbs to the Near East, Weninger implicitly associated them with the Turks, the quintessential racial and cultural "other" in the history of the Austrian Empire. Like Pöch and Eickstedt, Weninger used anthropology to narrow the category of "European" by tying the enemies of the Central Powers to regions and peoples outside of Europe.

The path to the conflation of liberal categories and the particular form it took thus depended on the personal perspective of the scientist and the particular context in which he worked. The German anthropologists Eickstedt and Reche produced racial portrayals that mobilized Germanness as an implicit standard. The Austrians, in contrast, assigned non-European racial identities to the enemies of the Habsburg Monarchy in an effort to fortify the distinction between Austria-Hungary and its eastern opponents. In each case, some form of nationalism or patriotism drove the process, but it always did so in combination with the practical experience in the camps. The camp milieu was crucial to the conflation of nation and race, because it collapsed earlier distinctions between "exotic" and "nonexotic" subjects and facilitated the racial study of national enemies. Thus, the experience of camp anthropology enlivened a discourse on race that in many

---

80. Josef Weninger, "Über die Verbreitung von vorderasiatischer Rassenmerkmale," *MAGW* 48 (1918): 43.

ways anticipated the directions anthropologists would take in the postwar period; it was a path that took them further afield from the tradition of liberal anthropology.

After the Camps

The defeat of the Central Powers and the consequent dissolution of the POW camps notwithstanding, wartime anthropology helped set the tenor for the anthropology of the Weimar period. Fully abandoning the liberal definitions of race, nation, and *Volk,* it was at that time that the discipline began to transform itself into *Rassenkunde,* the overtly racist brand of "racial science." The anthropologists who had worked in the camps were at the forefront of this development.

Rudolf Pöch died in 1921; but the formative experience of the POW studies continued to influence the work of Otto Reche and Egon von Eickstedt, and through them, the discipline as a whole. In the decades after the war, both scholars built successful careers based on the interconnected exploration of race, nation, and *Volk.* In so doing, they were part of a larger disciplinary trend that sought to determine the links between physical/racial and cultural/psychological qualities.[81] In 1925, for example, the Hamburg anthropologist Walter Scheidt founded the Nordic anthropological journal *Volk und Rasse,* which took the existence of "psychological *(seelische)* racial qualities" for granted. Positing that the "culture of a people *(Volk)* must be dependent on [its] racial character,"[82] the journal editors saw their task in the elucidation of their mutual connections. The adherents of *Rassenkunde* did not necessarily argue for complete congruence between *Volk,* race, and nation, but they had clearly abandoned the liberal prohibition on seeking connections between them. In this atmosphere, physical anthropology in the tradition of Rudolf Martin was increasingly viewed as outmoded.[83] By 1933, Eugen Fischer was able to affirm directly the connections between race and *Volk:* "While the concepts of race and *Volk* are indeed different, in reality, however, race and *Volk* are not to be divided."[84] This view obviously played well under National Social-

---

81. Proctor, "From *Anthropologie* to *Rassenkunde,*" 152–56.
82. Quoted in Hans Fischer, *Völkerkunde im Nationalsozialismus* (Berlin: Dietrich Reimer, 1990), 35.
83. See, for example, the introduction to Walter Scheidt, *Allgemeine Rassenkunde: Als Einführung in das Studium der Menschenrassen* (Munich: J. F. Lehmann, 1925), xi. Also see 342–44.
84. "Rasse und Volkstumsfragen in der Deutschkundlichen Woche: Rasse und Leitung, Prof. Eugen Fischer spricht," *Danziger Allgemeine Zeitung,* 11 October 1933.

ism, but the groundwork for such an assertion had been laid years before.

Camp anthropologists were centrally involved in this paradigm shift. Otto Reche, who became the editor of Scheidt's *Volk and Rasse* in 1927, had commenced research on the connections between race, language, and culture immediately after the war. In 1921, two years after completing his *Habilitation,* he published an article in the leading journal for physical anthropology, arguing that "language was part of the racial soul." While he conceded that race and *Volk* were not exactly congruent, language thus indicated to which racial group each people essentially belonged.[85] Discussing the article some eighteen years later during the Nazi era, one of Reche's students noted, "These views were hardly found anywhere in 1921, but today belong to the core of our racial thought!"[86] Reche continued to argue for close connections between *Volk* and race throughout his career. In 1934, he posited that every "change in the racial makeup of a people *(Volk)* must also result in a corresponding change in its culture."[87] And by 1939, his career was seen as an effort to clarify the "racial history of the Nordic race" in order to account for the "racial foundations of our *Volk.*"[88] The fusion of nation, race, and *Volk* that had characterized Reche's work in the POW camps came to form the intellectual basis of his entire professional life, channeling his work toward the virulently nationalistic and illiberal directions of *Rassenkunde.*

Eickstedt similarly drew on his experience in the POW camps in his move toward *Rassenkunde.* While he continued to pay lip service to the notion that race, nation, and *Volk* were unrelated concepts, his scholarly practice blurred the boundaries between these distinctions. In 1922, two years after he received his doctorate, Eickstedt produced a racial typology that linked racial types to various European peoples. There, he identified such entities as the brunette and short-skulled "Dinaric" race, whose members were found in Bosnia and Serbia. More generally, Eickstedt distinguished all of Eastern Europe from the rest of the continent by claiming the existence of an "Eastern race" *(Ostrasse)* that was a "pronounced hybrid."[89] Eickstedt was more cau-

---

85. Otto Reche, "Rasse und Sprache," *Archiv für Anthropologie* 46 (1921): 218.
86. Michael Hesch, "Otto Reche als Rassenforscher," in Hesch and Spannaus, *Kultur und Rasse,* 11.
87. Quoted by Katja Geisenhainer, "Otto Reche's Verhältnis zur sogenannten Rassenhygiene," *Anthropos* 91 (1996): 500.
88. Hesch, "Otto Reche als Rassenforscher," 9.
89. Egon von Eickstedt, "Die Rasse beim Menschen," *Die Umschau* 26 (1922): 5.

tious on the subject of Germans. He rejected the idea of a specifically Germanic race, pointing out that Germans were a mixture of the Nordic and Alpine types. Still, in his five-part typology of European races, he identified nearly all of Eastern Europe and parts of France as belonging to racial groups that were not found in the German racial mixture. Unlike anthropologists in the liberal tradition who stressed the interrelation of all Europeans, Eickstedt narrowed the racial space of Germans, setting them apart from other European peoples, particularly those in the East. Eickstedt promulgated his views in the *Archiv für Rassenbilder* (Journal for racial images), a periodical he founded in 1925 as a vehicle for the pictorial representation of racial typologies.

Reche and Eickstedt were not marginal figures. In the 1920s and 1930s, both became leading members of the discipline. In 1924, Reche accepted the prestigious chair of anthropology at the University of Vienna, the very position Pöch had held until his death three years earlier. In 1927, he was named to a professorship at the University of Leipzig, a position of considerable influence that involved the directorship of Leipzig's Ethnological-Anthropological Institute. Reche also enjoyed a great degree of professional success under National Socialism, working as an anthropologist for the S.S. Race and Settlement Office [Rasse und Siedlungsamt].[90] On the occasion of his sixtieth birthday in 1939, Reche's "students and friends" put together a commemorative festschrift that included forty-six contributors.[91] Eickstedt also gained positions of influence. In the late 1920s, he was an instructor of anthropology at the University of Breslau; and in 1933, a few months after the Nazi seizure of power, he was named full professor. Throughout the late 1930s, Eickstedt worked closely with the Nazi Office of Racial Policy, publishing an anthropological series entitled Race, Volk and Genetic Makeup in Silesia.[92] The approach the two men had developed in the camps at the very moment of their professionalization served them well throughout their careers, particularly during the Nazi era.

Conclusion

From 1914 to 1918, German anthropology was given a new direction by the war being fought around it. The European conflict not only cre-

---

90. Proctor, "From *Anthropologie* to *Rassenkunde*," 160–61.
91. Hesch and Spannaus, *Kultur und Rasse*.
92. Proctor, "From *Anthropologie* to *Rassenkunde*," 161.

ated the initial opportunity to examine captured soldiers, but increasingly informed the goals and results of anthropological research. During the war, the anthropologists who worked on the POW projects developed a new political outlook that reoriented their approach to the European context of race. Deep-seated wartime nationalism combined with the unique conditions in the camps to shape a view of the European enemies as racial "others." In the process, the liberal view of Europeans as interrelated and physically indistinguishable was replaced by a nationalist perspective that defined peoples according to their racial characters. Opposing the position articulated by Virchow and his followers in the late nineteenth century, camp anthropologists began to conflate the categories of race, nation, and *Volk,* thereby helping to prepare the intellectual atmosphere that was to produce the virulently racist *Rassenkunde* of the 1920s and 1930s.

This examination of the POW studies demonstrates the importance of World War I in the larger history of Germany anthropology. In the camps, several young anthropologists abandoned the central tenets of the liberal tradition, suggesting that a break between the liberal anthropology of the nineteenth century and the racist and nationalistic brand of the twentieth century did indeed occur. But more importantly, the story of camp anthropology demonstrates that the causes of this shift need to be examined in their multiplicity. It is clear, for example, that the disjuncture in German anthropology cannot be explained solely by events within the discipline, such as Rudolf Virchow's death or the debate over Darwinism. Nor can it be seen as a simple reflection of German liberalism's general decline. Changing circumstances and new experiences facilitated the rise of a different set of convictions, and thus no account of liberal anthropology's demise at the hands of *völkisch* race theories and eugenic programs can be complete without attention to the cataclysmic event of the era: World War I.

Colonizing Anthropology: Albert Hahl and the Ethnographic Frontier in German New Guinea

RAINER BUSCHMANN

German Anthropology's Colonialisms

A large literature exists on the relationship between anthropology and colonialism in English-speaking domains.[1] Unfortunately, this relationship has been examined less often in a German context, primarily because World War I cut short Germany's colonial reach. The few investigations available seem to concur that while anthropology profited immensely from German colonialism, the German colonial venture benefited only marginally from anthropologists. Reflecting on the intellectual trends of turn-of-the-century German anthropology in the context of colonialism, Woodruff Smith describes the relation in starkly negative terms: "Not only did the colonial authorities have no effect on the process that led to diffusionism's triumph, but the fact that a pattern of such little utility from their standpoint was dominant presumably discouraged them from emphasizing anthropological research in their request for appropriations."[2] In making this claim,

---

1. Two important collections of essays are Talal Asad, ed., *Anthropology and the Colonial Encounter* (Atlantic Highlands, N.J.: Humanities Press, 1973); and George W. Stocking Jr., ed., *Colonial Situations: Essays on the Contextualization of Ethnographic Knowledge* (Madison: University of Wisconsin Press, 1991).
2. Woodruff Smith, *Politics and the Sciences of Culture in Germany, 1840–1920* (Oxford: Oxford University Press, 1991), 170.

Smith summarizes the general findings of historians of German anthropology, who have long argued that the theoretical orientation of Wilhelmine ethnologists had little applicability for practical colonial matters.

Indeed, the scholarly consensus suggests that German anthropologists' colonial engagement was minimal at best. In his analysis of the Hamburg South Sea Expedition, Hans Fischer maintains, for example, that anthropologists appealed to colonial officials only for "opportunistic" purposes—that is, to further their own scientific agendas.[3] Building on Fischer's argument, Manfred Gothsch postulates that, in practical terms, anthropologists' impact on Germany's colonial agenda was insignificant, their contributions to the ideological formation and justification of colonial expansion notwithstanding. Gothsch was also the first to highlight the theoretical limitations of German anthropology in regard to colonial matters. Anthropological practitioners, concerned almost exclusively with indigenous material culture and adhering to evolutionary or diffusionist frameworks, were at a loss for a methodology that might assist colonial officials.[4] In this literature, we find the root of Smith's argument that, despite obvious intellectual connections, an active dialogue between anthropology and colonialism was virtually nonexistent.

At the heart of these investigations, however, lies a significant problem. While most of the aforementioned authors accept a significant degree of variability within the anthropological profession, few allow for similar variations within the German colonial edifice. In their writings, colonialism thus appears as both monolithic and idealized—the agendas of missionaries, traders, officials, and, of course, anthropologists, coalesced into one oppressive juggernaut. In historiographic practice, the agendas of particular groups participating in the colonial game are in turn contrasted with this theoretical type. German anthropologists, much like concerned missionaries and humanitarian colo-

---

3. Hans Fischer, *Die Hamburger Südsee Expedition. Über Ethnographie und Kolonialismus* (Frankfurt am Main: Syndikat Verlag, 1981); see also his *Völkerkunde im Nationalsozialismus. Aspekte der Anpassung, Affinität und Behauptung einer wissenschaftlichen Disziplin* (Berlin: Reimer Verlag, 1990).

4. Manfred Gothsch, *Die deutsche Völkerkunde und ihr Verhältnis zum Kolonialismus. Ein Beitrag zur kolonialideologischen und kolonialpraktischen Bedeutung der deutschen Völkerkunde in der Zeit von 1870 bis 1970* (Baden Baden: Nomus, 1983).

nial officials, are thus dissociated from a colonial field rendered too abhorrent to account for the actions of any individual agents.

Fortunately, the study of colonialism has made great strides over the last two decades. The assumption of a monolithic, abstract colonial edifice has come under close scrutiny in the face of recent investigations demonstrating colonialism's varied shapes and impacts. These investigations suggest that colonial agents were as often characterized by conflict as they were by cooperation. This insight spawned analytical tools that expose the multiple and local manifestations of colonialism. In the process, researchers have begun to talk of a culture (or cultures) of colonialism and proposed to undertake its anthropology.[5]

The German Empire exemplifies the varied nature and impact of colonialism. Hermann Hiery has recently argued that the German administration in the Pacific islands differed considerably from that in Africa. While Germany's African colonies experienced frequent indigenous insurrections, German New Guinea and Samoa had, comparatively speaking, few revolts. According to Hiery, this state of affairs had a number of implications for the German Pacific colonies. In economic terms, it meant that most German possessions in the Pacific operated on a shoestring budget, since the majority of government support went to Africa. By the same token, however, this situation lessened the German metropole's hold on its Pacific colonies, allowing greater latitude for colonial officials in New Guinea, for example, than was available to their counterparts in Africa. In turn, this relative liberty permitted the incorporation of "Melanesian Principles" in German colonial rule.[6] Hiery is somewhat vague about such principles, particularly as his description of administrative measures—involving, among other things, hostage taking and communal responsibility for individual criminal behavior—apply more to general,

---

5. See for instance, Nicholas Thomas, *Colonialism's Culture: Anthropology, Travel, and Government* (Princeton: Princeton University Press, 1994).

6. Hermann Hiery, *The Neglected War: The German South Pacific and the Impact of World War I* (Honolulu: University of Hawaii Press, 1995), 1–10; see also his *Das deutsche Reich in der Südsee (1900–1921). Eine Annäherung an die Erfahrungen verschiedener Kulturen* (Göttingen: Vandenhoeck und Ruprecht, 1995). Hiery certainly advocates a different type of comparative colonial studies than does Nicholas Thomas. Hiery proved himself as a thorough researcher in connection with the German colonies in the Pacific. His argument that German administration in the Pacific was comparatively better than that of other European powers, however, occasionally reminds the reader of Germany's apologetic colonial attitude during the interwar period. For a thorough critique on the politics in Hiery's writings, consult Klaus Neumann. "The Stench of the Past: Revisionism in Pacific Islands and Australian History," *Contemporary Pacific* 10 (1998): 31–64.

global patterns than to "Melanesian" ones. But his notion of German colonial flexibility in the Pacific helps account for the willingness of New Guinea's administration to consider anthropological experiments.

This essay investigates the implementation of such experiments during the tenure of Albert Hahl, the second Governor of German New Guinea. Hahl, I argue, not only engaged the German anthropological community to further his colonial agenda, but also actively rethought the discipline. And while Hahl tended to disagree with German anthropologists on the object and method of ethnographic research, there emerged in German New Guinea an active dialogue between colonialism and anthropology. In this essay I do not intend to follow in Hiery's footsteps by elevating his tenure to serve as a convenient counterpoint to the postulated less-than-accommodating British or French rule in the Pacific. Instead my exercise stands at the beginning of a different type of comparative project. I argue that the recovery of German anthropology's colonial rather than metropolitan influences allows for connections with other, better explored, national (American, British, French) traditions of this discipline.

German Anthropology and New Guinea

In German colonial consciousness, German New Guinea (Deutsch Neuguinea) occupied a secondary rank vis-à-vis the colonies in Africa. German anthropologists, however, viewed the matter differently, privileging New Guinea as a final frontier of ethnographic inquiry. Adolf Bastian, the director of the Berlin Museum of Ethnology, for instance, took great interest in the material culture returned from New Guinea and its surrounding islands. Although he never visited the region himself, samples of artifacts from the region convinced him of New Guinea's rich cultural manifestations; and he urged his peers to engage in "salvage anthropology" before Melanesia suffered the same fate as the Polynesian islands. Prolonged contact with the West, Bastian argued, had brought about the demise of traditional Polynesian society, and he feared that Melanesia, Oceania's last untouched area, would suffer a similar development.[7]

---

7. Bastian's views on New Guinea and Melanesia as a final frontier of ethnographic inquiry are best exposed in his *Inselgruppen in Oceanien. Reiseerlebnisse und Studien* (Berlin: Ferd. Dümmlers, 1883) and *Der Papua des dunklen Inselreiches im Lichte psychologischer Forschung* (Berlin: Weidmannsche Buchhandlung, 1885).

German colonial acquisitions in the Pacific islands would presumably assist Bastian's salvage agenda; but the main agents associated with the New Guinea Company (NGC) had other designs for ethnographic activity in the German colonies.[8] In an agreement with the Prussian Museum Administration, NGC officials pledged to offer collected indigenous artifacts to the Berlin museum before approaching other institutions. But while Bastian greatly enjoyed the opportunities afforded by this monopoly, his scientific enthusiasm was not shared by NGC director Adolph Hansemann. Whereas Bastian conceived of indigenous objects as ethnographica (i.e., scientific specimens), Hansemann regarded them as marketable commodities that would increase his company's profit margin. This conceptual tension made cooperation between the NGC and Bastian's institution tedious and difficult until the turn of the century, when the NGC surrendered its administrative duties to the German Reich.[9]

As the NGC and the Berlin museum argued over the quantity and quality of ethnographic acquisitions, New Guinea became the playground for German museological rivalries. Directors and curators at institutions located in Berlin, Bremen, Cologne, Dresden, Hamburg, Leipzig, and Stuttgart all tried to secure collections for their respective museums. They all subscribed to Bastian's salvage agenda, but not necessarily to the advantage of Bastian's own institution. As museums sought to increase their scientific standing by procuring rare "last" specimens, Melanesian artifacts emerged as precious possessions, and museums invested heavily in possible patrons among the colonial residents in the German territory. Money, German state decorations, or simply kind words contributed to a virtual collection frenzy; and by the

---

8. By 1885, the New Guinea Company had established itself throughout much of German Melanesia including the Bismarck Archipelago, the northeastern corner of New Guinea, and the northern Solomon Islands. These colonial boundaries shifted somewhat until 1914. In return for the acquisition of the western isles of Samoa, the German government relinquished some of the Solomon Islands to Great Britain around the turn of the century. The Spanish-American War provided for additional German annexations in Micronesia, whose islands were incorporated into German New Guinea. Stewart Firth in the opening chapters of *New Guinea under the Germans* (Melbourne: Melbourne University Press, 1982), provides a good overview of German New Guinea's territorial development.

9. For details of the disagreement, see Rainer Buschmann, "Exploring Tensions in Material Culture: Commercializing Artifacts in German New Guinea, 1870–1904," in *Hunting the Gatherers: Ethnographic Collectors, Agents, and Agency in Melanesia,* ed. Michael O'Hanlon and Robert Welsch (Oxford: Berghahn, 2000), 55–79.

late nineteenth century German New Guinea became a major arena in the museums' competitive games.[10]

When the Reich assumed complete administrative duties of German New Guinea from the NGC, the potential for new collectors increased even further. The administrative change of guard resulted in the appointment of German colonial civil servants to remote corners in the Bismarck Archipelago and throughout Micronesia, all regions of ethnographic interest to German anthropologists. Although most of these civil servants were bound by the Federal Council's resolution (*Bundesratsbeschluß*) of 1889 that ordered them to surrender collected artifacts to the Berlin museum, the great majority of them chose to ignore such restrictions, collecting instead for museums located in their home states or institutions that promised them prestigious state medals or other decorations.[11]

The collection frenzy contributed to a heightened awareness of ethnography throughout German New Guinea. Most of the colonial residents involved in ethnographic collecting, however, never developed any particular interest in indigenous cultures. "Among one hundred colonial residents," wrote one prominent ethnographer about German New Guinea, "you will find ninety-nine opportunists; and even if they do have interests beyond making money, it is usually not in the exploration of the life of the 'dirty Kanak.'"[12] One colonial official, however, rose above such sentiments. Recognizing the potential benefits of ethnography for the administration of the German colony, he sought to remodel the entire anthropological edifice within the German empire.

---

10. On the competitive atmosphere governing German ethnological museums, see Rainer Buschmann, "The Ethnographic Frontier in German New Guinea, 1870–1914," Ph.D. diss., University of Hawai'i, 1999, and "Franz Boluminski and the Wonderland of Carvings: Towards an Ethnography of Collection Activity," *Baessler Archiv N.F.* 44 (1996): 190–99; see also the important contribution by Glenn Penny, "Museum Displays: Civic Self-Promotion and the Development of German Ethnographic Museums, 1870–1914," *Social Anthropology* 6 (1998): 157–68.

11. The best treatment of the Bundesratsbeschluß and its implications is Wolfgang Lustig, "'Außer ein paar zerbrochnen Pfeilen nichts zu verteilen . . .': Ethnographische Sammlungen aus den deutschen Kolonien und ihre Verteilung an Museen 1889 bis 1914," *Mitteilungen aus dem Museum für Völkerkunde Hamburg N.F.* 18 (1988): 157–78.

12. Emil Stephan (Leader of the German Naval Expedition) to Felix von Luschan (Director of the Berlin Museum' African/Oceanic Division), 14 November 1907, Staatsbibliotek-Preußische Kulturstiftung (SB-PK), Felix von Luschan Papers (LuP), Emil Stephan file.

Albert Hahl's Attempt to Refigure German Ethnography

When Albert Hahl (1868–1945) assumed his post as second governor of German New Guinea, a new breed of administrator came to the forefront in the German colony. Hahl had been in the territory for over six years garnering experience as imperial judge and deputy governor. Having earned a doctorate in law in 1893, he also had extensive legal training; and his insights into the legal aspects of colonial rule brought him in contact with ethnography.[13]

During Hahl's tenure as imperial judge, he had begun to address legal concerns in an ethnographic context—a consequence of his interaction with indigenous people on the Gazelle Peninsula in New Britain. Having realized that German legal concepts did not translate well into the numerous indigenous languages of the territory, Hahl immersed himself in linguistic studies of the local groups.[14] Such studies inspired his appointment of chiefly representatives and indigenous elites to the posts of *luluai* and *tultul,* a form of indirect rule through local authorities. The two terms were borrowed from the vocabulary of the Tolai people with whom Hahl had close contact. *Luluai* originally designated local leaders whose skills were sufficiently tested in warfare to warrant leadership positions; *tultul* referred to a new elite group who had extensive contacts with the European community. The *tultul* emerged as important middlemen since they had an understanding of indigenous as well as European customs, while the *luluai* became colonial authority figures equipped with cap and staff to underline their position.[15] Hahl tried to apply the model elsewhere in the territory with mixed success.[16]

Hahl repeated his studies of local customs during his tenure as

---

13. Two important biographies dealing with Albert Hahl's impact on German New Guinea are Peter Biskop, "Dr Albert Hahl—Sketch of a German Colonial Official," *Australian Journal of Politics and History* 14 (1968): 342–57; and Stewart Firth, "Albert Hahl: Governor of New Guinea," in *Papua New Guinea Portraits: The Expatriate Experience,* ed. James Griffin, 28–47 (Canberra: Australian National University Press, 1978).

14. Albert Hahl, "Über die Rechtsanschauungen der Eingeborenen eines Theils der Blanchebucht und des Inneren der Gazellenhalbinsel," *Nachrichten über Kaiser Wilhelmsland* 13 (1897): 68–85; see also Biskop, "Dr Albert Hahl," 350–51.

15. For a review of Hahl's ideas of establishing local authority figures see Firth, *New Guinea under Germans,* 74–75; contrast that with Hiery, *Das Deutsche Reich,* 115–20.

16. Firth, "Albert Hahl," 32; and Peter Hempenstall, "The Neglected Empire: The Superstructure of the German Colonial State in German Melanesia," in *Germans in the Tropics: Essays in German Colonial History,* ed. A. Knoll and L. Gann (Westport, Conn.: Greenwood Press, 1987), 100–102, illustrate some failed examples of Hahl's system.

deputy governor in the Caroline Islands; and to convince others to follow his example, he published two articles with the Berlin-based *Ethnologisches Notizblatt*.[17] There, he discussed the situation in Pohnpei, where the Germans had assumed control following several wars between the indigenous people and the Spanish colonizers that had ravaged the island. Hahl tried to avoid such developments by gaining the thorough understanding of individual customs reflected in his articles. To that end, Hahl had also read the ethnographic accounts of German New Guinea, but generally found them wanting. In Hahl's view most ethnographic writing was cursory at best and yielded few insights for his administrative purposes. In particular, he chastised the "colorful and imaginative" renditions of German anthropologists, which had little in common with the type of research he envisaged. Nevertheless, despite the apparent lack of satisfying ethnographic work in his colony, Hahl had high hopes for the German anthropological community.[18]

As governor of German New Guinea, Hahl became a key figure for German ethnological museums, and a number of directors and curators courted him as a patron. But while Hahl did in fact collect for a great many museums, he refused to have his favors monopolized by a single institution. For instance, when the Leipzig museum director Karl Weule promised Hahl a decoration for his continuing patronage of the Saxon museum, the governor turned him down. He did not object to the decoration in principle, but he did "not want to be tied to [Weule's] museum in any other way than [his] will of giving freely."[19] Resisting such attempts at syndicating his collection efforts left Hahl open to engage with a number of German ethnological storehouses.

Interestingly enough, Hahl's dialogues with ethnological museums involved less collection practices than new ways of performing ethnographic research. Well versed in the intellectual discourse of German anthropology, Hahl openly conversed with museum officials about the "salvage paradigm." While the great majority of German anthropologists believed material culture to be the central text governing their dis-

---

17. Albert Hahl, "Mitteilungen über Sitte und rechtliche Verhältnisse auf Ponape," *Ethnologisches Notizblatt* 2 (1901): 1–13; and "Feste und Tänze der Eingeborenen von Ponape," *Ethnologisches Notizblatt* 3 (1902): 95–102.

18. The quote stems from Albert Hahl to German Colonial Office, 27 October 1911, Bundesarchiv (BArch) Lichterfelde, Reichskolonialamt (R 1001), 2994. Hahl referred to the ethnographic renditions of explorer Otto Finsch and local resident Richard Parkinson.

19. Albert Hahl to Karl Weule, 1 March 1910, Museum für Völkerkunde Leipzig (MfVL), Accession file 1909, Nr. 104 (1909/104).

cipline, Hahl attempted to convince them otherwise. In his words the salvage action based entirely on material culture had come to an abrupt end.[20] His correspondence abounded with assertions that entire island chains were "no longer a field for the collector";[21] he even suggested that it would be necessary to import ethnographic objects from Germany to New Guinea in order to find any in the territory.[22] Such statements hardly expressed nostalgia for a bygone era of ethnographic collection.[23] On the contrary, Hahl's correspondence with museum officials revealed an interesting dichotomy that thoroughly deprivileged a salvage paradigm centered on material artifacts. In his letters, Hahl often contrasted earlier collectors *(Sammler)* with contemporary scientists *(Wissenschaftler)*. To Karl Weule, for instance, Hahl wrote that the territory was now almost entirely depleted of artifacts. But "for scientific inquiry," he continued, "the field was wide open."[24]

Beyond his invocation of a new, "scientific" anthropology, Hahl also deployed the term *field* in conjunction with ethnographic work. Historians of anthropology have identified the period before and after the Great War as the origin of a new anthropological methodology commonly designated as "fieldwork." This method centered on the close investigation of a single indigenous society over a long stretch of time, a mode that replaced broad ethnographic surveys of large geographical areas.[25] Bronislaw Malinowski may not have invented this new methodology, but he certainly enshrined it. "The time when we

---

20. On the German anthropologists' bias toward material culture, see, for instance, Suzanne Marchand, "The Rhetoric of Artifacts and the Decline of Classical Humanism: The Case of Josef Strzygowski," *History and Theory* 33 (1994): 106–30.

21. Albert Hahl to Karl von Linden 9 September 1900, Linden Museum Stuttgart (LiMSt), Albert Hahl file.

22. Albert Hahl to Felix von Luschan, 10 March 1900, SB-PK, LuP, Albert Hahl file; Albert Hahl to Karl Weule, 1 November 1907, MfVL, Acquisition file 1907/113.

23. Renato Rosaldo, *Culture and Truth: The Remaking of Social Analysis* (Boston: Beacon Press, 1989), chap. 3, argues that the salvage paradigm amounts to an "Imperial nostalgia" whereby colonial actors could mourn and therefore negotiate their own involvement in the cultural demise of their subjects. While this assertion holds true to many museum officials in Germany, it cannot account for Hahl's views on ethnography.

24. Albert Hahl to Karl Weule, 1 November 1907, MfVL, Acquisition file 1907/113.

25. The literature on "fieldwork" in the Anglo-American tradition is vast. See for instance the collection of Akhil Gupta and James Ferguson, eds., *Anthropological Locations: Boundaries and Grounds of a Field Science* (Berkeley and Los Angeles: University of California Press, 1997); George W. Stocking Jr., *After Tylor: British Social Anthropology, 1888–1951* (Madison: University of Wisconsin Press, 1995), especially chap. 6; also his "The Ethnographer's Magic: Fieldwork in British Anthropology from Tylor to Malinowski," in *The Ethnographer's Magic and Other Essays in the History of Anthropology* (Madison: University of Wisconsin Press, 1992), 12–59. In the history of German anthropology such inves-

could tolerate accounts presenting us the native as a distorted, childish caricature of a human being is gone. This picture is false, and like many other falsehoods, it has been killed by Science."[26] Malinowski's words resembled the sentiments expressed by Hahl; but there were some differences to be found as well.

Hahl's emphasis on fieldwork was not dictated by Malinowski's scientific concerns, but resulted from the colonial realpolitik in the administration of German New Guinea. Material culture, as understood by the German anthropological community, supplied limited information for the colonial administration. This was in contrast to culturally homogeneous areas where colonial administrators could deploy material culture for their purposes. In the case of Fiji, for example, the British governor employed the display of artifacts to create "common denominators" uniting Fijian society, a practice that greatly facilitating his administrative work.[27] To attempt a similar task in German New Guinea was daunting, if not impossible. With hundreds of islands and an even larger number of indigenous languages and societies under his control, Hahl could hardly hope to find a common denominator by sorting through material culture. Whereas the British governor in Fiji had used material culture to express unity in the Fijian "mind," Hahl wanted to penetrate the very mind of his subjects.

Hahl's main concern was to create the category of "native" as a useful abstraction for colonial administration. In general terms, "native" included all non-Europeans within the colony and was usually applied to the indigenous male, whose mind was said to work in mysterious ways.[28] Linking a colonial agenda with the production of scientific knowledge, Hahl hoped to illuminate these "mysterious ways" through intensive research into native cosmologies—an investigative modality that would develop common legal denominators and statistical evidence for Hahl's subjects.[29]

---

tigations are still in their infancy. For an interesting starting point, consult Andrew Zimmerman, "Selin, Pore, and Emil Stephan in the Bismarck Archipelago: A 'Fresh and Joyful Tale' of the Origin of Fieldwork," *Pacific Arts* 21–22 (2000): 69–84.

26. Bronislaw Malinowski, *Argonauts of the Western Pacific* (New York: E. P. Dutton, 1961 [1922]), 11.

27. Nicholas Thomas, "Material Culture and Colonial Power: Ethnographic Collecting and the Establishment of Colonial Rule in Fiji," *Man* 24 (1989), 41–56.

28. Stewart Firth, "Colonial Administration and the Invention of the Native," in *The Cambridge History of Pacific Islanders,* ed. Donald Denoon et al. (Cambridge: Cambridge University Press), 262.

29. The term "investigative modality" is borrowed from Bernard Cohn, *Colonialism and Its Forms of Knowledge: The British in India* (Cambridge: Cambridge University Press, 1996),

Understanding the native mind through ethnography, however, was only one of the concerns of Hahl's administration. By the first decade of the twentieth century it had become apparent that the indigenous population was declining at least in some parts of the territory. This decline had ramifications for the labor market.[30] During NGC's tenure, officials had hoped to attract German settlers to New Guinea. Climate, disease, and company regulations, however, dashed these hopes, and the number of migrants dwindled. That left the main staple of the colonial economy: coconut plantations providing copra for European markets. Given this situation, a steady supply of low-paid labor remained the most pressing need for the German administration. There had already been a labor shortage during the tenure of the New Guinea Company, and this shortage continued well after the German state took over the colony in 1899. The steady increase of plantations in New Guinea, the Bismarck Archipelago, and, to a lesser extent, Micronesia made the labor issue even more pressing for the colonial administration.[31]

Much like the NGC, Hahl attempted to import laborers from East Asia, but their numbers fell well short of his expectations. As a result, German planters and settlers applied increased pressure on the administration to open up new recruiting grounds and to step up the process of indenture in those areas already contacted. Privileges granted to specific companies further complicated this effort. The NGC, for instance, had exclusive recruiting privileges on Kaiser Wilhelmsland, while the Deutsche Handels- und Plantagengesellschaft received several hundred recruits each year from New Guinea for its plantation operations in German Samoa. In light of the rising demands for labor power, Hahl turned his attention to the urgent problem of depopulation. Anthropological research could provide relevant information in this regard; and the information Hahl requested involved the "native"

3–15. The Foucauldian marriage between anthropological science and colonial execution of power is best described by Ernst Sarfert, directorial assistant and curator of the Oceanic/Indonesian division of the Leipzig museum: "To collect [vital ethnographic information] a trained gaze is needed to penetrate the most remote corners of the natives' bags and living-quarters and to understand native life in all its facets." Heinrich Schnee, ed., *Deutsches Kolonial-Lexikon* (Leipzig: Quelle und Meyer, 1920), vol. 3, Sammeln, ethnographisches.

30. Stewart Firth, "Labour in German New Guinea," in *Papua New Guinea: A Century of Colonial Impact, 1884–1984,* ed. Sione Latukefu (Port Moresby: National Research Institute, 1989), 179–202.

31. See for instance Doug Munro and Stewart Firth, "Company Strategies—Colonial Policies," in Clive Moore, Jacqueline Leckie, and Doug Munro, *Labour in the South Pacific* (Townsville: James Cook University, 1990), 5–7.

producers of material culture rather than material culture itself. "If science," Hahl wrote to a museum director, "can ultimately tell us what we have to do in order to not only save the native from extinction, but also to increase his numbers, [your research] will have contributed more than any discovery of large gold deposits."[32]

Colonial Ethnography Found: Richard Thurnwald's Engagement in German New Guinea

Hahl's agenda for useful ethnographic work in German New Guinea required a new type of researcher. This researcher was Richard Thurnwald, who arrived in the territory not to answer Hahl's call for a new ethnography, but as a response to Berlin museum officials' fear of competition from other institutions. Felix von Luschan, director of the African/Oceanic Division at the Berlin museum, had witnessed a sharp decline in ethnographic acquisitions from German New Guinea; and he decided to send a trained collector to the territory.[33] Hoping to gain a qualitative edge over other institutions, Luschan sought to limit collecting to geographical areas where the acquisition of material culture could be complemented with insights into indigenous society. Luschan called this research operation "monographic work," since the goal was not simply to amass artifacts, but to understand the indigenous meanings and worldviews. This process would, in turn, yield ethnographic monographs.[34]

Thurnwald's dispatch to German New Guinea was meant to reduce the collection gap in the Berlin museum. In Hahl's eyes, however, Thurnwald signified the implementation of colonial ethnography.

Luschan could have sent no better researcher than Thurnwald to further the dialogue between colonialism and anthropology in German New Guinea. Like Hahl, Thurnwald held a doctorate in law; and he had undertaken population studies for the Austro-Hungarian government in the protectorate of Bosnia-Herzogovina.[35] He was thus well

---

32. Albert Hahl to Georg Thilenius (Director of the Hamburg Museum of Ethnology), 6 December 1904, Museum für Völkerkunde Hamburg (MfVH), Südsee Expedition 1.
33. Felix von Luschan to Albert Hahl, 8 February 1905, Staatliche Museen zu Berlin-Preußischer Kulturbesitz (SMB-PK), Museum für Völkerkunde (MV), IB Australien/E 18/05; Felix von Luschan to Albert Hahl, 23 June 1906, LiMSt, Albert Hahl file.
34. See for instance, Felix von Luschan to Prussian General Museum Administration, 17 August 1909, SM-PK, MV, IB Australien, E 1648/09.
35. Marion Melk-Koch, *Auf der Suche nach der menschlichen Gesellschaft: Richard Thurnwald* (Berlin: Reimer Verlag, 1989), 30–34, 44–49.

equipped to discuss administrative concerns over indigenous law and population decline. Hahl took Thurnwald on several trips on the governmental steamer *Seestern* to familiarize him with different social and natural environments in the German colony. He also spoke extensively with Thurnwald about his experiences in the Balkans.[36] Although aware that Thurnwald was on a collection trip for the Berlin museum, Hahl used Thurnwald's dependency on the colonial administration as well as his interest in population studies to steer the research in directions that would aid the colonial administration. Thurnwald reluctantly continued to collect for Luschan in Berlin, but under Hahl's supervision, he also performed stationary research in northern New Britain and southern Bougainville.[37] There, Thurnwald even opened up new territory for colonial administration by facilitating a peace agreement between coastal and inland populations.[38] "It seems to dawn in our dark part of the world," Hahl enthusiastically reported to Luschan in Berlin. "May the commercial frontier keep the pace with the ethnographic one."[39]

As Thurnwald's ethnographic outlook came to correspond with Hahl's, he seemed to depart from Luschan's original research designs. Indeed, Thurnwald's collections of material culture were slow in reaching the Berlin museum, and soon Luschan's mission was in jeopardy.[40] Whenever Thurnwald and Luschan clashed over the issue of ethnographic research, however, Hahl shielded the young ethnographer. Hahl argued that Thurnwald's research into indigenous law and population statistics was not only vital to the colonial administration, but could also invigorate anthropology in Germany.[41] Thurnwald made an analogous point when he claimed that his fieldwork in German New Guinea redefined ethnographic research. Anthropologists and colonial officials had much in common, Thurnwald argued, yet they rarely connected intellectually. Anthropologists relied too heavily on indigenous

---

36. Ibid., 76–80.

37. For an ethnographic summary of his research see Richard Thurnwald, "Im Bismarck-Archipel und auf den Salomoneninseln, 1906–1909," *Zeitschrift für Ethnologie* 42 (1910): 98–147.

38. Melk-Koch, *Auf der Suche,* 80–87.

39. Albert Hahl to Felix von Luschan, 30 October 1908, SB-PK, LuP, Albert Hahl file.

40. Thurnwald's reluctant ethnographic collection policy was very much tied to his changing outlook on anthropology. For an analysis of his collection practices in German New Guinea, see Marion Melk-Koch, "Melanesian Art—or just Stones and Junk? Richard Thurnwald and the Question of Art in Melanesia," *Pacific Arts* 21–22 (2000): 53–68.

41. Melk-Koch, *Auf der Suche,* 131–32.

material culture and not enough on the social universe of the indigenous producers. Colonial officials, on the other hand, focused almost exclusively on economics. Thurnwald observed that economics and ethnographic knowledge were not mutually exclusive; in the tropics only a merger of these two aspects guaranteed both viable ethnography and a successful colonial economy.[42]

Thurnwald advanced the marriage of anthropology and colonialism in a number of publications. In these essays, he stressed the importance of understanding indigenous law and introduced the concept of a "gendered" native. While Thurnwald gave no prominent acknowledgment to Hahl, the German governor's ideas were clearly present in these writings, which enunciated the possibility of a colonial ethnography.

In terms of indigenous law, Thurnwald's long-term study of German New Guinea's peoples allowed him to support the important point made by Hahl ten years earlier: that colonial law had to emerge out of a compromise between indigenous and German concepts of legality.[43] The discovery of common denominators among the different legal concepts of the indigenous groups would aid such a syncretic vision. This was a rather difficult task in German New Guinea's linguistically diverse indigenous societies, exacerbated by Thurnwald's refusal of the contact languages in his studies. Much like Hahl, he derided "pidgin English," since the lingua franca lacked the elaborate vocabulary necessary to investigate the deeper intellectual meanings of indigenous people.[44] Only local studies carried out in the vernacular, Thurnwald contended in echoing Hahl's approach, could contribute to the formation of a common legal language that was applicable throughout the colony. For Thurnwald, the colonial advantages of such an endeavor were obvious: "As the native psyche offers the key for native justice, so the application of these insights form the prerequisite for a successful manipulation of the natives for the aims of the Europeans in a tropical colony."[45]

---

42. Ibid., 133–43.
43. Richard Thurnwald, "Das Rechtsleben der Eingeborenen der deutschen Südseeinseln, seine geistigen und wirtschaftlichen Grundlagen. Auf Grund einer im Auftrage des Berliner Museums für Völkerkunde unternommenen Forschungsreise 1906–1909," *Blätter für Vergleichende Rechtswissenschaft und Volkswirtschaftslehre* 6 (1910): 3–46; see also his "Ermittlungen über Eingeborenenrechte in der Südsee," *Zeitschrift für Vergleichende Rechtswissenschaften* 23 (1910): 309–64.
44. Thurnwald nicknamed this language "Bitchin-English," underscoring the limited applicability of this form of communication. Melk-Koch, *Auf der Suche,* 88.
45. Thurnwald, "Das Rechtsleben der Eingeborenen," 46.

Thurnwald's second contribution to colonial ethnography was the concept of a "gendered native." Building on Hahl's call to investigate the native producers of artifacts, Thurnwald developed the problematic category of the "native mother." In the British colonial realm, measures were already under way to intervene in the nurturing processes of the native mother—a colonial subject who was constructed in decisive opposition to the "normal" European woman. Indigenous women, the argument went, had few of the moral constraints of their European counterparts. Their open sexuality introduced venereal diseases, and their careless behavior led to a decline in childbearing as well as an increase in prostitution.[46] Thurnwald observed similar processes at work among the declining indigenous population of New Ireland. Native women, Thurnwald argued in this light, should not only be barred from the labor-recruiting process, but kept under close surveillance for venereal diseases. "There is no question in my mind that through drastic methods introduced both to restrict the recruiting process on Neu Mecklenburg [the German colonial name for New Ireland] and to cleanse the whole area of venereal disease, we will be able to manage the dangers of native depopulation. This should be in the interest of each planter, especially when similar surveillance is put in place in other recruiting areas as well."[47]

Hahl had a prominent presence throughout Thurnwald's essay, a function of their close collaboration. Hahl involved himself in writing the article, and he further assisted Thurnwald with the page proofs. "Finally science and exploration are coming together even here in New Guinea," he wrote to Thurnwald with evident satisfaction;[48] and in due time, he ordered three hundred offprints to be distributed in the German Reichstag.[49] With Thurnwald's help, Hahl had come a giant step closer to a colonial ethnography, and Thurnwald supported him throughout his tenure as German governor.[50] But the question

---

46. See Vicki Lugere, "The Native Mother," in *The Cambridge History of Pacific Islanders,* ed. Donald Denoon et al. (Cambridge: Cambridge University Press, 1997), 280–87; Margaret Jolly, "Other Mothers: Maternal 'Insouciance' and the Depopulation Debate in Fiji and Vanuatu, 1890–1930," in *Maternities and Modernities,* ed. K. Ram and M. Jolly (Cambridge: Cambridge University Press, 1998), 183–215.

47. "Die eingeborenen Arbeitskröfle im Südseeschutzpebiet," *Koloniale Rundschen* 10 (1910): 627.

48. Albert Hahl to Richard Thurnwald, 9 July 1910, cited in Melk-Koch, *Auf der Suche,* 135.

49. Melk-Koch, *Auf der Suche,* 134–35.

50. Ibid., 162–65.

remained whether the initial steps taken by Thurnwald could be sustained and nurtured by the German anthropological community.

Colonial Ethnography Lost: New Ireland as a "Colonial" Fieldsite

The opportunity to coordinate large-scale German ethnographic efforts presented itself to Hahl in New Ireland. There, he attempted to put into practice his own ethnographic designs, drawing on the insights generated during Thurnwald's visit to the German territory. A number of German ethnographic ventures in New Guinea proved helpful in Hahl's grand scheme of colonial ethnography. In chronological order, these expeditions were the German Naval Expedition (1907–9), the Geographical Commission Expedition (1908), the Hamburg South Sea Expedition (1908–10), as well as a number of smaller endeavors and privately sponsored travelers.

New Ireland is the second largest island in the Bismarck Archipelago. Long and relatively narrow, it stretches from northwest to southeast, covering roughly three thousand square miles. European settlements did not appear there until about 1880, when violent confrontations with the indigenous population became commonplace. By the turn of the century, the German administration had established a colonial outpost in northern New Ireland, followed a few years later by a second government station in the island's central region. Both stations increased the speed of the German pacification process. By the end of the first decade of the twentieth century, a rapid transformation of the island had occurred, bringing its population into the plantation economy. Beyond the local estates, New Ireland also supplied a large share of the indentured laborers for plantations all over German New Guinea.[51]

The transformation and incorporation of New Ireland into the German colonial economy was not without its problems. By the time Thurnwald arrived in the territory, the population was showing obvious signs of decline. Initial surveys, including Thurnwald's, suggested that this decline was partially the result of Western contact and the concomitant disruption of traditional societies. In Hahl's view, the

---

51. The transformation of New Ireland during the first decade of the twentieth century can be found in Rainer Buschmann, "Franz Boluminski," 185–210; Louise Lincoln, "Art and Money in New Ireland: History, Economy, and Cultural Production," in *Assemblage of Spirits: Idea and Image in New Ireland* (New York: Georg Braziller, 1987); and Peter Lomas, "The Early Contact Period in Northern New Ireland (Papua New Guinea): From Wild Frontier to Plantation Economy," *Ethnohistory* 28 (1981): 1–21.

ethnographic expeditions steaming to New Guinea could be put to good use in investigating this problem.

The value of ethnography for Hahl was clear. Aside from the customary collection of artifacts, the expeditions would provide careful census data for the area, most notably the ratio of males to females among the indigenous population.[52] Besides important data in connection with population decline, Hahl also desired a closer understanding of local languages in order to replace pidgin English with the more "meaningful" vernaculars. In Hahl's view, which was greatly informed by Thurnwald's initial research, language was an entrepôt on the way to indigenous cognition, yielding insights into local societies. At the same time, linguistic studies would provide a new administrative language in which both indigenous and German legal concepts were intelligible.[53] Since New Ireland was home to an estimated thirty language groups, this kind of linguistic and ethnographic work was crucial. As questions of population control and investigations into local languages emerged as the priorities of Hahl's colonial ethnography, New Ireland became the test case for its implementation.

Hahl hoped to find among the participants in the different German expeditions ethnographers of the type he had encountered in Richard Thurnwald. This proved difficult, however, as the organizers of these expeditions were clearly guided by the collection frenzy of Germany's ethnological museums. As a result, the organizers instructed the expeditions' members to neglect Hahl's prolonged colonial ethnography. Artifacts still reigned supreme, as museum officials hoped that their particular expedition would outshine the competitors.

The best-sponsored endeavor was by far the Hamburg South Seas Expedition. The aim of this ethnographic venture was to conduct an extensive survey of German New Guinea that had much in common with earlier salvage operations. Its budget of six hundred thousand marks allowed for the rental of a large steamer, crew, and scientific personnel and had no German equivalent.[54] Although the organizer of the expedition, Hamburg museum director Georg Thilenius, maintained

---

52. Albert Hahl to German Colonial Office, 23 April 1908, BArch, R 1001, 2373; Albert Hahl to Felix von Luschan, 9 August 1908, SMB-PK, IB 71/E 2092/08.
53. See, for instance, Cohn, *Colonialism,* chap. 2, "The Command of Language and the Language of Control."
54. The scientific program of this expedition is outlined in detail in Fischer, *Hamburger Südsee-Expedition.*

that his venture differed from earlier collection activities, Hahl failed to see its usefulness. Since it was to survey almost all of German New Guinea, the expedition was diametrically opposed to Hahl's agenda for the colonial ethnography of limited areas; and given that the expedition was to spend only a few weeks in any given place, Hahl deemed it a waste of time. The only tangible result of the venture, he thought, would be a steep increase of the territory's ethnographic prices. There was simply no room for such an extensive expedition in Hahl's colonial program.[55]

The German Naval Expedition, organized by Luschan in Berlin, was more agreeable to Hahl. Operating on a mere fraction of the Hamburg expedition's budget, the Naval Expedition was not a particularly mobile affair, remaining in one particular location for extended periods of time. But while this design came closer to Hahl's vision of colonial ethnography, he had strong reservations about expedition leader Emil Stephan. In previous years, Stephan had spent considerable time as a naval surgeon in the Bismarck Archipelago. He employed his leisure time for ethnographic collection and investigation resulting in two monographs that circulated widely among the German anthropological community.[56] When Stephan delivered the published monographs to the governor for inspection, Hahl's response was harsh:

> I had trouble keeping awake reading your booklet [*Südseekunst*], since I have no intention of interrogating the latest art theories. In the book about [New Ireland], I have underlined many questionable passages where the pidgin English has fooled you in your translation. Beware of this main enemy of research that prevents clear communication with the natives. ... The number of misunderstandings in my field are legion. For instance, how can we establish a language of legality if we are lacking even the most basic concepts.[57]

---

55. Hahl's opinion is contained in a letter of Emil Stephan to Felix von Luschan, 14 November 1907, SB-PK, LuP, Stephan file.

56. Emil Stephan's *Südseekunst. Beiträge zur Kunst des Bismarckarchipels und zur Urgeschichte der Kunst überhaupt* (Berlin: Reimer, 1907) advocated a recognition of indigenous material culture as "art" in its own right; his second book, coauthored with Fritz Graebner, *Neu-Mecklenburg (Bismarckarchipel). Die Küste von Umuddu bis Kap St. Georg. Forschungsergebnisse bei den Vermessungsarbeiten von SMS Möwe im Jahre 1904* (Berlin: Reimer, 1907) was a more traditional ethnographic survey of coastal southern New Ireland.

57. Albert Hahl to Emil Stephan, 26 January 1908, SB-PK, LuP, Hahl file.

This letter documented how Hahl sought to influence the research agendas of expeditions to New Guinea. Promoting his agenda of colonial ethnography, Hahl told Stephan to record indigenous languages and guard against pidgin English; he also used the metaphor of the field *(Feld)* to talk about his stationary research mode.

In addition to intervening in the expeditions' research agendas, Hahl determined research sites. Stephan's Naval Expedition was originally set to explore the lesser-known areas of New Britain (Neu Pommern) in the Bismarck Archipelago.[58] Hahl, however, invested considerable energy in redirecting the expedition to New Ireland, arguing that the harsh climate and difficult access to the originally targeted area would threaten the safety of the expedition. It was in New Ireland, of course, where Hahl saw the urgent need for linguistic study and research into population developments; and to maximize the results, he suggested that the expedition focus on the northern and southern portions of the island.[59]

Aside from advancing his agenda for colonial ethnography, Hahl sought to limit the Naval Expedition's survey area for another reason: he had reserved the central portion of New Ireland for a different expedition, organized by the Geographical Commission (Landeskundliche Kommission), a colonial organization created to further geographical knowledge of the German colonies. The original destination of that expedition had also been New Britain.[60] Hahl, however, saw an opportunity to combine the two expeditions' efforts on New Ireland, thereby advancing his own colonial goals. Specifically, the governor sought to complement Stephan's long-term stay (the Naval Expedition was scheduled for two years) with the insights of the more limited Geographical Commission Expedition. Its members, among them the geographer Karl Sapper and the ethnographer Georg Friederici, were particularly agreeable to Hahl, since their interests extended beyond a concern for the rising and falling commodity prices on the world market.[61]

But while Hahl was pleased with the division of New Ireland

---

58. Felix von Luschan to General Museum Administration, 7 March 1907, SMB-PK, MV, IB 71/E 435/07.

59. Emil Stephan Expedition Diary Entry, 4 September 1907, SMB-PK, MV, IB 71/ E 31/08.

60. Hans Meyer (Chairman of the Geographical Commission) to German Colonial Office, 16 August 1907, BArch, R 1001, 2373.

61. Albert Hahl to Karl von Linden, 20 April 1908, LiMSt, Hahl file.

between the Naval and Geographical Expeditions, his broader designs were hardly shared by their participants.[62] Naval Expedition member Edgar Walden, stationed in northern New Ireland, wondered why he had to compete with local colonial officials over the acquisition of ethnographica. For his part, Georg Friederici of the Geographical Commission Expedition complained bitterly about sending two expeditions into an area that was essentially pacified and thus had little to offer in terms of ethnographic research.[63] In Germany similar concerns could be heard. Hermann Singer, the editor of the important geographic-anthropological journal *Globus,* went so far as to employ the example of the two expeditions to criticize the spending policies of the entire German colonial administration.[64]

Hahl withstood such criticisms, not least because the expeditions' research produced desired results. Stephan heeded Hahl's warning regarding pidgin English, undertaking extensive research into the vernaculars of southern New Ireland, while Friederici investigated the uses and limitations of pidgin English.[65] Most important for Hahl's colonial ethnography, Stephan, in early 1908, provided the colonial administration of German New Guinea with a handwritten exposé on the causes of population decline in southern New Ireland. Based on the empirical evidence of long-term research, the report also presented suggestions for its halt.[66]

As promising as such results were, Hahl always had to contend with the competitive ethos of the individual expeditions. Although most of the ventures to German New Guinea stipulated to be pan-national, the initial impetus for their efforts always came from specific local museums. The German Naval Expedition, for instance, was a thinly disguised attempt by Berlin's Felix von Luschan to counter the Hamburg South Seas Expedition. Likewise, the Geographical Commission's

---

62. Albert Hahl to Heinrich Schnee, 13 March 1908, Geheimes Staatsarchiv, Schnee Papers.

63. Georg Friederici to Hans Meyer (Chairperson of the Geographical Commission), 18 October and 9 November 1908, BArch, R 1001, 2373; draft for a presentation on his travels in German New Guinea, 1908–10, MfVH, Friederici Papers.

64. Hermann Singer, "Die Verwendung des Afrikafonds," *Globus* 97 (1910): 110–11.

65. See Emil Stephan, Diary, 28 January 1908, SMB-PK, MV, IB 71/E 888/08; and Georg Friederici, "Das Pidgin-Englisch in Deutsch Neuguinea," *Koloniale Rundschau* 11 (1911): 92–102.

66. Emil Stephan, "Ursachen des Volksrückgange und Vorschläge zu seiner Erhaltung auf Grund von Untersuchungen über die Bevölkerung von Muliama," original in SMB-PK, MV, IB 71/E 995/08.

expedition was impelled by chairman Hans Meyer's opposition to the Berlin museum's monopoly over colonial artifacts.[67]

Much to Hahl's dismay, the vigorous competition among the expeditions ultimately undermined the usefulness of their findings. The rivalry threatened to disrupt the expeditions from the outset, but became acute when Stephan, the leader of the Naval Expedition, took ill. Suffering from blackwater fever, he passed away in late May 1908. Hans Meyer was quick to exploit the resulting instability and confusion. Operating behind the scenes, he sought to fuse the Naval Expedition with the venture of the Geographical Commission in order to "right," as he put it, "wrongs committed in the past."[68] Hurrying to prevent such a hostile takeover, Luschan quickly negotiated for a new leader. Augustin Krämer became the new leader, and rushed, together with his wife, to New Ireland to join the expedition.[69] Rather than bring stability, however, Krämer's dispatch triggered a wave of protests by the other expedition members, who wished to operate independently.[70] Fraught with personal and institutional conflicts, the naval venture was kept together by Krämer. But under increasing time pressure, he could do little more than, "prevent the ship from sinking" [die Karre aus dem Dreck zu ziehen].[71] As he embarked on a final ethnographic "romp" through New Ireland, Hahl's colonial agenda fell by the wayside.

Hahl was greatly disappointed with the outcome of the German

---

67. On the competitive issues surrounding German expeditions, see Buschmann, "Ethnographic Frontier," chap. 6.

68. Meyer was obviously referring to the centralization of artifacts in Berlin following the Federal Council's resolution of 1889. Felix von Luschan to General Prussian Museum Administration, 19 June 1908, SMB-PK, MV, IB 71/E 1258/08.

69. Felix von Luschan to General Prussian Museum Administration, 26 June 1908, SMB-PK, MV, IB 71/E 1258/08.

70. Their letters are contained in BArch, R 1001, 2370.

71. Augustin Krämer to Karl von Linden, 17 June 1909, LiMSt, Krämer file. In Krämer's defense one should point out, however, that he had already agreed to lead the Hamburg expedition's second year through the Micronesian portions of the German colony. There was thus considerable time pressure to bring the venture to a positive conclusion. The Naval Expedition convinced Krämer, like Stephan a naval surgeon, to terminate his employment with the German navy and to embark on a full-time anthropological career. In 1911 he would become the scientific director of the newly formed Linden Museum in Stuttgart. The best research on Augustin Krämer to date remains Dietrich Schleip's survey, "Ozeanistische Ethnologie und Koloniale Praxis: Das Beispiel Augustin Krämer," M.A. thesis, Tübingen University, 1989.

Naval Expedition. The grand experiment of colonial ethnography had failed and resignation took hold:

> I had expected an encompassing detailed picture of the peoples in northern and central [New Ireland] in addition to the coastal populations in the southern regions. I do believe this work will never be completed; the change in personnel was detrimental to the execution of the expedition. I also believe that the young researchers were not able to cope with the practical realities of their field of inquiry. They did not have enough time to engage intensively in their respective areas.[72]

Hahl ultimately believed that most of the members of the Naval Expedition, especially Otto Schlaginhaufen and Edgar Walden, were simply not up to the task: "Your gentlemen," Hahl reproached Luschan, "are lacking even the most basic notions of the tropics, tropical medicine, adaptation etc. Please make sure that such novices receive the proper instruction prior to departure. The struggle with the wilderness is hard. Capable people, such as Dr. Thurnwald, seem to be rare among your staff."[73]

The restructuring of the Naval Expedition put an abrupt end to Albert Hahl's vision of the "colonial field." His grand project for New Ireland had disintegrated, not for the lack of an appropriate theoretical framework, but because competition and personal issues made cooperation difficult. Although the New Guinea expeditions safely returned to Germany, their results would not advance Hahl's agenda for colonial ethnography. Hahl's correspondence with German ethno-

---

72. Albert Hahl to Felix von Luschan, 9 November 1909, SB-PK, LuP, Hahl file.
73. Albert Hahl to Felix von Luschan, 9 August 1908, SMB-PK, MV, IB 71/E 2092/08. To guard against criticism of his own administration, Luschan wrote in the margins of the letter: "Without Stephan I would have never sent them to the territory." Luschan actually removed Hahl's most scourging indictments against the Naval Expedition from the official museum files. The letters can be found in the Hahl file among the Luschan papers in SB-PK. Hahl was even more direct when he shared his opinions of the Naval Expedition personnel with Krämer, who faithfully recorded Hahl's outburst in his diary. Recalling a conversation with Schlaginhaufen, Hahl repeated his assertion, "What you are researching is common knowledge. You just don't believe us, so you send the researchers so they can publish about it." About Edgar Walden, Hahl condescendingly remarked, "He tried to conquer the world, but nothing came of it." August Krämer personal diary, undated entry "Hahlia," LiMSt, vol. 19.

logical museums, though quite extensive following his arrival in New Guinea, started to decline after 1910. As scholars with Richard Thurnwald's rare qualities—endurance, tenacity, and self-sacrifice—were not forthcoming, Hahl gradually withdrew from the German anthropological scene.

Not all was lost, though. Even if Hahl failed in his grand designs for colonial ethnography and was disappointed with the quality of researchers, methodologies resembling "fieldwork" took hold among some of the expeditions' participants. Performing ethnographic research in a mode approximating Hahl's design, Richard Thurnwald was one of the first anthropologists to experience the Malinowskian immersion of modern fieldwork. Emil Stephan also took some of Hahl's considerations into account when he set up his base camp in southern New Ireland. And while Edgar Walden did not enjoy Hahl's esteem, his research into the mortuary rituals of northern New Ireland focused on the deeper meanings of the artifacts associated with them.[74] In doing so, he criticized the endeavors of local resident ethnographers, such as Richard Parkinson, who collected objects without comprehending their meanings. Walden felt that Parkinson's work was riddled with mistakes, a function, in turn, of his linguistic ignorance.[75] Having discovered the advantages of fieldwork after Hahl had assigned him to northern New Ireland, Walden was also willing to share his methodological insights. In October 1908, the steamer of the Hamburg South Sea Expedition came upon Walden's area of research. Despite the tense competition embroiling the Hamburg and Walden's expedition (sponsored by Berlin), Walden followed an invitation to board the steamer. On the ship, Hamburg expedition member Wilhelm Müller listened carefully to what Walden had to say about the advantages of long-term stationary research. Criticizing the Hamburg expedition for its superficial surveying of all of German New Guinea, Walden explained that the "validity of his earlier notes" had become doubtful in the course of his ten-month stay in the region.[76] Apparently, Müller took the criticism to heart, and he subsequently complained to expedition organizer Georg Thilenius, "We are trying to write publications

---

74. Edgar Walden to Felix von Luschan 16 January 1908, SMB-PK, MV, IB 71/E 888/08.
75. Edgar Walden to Felix von Luschan, 18 July 1908, SMB-PK, MV, IB 71/E 1908/08. Walden refers in this passage to Richard Parkinson's classic, *Dreissig Jahre in der Südsee* (Stuttgart: Strecker und Schröder Verlag, 1907).
76. Wilhelm Müller to Georg Thilenius, 9 October 1908, MfVH, Südsee Expedition 6, 6.

after a mere few weeks of observation."[77] Both Walden and Müller had clearly come to realize the advantages of long-term studies of indigenous societies.[78] Hahl chose not to associate with these individuals; he deemed them unfit for study in the tropics, but his assigning of Walden to northern New Ireland did shape the ethnographic venture.

Conclusions

Two conclusions can be drawn from the present essay. One pertains to the more specific relationship between anthropology and colonialism in imperial Germany. The other is a more general finding concerning the origin of fieldwork in anthropology.

It is generally assumed that anthropological knowledge prior to the Great War was too abstract, too removed, too *weltfremd,* to be of any use for colonial administrators, and that they chose to ignore it. This essay documents that Hahl's experiences in German New Guinea led him to the realization that, on the contrary, ethnographic knowledge could be tremendously useful for his administration. His ensuing engagement with ethnography resulted in ongoing negotiations with German ethnological museums regarding the nature of anthropological research. In the process, Hahl sought to invigorate the discipline by advocating the study of actual people rather than material objects. The reoriented "salvage agenda" would still yield important insights for anthropologists, but the knowledge produced would also benefit colonial administrators.

Although Hahl's original designs for colonial ethnography ultimately succumbed to the competitive atmosphere of German museum anthropology, his contribution to fieldwork—as the intensive study of indigenous societies in limited geographical areas—was considerable. Hahl directly or indirectly influenced such anthropologists as Richard Thurnwald, Emil Stephan, Edgar Walden, and Wilhelm Müller, all of whom experienced a "Malinowskian moment" in German New Guinea.[79]

---

77. Ibid.

78. Unfortunately for German anthropology, Walden's and Müller's "Malinowskian moment" had limited impact, since both scholars became casualties of World War I. Walden was killed on the western front, and Müller contracted a deadly typhoid infection while interned on the island of Java.

79. On this Malinowskian moment, see James Clifford, *Routes: Travel and Translation in the Late Twentieth Century* (Cambridge: Harvard University Press, 1997), 64–74.

Historians of anthropology have given the origins of fieldwork a lot of thought.[80] Malinowski is no longer regarded as the sole originator of the fieldwork tradition; and the influence of the natural sciences on the formation of ethnography has been recognized.[81] There remains, however, a widespread notion that colonialism was a contextual rather than a direct intellectual influence on fieldwork, a position that is even more widespread in regard to German anthropology than other national traditions. This notion, I argue, was born out of an abstraction of colonialism that tends to ignore the sometimes competing projects existing at the heart of any nation's expansionistic drives. Hahl's relative remoteness from the German imperial authorities gave him time to negotiate new avenues for his colonial administration; and while the focus of German anthropology was removed from Hahl's particular designs, the governor managed to influence the anthropological agenda by attracting a number of young ethnographers to his project.

There are far-reaching implications for the recovery of German anthropology's colonial heritage. Not only does Hahl's engagement with German anthropology reveal the peripheral (colonial) contexts of this discipline, but it also allows for novel comparative dimensions. Hahl's situation is by no means unique for the colonial rule in the Pacific. Just across the border from German New Guinea, in the British portion of New Guinea, a similar union between anthropology and colonialism occurred. British New Guinea, initially a crown colony called "Papua," fell under Australian jurisdiction during the first decade of the twentieth century. By 1909, Hubert Murray, the lieutenant governor of Papua, started to emphasize that colonial administration must understand indigenous mentality. To further this goal, Murray established close contacts with the anthropological community in Britain; his main correspondents were Alfred Haddon, associated with Cambridge University and its Museum of Archeology and Ethnology, and Charles Seligman, the chair in ethnology at the University of London. Both Haddon and Seligman undertook extensive fieldwork, and Haddon in particular became a major proponent of the "intensive study of limited areas."[82] Unlike Hahl in German New

---

80. The main collection dedicated to this topic is Gupta and Ferguson, *Anthropological Locations*.
81. Stocking, "The Ethnographer's Magic"; Henrika Kuklick, "After Ishmail: The Fieldwork Tradition and Its Future," in Gupta and Ferguson, *Anthropological Locations*, 47–65.
82. Stocking, "The Ethnographer's Magic," 27–32.

Guinea, Murray was able to draw not only on museum practitioners, but also on established university-based scholars.

Murray's engagement with British anthropology produced two major results. First, following the Great War, his efforts led to the appointment of a government anthropologist for Papua. Second, to support the training of colonial officers destined for Papua, Australian authorities established a chair of anthropology at the University of Sydney in 1926. British social anthropologist Alfred Reginald Radcliffe-Brown was the chair's first occupant, holding it until 1931; Radcliffe-Brown was also responsible for the establishment of the well-known journal *Oceania*.[83]

Hahl and Murray clearly stand for two different national administrations in the colonial Pacific. Yet their similarities in commissioning anthropologists for their administrative tasks suggest alternative renderings of anthropology's histories. In the study of anthropology's formation intellectual-metropolitan influences on the discipline still reign supreme. A careful inclusion of colonial-peripheral effects allows for comparative dimensions between national traditions (in the above case British and German). In this sense the historical study of anthropology reveals much about nature of anthropology: a global discipline with distinct local expressions.

---

83. An increasing number of studies deal with the relationship between Murray and anthropology; see especially Ian Campbell, "Anthropology and the Professionalization of Colonial Administration in Papua and New Guinea," *Journal of Pacific History* 33 (1998): 69–90; Geoffrey Gray, "'Being Honest to My Science': Reo Fortune and J. H. P. Murray, 1927–1930," *Australian Journal of Anthropology* 10 (1999): 56–76. Murray's dealings with British anthropology also enter the pages of general histories of anthropology; see for instance, Henrika Kuklick, *The Savage Within: The Social History of British Anthropology, 1885–1945* (Cambridge: Cambridge University Press, 1991), 49; and Stocking, *After Tylor*, 385.

Gathering the Hunters: Bushmen in German (Colonial) Anthropology

ROBERT J. GORDON

> The Bushmen are of great ethnographic interest; however, because of their modest numbers, they play no role in the community life of Africa.
>
> —Fritz Jaeger, 1934

Shortly before Germany laid claim to that tract of real estate now known as Namibia, a young Swede, Gustaf de Vylder, set out with little scientific training and limited funds on a collecting venture sponsored by a Swedish museum. Almost immediately after leaving Cape Town, de Vylder met Dr. Theophilus Hahn (1842–1905), the son of a Rhenish missionary. Hahn had grown up in Namibia, and in 1870 he obtained his doctorate in Nama linguistics at Halle, the first doctorate on a Namibian subject. Afterward he returned to southern Namibia to set up shop as a trader.[1] De Vylder wrote in his journal that Hahn offered "to pay all expenses in return for half of what I collect, to be given to some museum in Germany," but de Vylder declined the offer.[2] A few months later he again met Hahn, who renewed his offer and upped the ante to include a wagon and all costs plus one thousand riksdaler if de Vylder would share half of what he collected, but he again declined.[3] At the end of March 1875, de Vylder boarded a schooner in Walfisch Bay together with his collection and adopted Bushman son. As fate would

---

1. Robert Gordon, "The Stat(u)s of Namibian Anthropology," *Cimbebasia* 16 (2000):1–23.

2. Ione Rudner and Jalmer Rudner, eds., *The Journal of Gustaf de Vylder, Naturalist in South-Western Africa, 1873–1875* (Cape Town: Van Riebeeck Society, 1998), 11.

3. Ibid., 183.

have it, Hahn was also on board. There, the following conversation reportedly took place: "Hahn declared that my collecting natural history specimens would not be of any use to Sweden because soon Germany would occupy Sweden and then take my collections. To this I replied it would be very flattering to me if people in Germany considered my collections so valuable that they would go to war against Sweden to get them." Bested, Hahn then pointed to de Vylder's adopted Bushman son and asked: "Does Mr. de Vylder believe he can make a Swede out of that Monkey?" "No, a German" de Vylder wryly replied.[4]

The interaction between de Vylder and Hahn, and particularly the last vignette, directs attention to the importance of possession, display, national self-promotion, and a theme that will be a constant in this essay: the varied connections between collecting, nationalism, and ethnic identity. It also foregrounds the important place of those people labeled "Bushmen" in such collections, and demonstrates the tension between the radically divergent registers of Bushmen as objects of classical colonial oppression and objects of romantic discourses sustained by the reified idea of the authentic primeval. What is it about the Bushmen that attracts so much scientific attention? Romanticization of Bushmen enabled scientists and officials, not only to imaginatively fantasize that the amateur field science they practiced found its purest representation in the pristine Bushmen, but crucially to gain moral absolution against of charges of racism when they went about the dirty business of colonial consolidation.

This chapter is focused on how German speakers in the former *Schutzgebiet* of Namibia—settlers, officials, travelers, and scientists—imagined the structure of "scientific" knowledge, and how this was articulated through both local and metropolitan visions of the Bushmen. It uses the case of the Bushmen to explore the dialogic nature of scientific discourse between the metropolitan center and the colonial periphery, and argues that it was not only academics who had a vested interest in promulgating the image of the "wild" Bushman but also the local *Feldwebels* of the state; these assorted settlers and farmers sustained and benefited from this image in the late nineteenth century, and in many ways continued to do so through most of the twentieth.

Historically, Namibia has been the site of numerous scientific collecting expeditions from the German-speaking world, and the complex interrelationships and politics between these expeditions and the estab-

---

4. Ibid., 258.

lishment of local museums and scientific societies (especially in Windhoek and Swakopmund) needs to be explored. Too much of the history of anthropology portrays the "founding fathers" as above the hoi polloi and somehow impervious to their messy and corrupting influences. Given its heavy museum-oriented artifact base and extensive use of *Fragebogen* to collect information, expatriates and settlers abroad, especially in Africa, provided vital inputs to the development of German anthropology.[5] Aspects of this complex relationship between settlers and metropole science in Namibia can be unpacked through a focus on the rather ambiguous status attributed to the Bushmen.

The Bushmen, as objects of science and the surrounding discourses, were used for a variety of often conflicting ends. Indeed, there was a dramatic tension between the metropole's desire for "salvaging" these "relics" and many settlers' wish to exterminate them. Because settlers gained a good deal of prestige by associating with German expeditions and scientific institutions, the Bushmen became one of the main vehicles for local settler science to gain respectability and assert a specific settler identity.

This chapter is thus about the abuse, celebration, and possession of Bushmen and the creation of a museum and settler society in Namibia, and in many ways it provides an alternative perspective from which to scrutinize the history of anthropology. It argues that the dynamic relationships between settlers, scientists, and indigenous peoples in South West Africa illustrates that the much vaunted center-periphery model that has characterized so much of historical writing needs to be collapsed. The imagined role assigned to science and museums in the continental *Heimat* was a key factor in the quality of treatment of indigenes, especially those labeled Bushmen. But local ethnography, patchy as it was, did not have a direct impact on colonialism or, for that matter, imperialism, except insofar as it reciprocally reinforced and shared the same representations with metropolitan science. Yet it is precisely the implications of this sharing, a mutually reinforcing working misunderstanding, that are important, because settler interpretations of metropolitan science led to what I have termed "shadow knowledge," a form of knowledge that allowed settlers to gloss over the contradictions inherent in the colonial experience.

---

5. Epitomized by L. Schultze-Ewerth and L. Adam, eds., *Das Eingeborenenrecht. Sitten und Gewohnheitsrechte der Eingeborenen derehemaligen deutschen Kolonien in Afrika un in der Suedsee,* 2 vols. (Stuttgart, 1930).

The Place of Bushmen in German Anthropological Thought

While much of German anthropological science and fantasy focused on South America and Oceania, those known generally as Bushman-Hottentot have long been central figures in the emergent German science of the Other.[6] The reason for their assigned importance is not hard to fathom. They were singled out both for their genitalia and for their ostensibly primitive character. Linnaeus used reproductive organs as the basis for his massive *Systema Naturae* (The system of nature) in the first edition (1735), where Hottentot-Bushmen were classified not as humans but as *Homo Monstrosis monochordiei* (human monsters with one testicle). The fact that this changed in subsequent editions is indicative of the keen interest taken in the topic. In particular, the notion that large genitalia led to increased libido, which was in turn linked to "primitive promiscuity," resulted in the Bushmen's enduring popularity among scientists.

The Bushmen's position as hunter-gatherers during the European industrial revolution further accounted for anthropologists' keen interest in the them; they were widely regarded by nineteenth-century scientists as remnants of the pre- or protohistoric forebears of contemporary Western society. Their genitalia remained important, but by the second half of the nineteenth century, their childlike, or paedomorphic, qualities were increasingly emphasized. As throwbacks to a distant past, Bushmen were regarded as a unique "window into how our ancestors lived." Indeed, in 1852 Wilhelm Bleek, a young philologist and first cousin of Ernest Haeckel, predicted that Africa would be as significant for philology in the second half of the century as the Orient had been during the first. The Bushman-Hottentot, he argued, was of critical importance for the understanding of human history, and his conviction that an adequate study of them was both crucial and long overdue was so strong that he expressed his willingness to spend years among them.[7] As he noted in his 1869 book, *On the Origin of Lan-*

---

6. See, for example, Robert Welsch, "One Time, One Place, Three Collections: Colonial Processes and the Shaping of Some Museum Collections from German New Guinea," in *Hunting the Gatherers: Ethnographic Collectors, Agents, and Agency in Melanesia*, ed. Michael O'Hanlon and Robert Welsch (Oxford: Berghahn, 2001); and Susanne Zantop, *Colonial Fantasies: Conquest, Family, and Nation in Precolonial Germany, 1770–1870* (Durham: Duke University Press, 1997).

7. J. Ryding, "Alternatives in Nineteenth-Century German Ethnology: A Case Study in the Sociology of Science," *Sociologus* 25, no. 1 (1975): 1–28.

guage, Bushmen were important to German science because "among all the hitherto discovered living species of men, the Australian Negroes in New Holland, and the Bushmen who are related to these in many ways, are the ones that stand nearest to the apes."[8] The first book that can be classified as an ethnography of peoples in southern Africa is Gustav Fritsch's magnum opus, *Die Eingeborenen Sued-Afrikas, Ethnographisch und Anatomisch Beschrieben* (1872), which was based on a research trip from 1863 to 1866. Fritsch assembled a large collection of photographs from the area and wrote extensively about the peoples he encountered in the *Zeitschrift für Ethnologie* and a number of other German journals. It was Fritsch who first coined the term "unfortunate child of the moment" in reference to the Bushmen. This act, coming from the man who was appointed to the first chair of comparative anatomy in Berlin in 1874, ultimately gave considerable scientific credibility to the colonialist distinction between "wild" and "tame" Bushmen.[9] Fritsch was not, of course, the first intellectual to romanticize the Bushmen, but he was widely cited by a range of scholars. The trope of the "unfortunate child of the moment," for example, was used by Siegfried Passarge to initiate his classic attack on the earlier generation of Bushman scholars.[10] Fritsch's romantic notions, however, were also transformed by the new contexts in which Passarge used his language. Fritsch's travels and writing took place before Germany acquired colonies, when the cultural leisure scene was enlivened by occasional visits by troupes of Africans including Bushmen who were dutifully measured, allowing emergent anthropologists to debate the implications of their genitalia. By the time Passarge went into the field in 1896–1898 and published his essay in 1905, Germany was an established colonial power and the settler colony of Namibia was embroiled in a bitter war with the local populace. Moreover, Passarge's statements about the Bushmen occurred just before he took up an appointment at the newly established Colonial Institute in Ham-

---

8. Wilhelm Bleek, *The Origins of Language,* ed. E. Haeckel (New York: Schmidt, 1869), 53. This stereotype has a remarkable persistence; even Ashley Montague in his classic *Man's Most Dangerous Myth: The Fallacy of Race* (Cleveland: World Pub. Co., 1964) writes, "If we were asked to name the two human types which would stand at opposite extremes physically, it would be the Hottentot or Bushman at one end and the European at the other" (214).

9. Robert Gordon, *Picturing Bushmen: The Denver African Expedition of 1925 (*Athens: Ohio University Press, 1997).

10. Edwin Willimess, *The Kalahari Ethnographies (1896–1898) of Siegfried Passarge* (Cologne: Rudiger Koeppe, 1997).

burg, where colonial interests were harnessed by local elites to create and justify its founding and where, as a consequence, "colonial science" was given some prominence. Within this new colonial context, Fritsch's definition of Bushmen as "unfortunate children of the moment" had two critical implications: either the Bushmen could be changed through sympathetic, paternalistic tutoring, or they were caught in some Peter Pan syndrome and hence should be eradicated—views that were widely reflected by segments of settler society.

Anthropologists' considerable interest in the Bushmen during the colonial period is given testament by the large number of articles listed in Nicholas J. van Warmelo's massive index.[11] Distinguished amateurs and academics such as Seiner, Pöch, Kaufmann, von Luschan, von Zastrow, Gentz, Mueller, Schulte, Vedder, Werner, and Schultz all wrote about Bushmen. The Austrian Rudolf Pöch, for instance, who eventually occupied the first chair of anthropology at the University of Vienna, is of particular importance. While making the first movie of Bushmen in 1909, he also amassed the world's largest collection of Bushmen skulls; and even though his work has been largely neglected by Anglo-American academics, he set the romantic parameters for film documentaries on Bushmen. Although the photographs that accompanied the triumphal interview he gave to the *Cape Times Weekly* on 3 November 1909 showed the Bushmen he had encountered during his expedition dressed in rags, his film showed them in their pristine state, decked out in loincloths, with no vestiges of "Western contamination." Entitled "The Bushman Tribes," this interview deserves citation if only for its portrayal of the anthropologist as hero.

While Pöch and others were setting new technical standards in their efforts to document the Bushmen, amateurs were also heavily involved, aided in large part by various *Fragebogen* developed in the metropole by Felix von Luschan and others. The *Anleitung,* 122 pages long, featured a complex and comprehensive checklist. It stressed the importance of *Mitarbeiter,* European (almost exclusively German) collaborators, and indicated that particularly effective associates could look forward to being elected a corresponding member of an ethnological/anthropological society, a matter of some prestige.[12] The *Anleitung* represented a major move to systematize collecting and enforce "sci-

---

11. Nicholas J. Van Warmelo, *Anthropology of Southern Africa in Periodicals* (Johannesburg: Witwatersrand University Press, 1977).
12. Andrew Zimmerman, "Anthropology and the Place of Knowledge in Imperial Berlin," Ph.D. diss., University of California, San Diego, 1998.

entific" parameters on Germans' long engagement with the region, particularly the Bushmen.[13] As late as 1949 *Fragebogen* and well-informed "alte Afrikaner," preferably German-speakers, were still seen as crucial for "colonial-ethnographic" research.[14]

Artifacts of German Identity in Namibia

In 1915, South West Africa was invaded by South Africa, and in 1920 it became a League of Nations mandated territory administered by the victors. During the mandate era, German science and a focus on the Bushmen helped the settlers retain a distinct identity separate from their South African neighbors. Hoarding and looting initially followed in the slipstream of invasion, so that shortly after South West Africa was successfully conquered, the South African minister of defense was forced to prohibit the removal or "plunder" of "specimens." Museums in South Africa competed aggressively with each other to secure the best "specimens" during this rare opportunity, and as a result, many artifacts, including several "Bushman" rock paintings, vanished.[15] In order to inventory its new territory, however, the administration needed experts, and thus in 1920 it included in its annual budget a small amount to fund basic anthropological research, of which the first allocation was used to pay for Bushman research, done under the aegis of the South African Museum. At the same time, however, and in response to visits from South African Museum personnel, Major O'Reilly of the Military Administration suggested that a small museum be established in South West Africa, "since charity begins at home." This was the beginning of an effort to create distinctions between South West Africa and its larger neighbor—an effort that

---

13. This *Anleitung* was made even more important by virtue of a Bundesrat decision in 1889 (ratified again in April 1903 by the DKB) that made the Berlin Museum the central collecting point while the state undertook to pay for shipping expenses. Colonial artifacts were in the future not to be seen as private property and disposed of as officials saw fit; rather, this centralized disposal underwrote nationalism insofar as working for an abstract "national organization" now took precedence over individual whims. These "Fragebogen" were supplemented by colonial vade mecums like Georg von Neumeyer's edited two volumes, which ran to at least three editions after 1875.

14. Hugo A Bernatzik, ed., *Afrika: Handbuch der Angewandten Völkerkunde* (Innsbruck: Schluesselverlag, 1949)

15. National Archives of Namibia (NAN), file SWAA A198/2, 2 November 1915. Much of the material in this section is derived from and discussed in greater depth in Gordon, *Picturing Bushmen*, 109–16.

depended explicitly on German science, the Bushmen, and an incipient nationalism.

Such was the demand for Bushman skeletons not only from South Africa but from Europe and elsewhere, that the administration was forced to pass the Bushman Relics Protection Proclamation to regulate the removal and export of Bushman "relics." And already in June 1921, a man who was to play a key role in propelling the science and Bushmen as key issues of local identity, the territorial medical officer Dr. Louis Fourie, was arguing that rather than send artifacts and skeletons out of the country, the administration should start its own collection:

> We are in a unique position with regard to the Bushmen and I would submit for serious consideration the question of starting a local collection, which I am sure would in time attract scientists from all parts of the world and place this country, as it should be, on the foreground as far as this subject is concerned.[16]

The administration officials agreed, and noted that

> everything should be done to preserve knowledge that will, in the anthropological line, be lost in a few years' time. In connection with the anthropological research we should bear in mind that we have in one of our own officers, Dr. Fourie, a gentleman who has collected an immense amount of knowledge about the Bushmen, which if not put on record, will be lost. With his scientific training his investigations should be of value.[17]

Fourie was clearly a man of influence. The youngest son in a large Afrikaans family, Fourie grew up on a family farm near Oudtshoorn, and after attending an English-language boarding school, he studied medicine in Scotland. He also spent a few months in Germany, where he studied pediatrics and thus developed a reasonable fluency in German. He returned very much an Anglophile, and accompanied by a wife descended from the Irish landed gentry, he decided to open a medical practice in Steynsburg, Cape Colony. Here, his interest piqued by stone implements, he became a keen amateur anthropologist. Appar-

---

16. NAN A198/3 memo, June 1921.
17. NAN A198/6 memo, 10 March 1924.

ently he disliked writing out accounts to patients, so in 1916 he came to the territory as medical officer, where his passion for matters "Bushmen" became well established and he began spending every vacation visiting with them. Obviously successful at his job, Fourie was awarded one of three Orders of the British Empire's in 1922.[18] His publications on the Bushmen, chiefly in the *Journal of the South West Africa Scientific Society* and in the famous *Native Tribes of South West Africa* (1928) were generally well received, and his articles were often used in classrooms at Harvard and other universities.

While Fourie was engaged in his research, a number of quasi-scientific expeditions that came from abroad were visiting the territory. These received wide publicity in the local settler press, stimulating controversy and initiating arguments about the need for well-supported local institutions.[19] The 1925 Denver Expedition was clearly the most important. This expedition, led by C. Ernest Cadle, a self-styled "doctor" with a flair for publicity, was originally meant to capture some "wild Bushmen" for American science, but settled for making a movie about them.

> Even as the Denver Expedition was making its way to SWA, Fourie was complaining that at the present time all the material collected in this happy hunting ground finds its way to institutions either in the Union or abroad. . . . It may be said that we are not competent to make such a collection to which one need only reply that museums have in the past always been most complimentary about the completeness of the specimens sent to them from this country.[20]

The government secretary agreed and added that the newly formed South West African Scientific Society could be responsible: "There is no reason why we should continue to finance other museums when we could . . . form an anthropological collection which would be unique

---

18. The others went to Native Commissioners Hahn and Manning.

19. What is striking is how many local inhabitants had, or at least thought they had, knowledge about the history and the people of Namibia far superior to that deployed by these scientific expeditions. For example, a series of lectures originally given in Windhoek in early 1925 by Prof. Griess, principal of the Deutsche Realschule, drew the comment from the English-language *Windhoek Advertiser,* 22 April 1925, that "the paper should be printed for the benefit, not only of people of this country, but of those in the Union and overseas interested in S.W. Africa."

20. NAN A198/3 memo, 23 September 1925.

and would probably attract anthropologists from all over the world in time."[21]

Fourie had touched on the sensitive nerve of incipient nationalism,[22] and his proposals quickly gained settler support. Just a few months later, for example, the Windhoek-based *Allgemeine Zeitung* published a strong plea for a museum, arguing that the country was in danger of being denuded of its scientific treasures.[23] Bushman skeletons, it wrote, were being sought after by South African museums, which had distressing implications for South West Africa and its worldwide reputation:

> If we keep these things in the country, scientists will be forced to come to SW Africa, and carry out their studies on the spot, and this would contribute in no small degree to make the land better known. . . . The ignorance of America as to this country is shown by the fact that the scientific Denver expedition left everything in Cape Town that is regarded as essential in civilized countries and only brought to Windhoek the equipment suited to an expedition into the Sahara, and the members of the expedition were astonished to find Windhoek a pretty little town with modern conveniences. We must therefore endeavor by every means in our power to make SWA known to the world. Advertisement is essential in these days. A museum would advertise us at no great cost.

This strong reaction to the Denver Expedition stemmed both from a desire for civic self-promotion that might, in the end, prove lucrative, and from the fact that within the context of the times (Germany was being admitted to the League of Nations) the administration was debating what sort of citizenship to give the erstwhile German citizens who had not been repatriated. As a Legislative Assembly was being created for European settlers, the one common ground these different settlers could agree on was the interests of "science."

---

21. NAN A198/3 memo, 23 September 1925.

22. Fourie's feelings of patriotism were long apparent. In one of his earliest letters to Dr. Peringuey, director of the South African Museum, he complained, "I understand that you have allowed Pöch of Vienna to steal a march on you and that Vienna now boasts the finest collection in existence. In this respect I consider that our national collection (if such you consider the SA Museum) should have pride of place and I am willing to assist you in every way to attain that object (moreover) I followed the route taken by Pöch and am delighted to be able to say that he did not obtain a single skeleton in the area visited by me." Fourie to Peringuey, 1 September 1919, SA Museum files.

23. *Allgemeine Zeitung,* 5 December 1925.

It was in this milieu of intellectual and nationalist fervor that the South West African Scientific Society was founded. A meeting chaired by Dr. Fourie and held in the newly founded library drew some seventy citizens, who quickly agreed that the society should be autonomous, rather than a "daughter organization" to the South African Association for the Advancement of Science. The aims and principles of the society were

> a) to contact all persons in the Territory interested in Science; b) create a basis for scientific research by systematic support; c) collect and preserve objects of scientific and historic interest; d) to assist in building up museum collections with a view of these becoming the Society's property and to make these collections accessible to the public.[24]

The society emphasized that "science" would be used to bridge ethnic animosities, at least among the three European sections of Afrikaner, English, and German. United in science, people would develop a common loyalty to the country; and indeed the society agreed to publish all its proceedings in both English and German (although financial constraints ultimately limited them to publishing papers in the language of the presenter). Its intended audience and clientele were clearly not professional scientists but amateurs, people like Fourie, who they all agreed could do a much better and more cost-effective job than many of the questionable professional experts visiting the territory. Moreover, they quickly gained substantial financial support: both the Roman Catholic diocese and the Rhenish Mission became corporate members, as did a number of large businesses. This was, in fact, a unique effort by private enterprise to subsidize government efforts to promote science.

Science and scientific associations, of course, had always been treated as ritually important by the state and its officials. Consider the visit of a contingent from the German oceanographic research vessel *Meteor* to Windhoek in 1926. Practically the whole town, led by the administrator and the mayor, waited at the railway station to officially welcome them. Both the German *Pfadfinder* and the South African Boy Scouts were there in full force, the former all waving German flags. After a march to the town hall done in terms of strict protocol accompanied by the ship's band and cheering along the route, the

---

24. H. J. Rust, "The South West Africa Scientific Society," *South West Africa Annual* 1974:61.

mayor, Councilor Menmuir, gave "an exceptionally eloquent speech" in which he stressed that the visit was important to the local citizenry because they can *"visualize in your presence a living link* with their old homes across the Sea, and also an actual expression of the ever-present pulsations of the civilization of their great Country." Even more importantly, they were welcomed by the town because they were "workers in that inscrutable and inexhaustible subject—SCIENCE." The mayor greeted them by explaining:

> You are *missionaries of Science,* and also let me say, of Peace, engaged upon a mission of research, the results of which will no doubt be of the greatest importance and benefit to Mankind. . . . We, as Laymen . . . can only dimly appreciate the enormous physical and mental energy required from you. We are here in Windhoek, isolated many hundred miles away from the big centres of civilization in the Union, but none the less we realize the importance and seriousness of the mission you are engaged upon.[25]

Within these and other public statements, the connection between science and colonization was accepted both implicitly and explicitly. This is perhaps best captured by Professor Fritz Jaeger, who had done research in South West Africa, and was later elevated to "hero" status by the Scientific Society. Jaeger explained in 1934:

> To colonize a country means to create a new, higher culture. This is only possible for superior cultures. Colonization is a process of cultural dissemination across the earth. Just as air flows from areas of high pressure, so culture spreads from geographical regions of high culture to those of low culture. . . . Military superiority allowed the European colonizing peoples to seize African colonies, but only their scientific and technological knowledge allowed them to develop the countries economically. It is to be hoped that they will also succeed in educating the natives to become a cultivated people.[26]

---

25. *The Windhoek Advertiser,* 4 August 1926, 2; emphasis added.
26. Fritz Jaeger, "Die Geographischen Grundlangen der Kolonisation Afrikas," in *Afrika, Europa und Deutschland,* ed. E. Wunderlich (Stuttgart: Fleischhauer und Spohn, 1934), 17. Thanks to John Noyes for this reference. The similarities to the justification that General von Trotha gave for his notorious extermination command against the Herero in 1905 are striking. It was, he said, the "law of nature" that the "weaker races must die out when they come into contact with the stronger ones." Cited in Mauritz Bonn, *Wandering Scholar* (New York: John Day, 1948), 137.

Fig. 1. The spectacle of science. The captain and crew of the *Meteor* are officially welcomed to Windhoek. (Source: National Archives of Namibia.)

Despite the resounding support for the project, and its longevity, however, Dr. Louis Fourie, who is widely regarded as having been the driving force behind the establishment of the Scientific Society, resigned in 1929 under conditions that are as yet unclear.[27] But as with many of his counterparts, two interlocking factors seem to have been crucial. The administration had started a policy of aggressively settling Afrikaner farmers in the territory. German-speakers, let alone English-speakers, had little chance of obtaining inexpensive government-subsidized farms, and this policy tended to marginalize Anglophiles like Fourie.[28] But it was the German-speaking sector who felt particularly threatened

---

27. He took up a position as chief pest control officer in the Transkei and by 1937 surfaces as assistant health officer for the City of Johannesburg. He seemed to have severed his ties completely with the territory except to accept an honorary life membership in the Scientific Society in 1937. His extensive Bushman collection he donated mostly to a minor provincial museum in Kingwilliamstown, South Africa, and the rest he placed on permanent loan to the University of the Witwatersrand. He died around 1953.

28. John Seymour, *One Man's Africa* (London: Eyre and Spottiswoode, 1955), 44.

Fig. 2. "A Most Eloquent Speech." Mayor Menmuir welcomes the crew of the German scientific vessel, the *Meteor* to Windhoek. (Source: National Archives of Namibia.)

by this land policy. Historically, the Germans in the territory had looked down upon the "Boers," who were now becoming a significant force in the political life of the territory, and the situation was further exacerbated by the Afrikaner-dominated administration's perceived inefficiency and disinterest.[29]

The antithesis of the administration's pro-Afrikaner action was of course scientific engagement, which also emphasized the German-speaking colonists' claims to being trustworthy colonizers. Within a few years, the Scientific Society had been transformed into a German enclave and English as a language of publication in the *Journal of the South West Africa Scientific Society* dropped into virtual nonuse after the third volume. This dovetailed nicely with a number of other organizations initiated at the time. The Deutsche Pfadfinder, for example,

---

29. Andree-Jeanne Totemeyer, *The State of Museums in Namibia and the Need for Training in Museum's Services* (Windhoek: University of Namibia, 1999), 60.

eschewed any contact with the Boy Scouts and rapidly became a major force. Avowedly nationalistic, the organization's members wore hats modeled after the *Schutztruppe,* emphasized *veldcraft,* or survival skills, and celebrated anniversaries of German colonialism like Francke's relief of Omaruru and the Battle of Waterberg.[30] Science, scientific societies, and scientific institutions were among a number of different vehicles harnessed to help promote a vigorous local identity during the mandate era—an identity that was distinctly German and, ironically, increasingly tied to the Bushmen.

The Place of the Bushmen in the Scientific Life of South West Africa

It is surely more than coincidence that the first public lecture sponsored by the Scientific Society was focused on the origins of Bushmen and that the Bushmen constituted a major focus of the society's activities throughout its existence.[31] The inaugural issue of the *Journal of the South West Africa Scientific Society* devoted half of its pages to the Bushmen, and they continued to dominate the ethnological articles published in the *Journal* right through the interwar period. The presence of living Bushmen was one of the few things that demarcated the territory from its powerful neighbor South Africa, and consequently the Bushmen became a major icon for important factions within the settler community.[32] Placing a special emphasis on the still surviving Bushmen in the territory drew legitimacy from German anthropologists' persistent emphasis on salvage anthropology, and it implicitly served as a critique of South Africa, where Bushmen were rapidly approaching extinction. Thus in many ways their focus on the Bushmen enabled German settlers to recoup some national esteem after being defeated by vastly superior numbers just a few years earlier.

This emphasis was also supported and extended in the following decades by the fact that the only serious research done by metropolitan anthropologists during the interwar years in the territory, that by Aus-

---

30. By 1932, however, it had been taken over and renamed the Hitler Youth Movement, and two years later the administration was forced to ban it. Resurrected under a slightly different format, it was again banned in 1939. Its impact was such that there are at present two private museums in Namibia devoted to Pfadfinder memorabilia.

31. Heinrich Vedder, *Kort Verhale uit 'n Lang Lewe* (Cape Town: A. A. Balkema, 1957).

32. Symptomatic of this iconicity is the map for South West Africa in the comprehensive *Das Eingeborenenrecht* (1930), edited by Schultze-Ewerth and Adam. In this map, the ethnic group labeled with the largest font and occupying the whole of the Northeast is the Bushmen.

trian Viktor Lebzelter and Italian Lidio Cipriani, had as its central concern the Bushmen.[33] Moreover, amateurs and dilettantes remained focused on the Bushmen as well, further promoting their particular importance. During this period a number of missionaries like the Reverends Underkoetter, Vedder, and Wulfhorst, as well as Pater Wuest, wrote about the need to bring Christ to the "sterbendes Volk" [dying people]. Indeed, Bushmen constituted one of the most popular cover stories for the *Berichte der Rheinischen Mission*.

This pattern of research/publicity continued after the Second World War. Apart from the U.S.-initiated Loeb Anthropological Expedition, which visited Ovamboland at the personal invitation of General Jan Smuts, and one or two minor glorified hunting trips disguised as scientific enterprises, the emphasis continued to be on Bushmen. Particularly noteworthy in this regard were the efforts of Pater Martin Gusinde, an erstwhile colleague of Wilhelm Schmidt, the various Marshall family expeditions,[34] as well as the efforts of the government ethnologist and later professor of Africanistics at Cologne, Oswin Kohler, who built his reputation on the Caprivi Bushmen in the early sixties.

One thing, however, set this postwar era apart. Because of the sensitive nature of the territory's international status, it was practically impossible for foreign anthropologists to get the necessary research visas. Only anthropologists with impeccably conservative credentials were allowed in, and then inevitably they were only permitted to engage in research on Bushmen in out-of-the-way areas like Nyae Nyae or the Caprivi. This administrative funneling served to distract attention from more pressing and embarrassing problems and issues in the more densely populated areas of the country. It also allowed the government to get around the completely inadequate budget of the newly appointed assistant government ethnologist by allowing rich foreign researchers like the Marshall family to undertake the relatively expensive work in out-of-the-way places. At the same time, those in the administration who controlled the permitting process genuinely (or perhaps cynically) believed that by encouraging research on the "wild" Bushmen they were doing their bit for promoting "scientific research." It is probably more than coincidence that the first (Afrikaner) ethnolo-

---

33. Influenced perhaps by Pater Wilhelm Schmidt's *Ursprung der Gottesidee* (Munich: Aschendarffsche Verlagsbuchhandlung, 1912), which had assigned empirical importance to Bushmen.
34. For an evaluation see Megan Biesele, Robert Gordon, and Richard Lee, *The Past and Future of !Kung Ethnography* (Hamburg: Helmut Buske Verlag, 1987).

gist appointed to the newly established state museum in Windhoek did his masters thesis on the Bushmen of Nyae Nyae.

But how did local settlers view the Bushmen and all this scientific interest in them? There was a strange duality at work in both popular conceptions of the Bushmen and popular assessments of scientists' ability to study and understand them. In a locally published book that aimed to encourage German settlers, Scientific Society stalwart Paul Barth proclaimed:

> Like a beast of prey the Bushman quietly stalks his victims, so that they are never even aware of his presence until his poisoned arrow has hit its mark. In this manner the Bushman also catches his four-legged prey, although primitive snares are also used. . . . The Bushman is so exceptionally frugal that he can go days enduring hunger and thirst without letting it seem to bother him. However, once he has his prey, he will stuff himself as full as he possibly can, so that with his wrinkled skin, bloated stomach, and sly cunning eyes he looks like a beast of prey himself. His speech, like everything else about him, is primitive, and composed mainly of consonants. . . . They seem therefore to be dying out, and no one will be any worse for their loss, as they are destroyers rather than producers.[35]

Undoubtedly Barth was echoing the dominant settler view, which tended to disdain the unproductive and deceptive Bushman; yet while many settlers regarded the Bushmen as "vermin," they also thought of them as cunning—so cunning, in fact, that they could easily hoodwink naive foreign visitors. Thus a 1930 article entitled "Of Wild and Tame Bushmen" and published in a small Windhoek-based German-language magazine by "Outis" (Afrikaans slang for an "old hand") described how he encountered the Denver Expedition in 1925 and recalled their Munchhausenesque bragging: They claimed, for example, to have "discovered" a completely unknown tribe of Bushmen who had never seen Europeans, and they were extremely pleased and proud of their film footage of wild war dances and secret religious rituals, which they confidently predicted would be a smash hit. As befits an experienced "colonial hand," Outis was skeptical. When shown the sacred Bushman religious relic, he dismissed it as a readily available

---

35. Paul Barth, *Südwest-Afrika* (Windhoek: John Meinert, 1926), 150.

ordinary Ovambo doll. He also claimed to have met the Denver Expedition interpreter on one of his trips through the Etosha Game Park, at which point he asked to see these "wild Bushmen." The interpreter obliged, complete with a staged mock attack. After satisfying their requests for cigarettes, the Bushmen performed their war dances, which Outis recalled was to the tune "Matiche," a Mexican song that had been popular with German troops during the 1904–7 war. Moreover he also recognized one of the dancers as "Jephter," the Bushman headman who had served as general factotum/interpreter for the same military company Outis had served in during the German era. After insisting on seeing their living quarters, Outis was first taken to a "primitive encampment," clearly constructed for tourist consumption, and then to their real abode, which consisted of tin shacks, included an old German military bed, and best of all, an old phonograph on which they played their only record, "Matiche!"

Such deception was all too common. Even ordinary settlers were aware of the special status of Bushmen in Europe and keen to capitalize on it: In January 1933, one settler, A. J. Meyer, wrote to the commissioner of the board of trade asking for advice.

> After many months of trouble, thirst and exertion, I have now managed to catch six wild Bushmen in the most deserted part of the Kalahari, I have trained and tamed them very well so that they are now quite used to the food of civilized people. I intend to take them to Europe and America for exhibition and performances in theatres. They can easily be numbered amongst the best dancers of the world in their peculiar way.[36]

The authorities, ever alert to the watchdog role of the League of Nations, investigated a possible charge of man-stealing against Meyer, but found that the six Bushmen were farmworkers on his father's farm. Upon discovering that they were "expert exponents of the art of Bushman dancing," Meyer junior "conceived the fertile idea that much money might be made out of this circumstance, if these Bushmen could be brought to Europe. Apparently in order to arouse further interest, he sought to convey the impression that these were wild and untamed Bushmen, kept in captivity by him."[37]

---

36. NAN SWAA A.50/76.
37. NAN SWAA A.50/76.

Despite the role that locals might play in such deceptions, "authentic" Bushmen and German settlers' desire to serve as spokesmen for their authenticity remained critical to Germans' local identities. As the Scientific Society's president remarked with regard to the first book they published (not surprisingly, on Bushmen):[38]

> This book represents a most interesting and important development. The subject matter is peculiar to this Territory, the author is a member of our own community and the book was produced entirely in this country. . . . Members of the Society do not need to be told that the opportunities to record Bushman lore and other information contained in this book, are fast disappearing, and that the author has rendered a service by placing them on the record.[39]

Clearly metropole-periphery relations in the interwar years were significant, and they served to develop a very strong sense of local *Deutschtum*. They were thus a means of combating the allegedly seditious efforts of South Africa in the mandate by invoking German culture for identity as both a rallying point and as a tool for enforcing conformity.

Indeed, the political situation made it essentially inevitable that reactions to outsiders would play a key role in the overt Germanization of the scientific community. As a reaction to the interloping actions of these outsiders, the Scientific Society soon began purging its ranks until only German science and scientists could continue to be numbered among their community. This homogenization was so extensive that in many ways, the society started to resemble the *Vereine* and *Gesellschaften* that were such an important part of the social scenery in small-town Wilhelmine Germany.

The Ritual Life of the Scientific Society

What is striking about the Scientific Society is its elaborate organization, which penetrated into multiple levels of territorial society and covered a variety of scientific fields. Equally impressive is the persis-

---

38. Fritz Metzger, *Narro and His Clan* (Windhoek: SWA Scientific Society, 1950).
39. J. S. Watt, "President Watt's Report to the Annual General meeting," SWA Scientific Society, mimeo, 1951.

tence of its staunchly German character—even during the decades when many people in the world of anthropology were eagerly abandoning those things thought to be most German. The Second World War marked a low point for the society, and a special meeting was held in 1947 to resurrect it. By making the administrator a patron, the society secured itself a more consistent source of government funds. But from the administrator at the apex, the society also had a number of different kinds of members, all of whom gained some mention in the *Journal:* namely fifteen honorary members (all German-speaking but including two affluent German Jews); six corresponding members (all German including luminaries like Prof. Eugen Fischer); five furthering members, generally local corporations who made large contributions; committee members, consisting of a president, vice president, and secretary plus seven "other members"; there is also a category called "co-opted members," in this case, one representing the Luderitz and Swakopmund work groups. The secretariat consisted of a secretary, a secretarial assistant, a librarian, a financial adviser and a book proofreader. After this are listed the various work groups with contacts: archaeology, botany, geology, herpetology, mineralogy, and ornithology. Later, other work groups in speleology, astronomy, and ethnology were added.

One of the problems the society continually faced was to find suitable papers for the *Journal,* and in some cases papers would be reprinted. Which papers were selected is quite telling: Dr. Fourie's "Preliminary Notes on Certain Customs of the Hei-Kom" is reprinted twice (in 1951 and 1964). Also reprinted were Frey's "Jonker Afrikaner and His Times" (1951) and Vedder's "Über die Vorgeschichte der Voelkerschaften" (1953). All of these are ethnographic and ethnohistorical by nature and feature "Bushmen" quite prominently.

Almost all the books and monographs the society has published until recently have been in German, and if the society has any "heroes," they are German-speaking ethnologists/ ethnohistorians. In terms of celebratory rituals, a number stand out: Heinrich Vedder, Eugen Fischer, and Martin Gusinde. They share a number of attributes: All are male German-speakers who specialized in Bushmen and represented ideas long abandoned in the metropole. Undoubtedly the most prominent was Heinrich Vedder, a Rhenish missionary who came to Namibia at the end of 1903. In 1912 he published some pioneering papers on Bushmen. Deported in 1919, he returned to Namibia in 1922. The next year the University of Tübingen awarded him an honorary doctorate for his research on indigenous languages and cultures in Namibia. In the same year, Hamburg University published his two-volume *Die Bergdama*. In 1928 he was the major author for an administration-sponsored volume, *The Native Tribes of South West Africa*. Six years later he published his classic *Das alte Südwestafrika,* the research for which was supported by the administration (Afrikaans [1937] and English [1938] versions rapidly followed). After the Second World War he became a leading spokesperson for the German community in Namibia, and he was appointed to the South African Senate.[40]

The Scientific Society celebrated Vedder in a number of ways: It made him an honorary member in 1937 and honored him in 1961 with the only festschrift it ever published. In addition, the society has republished in pamphlet form his "Zur Vorgeschichte Südwest-Afrikas" and ensured that *Das alte Südwestafrika,* an original and imaginative book, remains in print. Indeed, it is a fine example of what Brigitte Lau calls "colonial apologetic writing," which supports white settler myths and centers on the role and responsibility of the white (largely German) "race as the carrier of Christian civilization." Vedder's history, with its implicit glorification of German colonialism, meshed well with the militant nationalism that so suited the Nazis.

Eugen Fischer was another notable, and perhaps even notorious, celebrity. Fischer, while largely forgotten now, was a physical anthropologist of some fame. In 1959 he was invited to reminisce in the *Journal* to commemorate the fiftieth anniversary of his research among the Rehoboth bastards. This research was the first biological anthropological study to apply Mendelian genetics. In 1964, the newsletter *Mitteilungen* featured a special commemorative article to celebrate his ninetieth birthday, and an honored Fischer donated a personal copy of his recently reprinted book *Die Rehobother Bastards* as well as his album of Baster photographs and proclaimed a continued central interest in the Basters. Starting as professor at Freiburg, he coauthored a best-selling text on human genetics and then moved on, with Hitler's blessing, to be Rector Magnificus of Berlin University before becoming director of the Kaiser Wilhelm Institute for Anthropology, Human Genetics, Racial Hygiene, and Eugenics, where he perfected and

---

40. Officially he was appointed on account of his expert knowledge of the "native peoples" but in reality to represent the German community (Vedder, *Kort Verhale uit 'n Lang Lewe*).

taught, inter alia, the S.S. the science of "racial hygiene." When he retired in 1942 after obtaining the highest scientific honors the Nazis could bestow, a grateful Führer allowed the institute to be renamed after him.[41] As Franz Weidenreich noted in *Science,* he was among "the leading Nazi anthropologists who are morally responsible for the prosecution and extinction of the peoples and races the Nazis considered 'inferior.' . . . If anyone, he is the man who should be put on the list of war criminals."[42]

Compared to Fischer, Pater Martin Gusinde SVD (1886–1969) was a minor academic. Gusinde was inspired to become a missionary by a traveling colonial exhibition featuring live Africans. As a seminarian he soon fell in with Pater Wilhelm Schmidt, and he quickly developed a lifelong interest in the origin of the concept of God and diffusionism. He was sent off to Chile, where he made his reputation with a study of the Yahgan of Terra del Fuego, and later, like so many of Schmidt's supporters, he also undertook research on the Pygmies. In 1949 he was made a visiting professor at the Catholic University in Washington, D.C., and with support from the Wenner-Gren Foundation made his first visit to Namibia to study Bushmen. In the space of ten months, using Windhoek as a base, he undertook three tours; one to the Etosha, another to the Kavango, and a third to the central Kalahari in order to get a comprehensive picture. His expedition was heralded as the "first survey ever of Bushmen" and the *Cape Argus* portrayed him as somewhat of a hero because he, along with only two "half-Bushmen," spent months alone with "wild" Bushmen and examined over two thousand of them in only four months.[43] Two years later, in 1953, he spent the summer in Namibia traveling to places where, courtesy of the Oblates of Maria Immaculata, Bushmen were congregated. On his return to Austria he gave a slide show of his Bushman research to an applauding audience of over thirteen hundred and ceded his valuable material on Bushman genitalia to his friend Prof. Eugen Fischer.[44]

Gusinde obviously worked well with members of the Scientific Society and published three articles in their journal. He also got on well with a government-appointed commission that was looking into the

---

41. Niels C. Loesch, *Rasse als Konstrukt: Leben und Weck Eugen Fischers* (Frankfurt am Main: Peter Lang, 1997).
42. Franz Weidenreich, letter to the editor, *Science* 104 (1946): 399.
43. *Cape Argus,* 12 September 1951.
44. Fritz Bornemann, "Martin Gusinde, SVD (1886–1969), Eine biographische Skizze," *Anthropos* 65 (1970): 747–57.

question of the "Preservation of the Bushmen" and presented them with a memorandum that argued that blacks and Bushmen could not and should not live together on one reserve: "It is my conviction," he wrote, "that it is essential to prevent close dependency of the Bushmen on the Bantu. The natives are very clever and the Bushmen very childish and the Bushman has not enough courage to act against the superiority of the native. He is too childish to go to the Commissioner for help."[45] In short, he provided a benign argument in favor of apartheid.

Conclusion

In dealing with the local notables' curious obsession with the Bushmen, one could consider the dominant role of the field sciences in the listing of work groups of the society as well as the impact of the Pfadfinder on German cultural life in Namibia. That points to the myth that the "pristine Bushman" is the Pfadfinder and field scientist par excellence. The most popular book the society sells, and which has been translated from German into English and Afrikaans, is Henno Martin's *Wenn es Krieg gibt, gehen wir in die Wueste: Eine Robinsonade in der Namib.* The book chronicles the adventures of a young German geologist who in order to escape internment during the Second World War escaped for two years into the Namib Desert with a colleague and a dog—proof that scientific knowledge can help one triumph over the harshest adversity. Perhaps such fantasies are the stuff science is propelled by?

Clearly there were factors in the ideological preterrain that played a part in generating this particular obsession with Bushmen. But there were also material factors as well that funneled attention on Bushmen as scientific objects. While on a 1908 collecting expedition to German New Guinea on behalf of the Chicago Field Museum, an American anthropologist reported,

> Practically every German in the colony is a collector—the higher officials for the love of their local Museum at home—Berlin, Dresden, Munich, Cologne, Hamburg, Bremen, Strassburg, etc., etc.; the lesser officials for gain—shipping their material to dealers at home or in Sidney. Every traveler through here carries away old "curios"—a mask, a bundle of spears, a bundle of bows

---

45. NAN A50/46.

and arrows, a carved bowl, a carved drum. The missionaries are all collectors of ethnological material, and most of them "on the make." Every man's house here is a Museum.[46]

Namibia too, attracted collectors, but the "Afrika-Zimmer" that settlers and officials used to display their collected booty and finds focused largely on animal trophies and natural curiosities with only a few ethnological artifacts. This is not surprising, given the arid environment, the highly mobile lifestyles of the indigenes and the extensive nature of incorporation into the global capitalist system. Indeed, already by the turn of the century, there were very few "traditional" artifacts to collect. The one market of "traditional artifacts" that existed in South West Africa was in "Bushman relics," and the standard settler and scientific discourses of "vanishing primitives" surrounding Bushmen served to reciprocally enhance the value of these artifacts. In fact, the nature of the artifacts in turn, like a self-fulfilling prophecy, served to boost the credibility of the "vanishing primitive."

Clearly the South West Africa Scientific Society, while promoting science, was also associating it with Germanness. Its bimonthly or quarterly newsletter, started in 1962, is filled with the odd item of local research amid a mass of European or German scientific news items. Apart from German being the dominant language of business in the society, the genealogy of science was also regarded by the society's members as dominated by German-speakers.[47] Indeed, this was so much the case that when early English-speaking notables in the society are referred to, like Kreft and Gutsche, the fact that they are descended from German missionaries is conspicuously mentioned. Certainly the society facilitated *Deutschtum* by subscribing to the ostensible universal appreciation of "good science."[48] And good science in turn provided an important moral argument for the *Herrenvolk* to have their colonies returned to them—as any casual perusal of the pages of the *Koloniale Rundschau* from the interwar years attests.

---

46. Welsch, "One Time, One Place": 164.
47. Hans J. Rust, "Die Gruendung der S.W.A. Wissenschaftlichen Gesellschaft," in *Ein Leben für Suedwestafrika,* ed. W. Drascher und Hans J. Rust (Windhoek: SWA Scientific Society, 1961).
48. As Afrikaner nationalism consolidated itself in Namibia and nationalists made a play to control the State Museum and related activities in the midsixties, one of the most damning accusations they made was that the Scientific Society and its members were freely sending artifacts abroad and thus, by implication, were not loyal "South Westers" (Totemeyer, *State of Museums*). I have no doubt that these accusations were exaggerated.

Rituals perform, and in this case they helped freeze in time, some ideas of German ethnology from the late nineteenth century. What emerged from this complex interplay with metropolitan science was a way of conceptualizing problems with its own specialized vocabulary. The result was a colonial science that prided itself on its "practical applications." It was a "derivative," inventorying science done by supposedly lesser minds working on problems set by savants in Germany—or South Africa. As befits "low science," it was identified with fact-gathering done by amateurs, while the theoretical synthesis was still expected to take place in the metropole, either preferably Germany, or South Africa[49]—and it was not difficult to find savants to underwrite this particular stance. Thus what was absorbed was a biological science, one with a dark variation, that fit in rather well with the emerging policy of apartheid. And it is in this context that we have to understand the survival of the Peter Pan–like representations of Bushmen. The focus on Bushmen was fundamental to the activities of the Scientific Society, and this brought to the fore a tension: While Bushmen were the object of rather typical colonial abjection, they were also the main vehicle for the bestowal of respectability for the society insofar as reification of the Bushmen stands as the basis for the society's claim to be engaged in metropolitan science. Nevertheless, the Bushmen provide an important example of how the metropole can define the value of scientific artifacts. Locally, most settlers thought of them as a nuisance, indeed as vermin, and actively wanted to get rid of them; this was informal official policy as well. Yet as the metropole defined them as important scientific commodities, this led to a local ideological reappreciation of their role and place in society. Not only were they used as the measure from which colonial progress could be favorably and proudly gauged, but Bushmen also served as a key validation for the development of museums in Namibia to serve as repositories of what later became known as the "national heritage." In addition, all museums in Namibia have prominent Bushman displays of some kind or another. This fixation, indeed scholarly love of Bushmen, ironically serves to destabilize black claims to legitimacy because it is simply assumed that blacks exterminated Bushmen. But it is also shadow knowledge par excellence because Bushmen are seen in an essential-

---

49. E. L. Gill, "Biological Surveys," *Journal of the South West Africa Scientific Society* 2 (1926–27): 29–34; Roy MacLeod, "On Visiting the 'Moving Metropolis': Reflections on the Architecture of Imperial Science," in *Scientific Colonialism,* ed. N. Reingold and M. Rothenberg (Washington, D.C.: Smithsonian Institution, 1987).

ized, timeless, and decontextualized society in which colonial brutality is conveniently ignored. Indeed this shadow knowledge served to propel further studies of Bushmen as salvage. The notion that these artifacts and knowledge had to be collected "before it was too late," raises, as Virginia Dominguez points out, the question of too late for what?

> There is a historical consciousness here of a special sort. We hear an urgency in the voices of the collectors, a fear that we will no longer be able to get our hands on these objects, and that this would amount to an irretrievable loss of the means of preserving our own historicity. There is a two-fold displacement here. Objects are collected no longer because of their intrinsic value but as metonyms for the people who produced them.[50]

Moreover, and this should not be overlooked, these objects/artifacts that are taken to be representations of the other were selected by (quasi) scientists and not by the indigenes themselves and, as such, served to legitimize settlers' positions of power and privilege. The ideological importance, indeed fossilization, of the notion of "pristine Bushmen" was underlined in a dramatic fashion at the International Court of Justice in the Hague, where Ethiopia and Liberia were challenging South Africa's overrule of Namibia in 1965. The first expert witness South Africa called to justify its policy of "separate development" or apartheid was Werner Eiselen, D.Phil. (Hamburg), son of a German missionary, foundation professor of *Volkekunde* at the Universities of Stellenbosch and Pretoria, erstwhile secretary of the South African Department of Native Affairs and widely lauded as the "Architect of Apartheid." Asked to apply his concept of "multi-community" to South West Africa, he singled out the Bushmen:

> They have even to this day remained hunters and collectors of food; who have never settled down, who never endeavored to produce, but live merely by collecting, who are physically very different from the other people and also in their social structure, in their traditions, in their way of life.[51]

---

50. Virginia Dominguez, "The Marketing of Heritage," *American Ethnologist* 13, no. 3 (1986): 556.
51. International Court of Justice, *Pleadings, Oral Arguments, Documents: South West Africa Cases,* vol. 10 (1966), 109.

Queried on the viability of "separate development" in the territory, Eiselen felt that the one exception that proved the rule was the Bushmen: "no great strides were made in making them development-conscious and they still remain much as they have been ever since we came to know them centuries ago. They do not take kindly to leading a settled life and to becoming a productive people."[52] Indeed, when asked how many independent ethnic states he saw emerging as a result of apartheid he concluded that it would be "very difficult to say, some of the units are very small. Unfortunately the smallest one of the indigenous ones is also the most primitive, namely the Bushmen, so that it would be difficult to think in terms of such groups being viable communities if they once become independent."[53] Ultimately, when pushed, the two anthropologist expert witnesses, Eiselen and Bruwer, both used Bushmen as the example of innate group difference and thus the raison d'être for apartheid.

These imported discourses also provided lenses through which a descriptive confrontation with the realities of the process of colonization could be avoided. Science provided the means to fantasize about the nature of the colonial world. The image of scientific knowledge as portrayed by the South West African Scientific Society—objective, fair, and discerning—serves as an important counterpoint to the image of "the native"—impulsive, irrational, and undiscerning. To paraphrase Martin Chanock (1998), in an astonishing act of self-imagining, seen most prominently with the arrival of the crew of the good ship *Meteor,* and in the pages of their *Mitteilungen,* they saw themselves as part of a cosmopolitan world of science, as intellectual kin to the von Humboldt brothers and European scientists rather than individuals involved in the local instrumentalities of colonial oppression. Their "imagined community" was one based on the Renaissance. Their "scientific selves" helped them to evade Namibia's colonial realities. The discourse of science helped them evade reality and construct a sense of self and other as part of the development of "civilization." Such was the ideological hegemony of the "pristine Bushmen" that it was only in the late eighties that alternative representations of Bushmen as victims of genocide, as the most victimized of all southern Africa's bloody victims, started to challenge this representation.

---

52. Ibid., 110.
53. Ibid., 127.

Priests among the Pygmies: Wilhelm Schmidt and the Counter-Reformation in Austrian Ethnology

SUZANNE MARCHAND

In 1914, the eminent occupant of Vienna's chair for indology and comparative ethnology, Leopold von Schroeder, penned the following lines:

> The great battle *(Kampf)*—the greatest the new century has to fight—is not a world war, which many anticipate. One may well come—but I am thinking of an even bigger, even more decisive battle. It will not be about domination over East Asia, India, or Africa. Nor will it be the battle of nationalities, as fearful as are [the conflicts] partisans are perpetually inciting. This too will finally have to make way for a healthy future, because the interests of all are threatened by this path. Nor is the battle one for the economic overlordship of the Old or New World, of Europe or America; or the battle of the white and yellow races. Not the struggle between the haves and the have-nots, capitalism and the proletariat, the so-called social question and similar issues. These are all big and important questions, battles in which we are already entangled, that await us in the future, and that need to be

---

I would like to thank Matti Bunzl, Glenn Penny, Martin Rühl, and Manfred Laubichler for their exemplary comments on and criticism of this essay. I would like to dedicate it to George W. Stocking Jr., who inspired me to study the history of anthropology and whose scholarship continues to set the standard for the field.

decided. But the question of all questions is another one, a more central one. It is the question of the whence, where, and why of the evolution of humankind and the world, the question of the meaning and purpose of our lives, which science is unable to answer. The battle of all battles is the great battle over faith *(Glauben)*—in which science must assist, precisely where it, by nature, breaks off and demurs—the battle over *religion,* over *God,* over the question, if we want to have any religion, any faith, any god, and if so, what this religion should look like.[1]

Schroeder, a historically minded linguist by training, an unconventional but ardent Christian by conviction, and a Wagnerian Germanophile by overdetermined choice, was not an unusual practitioner of ethnology in Central Europe. Indeed, if we set aside the medically trained majority of physical anthropologists, we would probably find Schroeder's views widely shared among German-speaking ethnographic scholars from Hamburg to Trieste, Strasbourg to Budapest. Though deeply interested in racial types, their central concern remained the historical development of language and culture; though supporters of imperialism, their politics was shaped by nationality conflicts at home; though worried about world war, socialism, and America's newfound economic power, the big question was the history and future of religious belief. They came to ethnology by many different routes, from the humanities as well as the sciences. Some were believers; some (like Max Weber) were skeptics. But their careers were all shaped, in one way or another, by established religion's dramatic struggle with science and secularization. And nowhere did this struggle leave such deep scars as in Schroeder's adopted home, Austria.

To approach Central European ethnology through Austria rather than through Germany is to make the end point of Nazism less obvious—though, as we shall see, not at all irrelevant—and large sections of this essay will be devoted to teasing out similarities and differences between the German and Austrian scholarly worlds. Perhaps more importantly, however, to concentrate on Austria here is to diminish the centrality of colonialism, the political context in which this book is explicitly set. By examining the scholarly world through this lens, I do not mean to deny colonialism's critical role in anthropology's history. Clearly, the extension of European trade and settlement overseas cre-

---

1. Leopold von Schroeder, *Arische Religion,* vol. 1 (Leipzig, 1914), 1–2.

ated the conditions, intellectual, sociocultural, and material, for the professionalization of the ethnographic sciences; imperialism made anthropology "relevant," offered boundless new opportunities for ethnographic information gathering, and spurred neoromantic anxiety over the disappearance of unspoiled heathens. This was true, in part, for nations without overseas colonies (like Austria) as well as for those, like Germany, with short periods of imperial activity (and longer spells of colony-envy). But I also want to make the point that imperial ambitions and experiences were by no means the only forces shaping the cultural sciences from the 1880s to the 1940s; the fin de siècle crises in Christian theology, in particular, played an extremely important role in shaping twentieth-century German-language anthropology.

Of course, we are all aware that from the Spanish conquistadors to the nineteenth-century students of totemism, anthropological observers remained keenly interested in the subject of the religion (or lack thereof) of the "natives"; when we pass the notional date of 1880, however, religious issues seem to disappear in favor of colonial and racial ones. German historians, naturally, are particularly likely to follow this chronological progression. There are good reasons to stick with this trajectory—but it seems to me a mistake to write out religion entirely. Importantly, in German-speaking academia, *cultural* evolutionism—which taught that simple societies (and crude, promiscuous cultures) preceded complex, Victorian ones—never established strong roots. Here, midcentury positivism gave way after about 1890 to a neoromantic ethnology whose advocates were both critical of Western "progress" and desperate to find a regenerative spirituality. Primitivist this movement certainly was, but its practitioners were also often sincere admirers of the non-Christian cultures they studied. Some, like Rudolf Otto and Albert Schweitzer, came to ethnology and comparative religion by way of historicist biblical criticism; some, like Albrecht Dieterich, sought access to the Germanic ur-soul; some, like Hermann Graf Keyserling, pursued occult knowledge through its many global incarnations. If one reads the biographies and works of these men, it is evident that colonial politics provided the opportunity for their travels and gave additional resonance to their claims; but to explain the meaning of these works by reference exclusively to imperialism is to close one's eyes to the often more urgent hometown issues European ethnologists were determined to treat.

It may seem strange to include the famous theologian Albert Schweitzer and the obscure indologist Leopold von Schroeder in this account of German-speaking ethnology, but that is largely the result of the sifting processes of the history of anthropology, which tend to winnow out students of comparative religion and of ancient "high" cultures in favor of students of secular, "primitive" cultures. This does not do justice, however, to the richness of nineteenth- and early-twentieth-century ethnological thought, especially in historically oriented Central Europe. Here, debates raged among those trained as classical and biblical philologists, as "orientalists" or "Germanists," as theologians or geographers, and those who came to the field through exotic travel or local museum work. If, to reflect the complexities of these contemporary exchanges, we embrace in our histories of German anthropology not just Humboldt and Herder, Bastian and Virchow, but also the biblical philologist Julius Wellhausen, the classicist-folklorist Wilhelm Mannhardt, and the pan-Babylonists (archaeologists, theologians, and Assyriologists who speculated about Babylonian mythology and its spread), it quickly becomes apparent that the origins and uniqueness of Christianity was a subject absolutely central to their work, much as it was for others in the West, from Robertson Smith to Franz Cumont, from Jane Harrison to James Henry Breasted, from Frazer to Joseph Campbell.[2]

If we examine this broader history of ethnological thought, we may well arrive at a correspondingly broader understanding of the rise of radical anti-Semitism; here, scholars have all too often ignored important theological, ethnological and Assyriological debates in favor of fetishizing the biology of racism. We will also be confronted with the fact that modern anthropology has *völkisch,* religious, and romantic as well as progressive sources, and has not always been a left-wing discipline; in this way, it has a number of similarities to Central European social history, as James Van Horn Melton has beautifully illustrated.[3] Finally, a wider history of ethnology also extends the options for contextualizing the sciences; we can now see ethnology not just against the backdrop of imperial experience and the rise of biological determin-

---

2. I realize that this is an unconventional list of "ethnographers"—but in their day, these students of comparative religion would certainly have been considered at the forefront of ethnographic thought.

3. James Van Horn Melton, "From Folk History to Structural History: Otto Brunner (1898–1982) and the Radical-Conservative Roots of German Social History," in *Pathos of Continuity: Central European Historiography from the 1930s to the 1950s,* ed. Hartmut Lehmann and James Van Horn Melton (Cambridge, 1994), 263–92.

ism, but also as part of a world of multidirectional assaults on middle-class Christian and classical culture.

This enhanced backdrop is critical to a clear understanding of the new wave of German ethnological work (and speculation) produced in the period after about 1885, the era in which Germany's colonial quest began, as well as the period in which "spiritual" unification became a watchword among intellectuals and *materialism* shorthand for the new menace of socialism.[4] Articulated in reaction to Adolf Bastian's *Elementargedanken,* Wilhelm Mannhardt's discussion of vegetative gods, and, especially, Tylor's theory of animism, a neoromantic, historicist school took off from Friedrich Ratzel's diffusionist geography. Coupling Ratzel's critique of independent evolution with Herder's sensitivity to the particularities of spiritual development, this school emphasized the spiritual integrity of each culture while also insisting on the diffusion of particular elements.

In general, I would suggest, this model suited Central European nationalists' need for invented ethnic traditions as well as their institutions' preference for philological methods over the Darwinist model; historicist ethnology emphasized the spiritual uniqueness of each realm while acknowledging that many individual elements were widely shared. Replicated across the disciplines, the neoromantic historicism after 1890 also represented a retreat from the liberal materialism of the midcentury that closely paralleled political changes under way in the Habsburg and Hohenzollern Empires.

But these retreats took German and Austrian ethnologists down separate paths, their ways divided less by colonial engagements than by dissimilar academic cultures and religious politics. In Germany, the historicist-primitivist school remained firmly anchored in the *Kulturprotestantismus*[5] of Prussian academia; but in Austria, the historicist reaction to evolutionism provided the foundations for what I will call a counter-reformation in ethnology. Here, Austria, not Germany, took

---

4. For an interesting discussion of scientists' reaction to this context, see Anne Harrington, *Reenchanted Science: Holism in German Culture from Wilhelm II to Hitler* (Princeton, 1996).

5. David Blackbourn gives a beautifully clear discussion of German academia's pervasive Protestant ethic. "German culture," he writes, "*was* Protestant. . . . Even for those who saw themselves (in Max Weber's later phrase) as 'religiously unmusical' pride in German culture had an unspoken Protestant undertow." Blackbourn, *The Long Nineteenth Century: A History of Germany, 1780–1918* (Oxford, 1997), 293.

a *Sonderweg,* or special path; all over Europe and America, clerics tried to take back Darwin's turf, but only in Austria did they succeed. It is this Austrian *Sonderweg*—not the usual path to racial hatred—that forms the subject of this essay.

I use the term *counter-reformation* here quite deliberately, for the Austrian anthropological reaction led by Father Wilhelm Schmidt was not a rejection of modern learning, but an attempt to reorient it to the ends of the church. Taking off from a critique of cultural Darwinism very similar to that of Boas, Rivers, and Mauss, Schmidt and his followers also wanted to professionalize anthropology; but as ardent Catholics, they wanted to do so in order to turn the science of prehistory to Christian ends. Launched from *outside* the academy, this counter-reformation sought to take back territory lost to secular science by updating doctrine and mobilizing the faithful. The movement succeeded in Austria because, here, university life was both less secularized and less central to the nation's cultural identity than was the case elsewhere, and because Schmidt's connections, organizational skills, and intellect secured him political, social, and institutional power. This is a story not of paradigm makers, but of a national school that refused to play "normal" science's game; it is an unconventional one, but perhaps its telling will serve as a warning to those who have presumed the secularization and professionalization of science to be the inevitable outcome of modern experience.

Now, how did this counter-reformation succeed, and what was its intellectual content? I want first to sketch Austria's anthropological tradition to Schmidt's emergence as a scholar, then to describe Schmidt's intellectual agenda; the next section traces the consequences of his fascination with the "pygmies." In the final section, I show how the counter-reformation succeeded in the 1920s—the result of Schmidt's intellectual acumen and extraordinary flair for organization, on the one hand, and the structural peculiarities of Austrian academia, on the other. The essay is, in many ways, simply a case study. But I hope that this case study will help us see the Austrian tradition not as a failure to develop structural functionalism, but as a response to unique intellectual conditions, formulated by, in this case, one unique individual, whose career may also offer new insight into the significance of the "battle of battles" described by Leopold von Schroeder. As the concluding essay in this volume, the tale of Wilhelm Schmidt is intended to underscore the complexities of the colonial legacy, as well as the other, sometimes more pressing, political and cultural forces shaping Central European anthropology's entrance into the twentieth century.

Cultural Anthropology in Germany and Austria, 1869–1900

Understanding Schmidt and the Austrians requires some sorting out of Central European cultural similarities and differences. For centuries, of course, Austrians, Prussians, Bavarians, Saxons, and so on, had belonged to the same political entity, the Holy Roman Empire (and its successor, the German confederation); Prussia established its full independence only in 1866, by which time the Habsburg Empire's period of dominance had long since expired. United in 1871, Germany's day in the sun had not yet arrived.[6] Naturally, one of the most salient differences between the old empire and the new Reich was that Austria, a multiethnic monarchy, was ruled and overwhelmingly inhabited by Catholics; the new German state had a huge Catholic minority, but its politics and cultural affairs were dominated by Calvinists and Lutherans. In Germany, Protestants were particularly dominant in academic circles, where their neoclassicizing aesthetics remained de rigueur. Importantly, for our story, this tradition carried with it a kind of taboo on the discussion of religious matters (though Protestantism remained the ideal) and a penchant for underscoring the autonomy and rationality of the Greeks, two elements that hampered the development of the study of comparative religion.[7] Austrian—like Bavarian—classicism, on the other hand, tended to emphasize continuities in the humanistic tradition, from Greece to pagan Rome to medieval Christendom.[8] And, as German philhellenism increasingly became a means for asserting the uniqueness of the nation of "Dichter and Denker," in Austria, the classical tradition retained more of its liberal (but Catholic), cosmopolitan inheritance, an ambience that was not lost, for example, on Germanophile radicals like Josef Strzygowski.[9]

---

6. In John Boyer's pithy formulation: "If German history is the narrative of power gone awry, then Austrian history is the story of power gone away." John Boyer, *Culture and Political Crisis in Vienna: Christian Socialism in Power, 1897–1918* (Chicago, 1995), xiii.

7. Eric Sharpe notes that in 1905, Germany had fifty chairs of oriental studies, but none of comparative religion. Eric J. Sharpe, *Comparative Religion: A History* (London, 1975), 125–29.

8. Anthony Grafton, "The Origins of Scholarship," *American Scholar* 48 (spring 1979): 242–46.

9. See Suzanne Marchand, "The Rhetoric of Artifacts and the Decline of Classical Humanism: The Case of Josef Strzygowski," *History and Theory* 33 (1994): 106–30.

To generalize broadly, nineteenth-century German culture was scholarly, hierarchical, and philosophical; its practitioners were intensely sober, extremely diligent, and introspective; its tastes ran to the ascetic and the extreme. Austrian culture, by contrast, was characterized by a light-hearted festivity; its practitioners were inclined to pen feuilletons rather than research papers, to craft puns, not profound philosophy (though Austria has certainly had its share of great philosophers, too). Austrians demonstrated remarkable aptitudes for decoration and combination; they mixed their natural sciences and humanities more easily than others, and created, in Vienna, the most eclectic of modern capital cities. Unlike many of their north German neighbors, Austrians did not believe the material world to be permanently debauched; matter could be redeemed, or at least enjoyed. If the Germans were philosophical, the Austrians were theatrical, which does not mean that, underneath, there were no serious social dilemmas or psychological crises. On the contrary. But the Austrian way to face crisis was, in good Freudian style, to repress, to dissemble, to ignore.[10]

The anthropological traditions of the two nations, at least until about 1890, are more nearly alike. "Professional"[11] anthropology in Austria as in Germany at the turn of the century remained heavily dominated by studies of physical type. The first Austrian scholarly organization to devote significant attention to anthropological questions was the Royal Geographical Society, founded in 1855 on the German model. When an Austrian Anthropological Society split off from the geographical body in 1870, its first president was Carl Rokitansky, professor of anatomy at the University of Vienna and president of the Society of Medical Doctors. Like Berlin's Society for Anthropology, Ethnology, and Prehistory (founded in 1869), the Austrian society attracted many scholars, most of them natural scientists (especially geologists) or doctors; Rokitansky's successors, as professors and presidents, as well as the successive directors of the society's anthropological museum, were almost uniformly medically trained.

---

10. The ideas in the last two paragraphs owe much to conversations over the years with Carl Schorske, whose work, of course, has shaped the study of Austrian cultural history for the past three decades.

11. I use the quotation marks here to remind readers that by the 1890s, there were still very few chairs for ethnology in central Europe—or anywhere, for that matter. Those who would have been considered professionals in this era were chiefly men with medical degrees who wrote on ethnological or prehistorical subjects (e.g., Bastian and Virchow), geographers and seasoned travelers (e.g., Ratzel and Schweinfurth), or, perhaps most importantly, the growing contingent of museum assistants.

In the wake of Bismarck's leap into colonization in 1884, the Germans, however, did begin to create a few teaching posts and, especially, a large number of well-stocked ethnological museums.[12] The Austrians responded to the acceleration of colonizing activity more haltingly, and no new institutions arose to initiate disciplinary professionalization. Missionary societies—including Schmidt's religious order—made new plans for proselytizing, but the academy remained unmoved. Ethnology continued to fall within the purview of the Naturhistorisches Museum. No separate training for ethnographers was available, though many orientalists and Germanists with origin-fixations developed sidelines in the subject. In 1894, our old friend Leopold von Schroeder was hired at the University of Innsbruck with the title "professor for ancient Indian history and antiquities, with consideration of ethnography in general."[13] Faculties seem to have considered physical anthropology more scientifically respectable than cultural studies; in 1892, the ethnographer-orientalist Michael Haberlandt received permission to lecture at the University of Vienna, but when a regular post for anthropology was created in 1913, it was Rudolf Pöch, a specialist in tropical medicine, who got the job. Pöch, who spent the Great War making physical measurements of POWs, was elevated to full professor in 1919.[14]

If the academic positions fell to the anatomists, however, the anthropological society devoted most of its time and resources to the study of Austrian prehistory. Local patriotism was critical in the evolution of the scholarly fields supported by the society and its journal, *Mittheilungen der Anthropologischen Gesellschaft,* which covered prehistory, ethnology, anthropology, folklore studies, and natural history; prehistory in particular (*Urgeschichte,* or *Vorgeschichte*) owed both its popular prestige, and its institutional difficulties, to its origins in hometown patriotism.[15] The great importance of ethnicity for the

---

12. On the growth of ethnographic museums, see H. Glenn Penny III, "Cosmopolitan Visions and Municipal Displays: Museums, Markets, and the Ethnographic Project in Germany, 1868–1914," Ph.D. diss., University of Illinois, 1999.

13. Apparently the president of the anthropological society was instrumental in engineering Schroeder's call to Innsbruck. See Leopold von Schroeder, *Lebenserinnerungen* (Leipzig, 1921), 145.

14. See Christian Feest, "The Origins of Professional Anthropology in Vienna," in *Kulturwissenschaften im Vielvölkerstaat: Zur Geschichte der Ethnologie und verwandter Gebiete in Österreich, ca. 1780 bis 1918,* ed. Britta Rupp-Eisenreich and Justin Stagl (Vienna, 1995), 115–27.

15. For more on prehistory's unique status, see Suzanne Marchand, *Down from Olympus: Archaeology and Philhellenism in Germany, 1750–1970* (Princeton, 1996), chap. 5.

Habsburg Empire, as well as Austria's lack of overseas colonies, exacerbated tendencies to study the self, though the empire's proximity to the Ottomans and its long tradition of orientalist scholarship did introduce some diversity.[16] While in Germany passionate discussions about the divergent methodologies and social roles of the humanities and natural sciences made it increasingly necessary for anthropologists to take a side,[17] this was not so in Austria; nor was there here such a deep gulf between students of ancient "high" civilizations *(Kulturvölker)* and students of contemporary "primitives" *(Naturvölker)*. Carl von Rokitansky combined Darwinism and Bohemian Reform Catholicism in his insistence that, though all organisms sought to destroy their rivals, by imitating Christ, men could overcome suffering.[18] And Freud, of course, moved easily from medicine to classics, from Greek mythology to modern neuroses, from our ur-ancestors to ourselves.

Thus, Austrian students of culture tended to be less university-oriented than their German contemporaries, more interested in Asia and Europe than in Africa, and less concerned about divisions between the natural and cultural sciences and the *Naturvölker* and *Kulturvölker* than their neighbors to the north. But it is in the relationship between culture, politics, and religion that Austria really differed from Germany. Here we must recall Bismarck's attempt to destroy "disloyal" Catholic institutions in the so-called *Kulturkampf* of the 1870s, the National Liberal "war" on ultramontanism that succeeded only in creating a powerful new Catholic Center Party, able to play liberals, conservatives, and socialists off one another in pursuit of its own interests. The German Catholics' newfound political power, however, was not matched by a substantial new presence in *cultural* affairs. In Austria, on the other hand, the fin de siècle saw the emergence of an energetic, self-assertive Catholic political *and* cultural elite. Exemplified by Franz Martin Schindler, a liberal Catholic intellectual who served as profes-

---

16. On Austrian orientalism, see Karl Roider, "The Oriental Academy in the *Theresienzeit,*" in *Topic* 34 (fall 1980): 19–28; Marchand, "Rhetoric of Artifacts." The fact remains, however, that in Germany, too, the study of folklore, prehistory, and orientalia was vastly more popular than the study of the manners and customs of peoples beyond Eurasia. If the onset of colonization brought with it new excitement about "the other," funding for anthropological research did not increase appreciably as a result of Bismarck's new ventures, nor did ethnology replace classical art and languages as the mainstay of middle-class education in Germany or in Austria.

17. Leipzig is an important exception to this generalization.

18. William M. Johnston, *The Austrian Mind: An Intellectual and Social History, 1848–1938* (Berkeley and Los Angeles: University of California Press, 1972), 225.

sor of moral theology at the University of Vienna, this new generation, as John Boyer describes, abandoned old-fashioned anticapitalist politics for a more pluralist view. In doing so, they responded to current problems not by indulging in antimodernist maunderings but by developing "a Catholic science of society" and organizing and publicizing, within the academy and without.[19]

Small wonder then, that Father Wilhelm Schmidt, though born and bred a German, would choose Austria as the place to make his career. Indeed, his wide-ranging pattern of activity and his vision of science's modernizing (but still pious) function are highly reminiscent of Schindler's career. Though academics, both made their impact on Austrian society by forming and utilizing Catholic lay organizations (and publications) as forums; both were ardent seekers of a means to reconcile Catholicism with science; and both were tireless, skillful users of modern media. The political and cultural power of men like Schindler, and Schindler's disciple Ignaz Seipel (a priest cum professor who would become Austrian chancellor in the 1920s) made the anthropological counter-reformation possible. But it was Schmidt's hard work, intelligence, and obdurate leadership that made it actually happen.

An Unconventional Ethnologist: Pater Wilhelm Schmidt

Recent histories of anthropology make little mention of Wilhelm Schmidt, but in his Austrian context, he was at least as influential as any of his contemporary discipline-founders.[20] Like his counterparts Franz Boas, Marcel Mauss, and W. H. R. Rivers, Schmidt appeared on the anthropological scene in the 1890s, at a pivotal moment both in the history of anthropology and in the history of religion. In this decade, the ur-histories conjured by cultural evolutionists of the 1860s and 1870s came under new scrutiny, and major anthropological presumptions—the ur-existence of animism, promiscuity, simple languages, and irrationality—were increasingly contradicted by ethnographers' experiences and skeptical readings of the sources. The critical response to this double crisis—which made prehistory again both mysterious and crucial—was, for Schmidt and many of his contempo-

---

19. Boyer, *Culture and Political Crisis,* 304–8.

20. Ernest Brandewie has been trying for many years to give Schmidt his due. See Brandewie's two books *Wilhelm Schmidt and the Origin of the Idea of God* (London, 1983), and *When Giants Walked the Earth: The Life and Times of Wilhelm Schmidt, SVD* (Fribourg, 1990).

raries, the work of the Scottish scholar of comparative religion Andrew Lang. In his seminal *The Making of Religion* (1898), Lang argued for the ur-existence of monotheism and the nonexistence of primitive promiscuity (as well as the probable existence of telepathy). Lang impressed many readers, and challenged many to rethink the "primitive" mind. Only Schmidt, however, a man who firmly believed evolutionism to be a Protestant heresy, saw in Lang's work the plough that would prepare the ground for an anthropological counter-reformation.

Born in Germany in 1868, Schmidt had joined the Societas Verbi Divini—a recently founded order of Catholic missionaries—at age fifteen.[21] After his ordination, Schmidt was sent to the University of Berlin, where he devoted three semesters primarily to the study of the Arabic and Hebrew sources of medieval philosophy.[22] Although Adolf Bastian, the anti-Darwinian ethnologist, was a member of the Berlin faculty at the time, there is no evidence that the two Catholic scholars ever met. Indeed, Schmidt felt very isolated during his stay in Berlin; inside the mysterium of Prussian *Wissenschaft* in the years following the *Kulturkampf,* he experienced at close quarters the mutual hostility between primarily Protestant academia and the Catholic Church.[23] In 1895, he was sent to teach at the SVD's major seminary near Vienna, and soon thereafter, appreciative of Austria's Catholic culture and apparently wishing to avoid the Wilhelmine draft, he became a citizen of the Habsburg Empire.[24] Schmidt's first encounter with ethnology resulted from his study of Melanesian languages—a subject he began to pursue in the wake of the opening of an SVD mission in New Guinea in 1896. New Guinea, at the time, was formally administered by the German New Guinea Company; the empire would take over in 1899. Here, as elsewhere, the activities of the SVD order were intimately bound up with the extension of colonial dominion. The order's founder, Arnold Janssen, sent his first missionaries to China in 1879; in

---

21. Founded in 1875, this order was particularly active in colonies where German influence was strong. Brandewie, *Giants,* 15.

22. Schmidt's own discussion of his studies can be found in Fritz Bornemann, ed., *Remembering Arnold Janssen: A Book of Reminiscences* (Rome, 1978), 155.

23. Over the course of the rest of his long life, Schmidt would repeatedly plump for the creation of a Catholic university and urge his fellow Catholics to infiltrate the Protestant-dominated world of German science. See, e.g., Schmidt, "Die Grundgedanken der katholischen Universität für die Länder deutscher Zunge," *Schönere Zukunft* 51 (16 September 1934): 1345–47; 52 (23 September 1934): 1373–75.

24. Fritz Bornemann, *P. Wilhelm Schmidt, S.V.D., 1868–1954* (Rome, 1982), 14.

1892, SVD priests arrived in Togo; in 1906, they reached Japan. Missions to the "priest impoverished" nations of South America began in 1889.[25] Often, SVD members did entangle themselves, quite seriously, in colonial politics. In China, for example, the order's aggressive nationalism and proselytizing played an important part in unleashing the Boxer Rebellion.[26] Clearly, Schmidt's brethren used colonial settings to advance their spiritual cause, and his devotion to ethnology—and his superiors' toleration of his endeavors—owed a great deal to the exciting new prospects colonialism offered to ambitious European clerics. Ultimately, however, Schmidt's ethnology was intended not to assist in converting the heathen, but to secure faith in Europe; like Schroeder, he believed the big battle was to be waged over the European soul, not over colonial possessions.[27]

Like many other philologists of his generation, Schmidt gradually began to incorporate material culture into his linguistic studies. In his first works, he sought to classify Australian languages, using cultural as well as linguistic data. But it was none other than Leopold von Schroeder who acquainted Schmidt with Lang's work and pushed the priest into ethnology's path. In 1902, Schmidt attended a meeting of the Anthropological Society at which the Baltic-German Indologist delivered a lecture on the three sources of primitive religion—reverence for nature, cults of the dead, and belief in the highest Being. Seeking a means by which to appreciate the intricacies (and superiority) of early Aryan religion and mythology, Schroeder had invoked Lang against the cultural evolutionists. Like the Indologist, Lang held fast to a degenerationist worldview, in which animism, ancestor worship, and polytheism *followed* the dissipation of an original, universal belief in a higher God.[28] Importantly, too, for Schroeder, Lang had defended his claims with extensive ethnographic evidence, insisting that the evolutionists were simply sweeping contradictory accounts under the ani-

---

25. See Bornemann, *Remembering Arnold Janssen,* 146.
26. See Joseph W. Esherick, *The Origins of the Boxer Uprising* (Berkeley, 1987), 79–88, 123–26. Thanks to Michael Tsin for this reference.
27. Schmidt did, however, endorse German colonial efforts, especially in the wake of the so-called Dernbergian turn after 1906. See Edouard Conte, "Völkerkunde und Faschismus? Fragen an ein vernachlässigtes Kapitel deutsch-österreichischer Wissenschaftsgeschichte," in *Kontinuität und Bruch: 1938–1945–1955: Beiträge zur österreichischen Kultur- und Wissenschaftsgeschichte,* ed. Friedrich Stadler (Munich, 1988), 237–38.
28. It was logical, he wrote, for post-Adamic man "to 'go a whoring' after practically useful ghosts, ghost-gods, and fetishes" that could do him some good, leaving behind the one true God, who was not bribable. Andrew Lang, *The Making of Religion* (London, 1898), 282.

mist rug. Schmidt would later insist that it was Schroeder's lecture—and especially Lang's antievolutionist critique—that inspired his own (unrelenting) study of the idea of God.[29]

It is not difficult to see why Schroeder and Lang—both sharp critics of the Tylorian progression from animism to religion to science—appealed to the young scholar-priest. But crucially, Schmidt also immediately perceived that more ethnographic evidence would need to be amassed to defend their anti-Darwinian claims. For him, as for other German-speaking ethnologists, another pair of lectures would prove pivotal in this regard. In November 1904, the ethnologist Bernard Ankermann and the medieval historian turned ethnologist Fritz Graebner presented papers to the Berliner Gesellschaft für Anthropologie, Ethnologie und Urgeschichte, which, according to a 1938 reminiscence, "laid the foundations for culture-historical ethnology."[30] The papers sought to demonstrate historical connections between Oceania and southern Africa, and in arguing strenuously for diffusion, put another nail in Darwinian cultural evolution. "From this day forward," the 1938 account insisted, "faith in the decades-long hegemony of the idea of single-track evolution of all human culture began to wane."[31] Drawing on the earlier work of Friedrich Ratzel and Leo Frobenius, Ankermann and Graebner claimed to have identified cultural complexes so unique that they must have diffused and have traceable histories; Frobenius had called these complexes—which he believed to be organic entities with their own agency—*Kulturkreise;* and soon a term arose to describe this sort of diffusionist-historicist thinking: *Kulturkreislehre.*[32] If Ankermann, Graebner, Frobenius, and other members of this "school" perpetually criticized one another's formulations, the general principles of *Kulturkreislehre* appealed greatly to the young Schmidt and would remain his methodological

---

29. Schroeder, *Lebenserinnerungen,* 165. Lang's view of Schmidt's work—and of Schmidt's keen approval of his own writings—is worth noting. Lang cheered Schmidt's assistance in the campaign against "the anthropologically orthodox doctrine of the rise of religion in Animism," but insisted that his own objections to animism were not a priori (suggesting Schmidt's were), but based on a clear-eyed reading of the facts. See Andrew Lang, review of Schmidt, *L'Origine de d'Idee de Dieu,* in *Folk-Lore* 21 (1910): 523.

30. Editor, "Bernhard Ankermann," in *Zeitschrift für Ethnologie* 70 (1938): 129.

31. Ibid.

32. On Frobenius, see Suzanne Marchand, "Leo Frobenius and the Decline of the West," *Journal of Contemporary History* 32, no. 2 (1997): 153–70; and Janheinz Jahn, *Leo Frobenius: The Demonic Child,* trans. Reinhard Sander (Austin, 1974).

dogmatics long after—characteristically—its deficiencies had made it unpalatable to other scholars.[33] In Schmidt's hands, *Kulturkreislehre* would became the basis for a political as well as an anthropological worldview, the means by which Austria's nationality question could be solved.[34]

Having found his calling in historicist ethnology, Schmidt immediately assigned himself the tasks of synthesizer, organizer, tactician, drill sergeant, and publicist for this grand campaign. He quickly developed an organizational and intellectual plan of attack, one with both backward- and forward-looking features. He appealed to his superiors to allow him to follow his scientific star, and in 1906, having obtained the backing of the church, numerous Catholic lay organizations, and the German Colonial Office, he founded *Anthropos,* soon to become one of Central Europe's premiere anthropological journals.[35] He mustered missionaries to provide the raw data that would confirm Lang's claims; in calling these "field-workers" to participate in *Wissenschaft,* Schmidt made sure to distance his new work from the dilettantism of the clerical ethnographers of the past, issuing extensive instructions to missionary field-workers and defending their reports vigorously against secular critics. Again and again, in the pages of *Anthropos,* he vented his outrage at the contempt in which secular scholars increasingly held missionaries; for Schmidt, there was no reason to believe them any more biased than the agnostic "professionals."[36] Nor was there, in his eyes, any reason to assume the secularists would win. God, and the evidence, were on his side.

---

33. In 1936, Clyde Kluckhohn outlined four presumptions upon which *Kulturkreislehre* rested: (1) The poverty of man's ability to invent new means to deal with his environment; (2) man's imitativeness and the contagiousness of culture; (3) the mental uniformity of mankind; (4) the stability of groups of cultural elements. Clyde Kluckhohn, "Some Reflections on the Method and Theory of the Kulturkreislehre," in *American Anthropologist* 38, no. 2 (1936): 165.

34. See Bornemann, *P. Wilhelm Schmidt,* 116–29; Ernest Brandewie, "Wilhelm Schmidt and Politics during the First World War," in Rupp-Eisenreich and Stagl, *Kulturwissenschaft im Vielvölkerstaat,* 268–83.

35. The extremely interesting story of Schmidt's efforts to secure patronage for *Anthropos* is documented in Karl J. Rivinius, SVD, *Die Anfänge des "Anthropos": Briefe von P. Wilhelm Schmidt an Georg Freiherrn von Hertling aus den Jahren 1904 bis 1908 und andere Dokumente* (St. Augustin bei Bonn, 1981).

36. See, e.g., Schmidt's attack on J. G. Frazer for his dismissal of Reverend T. G. H. Strehlow's accounts of Australian totemism. Schmidt, "Is Ethnological Information coming from Missionaries Sufficiently Reliable?" *Anthropos* 6 (1911): 430–31.

Schmidt's first book, *L'Origine de l'Idee de Dieu,* appeared in 1908; having written this long-winded review of current anthropological thought in German, he translated it into French in hopes that it might be of assistance to beleaguered French Catholics.[37] Eventually, this book would become the introduction to a twelve-volume treatise, each segment of which had the same aim: to prove that all peoples believed in a single, high God. Despite Schmidt's repetitive conclusions, however, his contemporaries recognized his works to be full of important data and trenchant critiques of other ethnographers, and his journal continued to publish cutting-edge essays (especially those of continental scholars).

One might say that Schmidt's politics, before 1914, were essentially those of "Leonine accommodation" translated to the scientific sphere. Schmidt took seriously the church's attempt under Leo XIII to adjust its ideals to modern conditions—at least in the realm of science. Privately, he compared Catholicism's resistance to evolutionary theory to its now embarrassing early modern hostility to the work of Galileo.[38] During the period between 1909 and 1923, when modernism fell out of favor in Rome, Schmidt stuck to his conviction that "nature and revelation could never actually stand in contradiction with one another";[39] he refused to believe that science could in any way endanger faith in God. And to demonstrate the truth of his convictions, he was ready to go to ur-history's root and engage the "hottest" ethnological subject of his day: the pygmies.

Priests among the Pygmies

The "pygmies," in Schmidt's day, was a collective name for a number of small-sized peoples that included, primarily, the Andaman Islanders, the Eta of the Philippines, the Malaysian Semang, and the African Batchwa (Bushmen). Rumored to exist since the days of Herodotus and Aristotle, true African pygmies had been "discovered" by Georg Schweinfürth in the 1870s. A Europe-wide scholarly debate

---

37. Josef Franz Thiel, "Der Urmonotheismus des P. Wilhelm Schmidt und seine Geschichte," in Rupp-Eisenreich and Stagl, *Kulturwissenschaften im Vielvölkerstaat,* 257.

38. In his appeal to missionaries for help on *Anthropos,* he emphasized that "the law of absolute love of truth, which Pope Leo XIII proclaimed for history, writing in such marvelous words, must be likewise adopted by ethnology." Schmidt, "Einladung," in Rivinius, *Die Anfänge des "Anthropos,"* 194.

39. Ibid., 193.

then ensued: were they proper humans?[40] Controversy on this point raged for some time among physical anthropologists and linguists; among students of culture, it was presumed that pygmies, like other "primitives," had neither religion, nor morals, nor much in the way of culture. But the pygmies had their defenders, including the conservative French anthropologist A. de Quatrefages. In a posthumous publication of 1895, Quatrefages described the virtues of the Mincopies (Andaman Islanders), Aetas, and other "pygmies"; they were monogamous, respected private property, and most especially "have moral ideas similar to our own, and are attached to religious beliefs like those of the most civilized peoples."[41]

Schmidt, beginning his ethnological studies in the wake of Lang's assault on animism, took up the defense of pygmies where the conservative Frenchman left off, turning it into a powerful argument against cultural evolutionism. If he could show that the pygmies were the oldest surviving humans, and that they lacked neither religion nor morals, he could defeat the most threatening claim of the emerging human sciences, namely, that monotheistic religion was not an essential and indispensable part of humanness, but merely a social product. If he could suggest the probability of an ur-revelation and a primeval fall from grace, so much the better. For the young priest, who would later be known as "Pygmäen-Schmidt,"[42] these primeval "survivors" offered the opportunity to show that Darwinian agnosticism, not Catholicism, represented an ideologically motivated worldview. The pygmies, in short, could be the key to a modern, scientific apologetics.

It was Schmidt's contribution to ethnology to join together the skeptical comparative religion of Lang and new data on pygmy culture, collected largely by Catholic priests, to create a unique, anti-Darwinian portrait of prehistory.[43] He sketched this project in his *The*

---

40. Joan Mark, *The King of the World in the Land of the Pygmies* (Lincoln, Neb., 1995), 43. The pygmies also became sideshow fodder; at the St. Louis World's Fair in 1904, they were the main ethnographic attraction. William R. Everdell, *The First Moderns: Profiles in the Origins of Twentieth-Century Thought* (Chicago, 1997), 217.

41. A. de Quatrefages, *The Pygmies,* trans. Frederick Starr (1895; repr. New York, 1969), 122.

42. Bornemann, *P. Wilhelm Schmidt,* 78.

43. Ernest Brandewie suggests that Schmidt's pygmy portrait was heavily influenced by Alexandre Le Roy's *Les Pygmées Négrilles d'Afrique et Négritos de l'Asie* (c. 1900), in which this mission bishop in West Africa described pygmy belief in a high God (Brandewie, *Giants,* 70). Undoubtedly Le Roy did have an impact on Schmidt; but Quatrefages treated the topic first.

Place of the Pygmy-People in the Developmental History of Mankind of 1910 and continued to elaborate it for the rest of his life. The book opened with a discussion of the physical features of pygmies, the point of which was to show that all pygmies belonged to a single race, and thus must have a common origin and/or ancestor. Schmidt detailed the childlike characteristics of pygmies, including fetuslike lanugo and broad noses. The pygmies, according to Schmidt, also had childlike vices, like inconstancy and impetuousness. Schmidt then turned to another important point: the proof that pygmies were more ancient than Australian Aborigines, whose totemic rituals were, of course, a staple in every contemporary anthropologists' intellectual diet. But if older than other groups, the pygmies were not less intelligent than others; Schmidt, throughout his life, relentlessly opposed K. T. Preuss's theory of *Urdummheit,* or primeval stupidity.[44]

To answer the question, "If the pygmies are so smart, why had they failed to develop higher culture," Schmidt took his cues from Genesis. The original inhabitants of the Garden of Eden had not needed to exert themselves; likewise, the pygmies, living in tropical environs abundantly supplied with foodstuffs had not needed to abandon hunting and gathering for agriculture or animal raising. This life of Edenic leisure, however, had its drawbacks: "Life at the gathering stage has too little constancy, and the hunt has too many of the qualities of pleasurable occupation. Neither [gathering nor hunting] lends itself to the achievement of what is the basis of all cultural progress: constant work."[45]

But if pygmies failed to punch higher culture's clock, they did not lack the single most important component of culture: religion. Schmidt, as we have seen, obsessively collected and relentlessly reiterated evidence that the most primitive of peoples were monotheists. The pygmies, Adam's closest surviving kin, were monogamous and altruistic; they loved children and respected property; murder, theft, and sex before marriage were virtually unknown.[46] Indeed, one had to conclude, the ethnologist insisted, "that in many, very many ways, these

---

44. For example, Schmidt, *Der Ursprung der Gottesidee: Eine historische-kritische und positive Studie,* vol. 1, *Historisch-kritischer Teil* (Münster, 1912), 442–43.

45. Schmidt, *Die Stellung der Pygmäenvölker in der Entwicklungsgeschichte des Menschen* (Stuttgart, 1910), 112. Other members of the Austrian school had different theories on this question. Schebesta believed progress was the result of specialization and the division of labor. See Paul Schebesta, *Among the Forest Dwarfs of Malaya* (1928; repr. London, 1973), 243–44.

46. Schmidt, *Stellung der Pygmäenvölker,* 140–68.

little creatures are even 'better men' than the average [man] among the higher, more civilized peoples, not excluding many Europeans."[47] The lesson, in all this, for human history was the following: "We were not by nature imbeciles and libertines, and the development of this human race was not a process like the gradual healing of a madman or the disciplining of a prisoner."[48] By 1910, Schmidt was hardly alone in disputing the nineteenth-century's assumption that primitive peoples had had no religion at all. Continuing throughout his long life to beat a horse already dying at his career's outset, Schmidt made the Adamic pygmies the centerpiece of his long crusade against evolutionism.

By "evolutionism," however, Schmidt and his school meant less the Darwinian theory of biological evolution than the anthropologists who had spun out speculative histories of mankind from Darwin's theory. The Viennese ethnologists tended to divide evolutionary theory into two parts and to counsel agnosticism on the question of biological evolution, and absolute rejection of cultural evolution.[49] We do not know what man's body looked like in ancient times, Schmidt insisted, but we do know that the earliest humans possessed a unique spirituality not shared by apes. We should abandon the nineteenth-century's "ape fixation" *(Affen-Enthusiasmus)* and follow our evidence, not seek (nonexistent) transitional forms.[50] Reiterating Lang's accusation that evolutionary theory failed to explain the evidence increasingly being amassed by ethnographers, Schmidt and company emphasized their credentials as "objective" historians of culture. Trying to turn the tables on those who accused him of religious prejudice, Schmidt in 1912 suggested that the theory of animism was a Protestant fetish that had prevailed simply because Catholics lacked sufficient knowledge of ethnology to disprove it.[51]

This was, of course, a deficiency Schmidt was working hard to overcome, using his own (missionary) collectors and observers. Regrettably for Schmidt, however, missionary ethnography was precisely the sort of enterprise his generation of non-Austrian anthropologists scorned.

---

47. Ibid., 116.
48. Ibid., 299.
49. This tactic was very much the result of censorship on the part of the church; Schmidt otherwise was ready to concede the probability of biological evolution. See Bornemann, *P. Wilhelm Schmidt*, 81–83. The tactical phrasing was still being used by Wilhelm Koppers in *Primitive Man and His World Picture* (1949), trans. Edith Raybould (London, 1952), 41–54.
50. See, e.g., Schmidt, "Älteste Menchheit" (written 1935–37), in *Wege der Kulturen: Gesammelte Aufsätze* (St. Augustin bei Bonn, 1964), 46–50.
51. Schmidt, *Der Ursprung der Gottesidee*, 1:58–69, 89.

Missionaries had been central in the positivist, collecting stage of ethnology; but when interest turned to the "scientific" study of culture, they became both obsolete and a threat to the objectivity of the field. Already by 1914, "being there" had become central to British anthropologists, and the armchair ethnographer at the top of the missionary feeding chain (that is, Schmidt) had lost much credibility. Missionaries and officials, Rivers insisted, had other preoccupations and could not be expected to devote sufficient time to objective observation.[52] Indeed, most of the new professionals now presumed that missionaries, in particular, could *not* be objective observers at all. By the fin de siècle, French, British, American, and Prussian academics shared the presumption that religious conviction (especially Catholicism) compromised science; hence, the royal road to scientific respectability required the jettisoning of confessional baggage.

In Austria, where clerics still played a major role in higher and lower education, this supposition was not only insulting but also impracticable; with no overseas colonies or academic status, Austrian field-workers would be few and far between. But in trying to speak to the profession at large while retaining his clerical credentials, Schmidt faced insuperable odds: a modernizer in an antimodern institution and an antimodernist in a modernizing profession, his Catholic science was to be tried in a court in which God had been ruled a hostile witness.

That the fundamental issue of human religiosity could no longer be decided by anthropological evidence is apparent in a 1910 exchange between Schmidt and the young A. R. Brown in the journal *Man*. The topic was the mutually engrossing subject of religion and the pygmies. Trying to catch Brown in a contradiction, Schmidt had noted Brown's "ungrudging praise" for every statement in E. H. Man's book on the Andamanese, at the same time as he refused to credit Man's claims that the natives worshiped a single high God, Puluga. Brown, Schmidt argued, had every reason to accept Man's claims. Here, as elsewhere, Schmidt objected fiercely to modern attacks on early data collectors, arguing, sensibly, that to believe everything *except* accounts of religious belief and practice was something of a sleight of hand.[53] More-

---

52. George W. Stocking Jr., *The Ethnographer's Magic and Other Essays in the History of Anthropology* (Madison, Wis., 1992), 39.

53. The Austrians, for their part, implicitly tended to trust missionary accounts that suited their purposes; Schmidt and Koppers, for example, depended heavily on the accounts of the early missionary Bartholomäus Ziegenbalg in demonstrating the fundamental nature of Indians' belief in a single God. See Helmuth von Glasenapp, *Das Indienbild deutscher Denker* (Stuttgart: K. F. Koehler, 1960), 169.

over, Schmidt claimed, evidence drawn from Austronesian mythology suggested that Puluga had originally been a sky god, an idea shared by many pygmy peoples.[54] Brown had simply written God out of his story. "I regret very much that the *debut* of such a hopeful scholar as Mr. Brown was devoted to such partial aims, and that the results of his valuable and extremely interesting researches were not applied in a more independent and broad-minded spirit. It is to be hoped that in the book about his expedition Mr. Brown will free himself from all such aspirations and go straight along the path which his materials alone shall show him."[55]

Brown would not, of course, allow such an assault on his scholarly credentials to go unanswered, and his response, as David Tomas has noted, signaled less a revolution in anthropological method than the new authority of the "trained scientific student."[56] Brown attacked Schmidt for perpetually seeking "evidence of a pre-formed theory," for interpreting the beliefs of people of whom he had no personal knowledge, and for making unwarranted comparisons between groups. Denouncing Schmidt's historical reconstructions, Brown insisted on the importance of local knowledge and word usage and outlined the extremely limited conditions under which anthropologists could speculate about "survivals." Until we have proved, with direct evidence, that a modern belief could not arise in any other way than as a survival of an older one, we have no certainty, he insisted; "and this," he concluded, "is a task which is in nearly all cases quite impossible." In effect, Brown was saying that history was no concern of "scientific" ethnography. Indeed, the double threat of religious dogmatism and historical speculation in Schmidt's work made him, for Brown, the fledgling discipline's paradigmatic enemy. "As long as such arguments are tolerated and listened to," the British ethnographer thundered, "so long must ethnology remain in its unscientific stage."[57]

Now, it is certainly true that in a career that stretched from the 1890s to the 1950s, Schmidt did no fieldwork, traveled little outside Europe, and seems never to have met any Africans or Southeast Asians, much less any pygmies. But this did not mean that the Austrians despised fieldwork; on the contrary, Schmidt valued missionary

---

54. W. Schmidt, "Puluga, the Supreme Being of the Andamanese," *Man* 2 (1910): 6.
55. Ibid., 7.
56. David Tomas, "Tools of the Trade: The Production of Ethnographic Observations on the Andaman Islands, 1858–1922," in *Colonial Situations: Essays on the Contextualization of Ethnographic,* ed. George W. Stocking Jr. (Madison, Wis., 1992), 99.
57. A. R. Brown, "Puluga: A Reply to Father Schmidt," *Man* 217 (1910): 33–37.

anthropologists precisely because they lived among the natives for long periods of time.[58] He worked hard to acquire funding for his students to go to the field, especially to study pygmies. Far from being ignorant about other schools' methods and conclusions, Schmidt's students felt themselves to be fully accredited modern scholars. Three of the most noteworthy of Schmidt's SVD ethnologists, Wilhelm Koppers, Martin Gusinde, and Paul Schebesta, all completed extensive studies in the field, living, respectively, amongst the Bhils in India, the Yamana of Tierra del Fuego, and the Semang of Malaya (as well as the Bambuti of the Ituri forest). In 1949, Koppers was fulsome in his praise of Malinowski's fieldwork, saying, "We only regret that the good could not be achieved without the anti-historical extravagances."[59] But these accomplished fieldworkers were not likely to follow Malinowski's model, for they remained fundamentally committed to a historical and descriptive, rather than an interpretive science of anthropology.[60]

It should also be emphasized that *Kulturkreislehre* was very much a method oriented to the study of material culture. Ratzel had reached his diffusionist conclusions chiefly through comparing artifacts, and two of the school's leading theorists, Fritz Graebner and Leo Frobenius, were avid collectors and students of material culture. The museum continued to play a greater role in German ethnology than seems to be the case elsewhere, in part because of the empire's late appearance on the colonial scene and in part because of Germandom's peculiar intellectual and institutional traditions. Schmidt, himself, noted that the pursuit of *Kulturkreislehre* required the possession of good museums; those, like the French, who were hampered by their limited collections, were not likely to make much ethnological progress.[61] As the other anthropological founding fathers moved from the study of forms toward the study of meanings, however, this museum-oriented anthropology began to lose its relevance for the discipline's central debates.

Perhaps, had Schmidt been a less dictatorial type, or had another Austrian ethnologist been able to snatch away his powerful social and institutional positions in the interwar era, this historical school might

---

58. See Schmidt's "Einladung," 180.
59. Koppers, *Primitive Man*, 75, 18.
60. For a discussion of the latter-day Vienna School's critiques of Schmidt, see Henryk Zimon, "Wilhelm Schmidt's Theory of Primitive Monotheism and Its Critique within the Vienna School of Ethnology," *Anthropos* 81 (1986): 243–60.
61. Schmidt, "Die kulturhistorische Methode in der Ethnologie," *Anthropos* 6 (1911): 1017–18.

have provided a true alternative to the emerging orthodoxies of structural functionalism in Britain, Durkheimianism in France, and culture historicism in America.[62] But in the 1920s, the Germanic and Anglo-French traditions clearly parted company, and even the more historically oriented Americans began to emphasize their divergence from German models. Writing in 1936, Clyde Kluckhohn lamented the consistent unfairness Americans and especially Brits had exhibited in treating *Kulturkreislehre;* though these schools too had their biases, they had relentlessly harped on the Catholicism of the Viennese, and failed to read any of their post-1914 work.[63] Some of this, of course, had to do with politics; German-speaking scholars were very much isolated (and themselves retreated) from international discourse after the war's end. Moreover, the Germans had lost their colonies as well as many prewar sources for ethnological funding, and therefore found it harder than ever to convince others of their superior insight into the field.

In any event, introspection was the order of the day; the 1920s was the great era for the creation of chairs and national schools, most of them dominated by single figures (Boas in America, Radcliffe-Brown in England, Mauss in France). Germany did not, to my knowledge, have such a figure in the 1920s;[64] Austria had Schmidt. The intellectual as well as institutional consequences were momentous. In the next section, we will see how politics, institutions, and personality contributed to the exclusively Austrian success of Schmidt's "battle" against the all too Protestant theory of cultural evolutionism in the Great War period after World War I.

Counter-Reformation Triumphant

There have been many explications of structural-functionalism's rise, but few of historicist diffusionism's fall—which may not be the same

---

62. Writing in 1937, Robert Lowie could still insist that Schmidt's *Kulturkreislehre* really did not differ so much from the culture area theory of the Boasians. It was unfair, Lowie argued, to accuse the hard-working, wide-ranging Viennese scholars of coloring their ethnographies with Catholic prejudice. Robert H. Lowie, *The History of Ethnological Theory* (New York, 1937), 177.

63. Kluckhohn, "Some Reflections," 173–87.

64. German ethnology's great founding fathers, of course, arrived somewhat earlier: Rudolf Virchow and Adolf Bastian both belonged to the generation of 1848, not the generation of 1900. On Virchow's preeminence, see Benoit Massin, "From Virchow to Fischer: Physical Anthropology and 'Modern Race Theories' in Wilhelmine Germany," in *Volksgeist as Method and Ethic: Essays on Boasian Ethnography and the German Anthropological Tradition,* ed. George W. Stocking Jr. (Madison, Wis., 1996), 82–94.

story at all. Certainly, specialization played a very significant role in diffusionism's obsolescence. After several decades of Darwinian and anti-Darwinian culture histories, professional anthropologists increasingly found diffusionism impracticable and superficial. As avalanches of data and case after case of artifacts flooded Europe, it seemed less and less possible that one researcher could hold world prehistory in his head. Moreover, as ethnographic studies grew more intensive and sophisticated, epistemological and evaluatory problems grew more trenchant: did the blow gun mean the same thing in African cultures as in Melanesian ones? To those sensitive to these complex problems, diffusionism's grand attempts to re-create the history of mankind—like Grafton Elliot Smith's Egyptian fantasies, or Schmidt's history of the idea of God—seemed at best superficial, at worst absurd.[65]

In Austria, however, Schmidt stuck to *Kulturkreislehre,* and to the increasingly utopian project of reconstructing world prehistory. Schmidt's views prevailed (excepting 1938–45) long into the period after World War II. He became the arbiter of cultural anthropology at the University of Vienna (though he seems to have taught few courses), the editor of Austria's leading ethnological journal, and an important distributor of patronage. But scholarly success simply allowed him to enlarge his sphere of influence. Far from settling into a life of specialized scholarship, Schmidt in the 1920s threw himself into a wide range of political and cultural activities.

In the following section, we will see how Schmidt gained dominance over his field after the Great War, and in doing so, assured Austria's departure from the secularizing, and specializing, norm. It seems to me critical, here, not simply to write Schmidt out of the history of anthropology because he failed to keep step with "the West"; his obsolescence itself, and especially the institutionalization of his intransigence, should tell us a great deal about the cultural world of postwar Austria and, also, offer an illuminating contrast to the more familiar worlds of anthropology's other founding fathers.

Above all, Wilhelm Schmidt conceived of his role as that of a "mobilizer of auxiliary troops"[66] in what Schroeder called "the great battle over faith." As we have seen, in the years before the Great War,

---

65. In 1936, Kluckhohn did try to defend the importance of diffusionism's wide-angle view; "Perhaps the central reason for careful examination of the Kulturkreislehre is that it attempts to provide a schematization for the archaeological and ethnological facts of the whole world—at a time when the recognition that even very early peoples were no respecters of continents is being forced on us." Kluckhohn, "Some Reflections," 196.

66. Schmidt, *Der Ursprung der Gottesidee,* 1:72.

Schmidt devoted his extraordinary energy to a myriad of Catholic causes and secured for himself and for *Kulturkreislehre* a wide audience and influential patrons. In all of his endeavors, his ethnographic work, his politics, and his religious convictions were intertwined, often to the horror of his superiors. Indeed, they did occasionally try to reign in Schmidt, especially in the years before 1914. The war, however, brought Schmidt new prominence, both within his order and in wider Catholic sociopolitical circles. Charged by the royal family to accomplish a special mission, Schmidt applied his titanic energies to the organization of hundreds of homey library-canteens for soldiers. This close contact earned him the respect of Kaiser Karl, and in the war's last years, Schmidt served as the last Austrian kaiser's confessor. Although his order acted quickly to suppress the priest's two (anonymous) books on the causes of the war and the future of the Austrian Empire, by 1918, Schmidt was clearly becoming a politicocultural "player" with a high degree of notoriety and autonomy.[67]

In the years after 1918, Schmidt's career as Catholic scientific impresario took off. Soon after the war, he began organizing a series of international "Religion and Ethnology Weeks" for missionaries and scholars, which proved an exemplary means for the dissemination of Schmidt's own theories.[68] In 1921, he received the right to lecture on ethnology at the University of Vienna; in 1927, he and his close collaborator Wilhelm Koppers were put in charge of the university's new Institute for Anthropology (Institut für Völkerkunde). Through the good offices of their Catholic-conservative friend, Hermann Michel, the general director of Vienna's Naturhistorisches Museum, they were able to exert great influence on Austrian ethnological collections and exhibits.[69] Granted an audience with Pope Pius XI in 1923, Schmidt so impressed the pontiff that he not only subsidized Schmidt's journal and the pygmy fieldwork of his students, but also commissioned him to organize a Lateran Ethnology Museum, as well as a huge missionary ethnography exhibition in Rome. In the 1920s, Schmidt began contributing articles on political topics to *Schönere Zukunft* and *Hochland*, popular journals for well-educated Catholics.[70] He gave thousands of

---

67. For a description of these books, see Brandewie, "Schmidt and Politics."
68. Bornemann, *P. Wilhelm Schmidt*, 94–108.
69. Peter Linimayr, *Wiener Völkerkunde im Nationalsozialismus: Ansätze zu einer NS-Wissenschaft* (Frankfurt am Main, 1994), 27.
70. On the politics of *Schönere Zukunft*, see Erika Weinzierl, "Kirche und Politik," in *Österreich 1918–1938: Geschichte der Ersten Republik*, vol. 1, ed. Erika Weinzierl and Kurt Skalnik (Graz, 1983), 469–72.

lectures all over Europe, especially to lay audiences. In his ecosystem, Schmidt, who dominated Austrian ethnology until his death in 1954, was the equivalent of Franz Boas plus Father Coughlin, or Marcel Mauss plus Jacques Maritain. His modernist activism revived a dormant tradition of missionary ethnography and made *Kulturkreislehre* the cultural anthropology of choice in Catholic Central Europe.[71]

At this juncture, it is critical to underscore the ways in which Schmidt's institutional ambit differed from that of other anthropological "founding fathers." Unlike Boas, Mauss, and Malinowski, Schmidt was not primarily a university professor. A public intellectual, he spoke to groups of many different types on topics of contemporary relevance, as well as on scholarly subjects. He used Catholic intellectual circles to spread his message, and he tapped these "private" sources for funding.[72] Elsewhere, ethnographers had increasingly become dependent on public funds for their endeavors, a circumstance that made many liable to the charge of assisting in colonial oppression.[73] It is unlikely that Schmidt could have flourished in any other context than his own; but in Austria, the universities did not have the sort of cultural centrality they possessed, for example, in Germany, and the social power of Catholic organizations had not been broken, as in France. Austria's cultural infrastructure, too, played a big role in the making of this counter-reformation.

But it was Schmidt's personality that played the decisive part in prohibiting the adoption of the new social anthropology in Austria. His omnipresence in ethnological and Catholic cultural circles was the result not of circumstances but of colossal effort and of charismatic, intractable self-confidence. Schmidt, whose curriculum vitae already listed 166 items by 1911,[74] continued to produce essays, letters, lec-

---

71. *Kulturkreislehre,* according to one recent commentator, "shaped ethnological work in Central Europe during the whole first half of this century and can be described as the most significant methodological contribution of German-speaking anthropology *(Völkerkunde)* to the history of ethnology." Helmut Straube, "Leo Frobenius (1873–1938)," in *Klassiker der Kulturanthropologie von Montaigne bis Margaret Mead,* ed. Wolfgang Marschall (Munich, 1990), 167.

72. The work of Martin Gusinde in Tierra del Fuego, for example, was funded by the archbishop of Santiago (Koppers, *Primitive Man,* 136–38).

73. See, for example, the essays in Talal Asad, ed., *Anthropology and the Colonial Encounter* (London, 1973). If they now seem dated, some of these essays also rightly describe the ways in which social anthropologists developed critical positions on colonialism, a subtlety often overlooked in more recent literature.

74. Brandewie, *Giants,* 71.

tures, and books at an astonishing pace throughout his half-century career. Somehow, however, he found time to teach, preach, organize, and, especially, to endeavor, in print or in person, to stamp out dissent among his anthropological colleagues. His dictatorial tendencies increased as his institutional influence grew. Having taken over the Institute for Anthropology in 1927, he and his fellow Catholics prevented the ethnographer Michael Haberlandt from obtaining an academic position in ethnology; the "political Catholics" "drove the Protestant Haberlandt to the wall."[75]

Schmidt's tyrannical mien, however, was most evident in his dealings with his own SVD "brothers." Those who specialized in fieldwork, like Paul Schebesta, grew dissatisfied with the "big picture" approach of *Kulturkreislehre,* but were not permitted to step outside it.[76] Schebesta, in fact, would ultimately dispute Schmidt's central claim that all pygmies belonged to a single culture; but "disputing," here, simply meant wasting one's breath. Schmidt refused to listen when his field-workers challenged his idyllic reveries; on one occasion, he threatened to put a bullet through his brain rather than believe his pygmy paradise a fiction.[77] In the early 1930s, he and Koppers suppressed a historicizing movement launched by young Viennese scholars, leading one of them to compare the "law" under which they lived to that of "a medieval court, where every single one has to toe the line if he is not to be ostracized."[78] This "ethnohistory" movement would only be able to voice its criticisms of Schmidtian *Kulturkreislehre* in the later 1950s.[79] Still, his colleagues recognized that Schmidt had opened the way for them, intellectually as well as institutionally; his stubbornness, as Schebesta insisted in 1968, "in no way diminishes his importance for

---

75. Leopold Schmidt, quoted in Olaf Bockhorn, "Von Ritualen, Mythen, und Lebenskreisen," in *Völkische Wissenschaft,* ed. Wolfgang Jacobeit et al. (Vienna: Böhlau Verlag, 1994), 508.

76. For Schmidt, studies of single cultures were simply *Vorarbeit*—ethnology began where these studies were combined and shaped into an historical narrative. See Bornemann, *P. Wilhelm Schmidt,* 209. Schebesta's work, in particular, seems to have earned the respect of other professionals; if still tinged by religious romanticism, his studies contained much difficult-to-obtain information. For his romantic accounts of the Semang, see, for example, *Among the Forest Dwarfs,* 277–81.

77. Thiel, "Der Urmonotheismus des Schmidt, " 258–59.

78. Lebzelter quoted in Walter Hirschberg, "The Viennese Study Group for African Culture History (WAFAK) during the Years 1930–1932," in *Ethnohistory in Vienna: Forum,* vol. 9, ed. Karl R. Wernhart (Aachen, 1987), 16.

79. Walter Hirschberg, "'Culture and Dynamics' in Ethnohistory," in Wernhart, *Ethnohistory in Vienna,* 47.

310   *Worldly Provincialism*

our science, to which he gave an extraordinary stimulus and far-reaching goals."[80]

Schmidt's scientific inertia was accompanied by the deepening of his political conservatism over the course of the 1920s and early 1930s. As we have seen, Schmidt's prewar science and politics fit nicely into the world of Catholic "modernism," the educated clergy's attempt to beat liberalism at its own game. But increasingly, Schmidt turned to other causes and other enemies. His wartime political books showed that he had developed great faith in the multinational empire and new affection for his German birthplace. Naturally, the Versailles settlements put an end to his plans for the revitalization of the Habsburg Empire; but he remained a monarchist, as well as a Germanophile. In the wake of the war, he could not accommodate himself to the new social and political realities of republican rump Austria and "Red Vienna." Like his contemporary Ignaz Seipel, he grew more and more confident that liberalism was dead and that the real enemy lay to the far left.[81] That Schmidt was able, in this era, to deploy the pygmies for a new set of antiliberal causes gave his work a new lease on life and dangerous new relevance.

A few examples of Schmidt's popular essays should suffice to suggest the political dimensions of his work after the Great War—the period in which, it must be underlined, anthropology throughout the West gained academic status. In a 1925 essay on the origins of the family, for example, Schmidt clearly attempted to discredit the communal housing experiments of the Viennese socialist government. A second aim of the essay was to disparage attempts by feminists to gain equal rights for women.[82] In a later, synthetic analysis of the origins of matriarchy, the moral of Schmidt's ethnological parable was even clearer.[83] In the beginning—the closest approximation to which was pygmy culture—men and women were partners with defined spheres; it was now time to return to a modified version of the hunting and gathering stage,

---

80. Paul Schebesta, "P. W. Schmidts Studie über den Totemismus der Äquatorialen Waldneger und Pygmäen," in *Anthropica: Gedenkschrift zum 100. Geburtstag von P. Wilhelm Schmidt,* ed. Anthropols-Institut, Studia Instituti Anthropos, vol. 21 (St. Augustin bei Bonn: Verlag des Anthropos-Institut, 1968), 322.

81. On Seipel's rightward movement, see Klemens von Klemperer, *Ignaz Seipel: Christian Statesman in a Time of Crisis* (Princeton, 1972), 277–91.

82. Schmidt, "Familie," originally written for the *Handwörterbuch der Staatswissenschaft* (Jena, 1925), reprinted in *Wege der Kulturen,* 13–42.

83. Schmidt, *Das Mutterrecht,* Studia Instituti Anthropos, vol. 10 (Vienna, 1955), 185.

men working in the cities and women gardening and raising children in the suburbs. Nor did Schmidt simply spin out these politicized ur-fantasies from the quiet of his study; in 1934—in the wake of Dollfuss's coup from the right—he helped to found "Familienschutz," an organization that promoted lower taxes and greater influence for fathers of three or more children as a means to ward off the degeneration of the (German) *Volk*.[84] Clearly, the Durkheimian sociology and Freudian psychology that shaped new anthropological endeavors elsewhere did not suit this *völkisch*, Catholic plan. Thus Schmidt stuck with the pygmies and with hyperdiffusionism, and the Austrian school, now given official academic status, remained the captive of yesteryear's antievolutionist critique.

Like the eugenicists and Spenglerians of his day, Schmidt harbored a deep pessimism about the future of Western civilization. He, however, blamed incipient Western degeneracy not on miscegenation or city life, but chiefly on declining Catholicism and the advent of Bolshevism, whose way had been prepared by liberalism.[85] Similarly, although he pined for Austria's reunification with Germany, Schmidt's version of *Anschluss* was that of the "big Austria" advocated in 1848; that is, he longed for a return to the Holy Roman Empire in its pre-Lutheran glory days. He also longed for a strong state that would fight off the "Turkish threat" of socialism and take measures to ensure the survival of the German *Volksgemeinschaft;* but these measures were to involve conversion, not murder.[86] He sympathized with many of the policies of the Austrian fascist regime and was, unquestionably, an anti-Semite of the sort typical for right-wing Austrian Catholics of his generation. In one essay of 1934, Schmidt complained bitterly about the ways in which the Austrian people were being denied access to new, antievolutionist (and anti-Bolshevik) ideas by "the machinations of [the old, materialist party's] primarily Jewish leaders"; his recipe for combating these Jewish "machinations," however, was not expulsion but the establishment of a Catholic university.[87]

Schmidt knew a number of prominent Nazis and was apparently concocting a plan for church-state accommodation in the wake of

---

84. Bornemann, *P. Wilhelm Schmidt,* 253–57.
85. Schmidt, "Freiheit und Bindung des Christen in der Gesellschaft," *Schönere Zukunft* 9, no. 3 (15 October 1934): 53.
86. Ibid.
87. Schmidt, "Was vermag der Katholizismus der Wissenschaft zu bieten?" *Schönere Zukunft* 31 (29 April 1934): 794.

Hitler's annexation of Austria in March 1938.[88] But Schmidt failed the make-or-break test for Nazi anthropologists: he did not believe biology was destiny. Essentially a Lamarckian,[89] he held inheritance to be less decisive than environment. He thought Nazi racial hierarchies ridiculous, and said so, in the mid-1930s as well as after the war.[90] In an essay of January 1934 entitled "On the Jewish Question," he wrote: "The problem of the Jewish people as a race definitively cannot be understood according to the usual categories; its basis rests not on material but on spiritual factors (not in the physical factor of 'blood,' but in the spiritual factor of an historical disposition of the will)." The Jews had failed their national mission by denying Christ, he wrote, but through conversion they could join the Christian community, if not the German *Volksgemeinschaft*. The essay denounced Jewish cultural dominance (in schools, medical institutions, cinemas, law firms), but warned explicitly against solving the Jewish problem through force. Once converted, the Jews, like the Christian Africans, Chinese, Indians, and pygmies, belonged to *Christentum*. If they could never belong to *Deutschtum*, it was "not because they are lesser beings, but because they are other beings."[91] The semiuniversals of Catholic *Kulturkreislehre*, it seems, could be reconciled with the Austro-fascist corporate hierarchies, or even with Mussolini's colonial endeavors;[92] the worldview of Pygmy-Schmidt, however, could not be used to justify genocide.

The enthusiasm with which Austrians greeted Hitler's arrival in March 1938 meant that the Führer was not obliged to tolerate cultural or political deviations—militant Catholicism, of course, was both. Evidentially, Pope Pius anticipated that the *Anschluss* would not be good for his valued ethnological adviser, and thus sent a car to whisk Schmidt out of danger's way just as the German troops descended on

---

88. See Bornemann, *P. Wilhelm Schmidt,* 280–81; Schmidt also contributed extensively to *Schönere Zukunft* after 1933, though the editor's sympathetic stance with respect to Nazism must have been known to him.

89. Schmidt, *Rassen und Völker in Vorgeschichte und Geschichte des Abendlandes,* vol. 1, *Die Rassen des Abendlandes* (Lucerne, 1946), 147–48.

90. Schmidt, "Rasse und Weltanschauung" (1935), reprinted in *Wege der Kulturen,* 269–84.

91. Wilhelm Schmidt, "Zur Judenfrage," *Schönere Zukunft* 17 (21 January 1934): 408–9. Quotation reads: "nicht weil sie minderwertig wären, sondern weil sie anderwertig sind" (409).

92. On Schmidt's favorable attitude towards Italian fascism, see Conte, "Völkerkunde und Faschismus?" 241–42.

Austria.[93] Safely ensconced in a Swiss village, Schmidt continued to pursue his studies and his organizational work and to torment his brethren. Back in Austria, Wilhelm Koppers's chair at the University of Vienna was "temporarily suspended" in mid-1938; Koppers was officially dismissed in 1939, on grounds of being (unlike Schmidt) a well-known opponent of Germanization. The cleric-ethnologist took the opportunity to go to India to do fieldwork. His chair was taken over by Viktor Christian, an orientalist and member of the SS; the teaching of ethnology was passed on to young party members, many of whom had been students of Schmidt. Hardly had Schmidt left town when Walter Hirschberg published a tribute to Bernard Ankermann in which the "otherworldly Kulturkreis constructions" of the Vienna school were denounced in favor of Ankermann's more painstaking, and more racially oriented, ethnohistory.[94] The Germanophilic scholar of Mexican ethnology Fritz Röck survived denunciation by joining the Nazi Party and perpetually reiterating his hostility to the clerics of the *Kulturkreis* school.[95] By 1939, racial biology had achieved institutional hegemony, and confessional anthropology, like confessional folklore,[96] had been silenced.

Schmidt and his school do not look so bad in light of the antics of their colleagues in physical anthropology. While Schmidt's school had become dominant by mobilizing Catholic lay groups and utilizing non-university-related sources of funding, scholarly posts and museum collections in Austrian anthropology had remained heavily slanted toward anatomy and *völkisch* prehistory. The leading scholars in these schools were just as Germano-nationalist as Schmidt, but they were much more inclined to adopt racist principles. In 1933, the prehistorian Oswald Menghin published *Geist und Blut,* a volume of essays in which he identified Germans and Jews as two fundamentally different *Volkstypen,* the former agrarian, the latter nomadic. Menghin sympathized greatly with the *Anschluss* idea until it occurred, and Catholic neoconservatives like himself lost out to Nazi radicals.[97] Rudolf Much,

---

93. Bornemann, *P. Wilhelm Schmidt,* 281–82.

94. See Walter Hirschberg, "Bernard Ankermann," in *Zeitschrift für Ethnologie* 70 (1938): 131. Thanks to Glenn Penny for this reference.

95. Linimayr, *Wiener Völkerkunde im Nationalsozialismus,* 54–56, 75–116. Linimayr shows in detail how extensively Röck integrated Nazi ideology into the museum's programs and exhibits.

96. Bockhorn, "Ritualen, Mythen, und Lebenskreisen," 489.

97. On Menghin, see Richard S. Geehr, "Oswald Menghin, ein katholischer Nationaler," in *Geistiges Leben im Österreich der Ersten Republik* (Munich, 1986), 9–24.

Vienna's specialist in German *Altertumskunde* until his death in 1936, produced a cadre of pro-Nazi students.[98] The anthropology chair at the university was held by a series of men committed to racial classification; and two more anthropologists with Austrian origins, Felix von Luschan and Richard Thurnwald, were early and active members of racial hygiene societies.[99] Already by 1939, Vienna's Museum of Natural History had erected two exhibits suffused with Nazi racial ideology: "Austria's Contribution to the Study of German Colonial Regions" and "The Spiritual and Racial Physiognomy *(Erscheinungsbild)* of the Jews." An enormous caption for the physiognomic photos in the latter exhibition read: "The Jewish Question can only be solved by clearly differentiating the Jews from the non-Jews"[100]—an obvious incitement to ethnic cleansing.

The point not to be missed here is that Schmidt's politics were typical of the Christian Social Right of the 1920s and 1930s, which has its own sins to answer for. One of these, perhaps its most besetting, is that its ambiguous relationship with Nazism allowed conservative Austrians to learn nothing from World War II. Schmidt and his school were particularly culpable in this regard. Although the prominent priest's departure from Austria was arranged by the pope rather than an act of opposition on Schmidt's part, Schmidt ever after played the role of beleaguered exile. He blamed Nazism on Prussianism, thereby absolving German culture—and Catholic Germans and Austrians—of all responsibility; he also subscribed to the "first victim of Nazi aggression" view of Germany's annexation of Austria.[101] In his *Die Rassen des Abendlandes* (1946), he tried to show that race was not really a German concept at all; and he lumped Nazi barbarism together with other costs of civilization, such as the breakdown of families, blaming all on rampant materialism.[102]

---

98. See Bockhorn, "Ritualen, Mythen, und Lebenskreisen."

99. Marion Melk-Koch, "Zwei Österreicher nehmen Einfluß auf die Ethnologie in Deutschland: Felix von Luschan und Richard Thurnwald," in Rupp-Eisenreich and Stagl, *Kulturwissenschaften im Vielvölkerstaat,* 137.

100. Klaus Taschwer, "'Anthropologie ins Volk': Zur Ausstellungspolitik einer anwendbaren Wissenschaft bis 1945," in Herbert Posch and Gottfried Fliedl, eds., *Politik der Präsentation: Museum und Ausstellung in Österreich, 1918–1945* (Vienna, 1996), 249–51.

101. Schmidt, *Rassen und Völker,* 310–11, viii.

102. "The catastrophic reduction of human spirituality, which leads to the beastializing and mechanization of huge masses of mankind, means not only the exclusion of millions of men from cultural progress, but also produces a swamp of intellectual stagnation, moral rot, and social corruption, whose miasmas have the effect of poisoning and stunting the free [nations]" (ibid., 314).

The lesson our anthropological Loyola took from the Nazi experience was that it was essential for Germany to return to Catholicism; the Reformation had done its worst and it was high time to return to Germanic Christian unity.[103] In 1949, his successor, Wilhelm Koppers, echoed this sentiment; rather than waste our breath discussing the future of Western civilization, which had in any case given way to a new world order, "Would it not be better," Koppers asked, to say that we should use all our powers to bring about such a world civilization and to see to it that Catholic Christianity, which had repeatedly saved Europe from ruin, should play a decisive role in the shaping of its destinies? Christianity would then be called upon once more to save all that could be saved of our Western culture, while coming to an understanding with the mentality of India and the Far East and seeking to take over their cultural heritage. In doing so Christianity would fulfill a mission similar to that which it accomplished so successfully with regard to the intellectual heritage of classical antiquity.[104] There are, Schmidt pronounced in a postwar radio address, "healthy, even necessary catastrophes. They open eyes and prepare souls to see the eternal West and the roots of its existence, which reach millennia-deep into history's soil."[105] The cataclysm of the world war would permit the West to reroot itself in Catholicism and the land; redeemed from the sins of religious schism and hyperindustrialism, the West would be ready, once more, to take up the incomplete task of Christianizing the world.[106] In the era of decolonization, a theory that had once combated the hubris of evolutionism took on a grander and even more delusionary civilizing mission.

It was this sort of maudlin, conservative universalism, as well as the failure to see Nazism as anything other than a particularly virulent form of materialism, that characterized mainstream Austrian culture after 1945, the left's attempts at modernization notwithstanding. Even men and institutions deeply compromised by the *Anschluss* returned to power.[107] The Austrian school's resistance to Nazi racial determinism

---

103. Ibid., 31. Schmidt had begun this campaign already in 1919. See Bornemann, *P. Wilhelm Schmidt,* 37–40.

104. Koppers, *Primitive Man,* 135–36.

105. Schmidt, "Werdendes Abendland," in *Erbe und Zukunft des Abendlandes* (Bern, 1948), 7–8.

106. Schmidt does not explicitly state the new Christianizing mission, but it is heavily implied in the address; see, e.g., ibid., 14.

107. Brandewie gives an interesting account of the Africanist Hermann Baumann, who held a chair in Vienna's Department of Anthropology during the Third Reich. In 1945, Baumann, a Nazi, was prohibited from practicing his profession in museums or universities and

permitted it to smoothly reestablish its dominance (at the University of Vienna) after 1945, and Wilhelm Koppers returned to his chair. The octogenarian Schmidt, though he continued to reside in Switzerland, engaged in a furious new round of lectures, publications, and radio broadcasts; and his influence in Austrian Catholic circles remained considerable. But Schmidt, like many of his conservative colleagues, had fallen more and more out of step with changes in his profession. Indeed, by the time of his death in 1954, diffusionist historicism had begun to look distinctly quaint, and even slightly barmy, more and more evident as a relic of a dilettantish age. Now the secular path not taken in the 1910s and 1920s clearly defined the "scientific" approach to anthropology; in a postwar world of international agencies, declining missionary activity and church patronage, and continuing secularization and professionalization, the intellectual and institutional bases of Schmidt's achievements crumbled. In the long run, a counter-reformation in one country could not survive. The "battle of battles," in this field, in any event, had been lost.

It is not my purpose, here, to reopen the battle, but to admonish historians not to forget it. The centrality of religion as a subject for ethnographers in this century is not simply a meaningless "survival"; the attempt to treat religion and its history objectively lies at the heart of anthropology's professionalization story. The ways in which this issue could be treated varied, depending greatly on the institutional, political, and confessional structures of each nation. In Austria, the acquisition of anthropological authority did not necessitate the adoption of an agnostic stance. But Schmidt's departures from the "Western" norm, and especially his intellectual inflexibility, doomed his attempt to derail the secularization of cultural anthropology. Schmidt's counter-reformation ultimately failed, but at its height, it succeeded in making the study of ethnology more relevant to more Austrians than ever before or since. As always, local battles engage the public more passionately than distant ones; and if colonial questions shaped the wider context, for many early-twentieth-century ethnographers and their audiences, the battle nearest to their hearts remained the battle over the past, present, and future course of faith.

---

had to earn a living in a carpenter's shop making coffins. Perhaps partly on Schmidt's recommendation, Baumann was allowed to work at the Frobenius Institute, and by 1955 had been fully rehabilitated, and made professor at the University of Munich. Brandewie, *Giants*, 277.

Bibliography

Abrams, Lynn. *Workers' Culture in Imperial Germany: Leisure and Recreation in the Rhineland and Westphalia.* London: Routledge, 1992.
Ackerknecht, Erwin. *Rudolf Virchow: Doctor, Statesman, Anthropologist.* Madison: University of Wisconsin Press, 1953.
Althusser, Louis, and Étienne Balibar. *Reading Capital.* Trans. Ben Brewster. London: Verso, 1997.
Anderson, Warwick. "Climates of Opinion: Acclimatization in Nineteenth-Century France and England." *Victorian Studies* 35 (1992): 135–57.
Ankermann, Bernard. "Die Entwicklung der Ethnologie seit Adolf Bastian." *Zeitschrift für Ethnologie* 58 (1926): 221–30.
———. "Kulturkreise und Kulturschichten in Afrika." *Zeitschrift für Ethnologie* 37 (1905): 54–84.
Arendt, Hannah. *The Origins of Totalitarianism.* New York: Harcourt, Brace, Jovanovich, 1973.
Arens, Katherine. *Structures of Knowing: Psychologies of the Nineteenth Century.* Dordrecht: Kluwer Academic Publishers, 1989.
Arnold, Stefan. "Propaganda mit Menschen aus Übersee—Kolonialausstellungen in Deutschland 1869–1940." In *Kolonialausstellungen—Begegnungen mit Afrika,* ed. Robert Debusmann and János Riesz, 1–24. Frankfurt am Main: Verlag für Interkulturelle Kommunikation, 1995.
Asad, Talal, ed. *Anthropology and the Colonial Encounter.* Atlantic Highlands, N.J.: Humanities Press, 1973.
———. "From the History of Colonial Anthropology to the Anthropology of Western Hegemony." In *Colonial Situations: Essays on the Contextualization of Ethnographic Knowledge,* ed. George W. Stocking Jr., 314–24. Madison: University of Wisconsin Press, 1991.
Baker, Lee. *From Savage to Negro: Anthropology and the Construction of Race, 1896–1954.* Berkeley and Los Angeles: University of California Press, 1998.
Barratt, Glynn. *Russia in Pacific Waters, 1715–1825: A Survey of the Origins of Russia's Naval Presence in the North and South Pacific.* Vancouver: University of British Columbia Press, 1981.
———. *The Russian View of Honolulu, 1809–26.* Ottawa: Carleton University Press, 1988.

———. *Russia and the South Pacific, 1696–1840: The Tuamotu Islands and Tahiti.* Vancouver: University of British Columbia Press, 1992.
Barth, Paul. *Südwest-Afrika.* Windhoek: John Meinert, 1926.
Bastian, Adolf. *Der Mensch in der Geschichte.* Leipzig: Otto Wiegand, 1860.
———. "Meine Reise um und durch die Welt." *Illustrirte Zeitung* 35 (1860): 219–22.
———. "Das natürliche System in der Ethnologie." *Zeitschrift für Ethnologie* 1 (1869): 1–23.
———. "Darwin, The Descent of Man, 1871." *Zeitschrift für Ethnologie* 3 (1871): 133–43.
———. *Die Rechtsverhältnisse bei verschiedenen Völkern der Erde. Ein Beitrag zur vergleichenden Ethnologie.* Berlin, 1872.
———. *Geographische und ethnologische Bilder.* Jena, 1873.
———. "Ethnologische Erörterung." *Zeitschrift für Ethnologie* 19 (1877): 183.
———. *Führer durch die Ethnographische Abtheilung.* Berlin: W. Spemann, 1877.
———. *Inselgruppen in Oceanien. Reiseerlebnisse und Studien.* Berlin: Ferd. Dümmlers, 1883.
———. *Der Papua des dunklen Inselreiches im Lichte psychologischer Forschung.* Berlin: Weidmannsche Buchhandlung, 1885.
———. *Zur Lehre von den geographischen Provinzen. Aufgenommen in die Controversen.* Berlin, 1886.
———. *Ethnologie und Geschichte in ihren Berührungspunkten unter Bezugnahme auf Indien.* Vol. 2 of *Ideale Welten in Wort und Bild.* Berlin: Emil Felber, 1892.
———. *Controversen in der Ethnologie.* Berlin: Weidmannsche Verlagsbuchhandlung, 1893–94.
Belke, Ingrid, ed. *Moritz Lazarus und Heymann Steinthal: Die Begründer der Völkerpsychologie in ihren Briefen.* Tübingen: J. C. B. Mohr, 1971.
Ben David, Joseph. *The Scientist's Role in Society: A Comparative Study.* Englewood Cliffs, N.J.: Prentice Hall, 1971.
Benjamin, Walter. "Critique of Violence." In *Reflections,* trans. Edmund Jephcott. New York: Schocken, 1978.
Bennett, Tony. "The Exhibitionary Complex." *New Formations* 4 (1988): 73–102.
———. *The Birth of the Museum: History, Theory, Politics.* London: Routledge, 1995.
Benninghoff-Lühl, Sibylle. "Die Ausstellung der Kolonialisierten: Völkerschauen von 1874–1932." *Andenken an den Kolonialismus.* Ausstellungskataloge der Universität Tübingen, no. 17 (1984), 52–64.
———. "Völkerschauen—Attraktionen und Gefahr des Exotischen." *SOWI—Sozialwissenschaftliche Informationen* 15, no. 4 (1986): 41–48.
Berlin, Isiah. *Vico and Herder.* London: Hogarth Press, 1976.
———. *Against the Current.* Oxford: Oxford University Press, 1981.
Berman, Nina. *Orientalismus, Kolonialismus und Moderne: Zum Bild des Orients in der deutschen Kultur um 1900.* Stuttgart: Metzler, 1997.
Bernatzik, Hugo, ed. *Afrika: Handbuch der Angewandten Völkerkunde.* Innsbruck: Schluesselverlag, 1949.

Bhabha, Homi. *The Location of Culture.* London: Routledge, 1994.
Biesele, Megan, Robert Gordon, and Richard Lee. *The Past and Future of !Kung Ethnography.* Hamburg: Helmut Buske Verlag, 1987.
Biskop, Peter. "Dr Albert Hahl—Sketch of a German Colonial Official." *Australian Journal of Politics and History* 14 (1968): 342–57.
Blackbourn, David. *The Long Nineteenth Century: A History of Germany, 1780–1918.* Oxford: Oxford University Press, 1997.
Bleek, Wilhelm. *The Origins of Language.* Ed. E. Haeckel. New York: Schmidt, 1869.
Bley, Helmut. *South-West Africa under German Rule, 1894–1914.* Trans. Hugh Ridley. Evanston, Ill.: Northwestern University Press, 1971.
Boas, Franz. "The Occurrence of Similar Inventions in Areas Widely Apart." *Science* 9 (1887): 485–87.
———. "Museums of Ethnology and Their Classification." *Science* 9 (1887): 587–89.
———. "The Limitations of the Comparative Method in Anthropology." *Science* 4 (1896): 901–09.
———. "The Methods of Ethnology." *American Anthropologist* 22 (1920): 311–22.
———. *Race, Language and Culture.* New York: Macmillan, 1940.
Boas, Franz, and Ales Hrdlicka. "Facial Casts." *American Anthropologist* 7 (1905): 169.
Böckh, Richard. "Die statistische Bedeutung der Volkssprache als Kennzeichen der Nationalität." *Zeitschrift für Völkerpsychologie und Sprachwissenschaft* 4 (1866): 259–402.
Bockhorn, Olaf. "Von Ritualen, Mythen, und Lebenskreisen." In *Völkische Wissenschaft,* ed. Wolfgang Jacobeit et al., 477–526. Vienna: Böhlau Verlag, 1994.
Boehlich, Walter, ed. *Der Berliner Antisemitismusstreit.* Frankfurt am Main: Insel Verlag, 1965.
Bogden, Robert. *Freak Show: Presenting Human Oddities for Amusement and Profit.* Chicago: University of Chicago Press, 1988.
Bollenbeck, Georg. *Bildung und Kultur: Glanz und Elend eines deutschen Deutungsmusters.* Frankfurt am Main: Suhrkamp, 1996.
Bonn, Mauritz. *Wandering Scholar.* New York: John Day, 1948.
Boon, James. *Affinities and Extremes: Crisscrossing the Bittersweet Ethnology of East Indies History, Hindu-Balinese Culture, and Indo-European Allure.* Chicago: University of Chicago Press, 1990.
Bormann, Felix von. "Ist die Gründung einer europäische Familie in den Tropen zulässig?" *Archiv für Rassen- und Gesellschaftsbiologie* 31 (1937): 89–118.
Bornemann, Fritz. "P. Martin Gusinde, SVD (1886–1969), Eine biographische Skizze." *Anthropos* 65 (1970): 747–57.
———. *P. Wilhelm Schmidt S.V.D., 1868–1954.* Rome: Collegium Verbi Divini, 1982.
———, ed. *Remembering Arnold Janssen: A Book of Reminiscences.* Rome: Collegium Verbi Divini, 1978.

Bornhaupt, Christian von. "Die Vereidung von Eingebornen in den deutschen Schutzgebieten." *Koloniale Rundschau* 1 (1909): 427–32.
Bowlby, Rachel. *Just Looking: Consumer Culture in Dreiser, Gissing, and Zola.* New York: Methuen, 1985.
Boyer, John. *Culture and Political Crisis in Vienna: Christian Socialism in Power, 1897–1918.* Chicago: University of Chicago Press, 1995.
Brandewie, Ernest. *Wilhelm Schmidt and the Origin of the Idea of God.* Lanham: University Press of America, 1983.
———. *When Giants Walked the Earth: The Life and Times of Wilhelm Schmidt, SVD.* Fribourg: Fribourg University Press, 1990.
———. "Wilhelm Schmidt and Politics during the First World War." In *Kulturwissenschaften im Vielvölkerstaat: Zur Geschichte der Ethnologie und verwandter Gebiete in Österreich, ca. 1780 bis 1918,* ed. Britta Rupp-Eisenreich and Justin Stagl, 268–83. Vienna: Boehlau, 1995.
Bridgman, Jon. *The Revolt of the Hereros.* Berkeley and Los Angeles: University of California Press, 1981.
Brown, A. R. "Paluga: A Reply to Father Schmidt." *Man* 217 (1910): 33–37.
Bruckner, Sierra A. "The Tingle-Tangle of Modernity: Popular Anthropology and the Cultural Politics of Identity in Imperial Germany." Ph.D. diss., University of Iowa, 1999.
Bruford, Walter. *The German Tradition of Self-Cultivation.* London: Cambridge University Press, 1975.
Bunzl, Matti. "Franz Boas and the Humboldtian Tradition: From *Volksgeist* and *Nationalcharakter* to an Anthropological Concept of Culture." In *Volksgeist as Method and Ethic: Essays on Boasian Ethnography and the German Anthropological Tradition,* ed. George Stocking, 17–78. Madison: University of Wisconsin Press, 1996.
Burton, Antoinette. *Burdens of History: British Feminists, Indian Women, and Imperial Culture.* Chapel Hill: University of North Carolina Press, 1994.
Buschmann, Rainer. "Franz Boluminski and the Wonderland of Carvings: Towards an Ethnography of Collection Activity." *Baessler Archiv N.F.* 44 (1996): 190–99.
———. "Tobi Captured: Converging Ethnographic and Colonial Visions on a Caroline Island." *Isla* 4, no. 2 (1996): 317–40.
———. "The Ethnographic Frontier in German New Guinea, 1870–1914." Ph.D. diss., University of Hawai'i, 1999.
———. "Exploring Tensions in Material Culture: Commercializing Artifacts in German New Guinea, 1870–1904." In *Hunting the Gatherers: Ethnographic Collectors, Agents, and Agency in Melanesia,* ed. Michael O'Hanlon and Robert Welsch, 55–79. Oxford: Berghahn, 2000.
Buttmann, Gunther. *Friedrich Ratzel: Leben und Werk eines deutschen Geographen, 1844–1904.* Stuttgart: Wissenschaftliche Verlagsgesellschaft, 1977.
Campbell, Ian. "Anthropology and the Professionalization of Colonial Administration in Papua and New Guinea." *Journal of Pacific History* 33 (1998): 69–90.
Césaire, Aimé. *Discourse on Colonialism.* New York: Monthly Review Press, 1972.

Chamisso, Adalbert von. *Sämtliche Werke.* Ed. Jost Perfahl and Volker Hoffmann. Vol. 2. Munich: Winkler, 1975.

———. *Sämtliche Werke.* Ed. Werner Feudel and Christel Laufer. Vol. 2, *Prosa.* Munich: Hanser, 1982.

———. *A Voyage around the World with the Romanzov Exploring Expedition in the Years 1815–1818, in the Brig Rurik, Captain Otto von Kotzebue.* Trans. and ed. Henry Kratz. Honolulu: University of Hawaii Press, 1986.

Clifford, James. *Person and Myth: Maurice Leenhardt in the Melanesian World.* Berkeley and Los Angeles: University of California Press, 1982.

———. *Routes: Travel and Translation in the Late Twentieth Century.* Cambridge: Harvard University Press, 1997.

Cohn, Bernard. *Colonialism and Its Forms of Knowledge: The British in India.* Cambridge: Cambridge University Press, 1996.

Cole, Douglas. *Franz Boas: The Early Years, 1858–1906.* Seattle: University of Washington Press, 1999.

Conte, Edouard. "Völkerkunde und Faschismus? Fragen an ein vernachlässigtes Kapitel deutsch-österreichischer Wissenschaftsgeschichte." In *Kontinuität und Bruch: 1938–1945–1955: Beiträge zur österreichischen Kultur- und Wissenschaftsgeschichte,* ed. Friedrich Stadler, 229–64. Munich: Jugend und Volk, 1988.

Cook, Captain James. *A Voyage Towards the South Pole, and Round the World, Performed in his Majesty's Ships the Resolution and Adventure in the years 1772, 1773, 1774, and 1755.* 2 vols. London: Strahan and Cadell, 1777.

Cooper, Frederick, and Ann Laura Stoler, eds. *Tensions of Empire: Colonial Cultures in a Bourgeois World.* Berkeley and Los Angeles: University of California Press, 1997.

Crossick, Geoffrey. *Die Kleinbürger: Eine europäische Sozialgeschichte des 19. Jahrhunderts.* Munich: C. H. Beck, 1998.

Danziger, Kurt. "Origins and Basic Principles of Wundt's *Völkerpsychologie.*" *British Journal of Social Psychology* 22 (1983): 303–13.

Darnell, Regna. *And Along Came Boas: Continuity and Revolution in Americanist Anthropology.* Amsterdam: John Benjamins, 1998.

———. *Invisible Genealogies: A History of Americanist Anthropology.* Lincoln: University of Nebraska Press, 2001.

Däubler, Karl. *Die Grundzüge der Tropenhygiene.* 2d ed. Berlin, 1900.

Daum, Andreas. *Wissenschaftspopularisierung im 19. Jahrhundert: Bürgerliche Kultur, naturwissenschaftliche Bildung und die deutsche Öffentlichkeit, 1848–1914.* Munich: R. Oldenbourg, 1998.

Davidson, J. W. *Samoa Mo Samoa: The Emergence of the Independent State of Western Samoa.* Oxford: Oxford University Press, 1967.

Davis, Belinda. *Home Fires Burning: Food, Politics, and Everyday Life in World War I Berlin.* Chapel Hill: University of North Carolina Press, 2000.

Davis, Natalie Zemon. "The Rites of Violence: Religious Riot in Sixteenth-Century France." *Past and Present* 59 (1973): 51–91.

Debrunner, Hans-Werner. *Presence and Prestige: Africans in Europe—A History of Africans in Europe before 1918.* Basel: Basler Afrike-Bibliographie, 1979.

Deniker, Joseph. *Les Races de l'Europe: L'indice cephalique en Europe.* Paris, 1899.

Dernburg, Bernhard. *Zielpunkte des Deutschen Kolonialwesens.* Berlin: Ernst Siegfried Mittler und Sohn, 1907.

Dirks, Nicholas B., Geoff Eley, and Sherry B. Ortner, eds. *Culture/Power/History: A Reader in Contemporary Social Theory.* Princeton: Princeton University Press, 1994.

Dittrich, Lother, and Annelore Rieke-Müller, eds. *Carl Hagenbeck (1844-1913): Tierhandel und Schaustellungen im Deutschen Kaiserreich.* Frankfurt am Main: Peter Lang, 1998.

Doegen, Wilhelm. *Unter Fremden Völkern: Eine neue Völkerkunde.* Berlin: Otto Stohlberg, Verlag für Politik und Wirtschaft, 1925.

Dominguez, Virginia. "The Marketing of Heritage." *American Ethnologist* 13 (1986): 546-56.

Drechsler, Horst. *"Let Us Die Fighting": The Struggle of the Herero and Nama against German Imperialism (1884-1915).* Trans. Bernd Zöllner. London: Zed Press, 1980.

Drontschilow, Krum. *Beiträge zur Anthropologie der Bulgaren.* Braunschweig: Vieweg, 1914.

Dunkel, Harold. *Herbart and Herbartianism: An Educational Ghost Story.* Chicago: University of Chicago Press, 1970.

Dunmore, John. *Who's Who in Pacific Navigation.* Honolulu: University of Hawaii Press, 1991.

Ecker, Alexander. "Einige Bemerkungen über einen schwankenden Charakter in der Hand des Menschen." *Archiv für Anthropologie* 8 (1878): 67-74.

Efron, John. *Defenders of the Race: Jewish Doctors and Race Science in Fin-de-Siècle Europe.* New Haven: Yale University Press, 1994.

Eggeling, H. von. "Anatomische Untersuchungen an Den Köpfen von vier Hereros, Einem Herero- Und Einem Hottentottenkind." In *Zoologische und Anthropologische Ergebnisse Einer Forschungsreise im westlichen und zentralen Südafrika Ausgeführt in den Jahren 1903-1905,* ed. Leonard Schultze, 322-48. Jena: Gustav Fischer, 1909.

Eickstedt, Egon von. "Rassenelemente der Sikh." *Zeitschrift für Ethnologie* 52 (1920-21): 317-94.

Eksteins, Modris. *Rites of Spring: The Great War and the Birth of the Modern Age.* Boston: Houghton Mifflin, 1989.

Eley, Geoff. "Die deutsche Geschichte und die Widersprüche der Moderne." In *Zivilisation und Barbarei. Die Widersprüchlichen Potentiale der Moderne,* ed. F. Bajohr, W. Johe, and U. Lohalm, 17-65. Hamburg: Christians, 1991.

Enzensberger, Ulrich. *Georg Forster. Ein Leben in Scherben.* Frankfurt am Main: Eichborn, 1996.

Esherick, Joseph. *The Origins of the Boxer Uprising.* Berkeley and Los Angeles: University of California Press, 1987.

Essner, Cornelia. *Deutsche Afrikareisende im neunzehnten Jahrhundert: Zur Sozialgeschichte des Reisens.* Stuttgart: Steiner Verlag, 1985.

Evans-Pritchard, E. E. *A History of Anthropological Thought.* New York: Basic Books, 1981.

Everdell, William. *The First Moderns: Profiles in the Origins of Twentieth-Century Thought.* Chicago: University of Chicago Press, 1997.

Feest, Christian. "The Origins of Professional Anthropology in Vienna." In *Kulturwissenschaften im Vielvölkerstaat: Zur Geschichte der Ethnologie und verwandter Gebiete in Österreich, ca. 1780 bis 1918,* ed. Britta Rupp-Eisenreich and Justin Stagl, 115–27. Vienna: Boehlau, 1995.

Fiedermutz-Laun, Annemarie. "Aus der Wissenschaftsgeschichte: Adolf Bastian und die Deszendenztheorie." *Paideuma* 16 (1970): 1–26.

———. *Der Kulturhistorische Gedanke bei Adolf Bastian: Systematisierung und Darstellung der Theorie und Methode mit dem Versuch einer Bewertung des Kulturhistorischen Gehaltes auf dieser Grundlage.* Wiesbaden: Franz Steiner Verlag, 1970.

Field, Geoffrey. *Evangelist of Race: The Germanic Vision of Houston Stewart Chamberlain.* New York: Columbia University Press, 1981.

Finsch, Otto. *Gesichtsmasken von Völkertypen der Südsee und dem malayischen Archipel nach Leben abgegossen in den Jahren 1879–1882.* Bremen: Homeyer and Meyer, 1887.

Firth, Stewart. "Albert Hahl: Governor of New Guinea." In *Papua New Guinea Portraits: The Expatriate Experience,* ed. James Griffin, 28–47. Canberra: Australian National University Press, 1978.

———. *New Guinea under the Germans.* Melbourne: Melbourne University Press, 1982.

———. "Labour in German New Guinea." In *Papua New Guinea: A Century of Colonial Impact, 1884–1984,* ed. Sione Latukefu, 179–202. Port Moresby: National Research Institute, 1989.

———. "Colonial Administration and the Invention of the Native." In *The Cambridge History of the Pacific Islanders,* ed. Donald Denoon et al., 260–80. Cambridge: Cambridge University Press, 1997.

Fischer, Hans. *Die Hamburger Südsee Expedition. Über Ethnographie und Kolonialismus.* Frankfurt am Main: Syndikat Verlag, 1981.

———. *Völkerkunde im Nationalsozialismus. Aspekte der Anpassung, Affinität und Behauptung einer wissenschaftlichen Disziplin.* Berlin: Reimer Verlag, 1990.

Flemming, Johannes. *Völkerschau am Nil.* Hamburg, 1912.

Foucault, Michel. *Discipline and Punish: The Birth of the Prison.* Trans. Alan Sheridan. New York: Vintage, 1977.

Foy, Willy. *Führer durch das Rautenstrauch-Joest-Museum der Stadt Cöln.* Cologne: M. Dumont Schauberg, 1906.

———. "Das städtische Rautenstrauch-Joest-Museum für Völkerkunde in Cöln." *Ethnologia,* 1 (1909): 1–70.

———. "Ethnologie und Kulturgeschichte." *Petermanns Geographische Mitteilungen* 1, no. 3 (1911): 230–33.

Friederici, Georg. "Das Pidgin-Englisch in Deutsch Neuguinea." *Koloniale Rundschau* 11 (1911): 92–102.
Friedrichsmeyer, Sara, Sara Lennox, and Susanne Zantop, eds. *The Imperialist Imagination: German Colonialism and Its Legacy.* Ann Arbor: University of Michigan Press, 1998.
Fritsch, Gustav. *Die Eingeborenen Süd-Afrika's.* Breslau: Ferdinand Hirt, Königliche Universitäts- und Verlags-Buchhandlung, 1872.
———. Review of *Anthropologisch-ethnologisches Album in Photographien Herausgegeben mit Unterstützung aus der Sammlung der Berliner Anthropologischen Gesellschaft*, by C. Dammann. *Zeitschrift für Ethnologie* 6 (1874): 67–69.
Fritzsche, Peter. "Nazi Modern." *Modernism/Modernity* 3 (1996): 1–21.
Gall, Lothar. "Zur politischen und gesellschaftlichen Rolle der Wissenschaften in Deutschland um 1900." In *Wissenschaftsgeschichte seit 1900*, ed. Helmut Coing et al., 9–28. Frankfurt am Main: Suhrkamp Taschenbuch Verlag, 1992.
Gann, L. H., and Peter Duignan. *The Rulers of German Africa, 1884–1914.* Stanford: Stanford University Press, 1977.
Geehr, Richard. "Oswald Menghin, ein katholischer Nationaler." In *Geistiges Leben im Österreich der Ersten Republik.* Munich: Oldenbourg, 1986.
Geisenhainer, Katja. "Otto Reche's Verhältnis zur sogenannten Rassenhygiene." *Anthropos* 91 (1996): 492–512.
Gewald, Jan-Bart. *Herero Heroes: A Socio-Political History of the Herero of Namibia, 1890–1923.* Oxford: James Currey, 1999.
Gill, E. L. "Biological Surveys." *Journal of the South West Africa Scientific Society* 2 (1926–27): 29–34.
Gilson, R. P. *Samoa 1830 to 1900: The Politics of a Multi-cultural Community.* Oxford: Oxford University Press, 1970.
Goffman, Ervin. *Asylums: Essays on the Social Situations of Mental Patients and Other Inmates.* New York: Anchor, 1961.
Goldmann, Stefan. "Wilde in Europa." In *Wir und die Wilden: Einblicke in eine kannibalische Beziehung*, ed. Thomas Theye, 243–69. Reinbeck bei Hamburg: Rowohlt, 1985.
Goodbody, Bridget. "George Catlin's Indian Gallery: Art, Science, and Power in the Nineteenth Century." Ph.D. diss., Columbia University, 1996.
Goody, Jack. *The Expansive Moment: Anthropology in Britain and Africa.* Cambridge: Cambridge University Press, 1995.
Gordon, Robert. *Picturing Bushmen: The Denver African Expedition of 1925.* Athens: Ohio University Press, 1997.
———. "The Rise of the Bushman Penis: Germans, Genitalia, and Genocide." *African Studies* 57 (1998): 27–54.
———. "The Stat(u)s of Namibian Anthropology." *Cimbebasia* 16 (2000): 1–23.
Goschler, Constantin. "Rudolf Virchow. Eine biographische Studie über Naturwissenschaft, Liberalismus und die Kultur des Fortschritts." Habilitationsschrift, Humboldt-Universität, Berlin, 2001.
Gothsch, Manfred. *Die deutsche Völkerkunde und ihr Verhältnis zum Kolonialismus: Ein Beitrag zur kolonialideologischen und kolonialpraktischen Bedeutung*

der deutschen Völkerkunde in der Zeit von 1870 bis 1945. Hamburg: Institut für Internationale Angelegenheiten der Universität Hamburg, 1983.

Graebner, Fritz. "Kulturkreise und Kulturschichten in Ozeanien." *Zeitschrift für Ethnologie* 37 (1905): 28–53.

———. *Methode der Ethnologie.* Heidelberg: Carl Winter, 1911.

———. "Adolf Bastians 100. Geburtstag." *Ethnologica* 11 (1927): ix–xii.

Grafton, Anthony. "The Origins of Scholarship." *American Scholar* 48 (1979): 242–46.

Gray, Geoffrey. "'Being Honest to My Science': Reo Fortune and J. H. P. Murray, 1927–1930." *Australian Journal of Anthropology* 10 (1999): 56–76.

Grosse, Pascal. *Kolonialismus, Eugenik und bürgerliche Gesellschaft in Deutschland, 1850–1914.* Frankfurt am Main: Campus, 2000.

Gupta, Akhil, and James Ferguson. "Discipline and Practice: 'The Field' as Site, Method, and Location in Anthropology." In *Anthropological Locations: Boundaries and Grounds of a Field Science,* ed. Akhil Gupta and James Ferguson, 1–46. Berkeley: University of California Press, 1997.

Haberland, Eike, ed. *Leo Frobenius: An Anthology.* Wiesbaden: F. Steiner, 1973.

Haberland, Wolfgang. "Nine Bella Coolas in Germany." In *Indians and Europe: An Interdisciplinary Collection of Essays,* ed. Christian F. Feest, 337–82. Aachen: Rader Verlag, 1987.

———. "'Diese Indianer sind Falsch.' Neun Bella Coola im Deutschen Reich 1885/6." *Archiv für Völkerkunde* 42 (1988): 3–67.

Haberlandt, M. "Zur Kritik der Lehre von den Kulturschichten und Kulturkreisen." *Petermanns Geographische Mitteilungen* 1, no. 3 (1911): 113–18.

Hagenbeck, John. *Fünfundzwanzig Jahre Ceylon: Erlebnisse und Abenteuer im Tropenparadies.* Dresden: Deutsche Buchwerkstätten, 1922.

Hahl, Albert. "Über die Rechtsanschauungen der Eingeborenen eines Theils der Blanchebucht und des Inneren der Gazellenhalbinsel." *Nachrichten über Kaiser Wilhelmsland* 13 (1897): 68–85.

———. "Mitteilungen über Sitte und rechtliche Verhältnisse auf Ponape." *Ethnologisches Notizblatt* 2 (1901): 1–13.

———. "Feste und Tänze der Eingeborenen von Ponape." *Ethnologisches Notizblatt* 3 (1902): 95–102.

Harms, Volker. "Das Historische Verhältnis der deutschen Ethnologie zum Kolonialismus." *Zeitschrift für Kulturaustausch* 4 (1984): 401–16.

Harrington, Anne. *Reenchanted Science: Holism in German Culture from Wilhelm II to Hitler.* Princeton: Princeton University Press, 1996.

Harris, Marvin. *The Rise of Anthropological Theory.* New York: Thomas Crowell, 1968.

Harrison, Mark. "The Ordering of the Urban Environment: Time, Work, and the Occurrence of the Crowd, 1790–1835." *Past and Present* 110 (1986): 134–68.

Hartmann, Robert. "Untersuchungen über die Völkerschaften Nord-Ost-Afrikas." *Zeitschrift für Ethnologie* (1869): 23–45; 135–58.

Hasselmann-Kahlert, Margaret. "Über Menstruationsstörungen bei der gesunden

weißen Frau in der Tropen." *Archiv für Schiffs- und Tropenhygiene* 44 (1940): 124–33.
Hauschild, Thomas, ed. *Lebenslust und Fremdenfurcht: Ethnologie im Dritten Reich.* Frankfurt am Main: Suhrkamp, 1995.
———. "Christians, Jews, and the Other in German Anthropology." *American Anthropologist* 99, no. 4 (1997): 746–53.
Havelburg, V. "Klima, Rasse und Nationalität in ihrer Bedeutung für die Ehe." In *Krankheiten der Ehe. Darstellung der Beziehung zwischen Gesundheits-Störungen und Ehegemeinschaft,* ed. H. Senator and S. Kaminer, 89–144. Munich, 1904.
Haym, Rudolf. *Die Romantische Schule. Ein Beitrag zur Geschichte des deutschen Geistes.* 5th ed. Berlin: Weidmann, 1928.
Heger, Franz. "Die Zukunft der ethnographischen Museen." In *Festschrift für A. Bastian zu seinem 70. Geburtstag, 26. Juni 1896,* 585–93. Berlin: Reimer, 1896.
Heinrichs, Hans-Jürgen. *Die fremde Welt, das bin ich: Leo Frobenius, Ethnologe, Forschungsreisender, Abenteurer.* Wuppertal: P. Hammer, 1998.
Hemming, John. *Amazon Frontier: The Defeat of the Brazilian Indians.* Cambridge: Harvard University Press, 1987.
Hempenstall, Peter. *Pacific Islanders under German Rule: A Study in the Meaning of Colonial Resistance.* Canberra: Australian National University Press, 1978.
———. "The Neglected Empire: The Superstructure of the German Colonial State in German Melanesia." In *Germans in the Tropics: Essays in German Colonial History,* ed. A. Knoll and L. Gann, 93–117. Westport, Conn.: Greenwood Press, 1987.
Hennig, Edwin. *Württembergische Forschungsreisende der letzen anderthalb Jahrhunderte.* Stuttgart: Linden Museum, 1953.
Hensel, Reinhold. "Die Schädel der Corados." *Zeitschrift für Ethnologie* 2 (1870): 195–203.
Hesch, Michael, and Günther Spannaus, eds. *Kultur und Rasse: Otto Reche zum 60. Geburtstag.* Munich: J. F. Lehmann, 1939.
Hey, Barbara. "Vom 'dunklen Kontinent' zur 'anschmiegsamen Exotin.'" *Österreichische Zeitschrift für Geschichtswissenschaft* 8 (1997): 186–211.
Hiery, Hermann Joseph. *Das Deutsche Reich in der Südsee (1900–1921). Eine Annäherung an die Erfahrungen verschiedener Kulturen.* Göttingen: Vandenhoeck and Ruprecht, 1995.
———. *The Neglected War: The German South Pacific and the Impact of World War I.* Honolulu: University of Hawaii Press, 1995.
Hinsley, Curtis, Jr., *Savages and Scientists: The Smithsonian Institution and the Development of American Anthropology, 1846–1910.* Washington, D.C.: Smithsonian Institution Press, 1981.
Hirschberg, Walter. "Bernard Ankermann." *Zeitschrift für Ethnologie* 70 (1938): 129–43.
———. "The Viennese Study Group for African Culture History (WAFAK) during the Years 1930–1932." In *Ethnohistory in Vienna: Forum,* vol. 9, ed. Karl Wernhart, 15–35. Aachen: Editien Herodot, 1987.

———. "'Culture and Dynamics' in Ethnohistory." In *Ethnohistory in Vienna: Forum*, vol. 9, ed. Karl Wernhart, 45–53. Aachen: Editien Herodot, 1987.
Hog, Michael. *Ziele und Konzeptionen der Völkerkundemuseen in ihrer historischen Entwicklung.* Frankfurt am Main: Rit G. Fischer Verlag, 1981.
Honigsheim, Paul. "Adolf Bastian und die Entwicklung der ethnologischen Soziologie." *Kölner Vierteljahrshefte für Soziologie* 6 (1926): 59–76.
Huck, Gerhard. *Sozialgeschichte der Freizeit: Untersuchungen zum Wandel der Alltagskultur in Deutschland.* Wuppertal: Hammer, 1980.
Hueppe, Ferdinand. "Über die modernen Kolonisationsbestrebungen und die Anpassungsmöglichkeiten der Europäer in den Tropen." *Berliner klinische Wochenschrift* 38 (1901): 7–12, 46–51.
Humboldt, Wilhelm von. "Plan einer vergleichenden Anthropologie." In *Wilhelm von Humboldt—Werke in fünf Bänden*, ed. Andreas Flitner and Klaus Giel, vol. 1. Stuttgart: Cotta'sche Buchhandlung, 1980.
Irek, Malgorzata. "From Spree to Harlem: German Nineteenth Century Antiracist Ethnology and the Cultural Revival of American Blacks." Sozialanthropologische Arbeitspapiere, FU Berlin Institut für Ethnologie, Schwerpunkt Sozialanthropologie, 1990.
Jacknis, Ira. "Franz Boas and Exhibits: On the Limitations of the Museum Method of Anthropology." In *Objects and Others: Essays on Museums and Material Culture*, ed. George W. Stocking Jr., 75–111. Madison: University of Wisconsin Press, 1985.
Jackson, Robert. *The Prisoners, 1914–18.* New York: Routledge, 1989.
Jacobeit, Wolfgang, Hannjost Lixfeld, and Olaf Bockhorn, eds. *Völkische Wissenschaft: Gestalten und Tendenzen der deutschen und österreichischen Volkskunde in der ersten Hälfte des 20. Jahrhunderts.* Vienna: Böhlau, 1994.
Jaeger, Fritz. "Die Geographischen Grundlagen der Kolonisation Afrikas." In *Afrika, Europa, und Deutschland*, ed. E. Wunderlich, 105–7. Stuttgart: Fleischhauer und Spohn, 1934.
Jahn, Janheinz. *Leo Frobenius: The Demonic Child.* Trans. Reinhard Sander. Austin: African and Afro-American Studies and Research Center, University of Texas at Austin, 1974.
Jansen, Wolfgang. *Das Varieté: Die glanzvolle Geschichte einer unterhaltenden Kunst.* Berlin: Edition Hentrich, 1990.
Johnston, William M. *The Austrian Mind: An Intellectual and Social History, 1848–1938.* Berkeley and Los Angeles: University of California Press, 1972.
Jolly, Margaret. "Other Mothers: Maternal 'Insouciance' and the Depopulation Debate in Fiji and Vanuatu, 1890–1930." In *Maternities and Modernities*, ed. K. Ram and M. Jolly, 183–215. Cambridge: Cambridge University Press, 1998.
Kalmar, Ivan. "The *Völkerpsychologie* of Lazarus and Steinthal and the Modern Concept of Culture." *Journal of the History of Ideas* 48 (1987): 671–90.
Kant, Immanuel. "Von den verschiedenen Rassen der Menschen zur Ankündigung der Vorlesungen der physischen Geogaphie im Sommerhalbenjahre 1775." In *Schriften zur Anthropologie, Geschichtphilosophie, Politik und Pädagogik*, vol. 1, ed. Wilhelm Weischedel. Frankfurt am Main: Suhrkamp, 1996.

Katz, Jacob. *Out of the Ghetto: The Social Background of Jewish Emancipation, 1770–1870.* New York: Schocken, 1973.
Kelly, Alfred. *The Descent of Darwin: The Popularization of Darwinism in Germany, 1860–1914.* Chapel Hill: University of North Carolina Press, 1981.
Kennedy, Paul. *The Samoan Tangle: A Study in Anglo-German-American Relations, 1878–1900.* New York: Harper and Row/Barnes and Noble, 1974.
Klemperer, Klemens von. *Ignaz Seipel: Christian Statesman in a Time of Crisis.* Princeton: Princeton University Press, 1972.
Kluckhohn, Clyde. "Some Reflections on the Method and Theory of the Kulturkreislehre." *American Anthropologist* 38 (1936): 157–96.
Koepping, Klaus-Peter. *Adolf Bastian and the Psychic Unity of Mankind: The Foundations of Anthropology in Nineteenth Century Germany.* London: Queensland Press, 1983.
———. "Enlightenment and Romanticism in the Work of Adolf Bastian: The Historical Roots of Anthropology in the Nineteenth Century." In *Fieldwork and Footnotes: Studies in the History of European Anthropology,* ed. Han F. Vermeulen and Arturo Alvarez Roldán, 75–94. New York: Routledge, 1995.
Kolkenbrock-Netz, Jutta. "Wissenschaft als nationaler Mythos: Anmerkungen zur Haeckel-Virchow-Kontroverse auf der 50. Jahresversammlung deutscher Naturforscher und Ärzte in München (1877)." In *Nationale Mythen und Symbole in der zweiten Hälfte des 19. Jahrhunderts: Strukturen und Funktionen von Konzepten nationaler Identität,* ed. Jürgen Link and Wulf Wülfing, 212–36. Stuttgart: Klett-Cotta, 1991.
Kollmann, Julius. *Die Menschenrassen Europa's und Asien's.* Heidelberg: Universitäts-Buchdruckerei von J. Hörning, 1889.
Königliche Museen zu Berlin. *Führer durch das Museum für Völkerkunde.* 2d ed. Berlin: W. Spemann, 1887.
———. *Führer durch das Museum für Völkerkunde.* 6th ed. Berlin: W. Spemann, 1895.
———. *Führer durch das Museum für Völkerkunde.* 7th ed. Berlin: W. Spemann, 1898.
———. *Führer durch das Museum für Völkerkunde.* 8th ed. Berlin: W. Spemann, 1900.
———. *Führer durch das Museum für Völkerkunde.* 13th ed. Berlin: W. Spemann, 1906.
Koppers, Wilhelm. *Primitive Man and His World Picture.* Trans. Edith Raybould. London: Sheed and Ward, 1952.
Koshar, Rudy. "The *Kaiserreich's* Ruins: Hope, Memory, and Political Culture in Imperial Germany." In *Society, Culture, and the State in Germany, 1870–1930,* ed. Geoff Eley, 487–512. Ann Arbor: University of Michigan Press, 1996.
———. *Germany's Transient Pasts: Preservation and National Memory in the Twentieth Century.* Chapel Hill: University of North Carolina Press, 1998.
Kotzebue, Otto von. *Entdeckungs-Reise in die Süd-See und nach der Berings-Strasse zur Erforschung einer nordoestlichen Durchfahrt. Unternommen in den Jahren 1815, 1816, 1817 and 1818, auf Kosten Sr. Erlaucht des Herrn Reichs-*

Kanzlers Grafen Rumanzoff auf dem Schiffe Rurick unter dem Befehle des Lieutenants der Russisch-Kaiserlichen Marine Otto von Kotzebue... Weimar: Hoffman, 1821.

Krämer, Augustin. *Die Samoa-Inseln. Entwurf einer Monographie mit besonderer Berücksichtigung Deutsch-Samoas.* Vol. 1, *Verfassung, Stammbäume und Überlieferungen.* Vol. 2, *Ethnographie.* Stuttgart: E. Schweizerbartsche Verlagsbuchhandlung (E. Naegele), 1902–3.

———. *Hawaii, Ostmikronesien und Samoa. Meine zweite Südseereise (1897–1899) zum Studium der Atolle und ihrer Bewohner.* Stuttgart: Strecker und Schröder, 1906.

Krieger, K., and G. Koch. *Hundert Jahre Museum für Völkerkunde Berlin.* Berlin: Reimer, 1973.

Kroeber, Alfred. "Franz Boas: The Man." *American Anthropologist,* Memoir Series no. 61 (1943): 5–26.

Kuklick, Henrika. *The Savage Within: The Social History of British Anthropology.* Cambridge: Cambridge University Press, 1991.

———. "After Ishmail: The Fieldwork Tradition and Its Future." In *Anthropological Locations: Boundaries and Grounds of a Field Science,* ed. Akhil Gupta and James Ferguson, 47–65. Berkeley and Los Angeles: University of California Press, 1997.

Kuper, Adam. *Anthropology and Anthropologists: The Modern British School.* London: Routledge and Kegan Paul, 1983.

Lane, Adolf. "Deutsche Bauernkolonien im alten Russland." In *Unter Fremden Völkern: Eine neue Völkerkunde,* ed. Wilhelm Doegen, 267–74. Berlin: Otto Stollberg Verlag für Politik und Wirtschaft, 1925.

Lang, Andrew. *The Making of Religion.* London, 1898.

———. Review of Schmidt, *L'Origine de d'Idee de Dieu. Folk-Lore* 21 (1910): 516–23.

Lau, Brigitte. "Uncertain Certainties—the Herero-German War of 1904." In *History and Historiography.* Windhoek: Discourse/MSORP, 1995.

Lazarus, Moritz. "Über den Begriff und die Möglichkeit einer Völkerpsychologie." *Deutsches Museum: Zeitschrift für Literatur, Kunst und öffentliches Leben* 1 (1851): 113–26.

———. *Treu und Frei: Gesammelte Reden und Vorträge über Juden und Judentum.* Leipzig: Winter'sche Verlagshandlung, 1887.

———. *Die Ethik des Judentums.* 1898; Frankfurt am Main: J. Kauffmann, 1911.

———. *Moritz Lazarus' Lebenserinnerungen, bearbeitet von Nahida Lazarus und Alfred Leicht.* Berlin: Georg Reimer, 1906.

———. *Aus meiner Jugend: Autobiographie von M. Lazarus.* Ed. Nahida Lazarus. Frankfurt am Main: J. Kauffmann, 1913.

Lazarus, Moritz, and Heymann Steinthal. "Einleitende Gedanken über Völkerpsychologie, als Einladung zu einer Zeitschrift für Völkerpsychologie und Sprachwissenschaft." *Zeitschrift für Völkerpsychologie und Sprachwissenschaft* 1 (1860): 1–73.

Le Roy, Alexandre. *Les Pygmées Négrilles d'Afrique et Négritos de l'Asie.* c. 1900. Tours: A. Meme & Fils.
Leary, David. "The Historical Foundation of Herbart's Mathematization of Psychology." *Journal of the History of the Behavioral Sciences* 16 (1980): 150–63.
Leicht, Alfred. "Register zu Band I–XX: A. Autorenverzeichnis." *Zeitschrift für Völkerpsychologie und Sprachwissenschaft* 20 (1890): 373–86.
Levinas, Emmanuel. "The Temptation of Temptation." In *Nine Talmudic Readings,* trans. Annette Aronowicz. Bloomington: Indiana University Press, 1990.
Lichtblau, Albert. *Antisemitismus und soziale Spannung in Berlin und Wien, 1867–1914.* Berlin: Metropol, 1994.
Lichtenstein, Ernst. *Zur Entwicklung des Bildungsbegriffes von Meister Eckhart bis Hegel.* Heidelberg: Quelle und Meyer, 1966.
Liebersohn, Harry. "Discovering Indigenous Nobility: Tocqueville, Chamisso, and Romantic Travel Writing." *American Historical Review* 99 (June 1994): 746–66.
———. *Aristocratic Encounters: European Travelers and North American Indians.* Cambridge: Cambridge University Press, 1998.
Lifton, Robert Jay. *The Nazi Doctors: Medical Killing and the Psychology of Genocide.* New York: Basic Books, 1986.
Lincoln, Louise. "Art and Money in New Ireland: History, Economy, and Cultural Production." In *Assemblage of Spirits: Idea and Image in New Ireland.* New York: Georg Braziller, 1987.
Lindenberger, Thomas. *Straßenpolitik: Zur Sozialgeschichte der öffentlichen Ordnung in Berlin, 1900–1914.* Bonn: Verlag J. H. W. Dietz Nachfolger, 1995.
Lindfors, Bernth, ed. *Africans on Stage: Studies in Ethnological Show Business.* Bloomington: Indiana University Press, 1999.
Linimayr, Peter. *Wiener Völkerkunde im Nationalsozialismus: Ansätze zu einer NS-Wissenschaft.* Frankfurt am Main: Peter Lang, 1994.
Liss, Julia. "The Cosmopolitan Imagination: Franz Boas and the Development of American Anthropology." Ph.D. diss., University of California, Berkeley, 1990.
———. "German Culture and German Science in the *Bildung* of Franz Boas." In *Volksgeist as Method and Ethic: Essays on Boasian Ethnography and the German Anthropological Tradition,* ed. George W. Stocking Jr., 155–84. Madison: University of Wisconsin Press, 1996.
Livingston, David. "Human Acclimatization: Perspectives on a Contested Field of Inquiry in Science, Medicine and Geography." *History of Science* 25 (1987): 359–94.
Lomas, Peter. "The Early Contact Period in Northern New Ireland (Papua New Guinea): From Wild Frontier to Plantation Economy." *Ethnohistory* 28 (1981): 1–21.
Loomba, Ania. *Colonialism/Postcolonialism.* London: Routledge, 1998.
Lösch, Niels. *Rasse als Konstrukt: Leben und Werk Eugen Fischers.* Frankfurt am Main: Peter Lang, 1997.

Lowie, Robert. *The History of Ethnological Theory.* New York: Holt, Rinehart and Winston, 1937.

———. "The Progress of Science: Franz Boas, Anthropologist." *Scientific Monthly* 56 (1943): 184.

Lugere, Vicki. "The Native Mother." In *The Cambridge History of Pacific Islanders,* ed. Donald Denoon et al., 280–87. Cambridge: Cambridge University Press, 1997.

Luschan, Felix von. "Die anthropologische Stellung der Juden." *Correspondenz-Blatt der Deutschen Anthropologischen Gesellschaft* 23 (1892): 95.

———. *Beiträge zur Völkerkunde der Deutschen Schutzgebiete. Erweiterte Sonderausgabe aus dem "Amtlichen Bericht über die Erste Deutsche Kolonial-Austellung" in Treptow 1896.* Berlin: Dietrich Reimer, 1897.

———. "Anthropologie, Ethnologie und Urgeschichte." In *Anleitung zu Wissenschaftlichen Beobachtungen auf Reisen in Einzel-Abhandlungen,* ed. Georg von Neumayer, 1–123. 3d ed. Hannover: Dr. Max Jänecke, Verlagsbuchhandlung, 1906.

———. *Kriegsgefangene, Ein Beitrag zur Völkerkunde im Weltkriege: Einführung in die Grundzüge der Anthropologie.* Berlin: Dietrich Reimer [Ernst Vohsen], 1917.

Lustig, Wolfgang. "'Außer ein paar zerbrochnen Pfeilen nichts zu verteilen . . .': Ethnographische Sammlungen aus den deutschen Kolonien und ihre Verteilung an Museen 1889 bis 1914." *Mitteilungen aus dem Museum für Völkerkunde Hamburg N.F.* 18 (1988): 157–78.

Maase, Kaspar. *Grenzenloses Vergnügen: Der Aufstieg der Massenkultur 1850–1970.* Frankfurt am Main: Fischer Taschenbuch Verlag, 1997.

MacLeod, Roy. "On Visiting the 'Moving Metropolis': Reflections on the Architecture of Imperial Science." In *Scientific Colonialism,* ed. N. Reingold and M. Rothenberg, 217–50. Washington, D.C.: Smithsonian Institute, 1987.

Magnus, Shulamit. *Jewish Emancipation in a German City: Cologne, 1798–1871.* Stanford: Stanford University Press, 1997.

Malinowski, Bronislaw. *Argonauts of the Western Pacific.* New York: E. P. Dutton, 1961.

Mannschatz, Hans-Christian. "Mit Grassi auf dem Dach und Klinger im Hof— 100 Jahre Wilhelm-Leuscher-Platz 10/11: Die Geschichte eines Hauses," 1996 (unpublished paper in the Leipzig Staatsbibliothek).

Marchand, Suzanne. "The Rhetoric of Artifacts and the Decline of Classical Humanism: The Case of Josef Strzygowski." *History and Theory* 33 (1994): 106–30.

———. *Down from Olympus: Archaeology and Philhellenism in Germany, 1750–1970.* Princeton: Princeton University Press, 1996.

———. "Orientalism as *Kulturpolitik:* German Archeology and Cultural Imperialism in Asia Minor." In *Volksgeist as Method and Ethic: Essays on Boasian Ethnography and the German Anthropological Tradition,* ed. George W. Stocking Jr., 198–336. Madison: University of Wisconsin Press, 1996.

———. "Leo Frobenius and the Revolt against the West." *Journal of Contemporary History* 32 (1997): 153–70.

Mark, Joan. *The King of the World in the Land of the Pygmies.* Lincoln: University of Nebraska Press, 1995.

Martin, Rudolf. *Lehrbuch der Anthropologie in systematischer Darstellung.* Jena: Gustav Fischer, 1914.

———. "Anthropologische Untersuchungen an Kriegsgefangenen." *Die Umschau* 19 (1915): 1017.

———. "Germanen, Kelten, und Slaven." *Die Umschau* 20 (1916): 201–4.

Mason, Otis. "The Occurrence of Similar Inventions in Areas Widely Apart." *Science* 9 (1887): 534.

Massin, Benoit. "From Virchow to Fischer: Physical Anthropology and 'Modern Race Theories' in Wilhelmine Germany." In *Volksgeist as Method and Ethic: Essays on Boasian Ethnography and the German Anthropological Tradition,* ed. George W. Stocking Jr., 79–154. Madison: University of Wisconsin Press, 1996.

McCarthy, Daniel. *The Prisoner of War in Germany.* New York: Moffat, Yard, 1917.

McClintock, Anne. *Imperial Leather: Race, Gender, and Sexuality in the Colonial Contest.* New York: Routledge, 1995.

Mead, Margaret. "Apprenticeship under Boas." In *The Anthropology of Franz Boas: Essays on the Centennial of his Birth,* ed. Walter Goldschmidt, 29–45. Memoir no. 89 of the American Anthropological Association (1959).

———. *The Social Organization of Manua.* Rev. ed. Honolulu: Bishop Museum Press, 1969.

Meine Kriegs-Erlebnisse in Deutsch-Südwest-Afrika, Von Einem Offizier Der Schutztruppe. Minden, 1907.

Meinecke, Gustav, ed. *Deutschland und seine Kolonien im Jahre 1896.* Berlin: Dietrich Reimer, 1897.

Melk-Koch, Marion. *Auf der Suche nach der menschlichen Gesellschaft: Richard Thurnwald.* Berlin: Reimer Verlag, 1989.

———. "Zwei Österreicher nehmen Einfluß auf die Ethnologie in Deutschland: Felix von Luschan und Richard Thurnwald." In *Kulturwissenschaften im Vielvölkerstaat: Zur Geschichte der Ethnologie und verwandter Gebiete in Österreich, ca. 1780 bis 1918,* ed. Britta Rupp-Eisenreich and Justin Stagl, 132–40. Vienna: Boehlau, 1995.

———. "Melanesian Art—or just Stones and Junk? Richard Thurnwald and the Question of Art in Melanesia." *Pacific Arts* 21–22 (2000): 53–68.

Melton, James Van Horn. "From Folk History to Structural History: Otto Brunner (1898–1982) and the Radical-Conservative Roots of German Social History." In *Pathos of Continuity: Central European Historiography from the 1930s to the 1950s,* ed. Hartmut Lehmann and James Van Horn Melton, 263–92. Cambridge: Cambridge University Press, 1994.

Metzger, Fritz. *Narro and His Clan.* Windhoek: SWA Scientific Society, 1950.

Meyer, Michael. *The Origins of the Modern Jew: Jewish Identity and European Culture in Germany, 1749–1824.* Detroit: Wayne State University Press, 1967.

———. *Response to Modernity: A History of the Reform Movement in Judaism.* Oxford: Oxford University Press, 1988.
Meyer, Michael, and Michael Brenner, eds. *German-Jewish History in Modern Times.* Vol. 2, *Emancipation and Acculturation: 1780–1871.* New York: Columbia University Press, 1997.
Miller, Michael. *The Bon Marché: Bourgeois Culture and the Department Store, 1869–1920.* Princeton: Princeton University Press, 1981.
Montague, Ashley. *Man's Most Dangerous Myth: The Fallacy of Race.* Cleveland: World Pub. Co., 1964.
Morrell, W. P. *Britain in the Pacific Islands.* Oxford: Clarendon, 1960.
Mosen, Markus. *Der koloniale Traum: Angewandte Ethnologie im Nationalsozialismus.* Bonn: Holos, 1991.
Mosse, George. *Towards the Final Solution: A History of European Racism.* Madison: University of Wisconsin Press, 1985.
Mühlberg, Dietrich. *Arbeiterleben um 1900.* 2d ed. Berlin: Dietz Verlag, 1985.
Mühlmann, Wilhelm E. *Geschichte der Anthropologie.* 2d ed. Frankfurt am Main: Enke, 1968.
Müller-Hill, Benno. *Murderous Science: Elimination by Scientific Selection of Jews, Gypsies, and Others in Germany, 1933–1945.* Trans. George R. Fraser. Plainview, N.Y.: Cold Springs Harbor Laboratory Press, 1998.
Munro, Doug, and Stewart Firth. "Company Strategies—Colonial Policies." In *Labour in the South Pacific,* ed. Clive Moore, Jacqueline Leckie, and Doug Munro, 3–29. Townsville: James Cook University, 1990.
Neumann, Klaus. "Schlemihl's Travels: 'Hasty Contact' at Rapanui and the Context of a European Biography." *History and Anthropology* 10 (1997): 139–84.
———. "The Stench of the Past: Revisionism in Pacific Islands and Australian History." *Contemporary Pacific* 10 (1998): 31–64.
Nyhart, Lynn. "Civic and Economic Zoology in Nineteenth-Century Germany: The 'Living Communities' of Karl Möbius." *Isis* 89 (1998): 605–30.
Oelze, Berthold. *Wilhelm Wundt: Die Konzeption der Völkerpsychologie.* Münster: Waxmann, 1991.
Officieller Führer durch die Transvaal-Ausstellung am Kurfürstendamm und Stadtbahnhof "Savigny Platz" 1897. Berlin: Weylandt und Bauchwitz, 1897.
Olesko, Kathryn. "Civic Culture and Calling in the Königsberg Period." In *Universalgenie Helmholtz: Rückblick nach 100 Jahren,* ed. Lorenz Krüger, 22–42. Berlin: Akademie Verlag, 1994.
Oliver, Douglas. *Ancient Tahitian Society.* Vol. 3, *Rise of the Pomares.* Honolulu: University of Hawaii Press, 1974.
Osborne, Michael. *Nature, the Exotic, and the Science of French Colonialism.* Bloomington: Indiana University Press, 1994.
Osterhammel, Jürgen. *Kolonialismus. Geschichte-Formen-Folgen,* Munich: C. H. Beck, 1995.
Pagden, Anthony. *The Fall of Natural Man: The American Indian and the Origins of Comparative Ethnology.* Cambridge: Cambridge University Press, 1982.

Parkinson, Richard. *Dreissig Jahre in der Südsee.* Stuttgart: Strecker und Schröder Verlag, 1907.
Pels, Peter, and Oscar Salemink, eds. *Colonial Subjects: Essays on the Practical History of Anthropology.* Ann Arbor: University of Michigan Press, 1999.
Penny, H. Glenn, III. "Municipal Displays: Civic Self-Promotion and the Development of German Ethnographic Museums, 1870–1914." *Social Anthropology* 6 (1998): 157–68.
———. "Cosmopolitan Visions and Municipal Displays: Museums, Markets, and the Ethnographic Project in Germany, 1868–1914." Ph.D. diss., University of Illinois, 1999.
———. "Fashioning Local Identities in an Age of Nation-Building: Museums, Cosmopolitan Traditions, and Intra-German Competition." *German History* 17 (1999): 488–504.
Pöch, Rudolf. "I. Bericht über die von der Wiener Anthropolg. Gesellschaft in d. k. u. k. Kriegsgefangenlagern veranlaßten Studien." *Mitteilungen der anthropologischen Gesellschaft Wien* 45 (1915): 219–35.
———. "II. Bericht über die von der Wiener Anthropologische Gesellschaft in den k. u. k. Kriegsgefangenenlagern veranlaßten Studien." *Mitteilungen der anthropologischen Gesellschaft Wien* 46 (1916): 107–31.
———. "Anthropologische Studien an Kriegsgefangenen." *Die Umschau* 20 (1916): 989.
———. "III. Bericht über die von der Wiener Anthropologische Gesellschaft in den k. u. k. Kriegsgefangenenlagern veranlaßten Studien." *Mitteilungen der anthropologischen Gesellschaft* 47 (1917): 77–100.
———. Review of O. Stiehl's "Unsere Feinde." *Mitteilungen der anthropologischen Gesellschaft Wien* 47 (1917): 122.
———. "IV. Bericht über die von der Wiener Anthropologischen Gesellschaft in d. k. u. k. Kriegsgefangenlagern veranlaßten Studien." *Mitteilungen der anthropologischen Gesellschaft Wien* 48 (1918): 146–61.
Powell, John Wesley. "Museums of Ethnology and Their Classification." *Science* 9 (1887): 612–14.
Proctor, Robert. "From *Anthropologie* to *Rassenkunde* in the German Anthropological Tradition." In *Bones, Bodies, Behavior: Essays on Biological Anthropology,* ed. George W. Stocking Jr., 138–79. Madison: University of Wisconsin Press, 1988.
———. *Racial Hygiene: Medicine under the Nazis.* Cambridge: Harvard University Press, 1988.
Pulzer, Peter. *The Rise of Political Anti-Semitism in Germany and Austria.* New York: John Wiley and Sons, 1964.
Quatrefages, A. de. *The Pygmies.* Trans. Frederick Starr. New York, 1895.
Ranke, Johannes. *Der Mensch.* Vol. 2. Leipzig: Verlag des Bibliographischen Institutes, 1887.
Reche, Otto. "Zur Anthropologie der jüngeren Steinzeit in Schlesien und Böhmen." *Archiv für Anthropologie* 35 (1908): 220–37.
Reinharz, Jehuda, and Walter Schatzberg, eds. *The Jewish Response to German*

Culture: From the Enlightenment to the Second World War. Hanover, N.H.: University Press of New England, 1985.
Richardson, Ruth. *Death, Dissection, and the Destitute.* Chicago: University of Chicago Press, 2000.
Rieke-Müller, Annelore, and Lothar Dittrich. *Der Löwe Brüllt Nebenan: Die Gründung Zoologischer Gärten im deutschsprachigen Raum, 1833–1869.* Cologne: Böhlau Verlag, 1998.
Ripley, William. *The Races of Europe: A Sociological Study.* New York: D. Appleton, 1899.
Rivinius, P. Karl, SVD. *Die Anfänge des "Anthropos": Briefe von P. Wilhelm Schmidt an Georg Freiherrn von Hertling aus den Jahren 1904 bis 1908 und andere Dokumente.* St. Augustin bei Bonn: Steyler, 1981.
Roberts, J. S. *Drink, Temperance, and the Working-Class in Nineteenth-Century Germany.* Boston: Allen and Unwin, 1984.
Rodenwaldt, Ernst. "Das Geschlechtsleben der europäischen Frau in den Tropen." *Archiv für Rassen- und Gesellschaftsbiologie* 26 (1932): 173–94.
———. "Wie bewahrt der Deutsche die Reinheit seines Blutes in Ländern mit farbiger Bevölkerung." *Jahrbuch für auslandsdeutsche Sippenkunde* (1936): 62–67.
Roider, Karl. "The Oriental Academy in the *Theresienzeit.*" *Topic* 34 (fall 1980): 19–28.
Rosaldo, Renato. *Culture and Truth: The Remaking of Social Analysis.* Boston: Beacon Press, 1989.
Rosenbaum, Ron. "The Great Ivy League Nude Posture Photo Scandal." *New York Times Magazine,* 15 January 1995.
Rudé, George. *The Crowd in History: A Study of Popular Disturbances in France and England, 1730–1848.* New York: Wiley, 1964.
Rudner, Ione, and Jalmar Rudner, eds. *The Journal of Gustaf de Vylder, Naturalist in South-Western Africa, 1873–1875.* Cape Town: Van Riebeeck Society, 1998.
Rupp-Eisenreich, Britta, and Justin Stagl, eds. *Kulturwissenschaften im Vielvölkerstaat: Zur Geschichte der Ethnologie und verwandter Gebiete in Österreich, ca. 1780 bis 1918.* Vienna: Boehlau, 1995.
Rust, Hans. "Die Gruendung der S.W.A. Wissenschaftlichen Gesellschaft." In *Ein Leben für Südwestafrika,* ed. W. Drascher and H. J. Rust, 137–48. Windhoek: SWA Scientific Society, 1961.
———. "The South West Africa Scientific Society." *South West Africa Annual.* Windhoek: S. W. A. Publications, 1974.
Rydell, Robert. *All the World's a Fair: Visions of Empire at American International Expositions, 1876–1916.* Chicago: University of Chicago Press, 1984.
Ryding, J. "Alternatives in Nineteenth-Century German Ethnology: A Case Study in the Sociology of Science." *Sociologus* 25 (1975): 1–28.
Sahlins, Marshall. *Islands of History.* Chicago: University of Chicago Press, 1985.
Said, Edward. *Orientalism.* New York: Vintage, 1978.
———. "Representing the Colonized: Anthropology's Interlocutors." *Critical Inquiry* 15 (1989): 205–25.

Sajdi, Amadou Booker. *Das Bild des Negro-Afrikaners in der deutschen Kolonialliteratur: Ein Beitrag zur literarischen Imagologie Schwarzafrikas.* Berlin: Dietrich Reimer, 1985.
Schebesta, Paul. *Among the Forest Dwarfs of Malaya.* London, 1928.
———. "P. W. Schmidts Studie über den Totemismus der Äquatorialen Waldneger und Pygmäen." In *Anthropica: Gedenkschrift zum 100. Geburtstag von P. Wilhelm Schmidt,* ed. Anthropos-Institut, 303–22. Studia Instituti Anthropos, vol. 21. St. Augustin bei Bonn: Verlag des Anthropos-Institut, 1968.
Scheffler, Karl. *Berliner Museumskrieg.* Berlin: Cassirer, 1921.
Scheidt, Walter. *Allgemeine Rassenkunde: Als Einführung in das Studium der Menschenrassen.* Munich: J. F. Lehmann, 1925.
Schleip, Dietrich. "Ozeanistische Ethnologie und Koloniale Praxis: Das Beispiel Augustin Krämer." M.A. thesis, Tübingen University, 1989.
Schmidt, Pater Wilhelm, SVD. "Puluga, the Supreme Being of the Andamenese." *Man* 2 (1910): 2–7.
———. *Die Stellung der Pygmäenvölker in der Entwicklungsgeschichte des Menschen.* Stuttgart: Strecker und Schroder, 1910.
———. "Die kulturhistorische Methode in der Ethnologie." *Anthropos* 6 (1911): 1010–36.
———. "Is Ethnological Information Coming from Missionaries Sufficiently Reliable?" *Anthropos* 6 (1911): 430–31.
———. *Der Ursprung der Gottesidee: Eine historische-kritische und positive Studie.* Vol. 1, *Historisch-kritischer Teil.* Münster, 1912.
———. *Rassen und Völker in Vorgeschichte und Geschichte des Abendlandes.* Vol. 1, *Die Rassen des Abendlandes.* Lucerne, 1946.
———. *Erbe und Zukunft des Abendlandes.* Bern, 1948.
———. *Das Mutterrecht.* Studia Instituti Anthropos, vol. 10. Vienna, 1955.
———. *Wege der Kulturen: Gesammelte Aufsätze.* St. Augustin bei Bonn: Verlag des Anthropos-Instituts, 1964.
Schnee, Heinrich, ed. *Deutsches Kolonial-Lexikon.* Leipzig: Quelle und Meyer, 1920.
Schroeder, Leopold von. *Arische Religion.* Vol. 1. Leipzig, 1914.
———. *Lebenserinnerungen.* Leipzig, 1921.
Schultze, Leonhard. "Einleitung." *Zoologische und anthropologische Ergebnisse einer Forschungsreise im westlichen und zentralen Südafrika ausgeführt in den Jahren 1903–1905.* Jena: Gustav Fischer, 1908.
Schultze-Ewerth, L., and L. Adam, eds. *Das Eingeborenenrecht. Sitten und Gewohnheitsrechte der Eingeborenen derehemaligen deutschen Kolonien in Afrika un in der Südsee.* 2 vols. Stuttgart, 1930.
Schwalbe, Gustav. "Über eine umfassende Untersuchung der physisch-anthropologischen Beschaffenheit der jetzigen Bevölkerung des Deutschen Reiches." *Correspondez-Blatt der Deutschen Anthropologischen Gesellschaft* 34 (1903): 73–84.
Seed, Patricia. *Ceremonies of Possession in Europe's Conquest of the New World, 1492–1640.* Cambridge: Cambridge University Press, 1995.

Seymour, John. *One Man's Africa*. London: Eyre and Spottiswoode, 1955.
Sharpe, Eric. *Comparative Religion: A History*. London: Scribner's, 1975.
Singer, Hermann. "Die Verwendung des Afrikafonds." *Globus* 97 (1910): 110–11.
Sippel, Harald. "Rassismus, Protektionismus oder Humanität? Die gesetzlichen Verbot der Anwerbung von 'Eingeborenen' zu Schaustellungszwecken in den deutschen Kolonien." In *Kolonialausstellungen—Begegnung mit Afrika?* ed. Robert Debusmann and János Riesz, 43–64. Frankfurt am Main: IKO, Verlag für Interkulturelle Kommunikation, 1995.
Smith, Woodruff. "The Social and Political Origins of German Diffusionist Ethnology." *Journal of the History of the Behavioral Sciences* 14 (1978): 103–12.
———. "Friedrich Ratzel and the Origins of *Lebensraum*." *German Studies Review* 3 (1980): 51–68.
———. "Anthropology and German Colonialism." In *Germans in the Tropics: Essays in German Colonial History*, ed. Arthur J. Knoll and Lewis H. Gann, 39–58. Westport, Conn.: Greenwood Press, 1987.
———. *Politics and the Sciences of Culture in Germany, 1840–1920*. Oxford: Oxford University Press, 1991.
Smolka, Wolfgang. *Völkerkunde in München: Voraussetzungen, Möglichkeiten und Entwicklungslinien ihrer Institutionalisierung (c. 1850–1933)*. Berlin: Dunker und Humboldt, 1994.
Sorkin, David. "Wilhelm von Humboldt: The Theory and Practice of Self-Formation *(Bildung)*, 1791–1810." *Journal of the History of Ideas* 44 (1983): 55–73.
———. *The Transformation of German Jewry, 1780–1840*. Oxford: Oxford University Press, 1987.
Spannus, Otto. "Otto Reche als Völkerkundler." In *Kultur und Rasse*, ed. M. Hesch and G. Spannus, 249–53. Munich: J. F. Lehmann, 1939.
Speed, Richard, III. *Prisoners, Diplomats, and the Great War: a Study in the Diplomacy of Captivity*. Westport, Conn.: Greenwood Press, 1990.
Spivak, Gayatri. *A Critique of Postcolonial Reason: Toward a History of the Vanishing Present*. Cambridge: Harvard University Press, 1999.
Spraul, Gunter. "Der 'Völkermord' an den Herero: Untersuchungen zu einer neuen Kontinuitätsthese." *Geschichte in Wissenschaft und Unterricht* 39 (1988): 713–39.
Staehelin, Balthasar. *Völkerschauen im Zoologischen Garten Basel 1879–1935*. Basel: Basler Afrika Bibliographien, 1993.
Steinen, Karl von den. "Gedächtnisrede auf Adolf Bastian." *Zeitschrift für Ethnologie* 37 (1905): 236–49.
Steinmetzler, Johannes. *Die Anthropogeographie Friedrich Ratzels und ihre ideengeschichtlichen Wurzeln*. Bonn: Geographisches Institut, 1956.
Steinthal, Heymann. *Die Sprachwissenschaft Wilh. v. Humboldt's und die Hegel'sche Philosophie*. Berlin: Ferdinand Dümmler, 1848.
———. "Zur Charakteristik der semitischen Völker." *Zeitschrift für Völkerpsychologie und Sprachwissenschaft* 1 (1860): 328–45.
———. Review of *Das Judenthum und seine Geschichte*, by A. Geiger. *Zeitschrift für Völkerpsychologie und Sprachwissenschaft* 4 (1866): 225–34.

———. *Die Mande-Neger-Sprachen: Psychologisch und phonetisch betrachtet.* Berlin: Ferdinand Dümmler's Verlagsbuchhandlung, 1867.

———. "Der Semitismus, mit Rücksicht auf: Eberhard Schrader, *Die Höllenfahrt der Istar: Ein altbabylonisches Epos.*" *Zeitschrift für Völkerpsychologie und Sprachwissenschaft* 8 (1875): 339–50.

———. Review of *Philo, Strauß und Renan und das Urchristentum* and *Christus und die Cäsaren: Der Ursprung des Christentums aus dem römischen Griechentum,* by Bruno Bauer. *Zeitschrift für Völkerpsychologie und Sprachwissenschaft* 10 (1878): 409–69.

———. "Das fünfte Buch Mose: Ein Beitrag zur epischen Frage." *Zeitschrift für Völkerpsychologie und Sprachwissenschaft* 11 (1880): 1–28.

———. "Die erzählenden Stücke im fünften Buch Mose I." *Zeitschrift für Völkerpsychologie und Sprachwissenschaft* 12 (1881): 253–89.

———. "Die erzählenden Stücke im fünften Buch Mose II." *Zeitschrift für Völkerpsychologie und Sprachwissenschaft* 20 (1890): 47–87.

———. Review of *Jüdische Homiletik, nebst einer Auswahl von Texten und Themen,* by S. Maybaum. *Zeitschrift für Völkerpsychologie und Sprachwissenschaft* 20 (1890): 359–70.

———. *Über Juden und Judentum: Vorträge und Aufsätze, herausgegeben vom Gustav Karpeles.* Berlin: Poppelauer, 1906.

———, ed. *Die sprachphilosophischen Werke Wilhelm's von Humboldt.* Berlin: Ferdinand Dümmler, 1883.

Stephan, Emil. *Südseekunst. Beiträge zur Kunst des Bismarckarchipels und zur Urgeschichte der Kunst überhaupt.* Berlin: Reimer, 1907.

Stephan, Emil, and Fritz Graebner. *Neu-Mecklenburg (Bismarckarchipel). Die Küste von Umuddu bis Kap St. Georg. Forschungsergebnisse bei den Vermessungsarbeiten von SMS Möwe im Jahre 1904.* Berlin: Reimer, 1907.

Stocking, George W., Jr. *Race, Culture, and Evolution: Essays in the History of Anthropology.* Chicago: University of Chicago Press, 1968.

———. "The Aims of Boasian Ethnography: Creating the Materials for Traditional Humanistic Scholarship." *History of Anthropology Newsletter* 4 (1977): 4–5.

———. *Victorian Anthropology.* New York: Free Press, 1987.

———. *The Ethnographer's Magic and Other Essays in the History of Anthropology.* Madison: University of Wisconsin Press, 1992.

———. *After Tylor: British Social Anthropology, 1888–1951.* Madison: University of Wisconsin Press, 1995.

———, ed. *A Franz Boas Reader: The Shaping of American Anthropology, 1883–1911.* Chicago: University of Chicago Press, 1974.

———, ed. *Functionalism Historicized: Essays on British Social Anthropology.* History of Anthropology, no. 2. Madison: University of Wisconsin Press, 1984.

———, ed. *Objects and Others: Essays on Museums and Material Culture.* History of Anthropology, no. 3. Madison: University of Wisconsin Press, 1985.

———, ed. *Bones, Bodies, Behavior: Essays on Biological Anthropology.* History of Anthropology, no. 5. Madison: University of Wisconsin Press, 1988.

———, ed. *Colonial Situations: Essays on the Contextualization of Ethnographic Knowledge*. History of Anthropology, no. 7. Madison: University of Wisconsin Press, 1991.

———, ed. *Volksgeist as Method and Ethic: Essays on Boasian Ethnography and the German Anthropological Tradition*. History of Anthropology, no. 8. Madison: University of Wisconsin Press, 1996.

Stokvis, Barend Joseph. *De invloed von tropische gewesten op den mensch in verband met colonistie en gezondheid. Drei vordrachten*. Haarlem, 1894.

Stoler, Ann. *Race and the Education of Desire: Foucault's History of Sexuality and the Colonial Order of Things*. Durham: Duke University Press, 1995.

Straube, Helmut. "Leo Frobenius (1873–1938)." In *Klassiker der Kulturanthropologie von Montaigne bis Margaret Mead*, ed. Wolfgang Marschall, 152–69. Munich: C. H. Beck, 1990.

Taschwer, Klaus. "'Anthropologie ins Volk': Zur Ausstellungspolitik einer anwendbaren Wissenschaft bis 1945." In *Politik der Präsentation: Museum und Ausstellung in Österreich, 1918–1945*, ed. Herbert Posch and Gottfried Fliedl, 238–60. Vienna: Turid & Kant, 1996.

Taussig, Michael. *Shamanism, Colonialism, and the Wild Man: A Study in Terror and Healing*. Chicago: University of Chicago Press, 1987.

Thiel, Josef Franz. "Der Urmonotheismus des P. Wilhelm Schmidt und seine Geschichte." In *Kulturwissenschaften im Vielvölkerstaat: Zur Geschichte der Ethnologie und verwandter Gebiete in Österreich, ca. 1780 bis 1918*, ed. Britta Rupp-Eisenreich and Justin Stagl, 256–67. Vienna: Boehlau, 1995.

Thode-Arora, Hilke. *Für fünfzig Pfennig um die Welt: Die Hagenbeckschen Völkerschauen*. Frankfurt am Main: Campus, 1989.

———. "'Characteristische Gestalten des Volkslebens': Die Hagenbeckschen Südasien-, Orient-, und Afrika-Völkerschauen." In *Fremde Erfahrungen: Asiaten und Afrikaner in Deutschland, Österreich und in der Schweiz bis 1945*, ed. Gerhard Höpp, 109–34. Berlin: Das Arabische Buch, 1996.

Thomas, Nicholas. "Material Culture and Colonial Power: Ethnographic Collecting and the Establishment of Colonial Rule in Fiji." *Man* 24 (1989): 41–56.

———. *Entangled Objects: Exchange, Material Culture, and Colonialism in the Pacific*. Cambridge: Harvard University Press, 1991.

———. *Colonialism's Culture: Anthropology, Travel, and Government*. Cambridge: Polity Press, 1994.

Thomas, Northcote. Foreword to *The Natives of British Central Africa*, ed. Alice Werner. London: Archibald Constable, 1906.

Thompson, E. P. "The Moral Economy of the English Crowd in the Eighteenth Century." *Past and Present* 50 (1971): 76–136.

Thurnwald, Richard. "Ermittlungen über Eingeborenenrechte in der Südsee." *Zeitschrift für Vergleichende Rechtswissenschaften* 23 (1910): 309–64.

———. "Im Bismarck-Archipel und auf den Salomoneninseln, 1906–1909." *Zeitschrift für Ethnologie* 42 (1910): 98–147.

———. "Das Rechtsleben der Eingeborenen der deutschen Südseeinseln, seine geistigen und wirtschaftlichen Grundlagen. Auf Grund einer im Auftrage des

Berliner Museums für Völkerkunde unternommenen Forschungsreise 1906–1909." *Blätter für Vergleichende Rechtswissenschaft und Volkswirtschaftslehre* 6 (1910): 3–46.

"Die eingeboreren Arbeitskrafte im Südseeschutzgebiet." *Koloniale Rundschau* 10 (1910): 607–32.

Tomas, David. "Tools of the Trade: The Production of Ethnographic Observations on the Andaman Islands, 1858–1922." In *Colonial Situations: Essays on the Contextualization of Ethnographic Knowledge*, ed. George W. Stocking Jr., 75–108. Madison: University of Wisconsin Press, 1992.

Totemeyer, Andree-Jeanne. *The State of Museums in Namibia and the Need for Training in Museum's Services.* Windhoek: University of Namibia, 1999.

Trabant, Jürgen. *Traditionen Humboldts.* Frankfurt am Main: Suhrkamp, 1990.

Truettner, William. *The Natural Man Observed: A Study of Catlin's Indian Gallery.* Washington, D.C.: Smithsonian Institution, 1979.

Tschepourkovsky, E. "Zwei Haupttypen der Grossrussen, ihre geographische Verbreitung und ethnische Provenienz." *Correspondez-Blatt der Deutschen Anthropologischen Gesellschaft* 41 (1910): 84–85.

Tylor, Edward. *Primitive Culture: Researches into the Development of Mythology, Philosophy, Religion, Language, Art, and Custom.* 2 vols. London: John Murray, 1873.

———. "Professor Adolf Bastian." *Man* 75–76 (1905): 138–43.

Ucko, Sinai. "Geistesgeschichtliche Grundlagen der Wissenschaft des Judentums." In *Wissenschaft des Judentums im deutschen Sprachbereich*, ed. Kurt Wilhelm, 315–53. Tübingen: J. C. B. Mohr, 1967.

Van Warmelo, Nicholas. *Anthropology of Southern Africa in Periodicals.* Johannesburg: Witwatersrand University Press, 1977.

Vancouver, George. *A Voyage of Discovery to the North Pacific Ocean and Round the World, 1791–1795.* Ed. W. Kaye Lamb. 4 vols. London: Hakluyt Society, 1984.

Vaughan, Megan. *Curing Their Ills: Colonial Power and African Illness.* Cambridge: Polity Press, 1991.

Vedder, Heinrich. *Kort Verhale uit 'n Lang Lewe.* Cape Town: A. A. Balkema, 1957.

Vincent, Joan. *Anthropology and Politics: Visions, Traditions, and Trends.* Tucson: University of Arizona Press, 1990.

Virchow, Hans. "Graphische und plastische Aufnahme des Fusses." *Verhandlungen der Berliner Gesellschaft für Anthropologie, Ethnologie und Urgeschichte* 18 (1886): 118–24.

Virchow, Rudolf. "Anthropologie und prähistorische Forschungen." In *Anleitung zu Wissenschaftlichen Beobachtungen auf Reisen*, ed. Georg von Neumayer, 571–90. Berlin: Verlag von Robert Oppenheimer, 1875.

———. "Akklimatisation." *Verhandlungen der Berliner Gesellschaft für Anthropologie, Ethnologie und Geschichte, Zeitschrift für Ethnologie* 17 (1885): 202–14.

———. "Gesammtbericht über die Statistik der Farbe der Augen, der Haare, und der Haut der Schulkinder in Deutschland." *Correspondez-Blatt der Deutschen Anthropologischen Gesellschaft* 16 (1885): 89–100.

———. "Vortrag vor der Versammlung deutscher Naturforscher und Ärzte." *Tageblatt der 58. Versammlung deutscher Naturforscher und Ärzte in Strassburg,* 18–23 September 1885, 540–52.

———. "Zur Frankfurter Verständigung. XXII Versammlung der DAG, Danzig." *Correspondez-Blatt der Deutschen Anthropologischen Gesellschaft* 22 (1891): 121–24.

———. "Meinungen und Thatsachen in der Anthropologie." *Correspondez-Blatt der Deutschen Anthropologischen Gesellschaft* 30 (1899): 80–83.

———. "Über das Auftreten der Slaven in Deutschland." *Correspondez-Blatt der Deutschen Anthropologischen Gesellschaft* 31 (1900): 109–15.

Virchow, Rudolf, Adolf Bastian, et al. "Ratschläge für anthropologische Untersuchung auf Expeditionen der Marine." *Zeitschrift für Ethnologie* 4 (1872): 325–56.

Von Glasenapp, Helmuth. *Das Indienbild deutscher Denker.* Stuttgart: K. F. Koehler, 1960.

Weber, Max. *Gesammelte politische Schriften.* Ed. Johannes Winckelmann. Tübingen: Mohr/Siebeck, 1980.

Weindling, Paul. *Health, Race, and German Politics between National Unification and Nazism, 1870–1945.* Cambridge: Cambridge University Press, 1989.

Weinzierl, Erika. "Kirche und Politik." In *Österreich 1918–1938: Geschichte der Ersten Republik,* ed. Erika Weinzierl and Kurt Skalnik, 1:437–96. Graz: Styria, 1983.

Weissenberg, S. "Über die Formen der Hand und des Fusses." *Zeitschrift für Ethnologie* 27 (1895): 82–111.

Welsch, Robert. "One Time, One Place, Three Collections: Colonial Processes and the Shaping of Some Museum Collections from German New Guinea." In *Hunting the Gatherers,* ed. M. O'Hanlon and R. Welsch, 155–79. Oxford: Berghahn, 2001.

Weninger, Josef. "Über die Verbreitung von vorderasiatischer Rassenmerkmale." *Mitteilungen der anthropologischen Gesellschaft Wien* 48 (1918): 41–44.

Werner, Heinrich. "Hygienische Maßnahmen zum Schutze von deutschen und farbigen Frauen und Kindern im tropischen Afrika." *Deutsche medizinische Wochenschrift* 66 (1940): 729–31.

Westphal-Hellbusch, Sigrid. "Zur Geschichte des Museums." In *Hundert Jahre Museum für Völkerkunde Berlin,* ed. K. Krieger and G. Koch, 1–100. Berlin: Reimer, 1973.

Whitman, James. "From Philology to Anthropology in Mid-Nineteenth-Century Germany." In *Functionalism Historicized: Essays on British Anthropology,* ed. George W. Stocking Jr., 214–29. Madison: University of Wisconsin Press, 1984.

Wiener, Michael. *Ikonographie des Wilden: Menschen-Bilder in Ethnographie und Photographie zwischen 1850 und 1918.* Munich: Trickster Verlag, 1990.

Wildenthal, Lora. "Colonizers and Citizens: Bourgeois Women and the Woman

Question in the German Colonial Movement, 1886–1914." Ph.D. diss., University of Michigan, 1994.

———. *German Women for Empire, 1884–1945*. Durham: Duke University Press, 2001.

Winkelmann, Ingeburg. "Die Bürgeliche Ethnographie im Dienste der Kolonialpolitik des Deutschen Reiches (1870–1918)." Ph.D. diss., Humboldt-Universität zu Berlin, 1966.

Wundt, Wilhelm. *Völkerpsychologie.* 10 vols. Leipzig: Engelmann, 1900–1920.

Williams, Rosalind. *Dream Worlds: Mass Consumption in Late Nineteenth-Century France.* Berkeley and Los Angeles: University of California Press, 1982.

Willimess, Edwin. *The Kalahari Ethnographies (1896–1898) of Siegfried Passarge.* Cologne: Rudiger Koeppe, 1997.

Young, Robert. *Postcolonialism: An Historical Introduction.* Oxford: Blackwell, 2001.

Zantop, Susanne. *Colonial Fantasies: Conquest, Family, and Nation in Precolonial Germany, 1770–1870.* Durham: Duke University Press, 1997.

Zimmerman, Andrew. "Anthropology and the Place of Knowledge in Imperial Berlin." Ph.D. diss., University of California, San Diego, 1998.

———. "Anti-Semitism as Skill: Rudolf Virchow's *Schulstatistik* and the Racial Composition of Germany." *Central European History* 32 (1999): 409–29.

———. "German Anthropology and the 'Natural Peoples': The Global Context of Colonial Discourse." *European Studies Journal* 16 (1999): 85–112.

———. "Selin, Pore, and Emil Stephan in the Bismarck Archipelago: A 'Fresh and Joyful Tale' of the Origin of Fieldwork." *Pacific Arts* 21–22 (2000): 69–84.

———. *Anthropology and Antihumanism in Imperial Germany.* Chicago: University of Chicago Press, 2001.

———. "Looking beyond History: The Optics of German Anthropology and the Critique of Humanism." *Studies in History and Philosophy of Biological and Biomedical Sciences* 32 (2001): 385–411.

Zimon, Henryk. "Wilhelm Schmidt's Theory of Primitive Monotheism and Its Critique within the Vienna School of Ethnology." *Anthropos* 81 (1986): 243–60.

Zintgraff, Eugen. "Kopfmessungen, Fussumrisse und photographische Aufnahmen in Kamerun, vorzugsweise von Wei- und Kru-Negern." *Verhandlungen der Berliner Gesellschaft für Anthropologie, Ethnologie und Urgeschichte* 21 (1889): 85–98.

Zwernemann, Jürgen. *Hundert Jahre Hamburgisches Museum für Völkerkunde.* Hamburg: Hamburg Museum für Völkerkunde, 1980.

———. "Leo Frobenius und das Hamburgische Museum für Völkerkunde." *Mitteilungen aus dem Museum für Völkerkunde Hamburg* 17 (1987): 111–27.

Contributors

Sierra A. Bruckner completed her Ph.D. in 1999 at the University of Iowa with a dissertation entitled "The Tingle-Tangle of Modernity: Popular Anthropology and the Cultural Politics of Identity in Imperial Germany." She now works as a translator in Berlin and can be contacted at sierra.bruckner@gmx.de.

Matti Bunzl is Assistant Professor of Anthropology and History at the University of Illinois, Urbana-Champaign. Aside from the history of anthropology, his research interests include the ethnography of contemporary Central Europe and the culture and literature of fin de siècle Vienna. Bunzl is the coeditor of the volume *Altering States: Ethnographies of Transition in Eastern Europe and the Former Soviet Union* (University of Michigan Press, 2000). His book *Symptoms of Modernity: Jews and Queers in Late-Twentieth-Century Vienna* is forthcoming from the University of California Press.

Rainer Buschmann is a founding faculty member of the California State University at Channel Islands, where he teaches courses on Pacific Islands, European, and world histories. He has published widely on the development of German anthropology in the Pacific. Most recently, he edited a special issue of the *Journal of the Pacific Arts Association* on the interplay between Oceanic art and German anthropology. His manuscript "The Ethnographic Frontier in German New Guinea, 1870–1914: An Exploration into the Salvage Paradigm" is in preparation.

Andrew D. Evans received his Ph.D. in history from Indiana University and currently teaches at the State University of New York at New Paltz. His research interests include German imperialism, war and society, and German constructions of race. He is working on revising his dissertation, "Anthropology at War: World War I and the Science of Race in Germany," into a book manuscript.

Based at the University of Vermont, **Robert J. Gordon** has spent extended periods of time researching and teaching in Namibia, South Africa, Papua New Guinea, and Lesotho. He has written several books, including *Law and Order in the New Guinea Highlands* (with Mervyn Meggitt) and *The Bushman Myth*.

Pascal Grosse is a historian and neurologist, currently affiliated with the Institute of Neurology, University College London. He recently published a comprehensive study on the intersections between German colonialism and eugenics in *Kolonialismus, Eugenik und bürgerliche Gesellschaft in Deutschland, 1850–1918* (Colonialism, eugenics, and civil society in Germany, 1850–1918) (Frankfurt am Main: Campus, 2000). His current research projects are colonial migration in Germany, 1885–1945; and the gendered brain, 1750–1900.

Harry Liebersohn is a Professor of History at the University of Illinois, Urbana-Champaign. Among his publications are "Discovering Indigenous Nobility: Tocqueville, Chamisso, and Romantic Travel Writing," *American Historical Review* (June 1994), and *Aristocratic Encounters: European Travelers and North American Indians* (Cambridge University Press, 1998). He is now writing a history of scientific world travel from 1750 to 1850.

Suzanne Marchand is Associate Professor of European Intellectual History at Louisiana State University in Baton Rouge. She is the author of *Down from Olympus: Archaeology and Philhellenism in Germany, 1750–1970* (Princeton University Press, 1996) and is currently writing a book on German orientalism.

H. Glenn Penny is Assistant Professor of Modern European History at the University of Missouri in Kansas City. His essays on museums, identity formation, and the history of anthropology have appeared in *Central European History, Comparativ, German History, Social Anthropology, Osiris,* and *Pacific Arts*. In November 2000, he was awarded the Fritz Stern prize for the best dissertation in German history by the German Historical Institute in Washington, D.C. His book *Objects of Culture: Ethnology and Ethnographic Museums in Imperial Germany* was published by the University of North Carolina Press in 2002. He is currently working on a book tentatively titled the "German

Love Affair with the American Indian," which explores Germans' peculiar fascination with Native Americans over the last two hundred years.

Andrew Zimmerman is Assistant Professor of History at the George Washington University, where he arrived in 2000 after two years at the Society of Fellows in the Humanities at Columbia University. He is the author of *Anthropology and Antihumanism in Imperial Germany* (University of Chicago Press, 2001). His current research deals with science and state formation in British and German colonies in Africa and the role of the Tuskegee Institute in class formation in colonial Africa.

Index

Acclimatization, 180–97
Ammon, Otto, 205
Angerer, Fritz, 132, 134
Ankermann, Bernard, 90, 110–11, 114, 119, 296, 313
Anthropology: definitions of, 1n, 156–57n. 2, 180n, 199n. 7; professionalization of, 78–79, 124–25, 288, 305
Arendt, Hannah, 28
Asad, Talal, 26
Austrian Anthropological Society, 290

Barth, Paul, 272
Bastian, Adolf, 7, 11–13, 17–18, 22, 79–80, 83n. 120, 86–126, 157n. 2, 159, 161, 189, 233–34, 286, 287, 294
Belke, Ingrid, 50–51
Berlin Anthropological Society, 87, 163, 166–68, 189
Berlin Society for Anthropology, Ethnology, and Prehistory, 110, 137, 143, 290
Berman, Nina, 8
Bildung, 9, 22, 49, 58–61, 67, 71–85, 91, 124
Biological determinism, 180, 186–87
Bismarck, Otto von, 19, 73, 189–90, 291, 292
Bismarck Bell, 134
Bleek, Wilhelm, 259
Blumenbach, Johann Friedrich, 179
Boas, Franz, 6, 22, 44, 48n. 3, 52, 81–85, 90–92, 112, 118, 124–26, 288, 293, 305, 308
Böckh, August, 64, 66, 76
Bopp, Franz, 64
Boyer, John, 293
Brown, A. R., 302

Breasted, James Henry, 286
British Association for the Advancement of Science, 170
Bruce, J. C., 136
Bundesratsbeschluß, 235

Cadle, C. Ernest, 264
Campbell, Joseph, 286
Chamberlain, Houston Stewart, 201
Chamisso, Adelbert von, 32, 35–38
Chanock, Martin, 282
Chicago Field Museum, 105, 278
Choris, Louis, 34, 36, 41
Christian, Viktor, 313
Cipriani, Lidio, 271
Cities, civic society, and German science, 13, 15–16, 120–22
Cole, Douglas, 91
Cook, James, 31
Cooper, Frederick, 24
Cosmopolitanism, 2, 11–17, 35–38, 52, 88–126, 191
Crystal Palace, 106
Cultural pluralism, 1–2, 9, 11, 14, 18
Cumont, Franz, 286

Darwinism, 93, 118, 137, 200, 229, 287–88, 292, 294–96, 299, 301
Däubler, Carl, 192
Dernburg, Bernhard, 172, 176–77
Dieterich, Albrecht, 285
Diffusion, 89, 110–14, 119, 305
Dominguez, Virginia, 281

Efron, John, 204
Eickstedt, Egon von, 201, 209, 216–29

347

Eijkman, Christaan, 190
Eiselen, Werner, 281
Elementargedanken, 95–97, 287
Eschscholtz, Johann, 34, 36
Eugenics, 19, 182–83, 192–96, 311
Evolution, 1, 11, 91, 112, 137, 285, 299–301, 311, 314
Expedition: Denver, 264–65, 272–73; Geographical Commission, 245, 248–49; German Naval, 245, 247–49; Hamburg South Seas, 214, 231, 245–47, 249, 252

Fieldwork, 128, 238–55, 302–3
Finsch, Otto, 165
Fischer, Eugen, 27, 28, 157, 200–201, 205–6, 226, 275–77
Fischer, Hans, 231
Forster, Georg, 4, 38
Forster, J. R., 38
Foucault, Michel, 160
Fourie, Louis, 263–66, 268, 275
Foy, Willy, 90, 109, 112–18, 121
Frazier, James George, 286
Freud, Sigmund, 292, 311
Friederici, Georg, 248–49
Fritsch, Gustav, 162–63, 194, 260–61
Frobenius, Leo, 14, 110, 296, 304

Gedankenstatistik, 103, 117, 124
Gehring, Eduard, 134
Genocide, 19, 26, 28, 157, 172–78
Geographical provinces, 91, 96
German Anthropological Society, 38, 122, 167
German Army and Navy Exhibition, 144–51
German Colonial Exhibition, 130, 134, 152–53, 164
German Colonial Society, 141–43
Goffman, Erving, 213
Gorseh, Hersi Ergeh, 136
Gossler, Gustav von, 87–88, 102, 106
Gothsch, Manfred, 231
Graebner, Fritz, 90, 96, 110–14, 119, 296, 304
Grienpenkerl, Friedrich, 66
Grünwedel, Albert, 104
Gusinde, Martin, 271, 275, 277

Haberlandt, Michael, 291, 309
Haddon, Alfred, 254
Haeckel, Ernst, 94, 259
Hagenbeck, Carl, 132, 143, 148
Hagenbeck, John, 134
Hahl, Albert, 25, 233, 236–55
Hahn, Theophilus 256–57
Hambruch, Paul, 208, 214
Hansemann, Adolf, 234
Harrison, Jane, 286
Hartmann, Robert, 159–60
Havelburg, V., 193
Hensel, Rheinhold, 168
Herbart, Johann Friedrich, 56–57, 66–67
Herder, Johann Gottfried von, 11–12, 14–15, 62, 65, 286, 287
Herero, 157, 172–78
Herzfeld, Baruch, 64
Herzfeld, L., 65
Heyse, Carl, 64, 66–67
Hiery, Hermann, 232
Hirsch, August, 189
Hirschberg, Walter, 313
Historicism, 1, 9, 12, 93, 96, 305
Hitler, Adolf, 11
Humanism, 1, 9, 12, 17, 19, 52, 158–59
Humboldt, Alexander von, 4, 88, 93–95, 124, 286
Humboldt, Wilhelm von, 11, 56–58, 61, 64–65, 67

Jaeger, Fritz, 256, 267
Jagor, Fedor, 171
Janssen, Arnold, 294
Judaism, 22, 35–36, 45, 47–85

Kaiser Wilhelm Institute for Anthropology, Human Descent Theory, and Eugenics, 28, 276
Kalmar, Ivan, 84
Kant, Immanuel, 179
Kayser, Paul, 141
Keyserling, Hermann Graf, 285
Kluckhohn, Clyde, 305
Koch, Robert, 190
Köhler, August, 141–42
Kohler, Oswin, 271
Kollmann, Julius, 200, 205
Koppers, Wilhelm, 304, 307, 309, 313, 316

Kotzebue, Otto von, 34–35, 37
Krämer, Augustin, 32, 36, 38–46, 250
Kroeber, Alfred, 6n. 10
Krusenstern, Adam von, 34
Kulturkampf, 22
Kulturkreise, 110–15, 296, 304–7, 309, 313
Kulturschichten, 110, 296–97
Kulturvölker, 96–97, 113, 161, 292

Lang, Andrew, 294–96
Lapouge, Gustav de, 205
Lau, Brigitte, 276
Lazarus, Moritz, 12–13, 47–85
Lebensraum, 17, 28, 188–89
Lebzelter, Viktor, 271
Leenhart, Maurice, 23
Leo XIII, 298
Leutwein, Theodor, 173
Liberalism and science, 2, 9, 17–18, 28
Lowie, Robert, 6n. 10, 82
Luschan, Felix von, 104, 113, 123, 163–65, 167, 169–70, 174–77, 200, 202–3, 206–7, 209, 218, 220, 241–42, 247, 249, 261, 314

Maherero, Samuel, 135
Malinowski, Bronislaw, 6, 238–39, 253–54, 304, 308
Man, E. H., 302
Mannhardt, Wilhelm, 286–87
Marquardt, Carl, 134, 145, 148
Marquardt, Felix, 145
Martin, Henno, 278
Martin, Rudolf, 200, 203–4, 207, 214, 226
Mason, Otis T., 90, 92
Massin, Benoit, 118, 199–200
Mauss, Marcel, 288, 293, 305, 308
May, Karl, 8
Maybaum, Sigmund, 74
McLennan, John, 11
Mead, Margaret, 6n. 10, 43
Meinhof, Carl, 208
Melton, James Van Horn, 286
Mendelssohn, Moses, 62
Menges, Joseph, 134
Menghin, Oswald, 313
Meyer, A. B., 168
Meyer, A. J., 273
Meyer, Hans, 250
Michel, Hermann, 307

Möller, Willy, 138
Monogenism, 9, 95
Monotheism, 69–70
Much, Rudolf, 313–14
Müller, Wilhelm, 252–53
Murray, Hubert, 254, 255
Museums, Natural History, 5; in Berlin, 167; in Vienna, 291, 307, 314
Museums, Völkerkunde: in Berlin, 86–126, 167, 233, 241–43 ; in Cologne, 113–17; in Leipzig, 101, 121–23; in Stuttgart, 38

Nama, 26, 172–78, 256–57
National Socialism, 2, 18–22, 27–30, 176n. 68, 183, 195–97, 226–29, 277, 312–15
Naturalists, 5
Natural science, 18, 158–59
Naturvölker, 96–97, 103, 113, 137, 161, 292
Nazis. *See* National Socialism
New Guinea Company, 234–35, 240, 294

Orientalism, 8
Otto, Rudolf, 285

Parkinson, Richard, 252
Passarge, Siegfried, 260
Pius XI, 307, 312
Pöch, Rudolf, 201, 208, 210–13, 216–18, 221–26, 261, 291
Postcolonial studies, 8–10
Powell, John Wesley, 92–93, 124
Preuss, K. T., 300
Proctor, Robert, 199
Psychic unity of man, 95

Race, 2, 10, 45, 113, 199; and nation, 17–22, 201–29; and *Volk,* 20, 201–29
Race science, 2, 10, 20, 22, 118, 126
Radcliffe-Brown, A. R., 6, 255, 305
Ranke, Johannes, 200, 205–7
Ranke, Leopold von, 66
Rassenkunde, 27–28, 200, 226–29
Ratzel, Friedrich, 109–11, 191, 287, 296, 304
Reche, Otto, 201, 214, 217, 220–29
Religion and anthropology, 22–23
Renan, Ernst, 68–69
Rivers, W. H. R., 288, 293
Röck, Fritz, 313

Index

Rodenwaldt, Ernst, 196
Rokitansky, Carl, 290, 292

Said, Edward, 8, 24
Salvage anthropology, 12
Sapper, Karl, 248
Schebesta, Paul, 309
Scheffer, Dr., 37
Scheidt, Walter, 226–27
Schindler, Franz Martin, 292–93
Schlaginhaufen, Otto, 251
Schlagintweit, Hermann von, 164
Schlegel, August Wilhelm, 33
Schleiermacher, 65
Schlemiel, Peter, 33
Schmidt, Wilhelm, 29, 271, 277, 288–316
Scholz, Alfred, 149–50
Schrip, Fritz von, 138
Schultze, Leonard, 175
Schroeder, Leopold von, 283–85, 288, 291, 295–96
Schwalbe, Gustav, 201, 205–6
Schweinfurth, Georg, 298
Schweitzer, Albert, 285
Seed, Patricia, 31
Seligman, Charles, 254
Siepel, Ignaz, 310
Simmel, Georg, 44
Singer, Hermann, 249
Smith, Grafton Elliot, 306
Smith, Robert, 286
Smith, Woodruff, 110, 200, 230
Smuts, Jan, 271
Sonderweg, 2, 8, 183, 200, 288
Sorkin, David, 61
Steinthal, Heymann, 12–13, 47–85
Stephan, Emil, 247, 249, 252–53
Stöcker, Adolf, 73
Stocking, George W., Jr., 23, 84
Stoler, Ann Laura, 24
Stosch, Albrecht von, 165
Stovis, Barend Joseph, 190
Structural-functionalism, 6, 288, 305

Strzygowski, Josef, 289
Stuhlmann, Franz, 137
Stumpf, Carl, 208

Thilenius, Georg, 246–47, 252–53
Thurnwald, Richard, 241–46, 314
Toldt, Karl, 208
Tomas, David, 303
Treitschke, Heinrich von, 73, 75
Trotha, General Lothar von, 173–74
Tylor, Edward B., 11, 97, 110–12

U.S. National Museum, 90–92

Vancouver, George, 32
Viennese Anthropological Society, 208
Virchow, Rudolf, 7, 11, 17–19, 22, 83n. 20, 89, 91–93, 109, 118, 137–38, 140, 142–43, 156–57, 167, 169, 171, 181–82, 186–89, 200–205, 217, 229, 286
Volk, 10
Völkergedanken, 95–97, 103
Völkerpsychologie, 12, 22, 47–85
Völkerschauen, 5, 16, 18, 127–55, 199
Volksgeist, 12, 14–15, 55, 71
Volkskörper, 196
Vylder, Gustaf de, 256–57

Walden, Edgar, 249, 251–53
Waldeyer, Wilhelm, 176
Weber, Max, 44, 284
Weidenreich, Franz, 277
Wellhausen, Julius, 286
Weninger, Josef, 225
Weule, Karl, 121–23, 237–38
Wolf, Friedrich August, 66
Wundt, Wilhelm, 80–81

Zantop, Susanne, 8
Zoos, 5
Zunz, Leopold, 66–67
Zürn, Ralf, 174–77